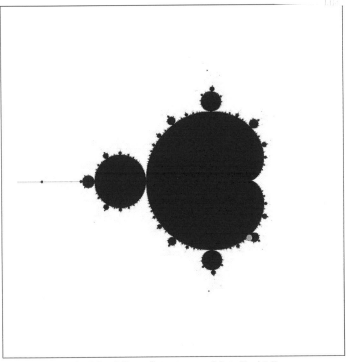

The Mandelbrot Set at $z = -0.5 + 0i$, ± 1.5.

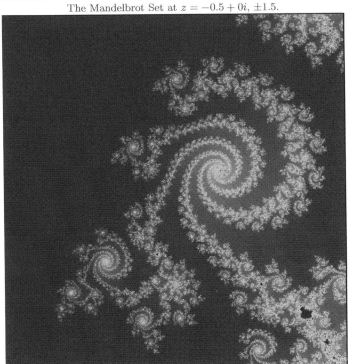

The Mandelbrot Set at $z = 0.2323 - 0.5345i$, ± 0.0025

The Boundary Between Light and Dark

The interior of the Mandelbrot set consists of all those points c in the complex plane for which fixed point iteration on the function $f(z) = z^2 + c$ converges. This region is filled with black in the figure on the top of the previous page.

The Mandelbrot set displays the properties of fractals: it is bounded; its edge has infinite self similarity; and its boundary has an infinite length.

A wide variety of interesting phenomenon occur on the boundary between light and dark, the edge of the Mandelbrot Set. The transition is dramatic in black and white, but seems almost transcendent when we map the number of iterations to a color scale. Mapping the region around the point $z = 0.2323 - 0.5345i$ (Python code on back cover; location indicated by a red dot on the top image on the previous page) in this way produces the front cover image.

About the Author

Bruce E. Shapiro teaches mathematics at California State University, Northridge, in the most challenging job he has ever had. For a while he collected degrees from various colleges, until his wife said uncle. In past lives he has been called a rocket scientist, a brain scientist, a computational scientist, a mathematical scientist, a data scientist, and a generally annoying and snarky pain in the ass. None of those pursuits were particularly challenging. Now he spends his spare time eating chocolate chip cookies, playing with imaginary friends in the complex plane, and pontificating about the poor state of public education in California while teaching his two Staffordshire Terriers, Bella and Romeo (pictured above), the finer points of Lebesque Integration.

Scientific Computation

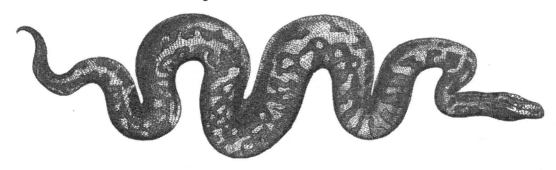

Python Hacking for Math Junkies

Second Edition, Revised

Bruce E. Shapiro

2015

Sherwood Forest

http://CalculusCastle.com

Scientific Computation: Python Hacking for Math Junkies
Second Edition, Revised
Bruce E. Shapiro, Ph.D.
California State University, Northridge
Sherwood Forest Books, Los Angeles, CA, USA

ISBN-13: 978-0692452004 / ISBN 10: 0692452001 (BW/Paper-Blue Cover)
ISBN-13: 978-0692366936 / ISBN-10: 0692366938 (BW/Paper-Orange Cover)
ISBN-13: 978-0692498552 / ISBN-10: 0692498559 (Color/Paper)
ISBN-13: 978-0996686006 / ISBN 10: 0996686002 (Hardbound)
ISBN-13: 978-0996686013 / ISBN 10: 0996686010 (Electronic)

Last Revised on: 1/17/16 (Version 2.5)

The drawing of the Python is from "Concerning Serpents" by Elias Lewis, Jr, *Popular Science Monthly* **4**(17):258-275 (Jan. 1874), published in the United States of America by D. Appleton & Co. The copyright has expired and this image is in the public domain.

The *Cat in the Hat* picture on the back cover was drawn by J. Fors.

The picture of the author in *About the Author* was drawn by A. Babahekian.

The cover image of the Mandelbrot Set was generated with the Python code on the back cover.

This is not an official document. Any opinions expressed herein are totally arbitrary, are only presented to expose the student to diverse perspectives, and do not necessarily reflect the position of any specific individual, the California State University, Northridge, or any other organization.

Please report any errors, omissions, or suggestions for improvements to bruce.e.shapiro@ csun.edu. Please include the version number and revision date listed at the top of this page on all communications.

And grateful thanks to the many useful suggestions and corrections provided by readers.

Contents

The Hacker's Codes

First Generation

- Computer access shall be unrestricted.
- Information shall be free.
- Judge others **only** by their acts.
- Computers shall produce beauty.
- Computers shall improve life.

Second Generation

- Do no evil.
- Protect data.
- Protect privacy.
- Conserve resources.
- Telecommunication shall be unrestricted.
- Share code.
- Strive to improve.
- Be prepared for cyber-attack.
- Always improve security.
- Always test and improve the system.

Preface

Almost everyone uses computers today. They improve our lives and produce wonderful works of art. Information is accessible and global communication is immediate. It is hard to imagine (or for some of us, remember) the days when you couldn't just look something up or chat with a friend or share your innermost thoughts with total strangers on the other side of the planet. We even have verbs for such things now: *to google, to skype, to tweet.*

The typical student uses at least three: a portable notebook computer that weighs no more than a textbook, a tablet, and a cell phone. None of these even existed before students in the class of 2016 were born. A lot has changed: ask your grandparents about AM radio, phone booths, or broadcast TV. Now when you feel an earthquake or see a fire plume or hear a siren the first place to go for information is Twitter.

Hacking and Programming

Naturally some computer literacy is expected of everyone; things like carbon copies of credit cards are mostly archaeological relics. Instant verification is here and now. Even paper and pencil are disparaged by many: "Shift or get off the pot. Seriously, it's not fair to the kids. It's tough at the outset to understand and learn all these tools, but you're doing a disservice to our students and these kid's futures if you don't."[1] Yet for many – including the teachers – computers are a source of trepidation and fear. This becomes especially true when computers are misunderstood or used improperly. And as math users, we know that the regardless of what some tech executives may want us to believe, we are still a very long way from letting go of paper and pencil.

The typical user needs to know how to run apps and keep the computer safe from infiltration. He or she need not be an expert on computer speak to do this. And as mathies, we need to know especially how we can use our computers to help us solve mathematics problems. This will involve a high-level understanding of how a computer works and what tools we can use to make it work optimally to solve our kind of problems.

It's like driving a car. You need to know to slow down for bumps and potholes and to take your car to a mechanic for regular service or when it is not working properly. You don't need to know anything about distributors or gaskets or struts (if those things even exist on cars today). Nor do you need to be an automotive engineer; you just need to know where to stick the key and what buttons to push and turn. If you are driving a truck or motorcycle, there are few differences to learn, but not so many that you need to become a mechanic (or anywhere close).

---

[1] L. De Cicco Remu, Director of Partners in Learning at Microsoft Canada, reported in straight.com, Stephen Hui, 15 May 2015, 4:28 PM, http://www.straight.com/life/452561/teachers-using-pens-and-paper-classroom-not-fair-students-microsoft-official-says.

Computers are similar. You need to keep your software up to date and avoid opening potentially dangerous attachments (the potholes). If it breaks, you take it in for service (the mechanic or IT guy). The people who design new software to sell you with your computer (programmers) are like the automotive engineers who design the cars. You need to know how to run their programs, not how they are designed. In fact, in most cases, the software design is kept secret (for arguable reasons).

What if you want to build your own car from scratch? Sure, you can become an engineer (computer programmer) and learn all the ins and outs of the ideal design. But what about the guy who is rebuilding an old Ferrari or motorcycle or speed boat in his garage around the corner? These individuals are true artists! They are *hackers*. They just do it.[2] They have managed to learn what they need to learn to get the job done and then have gone ahead and built their product. No bells and whistles. Just an elegant one-of-a-kind that gets the job done.[3]

Mathematical Hacking

This is a book about hacking, but not just any kind of hacking. It is about *mathematical hacking*, or *scientific computing*. If you like math and want to use computers to do math or solve mathematical problems, then this book is for you.

There are some commercial programs that will let you begin to do advanced mathematical computation without learning any "programming" at all. But they all have a complicated programming-like syntax or language and you will eventually need to learn this syntax if you want to anything beyond, say, solve a simple integral or perform an arithmetic calculation. So the question then becomes which programming syntax is the "best" one to learn. These syntaxes started to evolve in the middle of the twentieth century, with Fortran-like languages often being the preference of the scientific community; LISP-like languages being chosen by the artificial intelligence community; and COBOL-like languages being chosen by the data processing community. Since then, the distinctions have begun to blur and the number of languages had grown into the thousands.

Most of the early work on computation and computing grew from the *mathematical literati*. But market forces drive the industry: anything that makes money, or is exciting and glamorous, with growth potential, is what sells. These are things like business, social, and data manipulation applications. For most people, math is not glamorous. The typical "man on the street" tends to bunch math and computer types together in one big sticky mess in their brain, to be both feared and respected, but only to be approached carefully and with trepidation in matters of extreme urgency: "Please, my child needs help with advanced placement calculus" or "Why is my email so slow?" as if these subjects have any relation to one another.

Consequently, much of the beauty of computation – and what it can do for us math junkies – is largely ignored by both introductory computer science classes and introductory programming books as *irrelevant*. In industry, the "calcs" and the "squints" are expected to remain quietly in their dusty old offices and smelly laboratories (preferably on campus, so they don't have to be on the permanent industrial payroll) grinding out research reports until their specific expertise is actually requested on a need-to-know basis. Since neither undergraduate computer science nor mathematics curricula pay much serious attention to *mathematical* computing, many a promising student ends up as professional cappuccino *baristi*, substitute teachers, or insurance peddler.

---

[2] With apologies to Nike.

[3] To learn more about hacking and the Hacker's codes, see Levy S. (2010) *Hackers*. Sebastopol, CA: O'Reilly Media; Mizrach, S. "Is there a hacker ethic for 90s Hackers?" http://www2.fiu.edu/~mizrachs/hackethic.html

This book is designed rescue these math junkies and incipient mathematical literati from the dangerous shoals of computational irrelevance and confusion and lead them to the calm, clear waters of computational beauty.

Scientific Computing is not Programming

So you want to do scientific computing but have never taken a programming course, except maybe that Java 101 class you had as a freshman that was all about objects and interfaces and stuff and all you could say was wtf? huh? Or you want to do some data mining but the local college catalog says you need to take about eight courses first? Or looking at the books on Amazon it seems like you need to learn all about algorithms, databases, SQL, machine learning, cloud computing, statistics, visualization, interface design, graph theory, and so forth before you can do cull any meaningful results from your data set? And that you have learn a whole host of computer languages and styles, object oriented design, systems analysis, pair programming, and so forth.

None of that is true.

You have something that most programmers don't: love and knowledge of math.

Of course, learning as much as you can about any of those subjects (and more) will help you, but you don't need to learn about them before you start doing interesting, useful, creative, original and potentially publishable computational mathematics.

There is very little difference between writing a program to solve a problem and proving a theorem. In each case you need to produce a logical sequence of steps that takes you from input (assumptions) to output (conclusions). For most mathematicians, an understanding of the semantics, or meaning, of the statements in a computer program comes easily, once the logical analogues in mathematical analysis are understood. Usually the problem is understanding the *syntax*, and decoding of error messages.

Most scientific programs are written to be run only once and never again. Scientific programs often only have a single customer. The customer and programmer are frequently the same person. Niceties like idiot-proofing and fancy interfaces, which may consume the vast majority of the code in a commercial program, become unnecessary when you are your own customer.[4] Documentation becomes replaced by in-line comments and web pages. Copies of the source code go into open access repositories for the world to see, redact, and improve.

Students need to explore the limits of what is possible without the restrictions of a particular programming paradigm. Its the quality of their work that is important. Scientific computing is nothing like the stuff taught in introductory computer science classes.

Why Python?

I use Python as a teaching language for a number of reasons, chief among them that it is free on all operating systems. Thus students can install it on their laptops or home computers and are not chained to computer labs or expensive license agreements. Python has generic programming structures that are common to procedural, functional, and object oriented languages. If you already know another programming language, then Python is easy to learn. If you don't know how to program, then Python is free, it is completely documented online, and there are lots of books you can download for free to learn more about it.

---

[4]If you want to sell an app commercially, these are extremely important, of course. Nobody is going to *buy* something they can't understand or which crashes unexpectedly. But if you are the only one using it, you know the pitfalls of the program and how to avoid them.

Why *this* book?

There are a lot of books on Python, but unfortunately none of them are oriented towards the mathematical literati who can't program. There are books on advanced mathematical and scientific programming for advanced programmers, and there are (far too many) non-mathematical books on programming in Python for beginners. There are books on *programming* in Python for students at just about every level of prior experience. Unfortunately, very few say anything about Numpy, plotting, or vectors, and very nearly all of them completely give up the ghost when it comes to list comprehension and lambda functions. And if you want to try to learn about Voronoi diagrams, and draw them at them same time, well, you need to buy a whole shelf full of books.

So I've – ahem – hacked out a sort of *Math Hacker's Guide to the Pythonverse*.

I have included examples from a variety of disciplines that are usually relegated to advanced treatises on numerical analysis, machine learning, and the applied sciences, and have kept the amount of proof to a minimum. Some additional topics are introduced in the exercises.

Much of the material on Python is relegated to reference tables, rather than detailed how-to-do-its. Users are referred to the official documentation for further details. The goal of the tables is to collect some of the more relevant material so that students can focus their search into appropriate online documentation.

This book stems from my own professional experience. While some of the topics are stretched pretty far from the traditional undergraduate mathematics curriculum, I've included them for good reason. With the exception of the chapters on fractals and calculating the value of π,[5] **I have had to use virtually every single algorithm, method, hack, and technique presented in this book at some time in my professional life.**

A Note To My Students

Read Part I immediately, especially if you haven't programmed before or have been ruined by a single course in Java-based object-oriented design.

Read Part II as soon as you can, but no later than each section it is covered in class. Don't skip anything.

Read Part III as needed for reference.

Hacking is a hands-on experience. You can't expect to learn only by watching demonstrations or doing it in the lab. You have to take it home with you and practice it in your sleep. Live, think and dream in Python.

The Student's Imperative

Go forth and hack: but do no evil.

For Further Reading

Google it. Everything that's ever been done in Python is on the internet.

---

[5]I included both of these subjects because, well, they just sound like a lot of fun.

The Art of the Possible

"Politics is the art of the possible."[6] I've sometimes wondered if Stallman had that thought in mind when he defined hacking in his web article. Social media, for example, is changing the world in ways that Bismarck could not have even conceived.

More likely it was the voice of Juan Peron from *Evita* singing in his head:

> One has no rules, is not precise.
> One rarely acts the same way twice.
> One spurns no device, practicing the art of the possible.[7]

Either way, it makes you think.

Bella does Python.

---

[6] Die Politik ist die Lehre vom Möglichen (Otto von Bismarck, 1867).
[7] Andrew Lloyd Webber & Tim Rice (1979).

Notation

Typewriter Bold font is used to indicate single words code.

Full lines or multiple lines of code are enclosed in gray boxes.

```
this is a line of code
```

Code typed into the Python shell is enclosed in a gray box and preceded by the Python `>>>` prompt, which you should not type.

```
>>> print "Hello,␣World!"
Hello, World!
```

The underbracket character "␣" represents a blank space inside of a string literal.

The forward arrow symbol → is used as shorthand to represent the output of entering something in Python, as in **print x+y** → **23** is a short form of writing "if you type **print x+y** into the command shell now, then Python will return a value of **23**."

Algorithms have the following kind of format, and may use statements like **repeat**, **while**, **for**, and if.

Algorithm 0.1 The name of the algorithm.

---
input: The input variables are listed here
 1: $x \leftarrow a + b$
 2: **repeat**
 3:     do stuff
 4: **until** some condition is met
 5: **return** some value

An assigment statement in an algorithm like the $x \leftarrow a$ on line 1 means "calculate the value of $a + b$ and then replace x with the result."

Within mathematical expressions, scalar variables and functions, such as x y, and $f(x, y)$ are typeset in a *Roman italic* font. Vectors, matrices, and points such as **v**, **M**, and **P** are shown in san serif bold. Standard mathematical notation is used throughout, e.g., curly braces {} for sets, $\mathbb{R}$ for the real numbers, $\varnothing$ for the empty set, $\mathbf{M}^{-1}$ and $\mathbf{M}^{\mathrm{T}}$ for matrix inverse and transpose, etc.

Part I

Getting Started

Chapter 1

Programs and Programming

English (or any other language, for that matter) has rules about putting words together to form sentences.[1] If the words are not in the right order, or the inflection (in spoken language) is imprecise, the meaning will be altered.

When you mis-speak, people can usually figure out what you meant to say. For example, if you say "Please have napkin" to you friend during lunch, she will most likely pass you a napkin, figuring out that you meant to say "May I please have a napkin."

To tell a computer what to do you give it instructions in a **computer language**. The grammar and syntax of a computer language are precise, and do not leave any room for error. When you click on an application on you desktop, or an app on you cell phone, you are, in fact, **executing**[2] a computer program that has been written in some computer language. The author of the app has done the work of figuring out the necessary syntax for you; but by doing this, the programmer has traded the **flexibility** of full control over the computer for the **convenience** of mouse clicks.

The name of the language that we will use in this text is **Python**. Python is one of many different computer languages. There are so many different computer languages (thousands) that the Wikipedia has a list of Wikipedia pages containing lists of computer languages.[3] When we write a computer language like Python, our sentences are called **statements** and our conversations are called **programs**. A **computer program** is nothing more than a collection of precisely formatted statements telling the computer what we want it to do.

> **Definition 1.1. Program**
>
> A **Computer Program** is a sequence of instructions for a computer, so that it can perform a specific task.

It is useful to visualize the collection of all computer programs on a computer as providing several **layers of software** that lay on top of the physical **computer hardware** (figure 1.1). A program in any layer can be designed to access a program at any lower layer via **hooks**, special computer programming interfaces, written into the intermediate layers.

Computer programs can be broadly grouped into **application** programs and **system**

---

[1] If you have experience programming or understand the software development process, this chapter can be skipped without loss of continuity.

[2] When a computer program "does its thing" we say that that we are *executing* the program, derived from the verb *to execute*, to carry out or put into effect a course of action.

[3] As of 5 Dec 2014 there were fifteen different lists of programming languages on the "list of programming languages" page.

Figure 1.1: Several layers of computer software may be envisioned to sit on top of the physical computer hardware, with the operating system closest to the hardware and the application software furthest away.

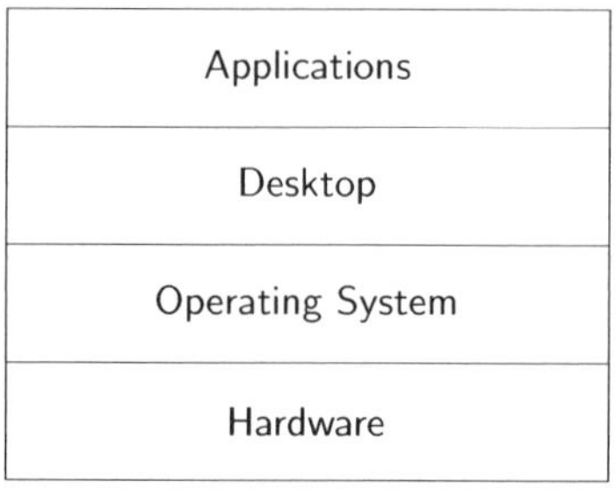

Applications
Desktop
Operating System
Hardware

software. **Application programs** are designed for the "end user."[4] Examples include spreadsheets, word processors, presentation programs, and web browsers. **System software** encompasses anything that makes the computer work, including the **operating system** and all the hardware interfaces. Most system software is invisible and runs in the background.

An exception is the **desktop environment**. Desktop environments control the look and feel of user interaction with the computer, through things like menus, icons, folders, task bars and launchers. Linux users have a variety of desktop environments to choose from, with names like gnome, KDE, x-windows, and so forth; many even choose to install multiple desktops on their computer and switch back and forth between them. Most Windows and Mac users identify their operating systems by their desktops, e.g., the Mac Desktop or the Windows Desktop. However, the desktop is only a small, though highly visible, part of the operating system, In most cases it is possible to replace the desktop environment on any computer while leaving the remainder of the operating system essentially intact.

A special class of application programs – **development software** – are tools that allow or assist users to create new computer programs. Examples are compilers and interpreters; text editors; and software development environments. The first part of this book will focus on how to use one of these tools: python.

Python is a computer language, which means it has both a **syntax** and **semantics**, as does English. But in this case, the reader of the language is not a human. When you speak in python (actually you will write **text** that is called **code**), the listener (technically, the reader) is a computer. So python is also **implemented** as a computer program that translates the the text that you write into stuff that the computer understands. When you type up a program in the python language and tell the computer to interpret it, you are creating a new program. We will use the same word – python – to refer to the language (the syntactical rules), the written language (the code or programs), and the computer program that translates your python code into machine

---

[4]The **user** is anyone uses or interacts with a computer. The **end user** typically refers to a customer who purchases a computer for themselves, or has a computer purchased for them by someone else such as the company they work for.

Figure 1.2: When you invoke the python interpreter to run your program, it first looks to see if a byte code version has already been created. The byte code versions is all ones and zeros and you cannot read it. If it does not exist, it will be created for you. If you change your Python source code, it will create and new byte code version and run that. We use the word *python* to refer to either the source code, the byte code, the program that performs the conversion, and the language itself.

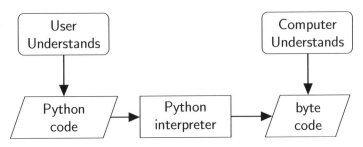

language or byte code.

> **Definition 1.2. Statement**
>
> The instructions in a computer program are called **statements**.

The down side of using a computer language is that the rules are **very precise**. There are no exceptions. These rules are called the **syntax** of the computer language.

If a rule is not followed, rather than being misunderstood, the program will likely either crash, or do something very unexpected.

Sometimes you will see an **error message** that seems totally unrelated to anything you did. This is because the computer interpreted things differently from the way you wanted. A comma replaced by a hyphen in spoken English will rarely throw off the listener, but it can lead to radically different interpretations by a computer.

There are two types of errors in computer programs: **syntactic errors** and **semantic errors**. The **syntax of a computer language** describes very precisely how to form statements the computer understands. If there is any deviation from the rules, even the smallest, the computer will recognize that there is an error, and it will tell you so. The **semantics of a computer program** describe what it is supposed to do. A semantic error that is not a syntactic error will not cause the program to halt. Instead, it will do something funny.

A common problem in Python is exponentiation. In many computer languages (such as Matlab), you can write exponentiation, such as 6^3, using the "carat" symbol, as in **6^3**. The statement **x=6^3** is syntactically correct in Python. However, it does not represent the number $6 \cdot 6 \cdot 6 = 216$. Instead you get the following somewhat peculiar result:

```
1  >>> print 6^3
2  5
```

What you should have typed (to get 216) was `x=6**3`

```
3  >>>print 6**3
4  216
```

The problem is that the carat operator is used in Python for the bitwise exclusive or operation.[5] (Yes, exponentiation in Python uses the same syntax as FORTRAN!)

Programming Paradigms

In the old days we used computer languages were classified by which **programming paradigm** or **style** they fit. As the number of different paradigms have grown, many of the languages have added features from other languages, so much so that the joke arose "the determined Real Programmer can write FORTRAN programs in any language."[6] Its actually quite difficult to even define the concept of programming paradigm, as (a) there are so many and (b) they overlap. Some of the better known paradigms (discussed very briefly below) include imperative, declarative, procedural, object oriented, and functional. Very few languages these days adhere to a single paradigm.

> **Definition 1.3. Imperative Language**
>
> A computer language or program is said to be **imperative** if control is based on a sequence of statements that change the **state** of the computer (e.g., values in particular memory locations[a]).
>
> ――――――――――――――
> [a]Typically called variables.

FORTRAN and C are imperative languages. Imperative programming is the primary focus of this book. It is based on the algorithms, or the sequences of steps, used to solve a problem. When we assign a value to a variable, do an `if`/`elif`/`else` test, or execute a loop with a `for` or `while`, we are programming imperatively.

> **Definition 1.4. Declarative language**
>
> A language is said to be **declarative** if programs consist of problem specifications. Typical examples are Prolog, Modelica, and SQL.

A declarative program says **what** you want to do, not **how** to do it. A declarative program might say something like "Solve the matrix equation $\mathbf{Ax}=\mathbf{b}$ for $\mathbf{x}$" while an imperative program might say "The solution of $\mathbf{Ax}=\mathbf{b}$ is $\mathbf{x}=\mathbf{A}^{-1}\mathbf{b}$."

――――――――――――――――――――――――――――――――
[5]See table 11.3: 6 xor 3 = $(0110)_2$ xor $(0011)_2 = (0101)_2 = 5$.
[6]Ed Post (1982)*Real Programmers Don't Use Pascal.*

Definition 1.5. Procedural Language

A computer language or program is said to be **procedural** if it can be broken down into one or more **procedures**[a] that can be **called** from a main program. A **procedure** is a sequential list of of instructions.

---

[a]Sometimes called functions or subroutines.

Procedural programs can actually be subclasses of other paradigms. Fortran and COBOL are both procedural.

When we define a function or class we are doing procedural programming. Object oriented programming is the ultimate in obsessive-compulsive procedural programming.

Definition 1.6. Object Oriented Language

A computer language or program is said to be **object oriented** (OO) if programs consist solely of (a) **object**[a] definitions and (b) sequences of operations on those objects via special procedures defined to change the objects.[b]

---

[a]Often called **data structures** or **classes**.
[b]Called **methods**.

Languages that support object oriented programming include C++, Java, and Ruby. The main advantage of object oriented programming is data encapsulation: all operations on an object are hidden and done by the method associated with its implementation. A new implementation can (in theory) be substituted for an old one with no impact on other parts of the program design. This is a programming implementation of the concept of **systems analysis**, in which the design of a large project is broken up into different parts that can be handed out to different teams who work independently. A different team can be brought in to replace the others and only has to learn about the interfaces with but not the details of the other parts of the project.[7]

Definition 1.7. Functional Language

A computer language or program is said to be **functional** if computation is based on a sequence of function calls.

Typical functional languages are Haskell, Curry, APL, and Lisp. A functional program is a sequence of function calls. The functions do not necessarily represent objects or object modifiers; nor do they necessarily represent a sequential breakdown of operations. However, a functional program can be both object oriented and/or procedural. Functional programming is mostly useful for formally proving program correctness. However, many of the features of functional programming are useful and elegant and can be used in Python.

---

[7]This has always been popular at NASA, and you know how many disasters that's lead to.

Which Paradigm is Right for Me?

It doesn't really matter what paradigm you believe is best or what is the coolest programming language. We take the algorithmic approach in this book because it is the most intuitive approach for mathematicians to follow.

The point of hacking is to get the job done. If you think you can get something done best by doing one part in SQL, another in R, a third in C++ and link then all together with Python and a bash front end, well then, by all means, do it that way.

Chapter 2

A Tour of Python

This chapter contains a whirlwind overview of Python. It won't tell you how to create a program or even run a single line of code in Python – that will come in later chapters. Don't even expect to learn Python by reading it. The purpose is to introduce some concepts that you might not be familiar with, and to give you a sense of just what Python is.

It is nearly impossible to introduce a new programming language linearly to a student with no prior experience in a short period of time. It will seem like we are jumping back and forth and referring to new concepts before they are actually introduced. While we will try to keep this to a minimum, that cannot be completely avoided in a textbook like this. One of the reasons for this chapter is to get you used to some of those unexpected concepts before their time.

Keep in mind that our goal is not to learn about programming, but to learn to use computer programs to do math. If we had all the time in the world we could spend a whole semester just learning about all the ins and outs of objects and interfaces (we'll get to what those words mean; see chapters 28 and 29, for example) before we even thought about calculating a singular value decomposition (we'll get to that, too, in chapter 40). But if we want to spend *most* of our time *actually doing math*, then we want to dive into programming as quickly as possible. This is why we choose the hacking approach. **A programmer builds a product. A hacker solves a problem.** We want to solve problems, not sell products.[1] We will learn what we need, as quickly as possible, so that we can write (or hack out) working programs that do math.

Programs and Statements

In definitions 1.1 and 1.2, we introduced the concepts of **computer program** and **statement**. These definitions are very broad, and intentionally so. *In this book*, when we use the term statement, we will mean any single line of Python code. We will use the word program to mean any sequence of (one or more) Python statements that do something. It may be a Python function (chapter 18), a Python class (chapter 29), a module (a file that contains one or more Python programs), something that can be run from the command line (such as the **terminal** program in linux or OSX, or **cmd.exe** or **powershell** in, Windows; see chapter 4), one or more lines of code in the python shell (chapter 4), a file created by the **idle** programming environment (page 26), a single cell in an iPython notebook, or even an entire iPython notebook (chapter 5). It may be a single line of code.

---

[1] There is no rule that says we can't sell our solutions, or that an individual can't be both a programmer and a hacker, but programming is not our primary concern.

Python statements can be roughly grouped into two categories: **simple** and **complex**. Simple statements are things that can be stated on a **single line**. Complex statements can't fit on a single line.

Simple Statements

A simple statement is something that can be done in a single line of code. For example, in Python version 2, we can print the expression "Hello, World!" on the screen by including the line of code

```
print "Hello,_World!"
```

in our program. In an **assignment statement** like

```
x = y-3*z+7
```

the value of the expression on the right hand side of the equation is computed, and then assigned to the variable on the left. In this example, the value of the variable **z** is multiplied by 3; then the result is subtracted from the value of the variable **y**; and finally, the number 7 is added to the previous result. The final result is stored in the variable **z**. The order in which the operations are computed is similar to the rules you probably learned in algebra class, but there are a few modifications because there are more operators than you probably expect. These rules are discusses in chapter 9. Assignments and other simple statements are discussed in more detail in chapter 10.

Numbers and Types

Python has three types of numeric representations: **int**, **float**, and **complex**. The **int** type is used for integers, which can take on any value between -2,147,483,648 and 2,147,483,647 on a 32 bit computer, and any value between -9,223,372,036,854,775,808 and 9,223,372,036,854,775,807 on a 64 bit computer.

The **float** type is used to represent anything that has a decimal point. These are called **floating point numbers**. Python floating point numbers can take on any value as large in magnitude as approximately 10^{308} and as small in magnitude as approximately 10^{-308}. Floating point numbers have approximately 17 digits of precision (see chapters 6 and 9 for more detail). A special complex number type (see appendix A for a review of complex numbers) does not really exist in Python. Instead, complex numbers are represented by a pair of **float**'s and the letter **j** (see page 58). For example, the number $2 - 3i$ would be represented by **2-3j**. The function **complex** can also be used to produce a complex number from a real number, or pair of real numbers.

In addition to the three numerical data types discussed, there is also a **boolean** data type. Boolean variables are used to represent expressions that have a truth value. A Boolean variable can take on one of two values, representing truth or falsehood. The special symbols **True** and **False** exist in Python to represent these values. In fact *any* numeric quantity can be used to represent a truth value; if the value is zero, the truth value is treated as **False**, and if it is non-zero, it is treated as true. Boolean expressions and data types are discussed in chapter 11.

Non-numeric data types include sequential data types like strings, lists, and tuplees. There are also objects called sets and dictionaries. Strings (data type **str**) are used to contain text like "My name is Fred" (chapter 15). A **list** is a comma delimited sequence of values enclosed in square brackets, like **[1,2,3]**. A **tuple** is similar to a list except that it is enclosed in parenthesis, as in **(8,3,42,99)**. The main difference between tuples and lists is that the lists are **mutable**, i.e., you can change the value of an element of a list after it has been assigned. Tuples are **immutable** (see chapter 14). A **set** is an unordered collection of unique items (chapter 16), analogous to a set in mathematics, Standard set manipulation operations like intersection and union can be applied to sets. A dictionary (data type **dict**) is organized like a printed dictionary: you can look up an entry by a key rather than a numerical index. For example, if you have a dictionary of phone numbers keyed by first name then **phone["Fred"]** would return Fred's phone number (chapter 24). Finally, you can always define your own data type with classes (chapter 29).

Lines and Indentation

Not all programming languages include the concept of lines; many of them ignore things like the carriage-return and line-feed characters in files or other hidden symbols in files that are used to represent the end of a line and the beginning of a new line. Python does not. Lines are significant in Python. The newline character in Python is **\n**, though in general you will not have to worry about this.

Not only are lines important, but so is spacing (indentation) within a line. Python implements **complex statements** (i.e., multi-line statements), to which we have alluded earlier, using **indentation**. A complex statement begins just before a block of indented lines, and ends with last indented line of code.

How you indent is just as important as **has far you indent**. When you use a word processor, you can indent paragraphs either with a tab key or some number of space characters. The tab key inserts a special character (represented by **\t** in Python). Python sometimes expects a line of code to be **indented**. **When you indent your code, you must use space characters, and not the tab key.**

Sometimes a sequence of lines of code, called a **block** or **suite**, are supposed to be indented at the **same level of indentation**. This means the same number of blank spaces must begin each line of code within the block. The expression "level of indentation" means "number of blank spaces" at the beginning of the line. The amount of indentation does not matter, but it must be the same for each line in the block.

Sometimes we will have a block within a block that requires further indentation. If you have chosen to indent by 4 spaces, and have another block within your first block, then the inner block will be indented 8 spaces, like this:

```
1   line of unindented code
2   line of unindented code
3       first line of block
4       second line of block
5       third line of block
6           start of block within a block
7           second line of inner block
```

8	end of inner block
9	return to outer block
10	more of outer block
11	end of outer block
12	line of unindented code
13	line of unindented code

There is one block that starts on line 3 and ends on line 11. The block on line 6 ends on line 8; after it ends, the flow returns to the block from which the original code started, on line 9, which should agree with the indentation level on line 5. Examples of statements that require indentation are **if**, **while**, **for**, **with**, **try** and **def**.

Conditional Expressions and Statements

Conditional expressions and statements, discussed in chapter 11, perform an action based on the value of a Boolean (i.e., True/False) decision. Examples of Boolean decisions are questions like "is $x > 15$?", "is $(x + y)/2 < z^2$?", and "is $i + j$ even?"

The ternary operator (page 87), for example, can be used to define the step function

$$z = \begin{cases} 1, & \text{if } x > 0 \\ -1, & \text{if } x \leq 0 \end{cases} \tag{2.1}$$

with a single line of code:

```
z = 1 if x > 0 else -1
```

The more traditional **if/elif/else** suites can be used to formulate more complex decisions trees. For example, a graduated income tax code that does not tax income below \$1000, taxes at a 10% rate all income after the first \$1000, up to \$10,000, a 20% rate after that up to \$30,000, and at a 30% rate on additional income, might be implemented as follows.

```
if income < 1000:
    tax = 0
elif income < 10000:
    tax = 0.1*(income-1000)
```

```
elif income < 30000:
    basetax = 0.1*(10000-1000)
    tax = basetax + 0.2*(income-10000)
else:
    basetax = 0.1*(10000-1000)+0.2*(30000-10000)
    tax = basetax + 0.3*(income-30000)
```

The **if** statement is discussed in chapter 11.

Functions, Classes, and Packages

Functions (chapter 18) and classes (chapter 29) give us a way to easily execute computer programs with a standardized interface. Functions describe how things are computed. Classes describe objects that functions operate on. It is not really necessary at this level to learn a lot about classes, since a sufficient number of data types are built into Python. As your hacking skills improve you will want to learn all about classes, because you can develop very elegant and efficient code using classes (e.g., object oriented programming), but that is the subject of other books. Functions, however, play a central role in scientific computing.

Functions have a form that looks like

```
somefunction(variable, variable, variable, ..., variable)
```

An example of a function that already exists in Python is the absolute value function, **abs(x)**. The function **abs(x)** implements the mathematical function $|x|$. Other typical functions that you will become familiar with are in the Python **math** package, such as **sqrt** (square root), **factorial**, and **atan** (arctangent) (see chapter 9).

Functions have both a domain and a range, just like in math. The domain variables are specified in the argument or parameter list, and the range values are given by the function itself. In math we say $f(x) = |x|$ maps the real numbers to the non-negative real numbers. In programming we say the function **abs(x)** returns a value that is the absolute value of **x**. The **return value** is in the range of the function. We obtain the return value by setting the function equal to a variable:

```
y=abs(x)
```

The value of **y** will contain the result calculated by the function **abs(x)**. It is very easy to define our own function in Python; consider the tax table introduced earlier. We could define a function **tax(income)** as follows:

```
def tax(income):
    if income < 1000:
        tax = 0
    elif income < 10000:
        tax = 0.1*(income-1000)
```

```
    elif income < 30000:
        basetax = 0.1*(10000-1000)
        tax = basetax + 0.2*(income-10000)
    else:
        basetax = 0.1*(10000-1000)+0.2*(30000-10000)
        tax = basetax + 0.3*(income-30000)
    return tax
```

We could save this in a file (a package) and then use it later as discussed in chapter 18. Whenever we wanted to use it we could call the function with the statement **y=tax(income)**, for whatever value of **income** we choose.

Loops

Computer programs use loops to repeat the same sequence of operations over and over again. There are four basic types of loops in Python: **for** loops, **while** loops, list comprehension, and generators. The first two types of loops are the most popular, and are present in nearly every mathematically oriented programming language in one form or another.

The **while** loop (chapter 12) is pretty similar to its analogues in other computer languages. The concept is this: while some boolean condition is true, continue to execute some suite of code. Each time the suite is executed (run) is called an **iteration**. As soon the boolean condition becomes false (even if it is false before the first iteration) stop and exit the loop. The following will add up the numbers 5, 10, 15, ..., 100 and print the sum, using a **while** loop.

```
total=0
n=5
while n <= 100:
    total = total + n
    n = n+5
print total
```

The **for** loop (chapter 17) iterates over a sequence and performs an action on every item on that set. The logic is this: for every item **x** in some sequence **S** perform the operations **f(x)**. To add up the numbers 5, 10, 15, ..., 100 using a for loop

```
total=0
for x in range(5,101,5):
    total = total + x
print total
```

One of the key differences between the two types of loops is that some sort of incrementation of the loop index is required in the **while** loop while it is done implicitly in the **for** loop. The incrementation is done by the statement **n=n+5** in the **while** loop, which takes the current value of **n**, adds 5 to it, and then points the variable to the new value.

To understand **list comprehension** (chapter 20) you need to understand Python list data types and mathematical set notation. Think of a Python list as a sequence of numbers separated by commas and enclosed in square brackets, such as

```
S=[2,4,6,8,9,11,15]
```

Suppose we want to generate a new list, **R**, that contains the square of every element in **S**. If these were sets, we could specify this mathematically by

$$R = \{x^2 | x \in S\} \tag{2.2}$$

We can write that almost literally in Python, replacing the $\in$ with the word **in**, the vertical line | with the word **for**, the expression x^2 with equivalent Python code **x**$**2**, and the curly brackets with square brackets:

```
R=[x**2 for x in S]
```

Finally, we have generators. Generators are produced by any function that uses a **yield** rather than a **return** statement. This is analogous to lazy evaluation in functional programming (see chapter 28).

Libraries

There are many functions that extend the capability of Python, but which are not part of the basic definition of the language. To use these functions you must access a library with an **import** statement. The **import** must be executed before any function in the library is executed. (See chapters 10 and 18.)

There are two types of libraries: Python Standard Libraries, and other libraries. The only difference is that the Standard Libraries are defined in the language documentation at python.org and should be part of any standard Python installation. Other libraries may require additional software installation. The most common ways of installing these additional libraries are by using the programs **pip** or **easy_install**, although in some cases, a special install procedure is needed.[2]

Libraries are defined hierarchically and sometimes you will only need to install part of a library. The sub-parts are separated in the name by dots. Thus if you import the library **matplotlib.pyplot** that means you are importing only the **pyplot** sublibrary of **matplotlib**, and not all of **matplotlib**.

A list of some commonly used libraries is given in table 2.1.[3].

---

[2] An index of which packages can be installed by **pip** is maintained at https://pypi.python.org/pypi. As of 23 Dec. 2015, 71626 packages were listed.

[3] A complete list of the Python Standard Libraries is given at https://docs.python.org/2/library/. A list of non-standard but useful scientific libraries is maintained on the wiki at https://wiki.python.org/moin/NumericAndScientific/Libraries

Table 2.1. Some Python Libraries

Some Commonly Used Standard Libraries

`math`	Math	Table 9.6.
`cmath`	Complex Math	Table 9.7.
`fractions`	Rational Numbers	Table 9.8.
`random`	Random numbers	Table 9.9.
`operator`	Function equivalents of Operators	Table 9.10.
`itertools`	Permutations, Combinations	Table 28.1.

Other Commonly Used Libraries Mentioned in the Text

`matplotlib`	Plotting	Chapter 22.
`matplotlib.pyplot`	Plotting	Chapter 22.
`numpy`	Numerical Analysis	Chapter 21.
`numpy.linalg`	Linear Algebra	Table 30.1.
`numpy.random`	Random Numbers	Chapter 34.
`scipy.integrate`	Numerical Integration	Tables 36.1 -36.3.
`scipy.interpolate`	Interpolation	Table 32.1.
`scipy.spatial`	Spatial Geometry	Chapter 31.
`statsmodel`	Statistical Analysis	Chapter 34.
`Image`	Python Imaging Library	Chapter 43.

Other Commonly Used Libraries (Not Mentioned in the Text)

`pandas`	Data Analysis
`sympy`	Symbolic Mathematics
`scikit-learn`	Machine Learning

Chapter 3

The Babylonian Algorithm

Suppose you want to find $\sqrt{2}$. Make a first guess, and call it x_1. Then if your guess is any good,

$$x_1 \approx \sqrt{2} \tag{3.1}$$

Therefore

$$x_1 \cdot x_1 \approx 2 \text{ or } x_1 \approx \frac{2}{x_1} \tag{3.2}$$

If x_1 is a reasonably good guess, then it is very close to $\frac{2}{x_1}$. Even if it is a poor guess, based on (3.2), we have no way to justify either of the following statements:

1) x_1 is a better guess than $2/x_1$.

2) $2/x_1$ is a better guess than x_1.

Since we have two equally good guesses for $\sqrt{2}$, why not take their average? It turns out that

$$x_2 = \frac{1}{2}\left(x_1 + \frac{2}{x_1}\right) \tag{3.3}$$

is always a better estimate of $\sqrt{2}$ than either x_1 or $2/x_1$, regardless of the value of x_1. Next, we apply the same argument to x_2. We arrive at the same conclusion. Repeating this process ad-infinitum,

$$x_3 = \frac{1}{2}\left(x_2 + \frac{2}{x_2}\right) \tag{3.4}$$

$$x_4 = \frac{1}{2}\left(x_3 + \frac{2}{x_3}\right) \tag{3.5}$$

$$x_5 = \frac{1}{2}\left(x_4 + \frac{2}{x_4}\right) \tag{3.6}$$

$$\vdots$$

$$x_{n+1} = \frac{1}{2}\left(x_n + \frac{2}{x_n}\right) \tag{3.7}$$

where each guess is better than the one preceding it.

We can stop when we reach our desired level of precision. For example, suppose we want to know the answer with a precision of six digits to the right of decimal point. Then we keep repeating this process until

$$|x_{n+1} - x_n| < 10^{-6} \tag{3.8}$$

The same argument applies to finding $\sqrt{a}$. The only difference is that instead of averaging x_1 and $2/x_1$, we average x_1 and a/x_1. The result is

$$x_{n+1} = \frac{1}{2}\left(x_n + \frac{a}{x_n}\right) \tag{3.9}$$

We will return to this iteration formula again and again throughout this book.

Bablylonian Algorithm

To find $\sqrt{a}$, let $x_1 = a$ and then iterate using

$$x_{n+1} = \frac{1}{2}\left(x_n + \frac{a}{x_n}\right) \tag{3.10}$$

Here's how we might write this up as an **algorithm**.

Algorithm 3.1 The Babylonian Algorithm.

input: a, tolerance ϵ
1: $x \leftarrow a$
2: **repeat**
3:　　$x_{new} \leftarrow 0.5(x + a/x)$
4:　　$\Delta \leftarrow |x_{new} - x|$
5:　　$x \leftarrow x_{new}$
6: **until** $\Delta < \epsilon$
7: **return** x

The list of instructions above is not written in any computer language. It is an algorithm that is meant to be read by humans, and not by computers. It is written in a standard symbolic language that is midway between mathematics and computer programming. The format of the algorithmic language is designed to make it easy to translate directly into any computer language you like while retaining the basic mathematical content. Details like where you put semicolons and commas are omitted from this language.

Definition 3.1. Algorithm

An **algorithm** is a step by step procedure for performing a computation. It must contain an **identifiable entry point** and must **terminate after a finite number of steps**.

Here is what some of the symbols in algorithm 3.1 mean:

0) **input:** gives the list of numbers that must be provided before you can begin the algorithm.

1,3,4,5) $x \leftarrow a$ means replace the symbol x with the value of symbol a. The arrow is used to indicate which direction the copying goes: the symbol at the arrowhead is changed, while the symbol or expression at the foot of the arrow is not affected. In lines 3, 4, and 5, a computation is performed first, and the result of the computation is then copied into the symbol on the left.

2...6) **repeat..until**: the entire sequence of steps is repeated, in order, over and over again. After each repeat, the expression after the **until** is evaluated. If it is true, then the repetition is terminated. If it is false, the sequence is evaluated again.

7) **return**: gives the quantity that is returned. Everything else is invisible to the outside world except for the value returned.

Algorithms are often represented by flow charts. An flow chart of the Babylonian algorithm is shown in figure 3.1.

Figure 3.1: Flowchart for the Babylonian algorithm.

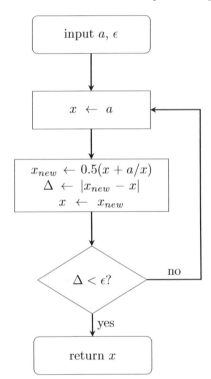

Flowcharts have a standardized format to make them easier to read at a glance (figure 3.2). **Start** and **stop** nodes are drawn as rounded rectangles or ovals. Usually start is at the top and stop is at the bottom but this is not always true. **Diamonds** represent **decisions**. Single or sequences of statements are collected together in rectangles which are called **process** boxes. Sequential flow is represented by the direction of the arrows, generally from top to bottom and left to right.[1] Arrows are generally aligned along horizontal and vertical paths and intersecting lines should be avoided. Additional standard boxes are defined for data, storage devices, documents, and manual entry.

---

[1]The top-to-bottom and left-to-right flow is often modified for typesetting purposes, so that an entire chart can fit into a smaller area. Of course loops require arrows pointing against the flow, so if there is anything really interesting going on there will be arrows in more than one direction.

Figure 3.2: Some standard flow chart symbols.

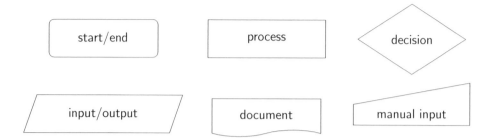

Exercises

1. Estimate $\sqrt{20}$ to 7 significant figures using the Babylonian algorithm. Use your calculator or a spreadsheet to do the calculations. Compare with the correct answer. How many iterations do you need to get all 7 digits to match? How many additional digits do you get on each iterations?

2. Look up Newton's method in your freshman calculus book. Newton's method says that the root of a function $f(x)$ is given by successive iterations on the function $x_{n+1} = x_n - f(x_n)/f'(x_n)$. Show that the Babylonian algorithm can be derived from Newton's method.

3. Let $g(x) = \frac{1}{2}\left(x + \frac{2}{x}\right)$. Suppose $x = g(x)$. Find x.

4. Let $g(x) = \frac{1}{2}\left(x + \frac{a}{x}\right)$. Suppose $x = g(x)$. Find x.

5. Let $g(x) = \frac{1}{2}\left(x + \frac{a}{x}\right)$. For any fixed $a > 1$, show that there exists some number $K < 1$ such that $|g'(x)| \leq K$ in some neighborhood of $x = a$.

6. Suppose you use $g(x) = \frac{1}{2}\left(x + \frac{a}{x}\right)$ to generate a sequence of iterations $p_0, p_1, p_2, ...$ that are estimates for the root. Show that for each value of i there exists some number c_i such that

$$|g(p_{i-1}) - g(p)| = |g'(c_i)||p_{i-1} - p|$$

where $p = g(p)$ is called the fixed point of $g(x)$ (you found this in exercise 4).

7. Use the results of exercises 5 and 6 to show that

$$|g(p_{i-1}) - g(p)| \leq K|p_{i-1} - p|$$

Use the fact that $p_i = g(f_{i-1})$ to show that

$$|p_{i-1} - p| = |g(p_{i-2}) - g(p)|$$
$$\leq |p_{i-2} - p|$$
$$\leq K^2|p_0 - p|$$

where p_0 is your first guess. Use this to prove that the sequence $p_0, p_1, ...$ converges to p.

8. Write an algorithm for your typical morning. Include things like turning off the alarm clock, taking a shower, getting dressed, eating, making the coffee, feeding the dog, etc. Are there decisions that need to be made? Repeated processes (check to see if the dog needs to go out? is ready to come back in? did I turn the water off?).

9. Sketch a flow chart for filling up a bath tub. Things to consider: is the water hot enough? Did I put the drain stopper in? Is the tub full? Did I turn the water off?

10. Write down the steps and draw a flow chart for getting getting gas when you pay at the pump.

11. What is the big deal about the Babylonian algorithm? Why don't we just write down an expression for the the Taylor series for $f(x) = \sqrt{x}$ and add up terms until it converges numerically?

Chapter 4

The Python Shell

Shells and Stuff

You are probably most familiar with opening your apps by **point and click**. You find the right icon and click (or double click, depending on the operating system) to open it. Variations may include some level of navigation through the file hierarchy or menus (e.g., an application or start menu); a dock, task or launcher bar; or a heads-up display, in which you type an option key followed by the first one or two letters of the application's name. Typical applications you would open this way might include word processors, spreadsheets, presentation software, draw and paint programs, and web browsers. Nearly everything can be run this way, and for most people, this will be sufficient. On hand-held systems, such as phones and tables, this is the only way that applications are intended to be run.

However, on full-fledged computing platforms, like laptop and desktop computers, there is another way to run your application. This is via the **command shell** program on your operating system. The command shell is itself an application that you will normally open by one of the methods described in the previous paragraph. But it is a special application that allows you to run any other application on your computer *by typing in the name of the application*.[1] For example, I can open the Firefox web browser on my computer in any of the following ways (see fig. 4.1):

1. Click on the **Firefox** icon on my desktop.
2. Click on the **Firefox** icon on my launcher, dock, taskbar, or start menu (which one will depend on the operating system I am using).

---

[1]Sometimes a slight variation on the name of the application is required.

Figure 4.1: Three different ways to open the firefox web browser on Windows.

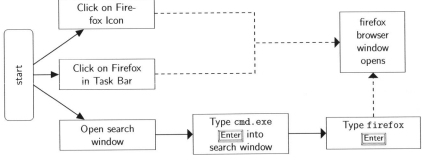

3. Open my command shell application and then type **firefox**, followed by the [Enter] key.

The name of the command shell program on will depend on your operating system. On mac and linux operating systems, it is called **terminal**. On windows, you can use either **cmd.exe** (based on the old DOS operating system) or **powershell** (a more advanced shell). When the command shell application is open, it will look like some variation of figure 4.2. The command shell is just an empty palette for typing in commands. All of the commands are in text, and must be entered from the keyboard.[2]

Figure 4.2: The command shell in linux. There may be some variations in colors. White writing on a black background is typically default, and you may see a copyright message at the top. In Windows the **$**, for example, is replaced by a **>**, and may be preceded by the name of the current directory.

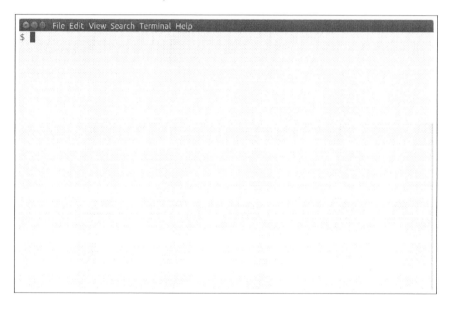

From within the command shell you can open any program on your computer by typing in the name of the program.

The program we will be using first in this book is called the **python shell**. You get to the python shell by typing **python** [Enter] in the command shell (fig. 4.3). When you do this the **prompt** character (the **$** or **>** in the command shell) is replaced by a new prompt, **>>>** (figure 4.4). When you are in the python shell, you can only enter python commands. You may not open other applications from this window, and you may not enter operating system commands. You may open additional command shell windows

---

[2]For windows users, a good place to learn about the command shell quickly is *The CLI Crash Course* by Zed Shaw, which you can read on line for free at http://cli.learncodethehardway.org/. The Mac OS uses a variation of the linux bash command shell, but one place to start learning about it is the book by Joe Kissell, *Take Control of the Mac Command Line with Terminal, 2nd Ed.* For Linux users I suggest Machtelt Garrels' *Bash Guide for Beginners*.

Figure 4.3: The python shell can be entered in different ways: through the command shell, through idle, through a language sensitive editor, dashboard, or interactive development environment.

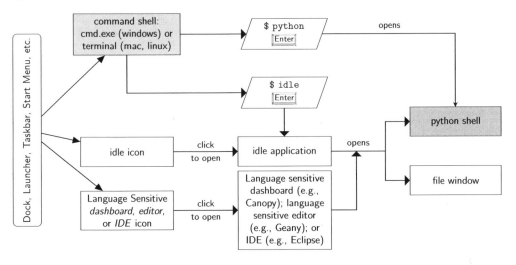

if you want to do these things while the python shell is open.

Sometimes you will use an interactive development environment. The simplest one is called **idle**, and it comes with all python installations. When you open **idle**, either from the command line or from an icon, you will also see a python shell, though it will look a little bit different from the python shell you saw in the previous paragraph. Again, you can only run python commands and not execute other programs from python shell in idle. Additionally, idle has a text editor that allows you edit, save, and run programs, as described later in this chapter. Proprietary environments like anaconda or canopy have their own dashboards and programming environments, which we will not discuss further in this text.

So Let's Do it in Python

How might we implement the Babylonian algorithm Python? Lets start by opening the Python shell. First you need to open a command line program on your operating system (e.g., **cmd.exe** (on Windows) or **terminal** (on Linux or Mac)) and then type in **python** (see figure 4.4). Your computer might have other versions of Python installed as well, like iPython or qtPython that you can open from icons on your desktop. **Do not use these now**. You can use these later; for now you should learn the basic Python window.

In windows: open a search menu, and search for **cmd.exe**. This will open the command line.

On a mac: from the applications > utilities menu, look for **terminal**. This is the command line program.

In the **Python shell** you will see a **>>>** at the beginning of each line. This **>>>** is called a **prompt**. When you see the prompt, it means that Python is waiting for you to do something. If you see a different prompt, like **$**, then you are not in the Python shell.

To leave the Python shell and return to the **command line program** you can always type in **exit(0)**, in any operating system. In Linux you can also use ⌈Ctrl⌉ ⌈D⌋ .

We will often need both a command line window and a Python window open at the same time. To do this, open Python as described above in the first window. Then, if you are in Windows, go to the search window and select **cmd.exe** to open a second command shell. From Linux or Mac you can open a second command window from the file menu (see 4.5).

Figure 4.4: Opening the Python shell from the Windows 8 command prompt.

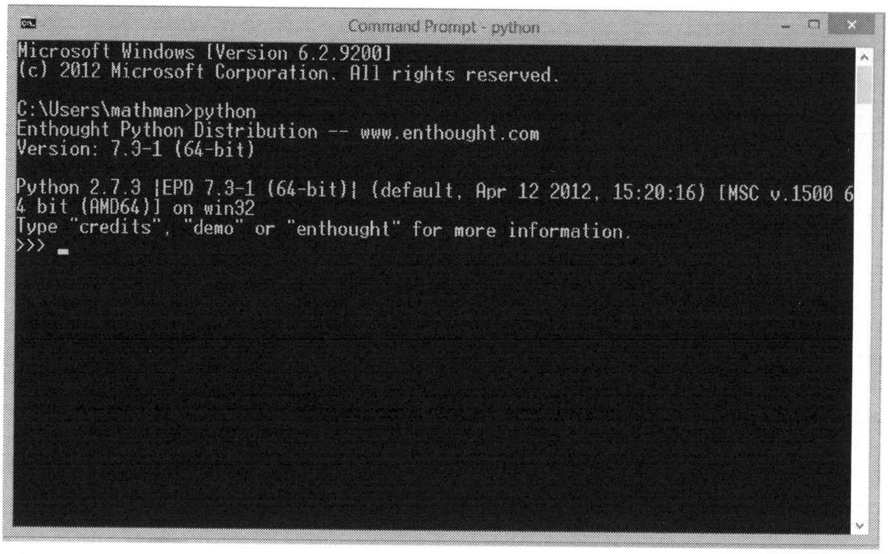

Figure 4.5: A Python shell and a command shell in Ubuntu linux.

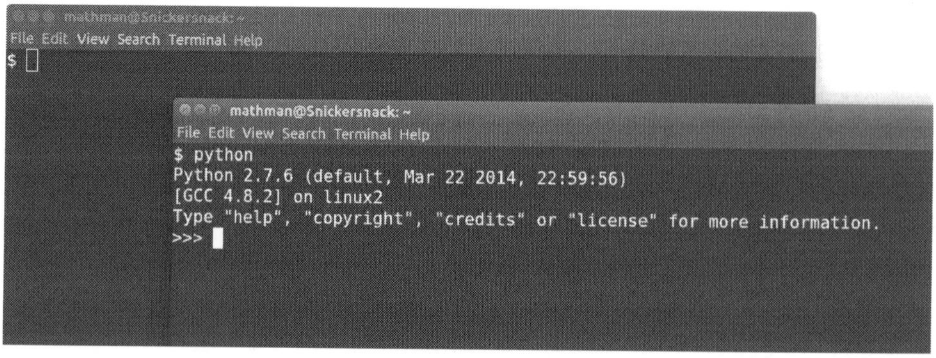

Now type the first three lines of the following code into your Python shell. **Do not type in the >>> prompts**. After each line, type the [Enter] key. A new prompt will appear. When you press [Enter] after the **print** statement, the number **1.5** should be returned by the computer. Since there is no prompt before the **1.5**, you know that the computer printed this number and you did not type it in yourself.

```
>>> x1=2
>>> x2=0.5*(x1+2/x1)
>>> print x2
1.5
```

Now open a text editor like gedit, eclipse, komodo, bbedit, textwrangler, Bluefish, jEdit, Kate, Notepad++, textedit, lightable, bracket, sublime text, ultra edit, geany, scribes, and so forth. Notepad will do but you have to make sure to save you file as a text file. If you are already familiar with them, feel free to use emacs or Vim, but if you don't, leave these for later.

Open up a new file and type in the following code.

```
x1 = 2
x2 = (x1+2.0/x1)*0.5
print "x2=",x2
x3 = (x2+2.0/x2)*0.5
print "x3=",x3
x4 = (x3+2.0/x3)*0.5
print "x4=",x4
x5 = (x4+2.0/x4)*0.5
print "x5=",x5
x6 = (x5+2.0/x5)*0.5
print "x6=",x6
x7 = (x6+2.0/x6)*0.5
print "x7=",x7
```

Save the file as **babyl.py** and verify that the program you are using doesn't try to append a different file type to it like **.txt**. Exit the editor and go to to the command shell (not the python shell). You should see the file you just saved.

In windows, type

```
$ dir babl.py
```

On a mac or in linux, type

```
$ ls babyl.py
```

You just asked the computer to show you a list of all the programs in the local folder (directory) named **babyl.py**. You should see one line, which looks something like this:

```
babyl.py
```

If you do not see your program listed then you are not in the appropriate folder. Go back and figure out where you saved your program and open a new command shell there, or find the folder where you did save the program to and then type

```
$ cd PATHNAME
```

in the command line. The same command will work on all operating systems. You need to replace **PATHNAME** with the full path of the folder where you saved your file. Repeat the previous paragraph until you succeed.

When you have found your file, type the following:

```
$ python baby1.py
```

As soon as you press [Enter] , the computer will spit out several lines, like this:

```
x2= 1.5
x3= 1.41666666667
x4= 1.41421568627
x5= 1.41421356237
x6= 1.41421356237
x7= 1.41421356237
```

If your output looks something like this, then you have succeeded in running your program from the command line.

Now for one more run. Go to the command line again and type

```
$ idle
```

followed by [Enter] .

A new and slightly different looking Python shell will open up. You may also be able to find an [idle] icon on your computer. On the idle menu select **file** > **new** (or equivalently, [Ctrl] [n]). A new window will pop open. Copy the entire text of the **baby1.py** program into this window. Then hit the [f5] key. You will be prompted for a file name - save the file this time as **baby12.py**. When you click OK, the program will run in the idle-python window. See figure 4.6.

We've implemented the repeated calculations of the Babylonian algorithm by brute force, namely, by typing the same thing in over and over again. This works fine if you only have to do it a few times. In later chapters we will revise the implementation so that you don't have to type the same thing over and over again.

File Extensions for Windows Users

In all versions of Windows operating systems, the portions of the file name following the period are normally hidden from the user. This is because Windows thinks it is smart enough to figure out what those extra letters means. Sometimes it does, and sometimes it doesn't. If you want to be able to tell which files are Python programs at a glance, you will want to be able to see the file extension, which must be **.py**. To display file extensions, search for the string **file extensions** in the control panel (or just open up a search window). From the Folder Options Menu (figure 4.7), remove the check mark next to the line that says "**Hide file extensions for known file types**" and then click on **Apply**

Figure 4.6: The idle Python window.

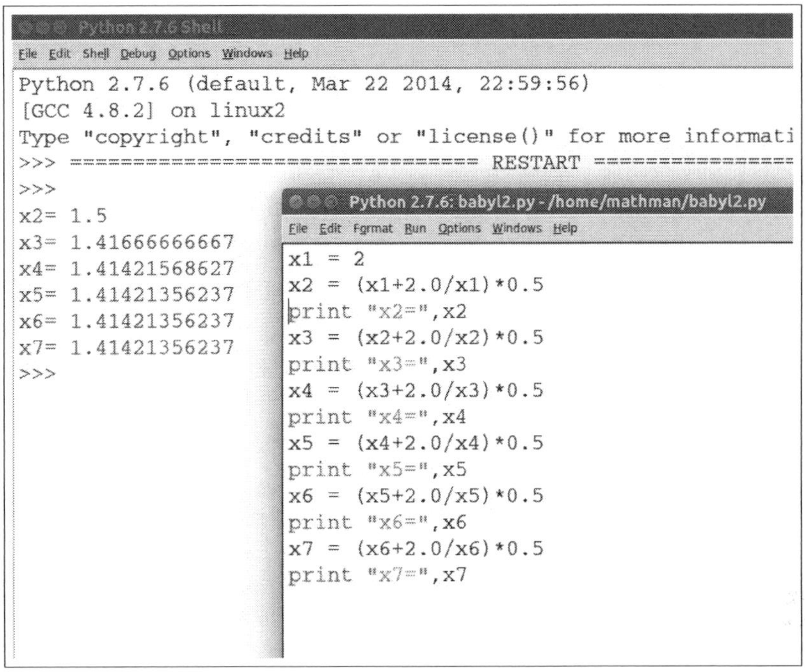

```
Python 2.7.6 Shell
File  Edit  Shell  Debug  Options  Windows  Help
Python 2.7.6 (default, Mar 22 2014, 22:59:56)
[GCC 4.8.2] on linux2
Type "copyright", "credits" or "license()" for more informati
>>> ================================= RESTART ==================
>>>
x2= 1.5
x3= 1.41666666667
x4= 1.41421568627
x5= 1.41421356237
x6= 1.41421356237
x7= 1.41421356237
>>>
```

```
Python 2.7.6: babyl2.py - /home/mathman/babyl2.py
File  Edit  Format  Run  Options  Windows  Help
x1 = 2
x2 = (x1+2.0/x1)*0.5
print "x2=",x2
x3 = (x2+2.0/x2)*0.5
print "x3=",x3
x4 = (x3+2.0/x3)*0.5
print "x4=",x4
x5 = (x4+2.0/x4)*0.5
print "x5=",x5
x6 = (x5+2.0/x5)*0.5
print "x6=",x6
x7 = (x6+2.0/x6)*0.5
print "x7=",x7
```

File extensions are normally shown on Mac and Linux systems so no additional modification is required.

Exercises

1. Explain the steps needed to open the python shell on your computer. What is the difference between python and idle?

2. Compare and contrast the python shell and the command shell.

   (a) List at least three things you can do in the command shell that you can not do in the python shell.

   (b) Describe something you can only do in the python shell.

   (c) Explain how to the open the python shell and how to open the command shell.

3. Explain the difference between command shell and command line. How do you write a command line program on your computer?

4. What is the difference between an interactive program and a command line program? A command line program and an application?

5. Figure out how to open up the command shell on your computer. Open the command shell and from the command shell do each of the following:

   (a) print the name of the current directory (folder)

   (b) print the names of all the files in the current directory

   (c) print a list of the names of all the files in the current directory with only one name per line and nothing else on the line

   (d) print a list of the files in the current directory showing the file size, creation date, and file protection

Figure 4.7: Show file extensions for removing the check box next to **hide extensions for know file types**, then click **Apply**.

(e) without changing the current directory, print the name of the parent directory

(f) print a list of all files of extension **.png** in the current directory. If there are no **.png** files there, find a picture on the internet, and save one to the current folder using your web browser and then repeat this task.

(g) change your current directory to the parent directory

(h) show the new directory

(i) set your directory to your home folder

(j) create a new folder called **python-homework**

(k) set your directory to **python-homework**

(l) open the Python shell by typing **python** in the command line

6. In the Python shell,

(a) Assign a values of 7 and 10 to variables **p** and **q**

(b) Calculate and print out $p + q$, $p - q$, pq and p/q. For the quotient, calculate the result both using integer and floating point division.

(c) Find 10 mod 7 and 7 mod 10 using Python

(d) Type in the line **import math** and then hit the enter key

(e) Find $\sqrt{2}$ by typing **sqrt(2)**

7. Type in the code for a single calculation of the Babylonian algorithm for $\sqrt{7}$. Let $x_0 = 7$. Find x_1. Repeat several calculations. Try to get the algorithm to converge to 7 places.

8. Create a text file that contains the code for ten iterations of the Babylonian algorithm for $\sqrt{37}$. Have it print the output after each iteration, as we did on page 25. Save the file and run it from the command line.

9. It is traditional in programming classes for your first program to be one that prints out the string "Hello World!" to the screen. Write a "Hello World!" program and save it to a file **hello.py**. Run it from the command line.

Chapter 5

iPython Notebooks

IPython notebooks are not really part of Python, and you may wish to skip this chapter entirely. Notebooks provide a way to combine Python code, documentation, analysis, output, and figures all together in one file. They are particularly convenient for student projects. To a certain extent they resemble the type of interface you might see in a commercial program like Mathematica or Matlab.

The key to iPython notebooks is the iPython notebook viewer, which is implemented using a program called **jupyter** in your web Browser. Notebooks are stored in a special file format called JSON. That means that you can't edit them or change them except using special software. If you have a web browser on your computer like Firefox, Internet Explorer, or Safari, you can install iPython. Chances are, iPython was automatically installed when you installed Python.

Figure 5.1: The iPython-jupyter iterface on a mac. Open this interface by typing **ipython notebook** in a terminal window, such as **cmd.exe**. When you first open the interfae all you see is a listing of accessible files and folders. Notebooks will end with the letters **.ipynb**.

To open the notebook interface you need to go to the command line (the terminal program such as **cmd.exe**, **terminal** or **powershell**) and type in the line[1]

---

[1]Some python distributions, such as Enthought, will come with launchers. You avoid these interfaces until they know what they are doing, because they add in shortcuts that break Python standards, such as including all of **pylab** without telling you. Notebooks created in this manner are not compatible with standard Python, and should be used with caution. Don't be surprised if you create a notebook

```
ipython notebook
```

This command will start a local web server running on your computer that can read
and write iPython notebooks. Don't worry – you are not setting up a web site. This is
a special type of web server that you can only access from your computer. Just ignore
the stuff that scrolls down the terminal. At the same time, a new browser window will
open in whatever is the default browser in your operating system. An example of what
you will see is shown in figure 5.1.

Figure 5.2: Creating a new notebook from the menu.

To create a new notebook, click on the drop-down menu labeled **New** and select **python
2** (fig. 5.2). Your new notebook appears in a tab labeled **Untitled** (fig. 5.3).

Figure 5.3: A new empty notebook.

Notebooks are organized in pieces that are called cells; these are like paragraphs or
chapters in a book. Each cell can contain whatever you want: a function, a piece of
code, a picture, an essay, some documentation, or some program output. The empty
notebook we have just created has a single empty **cell** in it labeled(for now) **In [ ]:**.
The word **In** means it is an input cell, and the fact that nothing is written between the
square brackets means that we have not executed the cell.

The numbers inside the brackets are filled in sequentially in the order in which they are
are run. So if you go back to an earlier cell in your notebook, modify the value, and
re-run it, the output of that cell will show the output with the new value. If subsequent

---

in Canopy and turn it in only to get a failing grade because it crashed when your professor rand
the program, because you didn't know you had to include some library that Canopy automatically
included without telling you!

cells in the notebook depend on this value, but are not re-run, any output they have calculated will remain unchanged. This can lead to some confusion in reading notebooks if you scroll back-and-forth making changes.

Figure 5.4: One calculation of the Babylonian Algorithm in an iPython notebook.

A cell is executed by putting the cursor anywhere in the cell (with the mouse) and then typing `Shift ⇑` - `Enter` (i.e., by hitting the `Shift ⇑` and `Enter` keys simultaneously). Hitting the `Enter` key alone will just add a new line to the cell. Thus it is possible to execute cells out of order in a notebook.

Suppose we enter the code `x=99` and then press `Shift ⇑` - `Enter` . Nothing much happens except that the number 1 appears between the brackets. But then this is what we would also expect in the Python shell. If we now try to calculate one iteration of the Babylonian algorithm and print out the result, we see something different. It creates output cells (figure 5.4).

Notebooks are particularly useful for combining both text and graphics. Instead of using a **show()** command (chapter 22) all graphics output can be redirected to the notebook and the corresponding **show()** call omitted if you include the command

```
%matplotlib inline
```

before your first graphics command (fig. 5.5).

Additional cells can be added for documentation. If these cells are labeled as markdown using the drop-down menu in the center of the toolbar that is normally listed as code, then formatting commands can be added using both html and latex.

Complete documentation of the iPython notebook is given on the official website at `http://ipython.org/documentation.html`.

Figure 5.5: Including graphics in the notebook requires using the "magic" command.

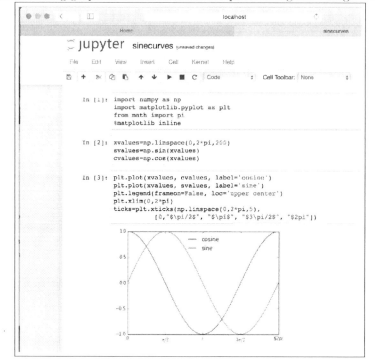

Exercises

1. Create a new ipython notebook on your system.

2. Inside your notebook create a cell that defines a function **f(x,a)** to do one update of the Babylonian algorithm for $\sqrt{a}$.

3. Write a program, in a different cell, that calculates $\sqrt{42}$ using the function you created in exercise 2.

4. Go back to the top of your notebook and insert a new cell. Write the line **import math**, and then execute the cell

5. Scroll back down to the bottom of the notebook, and calculate $\sqrt{42}$ using **math.sqrt(42)**. Compare your answer with the number you calculated using the Baybylonian algorithm. Create a new Markdown cell and type in your observations.

Chapter 6

Numbers in Computers

Binary Numbers

The information in a computer is stored in binary (base 2). This is because of the hardware design of all computers used today, which are based on switching circuits. At the very heart of their circuits are simple components called **switches** which can be in either of two states: **on** or **off**. These two states are used to represent the numbers zero and one. The term **bit** is a shortened form of the oxymoronic term **binary digit**.[1] Consequently, modern computers are called **digital computers** (again oxymoronically, since they are really binary).

Consider the base ten number 117.[2] To understand how 117_{10} is stored in the computer, we first recall from elementary school arithmetic that

$$117_{10} = (1 \times 10^2) + (1 \times 10^1) + (7 \times 10^0) \tag{6.1}$$

To represent the same number in base two, we need to expand it in **powers of 2** instead of **powers of 10**. Since

$$117 = 64 + 32 + 16 + 4 + 1 \tag{6.2}$$
$$= (1 \times 2^6) + (1 \times 2^5) + (1 \times 2^4) + (0 \times 2^3) + (1 \times 2^2) + (0 \times 2^1) + (1 \times 2^0) \tag{6.3}$$

we know that there must be 1's in the 1, 4, 16, 32, and 64 places, and zeros in the 2's and 8's places. So we have

$$117_{10} = 0111\ 0101_2 \tag{6.4}$$

When typesetting binary numbers, a space is typically left every fourth bit. This space is analogous to the comma[3] that is normally used every third place when typesetting decimals. The four-bit grouping is useful because it makes conversion to **hexadecimal** (base 16) much easier. In addition to the digits 0 through 9, hexadecimal also uses the letters A through E to represent the numbers 10 through 15:

---

[1] The term **digit** refers exclusively to base 10, because we have ten fingers (digits).

[2] When there is any confusion about the base, we use a subscript next to the number to represent the base. Instead of writing "117 in base 10" we write 117_{10}.

[3] Commas are used every third digit, and a period is used for a decimal point, in North America. In much of the rest of the world, however, the period and the comma are interchanged, so that 5,678.45 becomes 5.678,45.

$$0 \cdots 9 \text{ represent } 0 \cdots 9$$
$$A \text{ represents } 10$$
$$B \text{ represents } 11$$
$$C \text{ represents } 12$$
$$D \text{ represents } 13$$
$$E \text{ represents } 14$$
$$F \text{ represents } 15$$

Since

$$117_{10} = (7 \times 16^1) + (5 \times 16^0) \tag{6.5}$$

we can write

$$117_{10} = 75_{16} \tag{6.6}$$

We can also convert 4 bit grouping individually to hexadecimal:

$$117_{10} = \underbrace{0111}_{7} \ \underbrace{0101}_{5} = 75_{16} \tag{6.7}$$

A similar direct conversion to **octal** (base 8) could be made by collecting the bits in groups of three instead of groups of four.

Nibbles, Bits, and Bytes

The basic hardware unit of memory is a **byte**, which represents eight bits. It is convenient, sometimes, to think of a byte as a place with eight "slots," each of which can contain a one or a zero. For example, we might write 117_{10} as

$$117_{10} = \boxed{0|1|1|1} \ \boxed{0|1|0|1} \tag{6.8}$$

Each block of four bits is called a **nibble**.

Since a nibble has four slots, it can represent any of $2^4 = 16$ different numbers.

A byte has 8 bits or can represent any of $2^8 = 256$ different numbers.

A **word** consists of 4 bytes or 32 bits, and can represent up to $2^{32} = 4,294,967,296$ different numbers. The four-gigabyte limit on old computers was a result of a computer addressing scheme that counted memory locations using a single 32 bit word.

A **double-word** consists of 2 words, or 64 bits, and can represent up to $2^{64} = 18,446,774,073,709,551,616$ different numbers. Most computers sold today use 64-bit memory.

Because $2^{10} = 1024 \approx 1000$ the word "kilo" became popular to represent chunks of 1024 bytes in the early days of computing, in analogy with its use in the metric system to represent chunks of 1000 litres or 1000 metres. This led to a relatively small error (2.4%) that most people did not care about. But this error is compounded when larger amounts of memory are computed. Consequently, to represent memory correctly, the correct nomenclature (rarely used) is that $2^{10} = 1024$ bits = 1 **Kibibit**, while 1000 bits = 1 **kilobit**. Unfortunately these terms are almost always used incorrectly.

Value	Letter	Name	Value	Letter	Name
1000	k	kilo	1024	Ki	kibi
1000^2	M	mega	1024^2	Mi	mebi
1000^3	G	giga	1024^3	Gi	gibi
1000^4	T	tera	1024^4	Ti	tebi
1000^5	P	peta	1024^5	Pi	pebi
1000^6	E	exa	1024^6	Ei	exbi
1000^7	Z	zetta	1024^7	Zi	zebi
1000^8	Y	yotta	1024^8	Yi	yobi

Example 6.1. Misleading Computer Hardware Labels. You purchase a new hard disk for your computer. The label on the box says 1.5 terabytes, and one terabyte $= 1000^4$ bytes. You plug it into your computer and it says it has a capacity of only 1.36 TB. What happened to the other 140 MB?

The computer is calculating the memory in tebabytes:

$$1.5 \text{ terabytes } \times \frac{(1000)^4 \text{ bytes/terabyte}}{(1024)^4 \text{ bytes/tebabyte}} = 1.36424 \text{ tebabytes} \qquad (6.9)$$

All operating systems display memory in units of 1024 Bytes. The manufacturer is being honest when it says that it is selling you 1.5 terabytes - because a terabyte is 10^{12} bytes. Your computer is also being honest, because it is not displaying the information in terabyptes but in tebibytes, and a tebibyte is $1024^4 = 1.024^4 \times 10^{12}$ bytes. Thus 1.5TB $=$ 1.36TiB. Manufacturers are always going to label things in the largest possible number, to make it look like you are getting the most for your money. To the computer, however, that 1.5 has no significance, and it only measures things in units of 1024 bytes.

Integer Representation

Computer words are just strings of ones and zeros, so there is no way intrinsically to represent a negative number. Suppose, for example, that we have a computer with 4-bit words. Every word in our hypothetical computer can take on up to 16 different values. If we write these as

$$0000_2 = 0_{10}, \ 0001_2 = 1_{10}, \ 0010_2 = 2_{10}, \dots, 1110_2 = 14_{10}, \ 1111_2 = 15_{10} \qquad (6.10)$$

then we are only representing the non-negative numbers $0 \leq n \leq 15$. What we would really like is to have around half of the numbers represent negative numbers, and around half represent positive numbers.

There are several common ways that the interpretation of the number stored in memory can be changed so that we treat half of the numbers as negative. The actual representation varies from computer to computer.

Use a Sign Bit. We can use let the first bit represent the sign: If the sign bit is 0, treat the rest of the number as positive; if the sign bit is 1, treat the rest of the number as negative.

$$
\begin{array}{ll}
0000 = 0 & 1000 = \text{-}0 \\
0001 = 1 & 1001 = \text{-}1 \\
0010 = 2 & 1010 = \text{-}2 \\
0011 = 3 & 1011 = \text{-}3 \\
0100 = 4 & 1100 = \text{-}4 \\
0101 = 5 & 1101 = \text{-}5 \\
0110 = 6 & 1110 = \text{-}6 \\
0111 = 7 & 1111 = \text{-}7 \\
\end{array}
$$

As we can see there are two different representations for zero, but we can represent all integers from $-7 \leq n \leq 7$ with this scheme.

One's complement. In one's complement notation, we use a sign bit as well, but if the sign bit is 1, we first flip all the bits and then treat the number as negative. If the sign bit is zero we read the number as is and treat it as positive.

$$
\begin{array}{ll}
0000 = 0 & 1000 \rightarrow 0111 = -7 \\
0001 = 1 & 1001 \rightarrow 0110 = -6 \\
0010 = 2 & 1010 \rightarrow 0101 = -5 \\
0011 = 3 & 1011 \rightarrow 0100 = -4 \\
0100 = 4 & 1100 \rightarrow 0011 = -3 \\
0101 = 5 & 1101 \rightarrow 0010 = -2 \\
0110 = 6 & 1110 \rightarrow 0001 = -1 \\
0111 = 7 & 1111 \rightarrow 0000 = -0 \\
\end{array}
$$

The consequence is the same as before; we still have two representations for zero, and range of -7 to 7.

Excess-p notation. Let $p = 2^{n-1} - 1$ where n is the number of bits. For our four-bit machine, we have $p = 7$. We assume that the number represented by the computer is just off by 7.

$$
\begin{array}{ll}
0000 = 0\text{-}7 = \text{-}7 & 1000 = 8\text{-}7{=}1 \\
0001 = 1\text{-}7 = \text{-}6 & 1001 = 9\text{-}7{=}2 \\
0010 = 2\text{-}7{=}\text{-}5 & 1010 = 10\text{-}7{=}3 \\
0011 = 3\text{-}7{=}\text{-}4 & 1011 = 11\text{-}7{=}4 \\
0100 = 4\text{-}7{=}\text{-}3 & 1100 = 12\text{-}7 = 5 \\
0101 = 5\text{-}7{=}\text{-}2 & 1101 = 13\text{-}7{=}6 \\
0110 = 6\text{-}7{=}\text{-}1 & 1110 = 14\text{-}7{=}7 \\
0111 = 7\text{-}7{=}0 & 1111 = 15\text{-}7{=}8 \\
\end{array}
$$

This time we only have one representation of zero, and we have gained an extra integer: $-7 \leq n \leq 8$.

Two's complement notation. In this representation, positive numbers are represented normally and negative numbers are represented by flipping their bits and adding 1. This if the first bit is a 1 we automatically know the number is negative.

$$0000 = 0 \quad 0111 + 1 \rightarrow 1000 =\text{-}8$$
$$0001 = 1 \quad 1110 + 1 \rightarrow 1111 =\text{-}1$$
$$0010 = 2 \quad 1101 + 1 \rightarrow 1110 =\text{-}2$$
$$0011 = 3 \quad 1100 + 1 \rightarrow 1101 =\text{-}3$$
$$0100 = 4 \quad 1011 + 1 \rightarrow 1100 =\text{-}4$$
$$0101 = 5 \quad 1010 + 1 \rightarrow 1011 =\text{-}5$$
$$0110 = 6 \quad 1001 + 1 \rightarrow 1010 =\text{-}6$$
$$0111 = 7 \quad 1000 + 1 \rightarrow 1001 =\text{-}7$$

Two' complement has the advantage that mathematical operations work normally – no special hardware is needed. The math just comes out right. Furthermore, there is only a single representation for zero; there is no "negative zero," like there is in the one's complement notation. Nearly all computers implement the two's complement method in their hardware, although some early computers used the other techniques.

Numbers with Decimal Points

There is no decimal point in a computer word so we cannot represent anything except for integers directly. Instead, we approximate real numbers by their **floating point representation**

$$x = (\pm 1) \times (m) \times 10^{E} \tag{6.11}$$

where E is an integer **exponent**, m is an integer **mantissa**, and one bit is reserved for the **sign**.

There are three standard ways of doing this, depending upon whether one, two or four words of 32 bit memory are used. Understanding these implementations will help you to understand why computations work the way they do.

In the **IEEE 32 bit standard**[4] a single 32 bit word of memory is used to represent a floating point number.

sign, s	exponent, e	mantissa, f
one bit	8 bits	23 bits

Since there are $2^8 = 256$ possible exponents, there is a range of approximately $10^{\pm 38}$ values;[5] and since there are 23 bits in the mantissa, there are $2^{23} = 8,388,608$ possible mantissas, which gives approximately 7 significant figures. This is called **single precision** in some languages, but is not used in Python.

In the **IEEE 64 bit standard** two 32 bit words of memory (on older computers) or one 64 bit word of memory is used to represent a floating point number. This is the representation used by Python.

sign, s	exponent, e	mantissa, f
one bit	11 bits	52 bits

[4]IEEE Standard for Binary Floating-Point Arithmetic, IEEE Standard 754, revised 2008.
[5]To get this solve $10^n \approx 2^{127}$ for n - reserving one exponent bit for the sign.

There are 11 bits in the exponent, so that $2^{11} = 2048$ possible exponents. This gives a range of approximately $10^{\pm 308}$. The 52 bit mantissa has $2^{52} \approx 7.2 \times 10^{16}$ possible values, giving approximately 15 significant figures. This representation is called **double** or **double precision** in some languages.

In the **IEEE 128 bit standard** four 32 bit words, or two 64 bit words are used for a total of 128 bits.

There are $2^{15} = 32,768$ possible exponents, giving a range of approximately $10^{\pm 4931}$. There are $2^{112} \approx 5.2 \times 10^{33}$ possible mantissas, for approximately 33 significant figures. This representation is called **quadruple precision** in Fortran or **long double** in some C/C++ compilers.

Exercises

1. Convert from decimal to binary:
   (a) 100   (b) 142   (c) 1/3   (d) 0.1

2. Convert from octal to binary:
   (a) 73   (b) 462   (c) 7632   (d) 101.101

3. Convert from binary numbers to decimal, octal and hexadecimal:
   (a) 110101   (b) 1101.111
   (c) 110110111   (d) 1.101010101

4. Convert from hexadecimal to decimal:
   (a) 10   (b) A1   (c) FF1A   (d) 1A

5. Referring ahead to chapter 9, write python representations of:

   (a) Each octal integer in exercise 2.
   (b) Each binary integer in exercise 3.
   (c) Each of the hexadecimal numbers in exercise 4.

Chapter 7

When Numbers Fail

In Python the standard floating point representation gives us about 15 significant figures. Why do we need so much precision in floating point numbers?

There are two basic problems. First, not all decimal numbers can be represented precisely in binary. For example, $1/10$ is a repeating decimal in base 2, and whenever we truncate, we get an error:

$$0.110 = 0.0001\ 1001\ 1001\ \overline{1001}_2 \tag{7.1}$$

Second, most numerical computations will include a large number (millions or billions or more) of repeated calculations, and even small errors can build up over time.

Roundoff Error

To understand roundoff error, we will consider a computer that stores its numbers in base 10 rather than base 2, because as human beings we can understand base 10 more easily. Let's use the Babylonian algorithm to calculate $\sqrt{a}$ with 3-digit truncation. This means we truncate every calculation to 3 digits. In the algorithm, we start with some initial guess x_0 and then iterate on

$$x_{n+1} = \frac{1}{2}\left(x_n + \frac{a}{x_n}\right) \tag{7.2}$$

until $|x_{n+1} - x_n| < \epsilon$ for a desired tolerance ϵ. For example, here are some possible iterations for several values of a and different starting values.

a	4.00	1.00	0.800	0.950	0.999
x_0	2.50	0.500	0.900	0.970	0.995
x_1	2.05	1.25	0.890	0.970	0.995
x_2	2.00	1.02	0.890	0.970	0.995
x_3	2.00	1.00	0.890	0.970	0.995
exact	2.00	1.00	0.894	0.970	0.999

In each case, if there are extra digits, they just fall off the right end of the storage space for the number and are lost. This is equivalent to dropping (or truncating) the last digits.

In the third column,

$$x_1 = (0.900 + .800/.900)/2 = (.900 + .888)/2 = 1.78/2 = 0.890 \tag{7.3}$$

In the fourth column,

$$x_1 = (0.970 + .950/.970)/2 = (0.970 + .979)/2 = 1.94/2 = 0.970 \qquad (7.4)$$

In the last column the error is even worse, as it moves *away* from the correct answer.

$$x_1 = (0.995 + 0.999/.995)/2 = (0.995 + 1.00)/2 = 1.99/2 = .995 \qquad (7.5)$$

The answer is worse than the first guess, even though we know the algorithm is *mathematically* guaranteed to converge to the correct answer.

The problem in all of these cases is that we are calculating the average of two numbers, and the formula $(a + b)/2$ will not always work. A worst-case scenario would be something like the average of 0.501 and 0.503:

$$\frac{0.501 + 0.503}{2} = \frac{1.00}{2} = 0.5 \qquad (7.6)$$

which is not even between 0.501 and 0.503. This is because $0.501 + 0.503 \neq 1.004$, because we are only using three digits. The fourth digit is lost. So we end up with an average that is not even between the two original numbers. A better formula for the average would be

$$\text{average} = a + \frac{b - a}{2} \qquad (7.7)$$

Then

$$.501 + \frac{.503 - .501}{2} = .501 + \frac{.002}{2} = .501 + .001 = .502 \qquad (7.8)$$

The worst case happens when the average falls on one endpoint, e.g.,

$$.501 + \frac{.503 - .502}{2} = .501 + \frac{.001}{2} = .501 + .000 = .501 \qquad (7.9)$$

At least now the average is between the two end points (inclusively).

Numerical Errors: Dhahran, 1991

From the New York Times:

> DHAHRAN, Saudi Arabia, Tuesday, Feb. 26, 1991 In the most devastating Iraqi stroke of the Persia Gulf war, an Iraqi missile demolished a barracks housing more than 100 American troops on Monday night, killing 27 and wounding 98, the American military command in Riyadh said early today.

Three months later, on May 29, the same newspaper printed this:

> The Iraqi missile that slammed into an American military barracks in Saudi Arabia during the Persian Gulf war, killing 28 people, penetrated air defenses because a computer failure shut down the American missile system designed to counter it, two Army investigations have concluded ... The radar system never saw the incoming missile, said Col. Bruce Garnett, who conducted one of the investigations...

What was behind this failure of the American PATRIOT[1] anti-missile system to shoot down the incoming Iraqi Scud missile? The Scud missile was travelling at Mach 5 (five times the speed of sound), approximately 6000 km/hour or 1700 meters per second. The PATRIOT uses a radar system to track and shoot down precisely this type of missile.

The software in the PATRIOT stored time as a 24-bit number in units of 1/10 of a second. Since 1/10 cannot be represented exactly in based 2 it was truncated as

$$0.1_{10} \approx 0.0001\ 1001\ 1001\ 1001\ 1001\ 100_2 \tag{7.10}$$

or

$$0.1 \approx 2^{-4} + 2^{-5} + 2^{-8} + 2^{-9} + 2^{-12} + 2^{-13} + 2^{-16} + 2^{-17} + 2^{-20} + 2^{-21} \tag{7.11}$$

$$= \frac{209,715}{2,097,152} \tag{7.12}$$

Therefore the error that was made with each tick of the clock was

$$\epsilon = \frac{1}{10} - \frac{209,715}{2,097,152} = \frac{1}{10,485,760} \approx 9.54 \times 10^{-8} \tag{7.13}$$

every 0.1 second:

- After one second, the accumulated error in time is 9.54×10^{-7} seconds
- After one minute, the accumulated error is 0.0000572205 seconds
- After one hour, the accumulated error is 0.00343323 seconds
- After one day, the accumulated error is 0.0823975 seconds
- After 100 hours, the accumulated error is 0.343323 seconds

At the time of the attack, the computer had been running for approximately 100 hours without being reset. So there was an accumulated error of 0.3433 seconds. Since the Scud was travelling at approximately 1.7 km/second, the radar was expecting the missile to be approximately 580 meters away from where it actually was. Since it wasn't where it should have been, it was not classified as a threat.

The programmers knew about the accumulated error problem but this information had not been communicated to the operators of the system in combat for undetermined reasons (chain of command, security, who knows?) A fix for the software was in transit at the time of the attack. Had the attack occurred a week later the PATRIOT would have intercepted the incoming missile.

Atlanta Airport, 2009

From the Los Angeles Times, 20 Nov 2009:

> **U.S. flight delays hit Atlanta airport especially hard: The FAA blames a computer glitch in Salt Lake City.** Hundreds of flights

---

[1] *Phased Array Tracking Radar to Intercept Of Target*, aka *Protection Against Threats, Real, Imagined, or Theorized.*

around the country were canceled or delayed Thursday after a communications failure at a Federal Aviation Administration computer center, leaving passengers scrambling to revise travel plans. The glitch, which occurred about 5 a.m. Eastern time, prevented airlines from electronically entering their flight plans into an FAA computer in Salt Lake City that air traffic controllers nationwide rely on.

But what is a **computer glitch**?

There is no such thing as a computer glitch. The word glitch has no meaning. **Either someone wrote an incorrect program, or someone did not run the program properly**. Someone did not do his or her job correctly. The only reason we use a word like glitch is that we then do not have to hold anyone accountable. (Tom Impelluso, Los Angeles Times, 24 Nov. 2009)

A computer glitch is a problem that has not been solved. It is not a problem with the computer. It is because the computer was incorrectly used. In the case of the PATRIOT missiles, the error was leaving on the system for too long but not telling the users that was not a good thing. The error in the FAA software was not identified.

USS Yorktown, 1997, and Windows NT: Dead in the Water

The USS Yorktown was a Aegis missile cruiser in the US Navy launched in 1984. In the early 1990's it was retro-fitted with a new Engineering Control and Integrated Bridge System built by Litton Industries in Woodland Hills, California, at a cost of nearly $140 Million. In these "smart ships" all on-board systems were controlled by applications running under Windows NT. However, when bad data was fed into one of the computers during maneuvers off Cape Charles, VA, on 21 Sept., 1997, a division by zero error occurred in the system software. This error caused the entire on-board computer network to crash; the ship's crew were unable to bring systems back up again. This made the ship entirely "dead in the water" for about two and half hours (quote from Commander John Singley of the Atlantic Fleet Surface Force, archived in *Wired*). The ship had to be towed to port. The Yorktown was decommissioned in 2004.

F-22 Raptors, 2007: The International Date What?

In the first deployment of twelve new F-22 Raptors to Okinawa, while en-route from Hawaii in 2007, as they crossed the international dateline all their systems failed because of a software error that assumed this event would never occur. The pilots managed to navigate the aircraft back to Hawaii by manually following a tanker.

Google, 2009: The entire internet is spam

On Jan 30, 2009, a programmer at Google accidentally entered "/" as the address of a malware site. Since this designation is used to represent the top-level directory (root) of a computer, the effect was to designate the entire internet as malware. For all practical purposes, Google had shut down internet searches for 40 minutes.

Therac-25, 1987: Killing Cancer Patients with x-Rays

The Therac-25 was used to treat cancer patients in the 1980's with radiation therapy, but the error messages were ambiguous and confusing to operators. Under certain conditions the radiation beam could become thousands of times stronger than expected. Rather than shutting off the machine when this happened, the failsafe software merely printed a message "MALFUNCTION n," where n was a number between 1 an 64. Users did what they do best, which was to ignore the error messages, and several patients were killed.

Numerical Error

Even if your program is completely perfect and error free, there could still be some numerical inaccuracy to it. These **inherent numerical errors** in computations have two general sources. First, there may be some inaccuracies in the input data. This error is then propagated forward, and compounded, by successive computations. This type of error is called **data error**. Data error is causes by errors that are already present before a computation begins. Sources include:

1. **Measurement errors**: The number supplied to the program could be wrong.
2. **Previous computations**: Successive computations depend on earlier computations. If the result of one computation that has an error in it, and is used as the input to another computation, this causes a data error.
3. **Modeling errors**: The theory behind the implementation could be approximate. For example, one might model a gravity force by $\mathbf{F} = -m\mathbf{g}$, an approximation that is only valid near the surface of the earth, instead of $\mathbf{F} = -GMm/r^2$.

A second type of errors are those introduced by the computation itself. These **computational errors** are usually due to the limitations of the actual hardware or software implementation. Computational errors may be caused by

1. **Roundoff errors**: Errors due to the fact that computers use a finite number of digits to represent numbers.
2. **Truncation errors**: Errors due to the truncation of an infinite process, such as calculating only a finite number of terms in a Taylor Series approximation.

Of course, there can always be a bug in your program that will lead to a numerical error; for example you might transcribe a formula incorrectly when you implement it, or use a particular programming construct incorrectly.

Lets assume your program is perfect and bug free, and try to quantify the inherent error.

Definition 7.1. Absolute Error

The absolute error in a numerical approximation is

$$\textbf{absolute error} = |\text{approximate value - true value}| \qquad (7.14)$$

Definition 7.2. Relative Error

The relative error in a numerical approximation is

$$\textbf{relative error} = \frac{\text{absolute error}}{\text{true value}} \qquad (7.15)$$

This gives us the useful result

$$\text{approximate value} = (\text{true value}) \times (1 \pm \text{relative error}) \qquad (7.16)$$

We will sometimes use the term **unit in the last place** or **ulp** to represent the value of a 1 when placed in the rightmost digit of a numerical representation of a number.

Definition 7.3. ULP

One ULP - Unit in the Last Place – is the value of a 1 in the rightmost digit of a number.

Example 7.1. Suppose that $e = 2.718281828459045...$ is represented in a computer with a 23 bit mantissa. Find the ULP.

$$\text{True Value: } e = 2.718281820459045...$$
$$\text{Approximate Value: } \hat{e} = 2.71828135 = 10.\underbrace{1011 \cdots 101}_{21 \text{ bits}}{}_2$$
$$1 \text{ ULP} = 2^{-21} \approx 4.768 \times 10^{-7}$$

Here is a program to find the ULP in Python.

```
1  ulp = 1.0
2  iterations = 0
3  while ((1+ulp) - 1) > 0:
4      ulp = ulp/2
5      iterations += 1
6  print ulp
7  print iterations-1
```

This loop will terminate after 55 iterations with an ulp of approximately 1.1×10^{-16}. When that number is added to 1, the result is 1, and so `((1+ulp)-1)` gives zero and the loop terminates.

If we had written line 3 in the above loop as **while ulp >0:** the loop would always return zero, because the number **ulp** will continue to divide by 2 until the program reaches 4.9×10^{-324} after 1075 iterations. When this is divided by 2, it falls beneath the lowest precision available and returns zero.

Definition 7.4. Decimal Places of Accuracy

$$\textbf{decimal places of accuracy} = \lfloor -\log_{10}(\text{absolute error}) \rfloor \qquad (7.17)$$

The notation $\lfloor x \rfloor$ means the greatest integer less than or equal to x (the floor function).

The decimal places of accuracy gives approximately the number of digits that are accurately represented to the right of decimal point. In example 7.1 we had 1 ulp $= 4.768 \times 10^{-7}$, so that an error of 1 ulp represents $\lfloor (-\log 4.768 \times 10^{-7}) \rfloor = \lfloor 6.322 \rfloor = 6$ decimal places of accuracy.

We are sometimes only interested the total number of correct digits, not just the number of digits to the right of decimal point that are correct. This is derived from the relative error.

Definition 7.5. Digits of Accuracy

$$\textbf{digits of accuracy} = \lfloor -\log_{10}(\text{relative error}) \rfloor \qquad (7.18)$$

The digits of accuracy gives approximately the total number of digits of accuracy, starting from the first nonzero digit. So 3.124, 3124, and 0.003124 all have 4 digits of accuracy, whereas they have 3, 0, and 6 decimal places of accuracy, respectively. In example 7.1 we had a relative error of $r \approx (4.768 \times 10^{-7})/e \approx 1.75 \times 10^{-7}$. Since $\log(4.768 \times 10^{-7}) \approx -6.76$, there are 6 digits of accuracy to this estimate.

Once there is an error in a quantity, it will be propagated by the program. We can quantify this as the propagated data error.

Definition 7.6. Propagated Data Error

Let x be a true value of some quantity, and $\tilde{x}$ be the same quantity with data error in it, and let the function $f(x)$ represent the thing we are trying to compute. Then the

$$\textbf{propagated data error} = f(\tilde{a}) - f(a) \qquad (7.19)$$

Note that the propagated data error defined in this way has nothing to do with the computer implementation of how we calculate f: it only depends on the true definition of f.

Example 7.2. Estimate the propagated data error due to calculating $\cos(\pi/3)$ using $\pi = 3.1416$ Since we have approximated π at the fourth decimal place, this is inherently inaccurate.

$$\text{propagated data error} = \cos(3.1416/3) - \cos(\pi/3) = -2.12 \times 10^{-6} \qquad (7.20)$$

The computational error depends on the way in which we calculate f.

Definition 7.7. Computational Error

Let x be some input data, f describe a function we are computing, and $\hat{f}(\tilde{x})$ the computed value using an approximate value $\tilde{x}$ for x. Then

$$\text{computational error} = \hat{f}(\tilde{x}) - f(\tilde{x}) \tag{7.21}$$

Example 7.3. Estimate the computational error for $\cos(\pi/3)$ using a three-term Taylor approximation for $\cos x$ and $\pi \approx 3.1416$.

We have $\hat{f}(x) = \cos x \approx 1 - \dfrac{x^2}{2} + \dfrac{x^4}{24}$ and therefore the computational error is

$$\text{error} \approx 1 - \frac{(3.1416/3)^2}{2} + \frac{(3.1416/3)^4}{24} - \cos\frac{3.1416}{3} \tag{7.22a}$$

$$\approx 0.5017941058109612 - 0.4999978792725457 \approx 0.001796 \tag{7.22b}$$

Exercises

1. Suppose you have a computer that stores numbers with three digits of accuracy. Suppose it uses truncation error (lopping off the extra digits) when overflow occurs. How does it store (or calculate, and then store):
   (a) 5/9   (b) 5/7
   (c) (5/9)+(5/7) (d) (5/9)-(5/7)

2. Repeat the previous problem assuming that there is some kind of special hardware that performs round-off after each calculation.

3. Suppose you have a digit that stores numbers with 3 digits of accuracy. Let $x = 566$, $y = 568$, and $z = 999$. What would your computer calculate for the average of u and v, where $u = x/z$ and $v = y/z$, assuming it uses each of the following formulas:
   (a) average $= (u + v)/2$
   (b) average $= u + (v - u)/2$

4. Suppose you have a computer that does calculations to 4 significant figures. Calculate the first iterations to $\sqrt{1}$ in the Babylonian algorithm using (a) $x_0 = 0.999$; (b) $x_0 = 1.001$

5. In the Python shell type in the following expression:

   ```
   >>>  3.0/10-3*.1
   ```

   Observe and explain your results.

6. If a SCUD missile should have been within 50 meters of its predicted positions for it to be classified as a danger, what is the maximum amount of time the system could be left on without a reset?

7. Determine the ULP of your computer.

8. Suppose you were writing a program to calculate $\cos(x)$ using the Taylor series approximation. How many terms would you have to include to calculate the result to machine accuracy? Hint: this is an alternating series. Look up the theorems for convergence of an alternating series in your calculus book.

9. Consider the quadratic $x^2 + 500x + 1 = 0$.

   (a) Find the roots in a four-digit truncation system using the quadratic formula in the following form:

   $$x = \frac{-b \pm \sqrt{b^2 - 4ac}}{2a}$$

   (b) Repeat part (a), but this first rearrange the quadratic equation (analytically) by rationalizing the numerator, and use the resulting formula.

   (c) Compare your two sets of results. The actual roots are at $-1/(250 + \sqrt{62499}) \approx -.002$ and $-250 - \sqrt{62499} \approx -499.998$. Can you come up with a general rule about when to use the normal formula and when to rationalize the numerator?

Chapter 8

Big Oh

Algorithms (definition 3.1) describe how computers process information. They specifically state **what happens** at each step, but are **implementation independent**. To be useful an algorithm should be **correct**, **efficient**, and **implementable**.

One important measure of an algorithm's efficiency is the number of steps it takes to complete. By counting the number of **basic operations** performed by the algorithm, we can get a device-independent measure of how fast an algorithm works.

For non-mathematical algorithms, the number of operations is the number of lines of code executed. Thus if a **for** loop that contains a suite of 15 executable lines of code loops through 20 iterations, the number of basic operations is $20 \times 15 = 300$. If any of those lines of code were function calls (chapter 18), the weight of the line of code for each function would have to be replaced by the number of basic operations performed within the function.

For mathematical computations, basic operations are multiplications and additions. Consider matrix multiplication (definition B.9 or example 17.6). Let c_{ij} be the ij^{th} element of the product of two square $n \times n$ matrices $\mathbf{A} = [a_{ij}]$ and $\mathbf{B} = [b_{ij}]$. Then

$$c_{ij} = \sum_{k=1}^{n} a_{ik} b_{kj} = a_{i1} b_{1j} + a_{i2} b_{2j} + \cdots + a_{in} b_{nj} \tag{8.1}$$

Just to calculate c_{ij} there are n multiplications and $n-1$ additions, or $2n-1$ operations. Since we have to repeat this operation $n \times n = n^2$ times, the total number arithmetic operations are $n^2(2n - 1) = 2n^3 - n^2$.

To get an idea of what this means for real calculations, we need to know the machine speed. An Intel Core i7 5960x Haswell chip (the state of the art desktop PC in 2015) runs at approximately 300,000 **MIPS**. A MIP is a million instructions per second, so the Haswell completes approximately 3×10^{11} instructions per second (IPS). The K-computer, with over 700,000 cores, and which was ranked the fastest computer in the world in 2011, ran at 10^{10} MIPS or 10^{16} IPS. Early personal computers in the 1980's ran at about 1 to 3 MIPS, while the UNIVAC 1 completed approximately 2000 IPS. Table 8.1 compares the run times for different machines as a function of matrix size. Figure 8.1 shows the experimentally determined calculation times on the computer that was used to write this book.

The number of basic operations or lines of code executed tell us how well an algorithm will **scale** with the size of the data set in a machine independent manner. Matrix multiplication scales proportionally to n^3 (for large n), since as n becomes large, $n^3 \gg n^2$ and therefore

$$2n^3 - n^2 \sim 2n^3 \sim O(n^3) \tag{8.2}$$

Table 8.1: Comparison of run times for matrix multiplication different machines.

n	Univac I	Early PC	Haswell	K Computer
10	950 mS	950 μS	6.3 nS	0.02 pS
100	16.6 min	995 mS	6.6 μS	20 pS
300	7.5 hrs	27 sec	180 μS	540 pS
1000	11.6 days	16.6 min	6.66 mS	20 nS
10 000	31.7 years	11.6 days	6.66 sec	20 μS
100 000	31709 years	31.7 years	1.85 hrs	20 mS
1 000 000	3.2×10^7 years	31709 years	11 weeks	20 sec

Figure 8.1: Time to multiply to two $n \times n$ matrices on an Intel Core i7 3770K machine running at approximately 100,000 MIPS using Numpy for array multiplication.

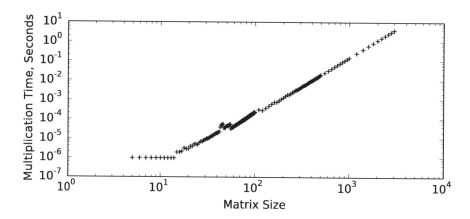

and we say that "matrix multiplication scales at big-Oh of n^3." This means that when we double the size of the input, it takes $2^3 = 8$ times as long to complete the program.

Definition 8.1. Big Oh

We say that an algorithm scales as $O(f(n))$ if there exists some constant c and some number N such that $cf(n)$ is an upper bound on the number of steps where the input size is n for all $n > N$

Definition 8.2. Little oh

We say that an algorithm scales as $o(g(n))$ if there exists some constant c and some number N such that $cg(n)$ is a lower bound on the number steps when the input size is n for all $n > N$.

In fact, we will mostly just look at big-Oh because big-Oh gives us a worst case scenario.

As we know from the study of limits in calculus, its really only the highest order term that dominates. Since matrix multiplication takes $2n^3 - n^2$ steps, then we know that for really large n, the $2n^3$ term is a lot more important than the n^2 term. Thus matrix multiplication, for example, scales with $O(n^3)$.

Now that we have a metric to use for measuring the speed of algorithm, the natural question to ask is what are good values for the metric, and what are bad values for the metric. If we start naively implementing a lot of the existence proofs from calculus or number theory, it will turn out that our calculations will take a very, very long time to run. It turns out that in very many cases we can do a lot better than these naive implementations.

- $O(n)$ - Find the largest number in a list of unsorted numbers by examining every number in the list, or looking up a word in the dictionary by starting at A and proceeding, one by, one, until we find the word we want. We say that these algorithms scale **linearly**.

- $O(\log n)$ - Look up a word in the dictionary using a **binary search**. These algorithms are a lot faster than linear algorithms. We say that these algorithms scale **logarithmically**.

- $O(n^2)$ - Any algorithm that looks at all pairs of numbers in a set of length n. **Naive sorting algorithms** scale **quadratically**.

- $O(n \log n)$ - These are faster than $O(n^2)$ but slower than $O(n)$. Examples include **efficient sorting algorithms**.

- $O(n^3)$ - An algorithm that looks at all triples of elements in a set of size n, like **matrix multiplication**, is said to scale **cubically**

- $O(a^n)$ - An algorithm that requires generating all possible subsets of any length scales **exponentially** (here a is a fixed constant, usually 2). These algorithms are excruciatingly slow.

- $O(n!)$ - Generate all possible permutations of n items. These are even worse than exponentially slow algorithms.

Really hard problems typically fall into the last two cases. To understand this combinatoric growth, consider the following table. It shows the expected time for a Haswell 5960 to complete the specified number of operations. The scaling of an algorithm can be seen by following a column in this table. For example, to see how an $O(n^3)$ algorithm scales with n, follow the values under the n^3 column.

n	$\log(n)$	n	$n \log n$	n^2	n^3	2^n	$n!$
20	14 pS	67 pS	290 pS	1.3 nS	27 nS	3.5 μS	91 D
30	16 pS	100. pS	490 pS	3. nS	90. nS	3.6 mS	2.8×10^{13} Y
50	19 pS	170 pS	940 pS	8.3 nS	417 nS	1.0 H	3.2×10^{45} Y
70	20 pS	230 pS	1.4 nS	16 nS	1.1 μS	130 Y	1.3×10^{81} Y
100	22 pS	330 pS	2.2 nS	33 nS	3.3 μS	1.3×10^{11} Y	9.9×10^{138} Y
1000	33 pS	3.3 nS	33 nS	3.3 μS	3.3 mS	1.1×10^{282} Y	4.3×10^{2548} Y
10^6	66 pS	3.3 μS	66 μS	3.3 S	39 D	10^{301011} Y	9×10^{5565689} Y

Here S=seconds; H=hours; D=days; and Y=years. As you can see, the really hard problems in the last two columns scale really poorly. Exponential and factorial order algorithms should be avoided if at all possible – even a modest $n = 30$ calculation that expands all permutations $(O(n!))$ will take longer than the known age of the universe to complete.

Exercises

1. Suppose algorithm f_1 has complexity $100,000n + 0.01n^2$, while algorithm f_2 has complexity $0.1n + 1000n^2$. If you are processing 50 data records, which algorithm is more efficient? 100 data items? 1000 data items?

2. Suppose an algorithm that has complexity $\sim 10n^2$ takes 30 seconds to process 1000 data records. How long will it take to process 10,000 records? One million records?

3. Prove that for a sufficiently large data set, an algorithm that has $O(e^x)$ will always

take longer to run than an algorithm that has $O(x^n)$, regardless of the value of n.

4. (Requires chapter 12). Estimate the complexity of the implementation of the Babylonian algorithm used in example 12.2.

5. (Requires chapter 17). Estimate the complexity of algorithm 17.1 for the dot product.

6. (Requires chapter 17). Estimate the complexity of algorithm 17.2 for matrix multiplication.

Part II

Hacking in Python

Chapter 9

Identifiers, Expressions & Types

Identifiers

An **identifier** is the name of a variable (or other object in a computer program). In addition to variables, identifiers are the names of other things, such as functions (e.g., the sine and cosine functions in mathematics). In Python, identifiers are made up of any combination of the letters **A-Z**, **a-z**, **0-9**, and the underscore character _. A variable must begin with a non-numeric character, i.e., a letter or the underscore. **Identifiers are case sensitive**. Thus the variables **abc**, **ABC**, and **aBc** are all different.

Identifiers

- **Must** start with either a letter or an underscore character **"_' "**
- **May not** start with a number
- **May** contain both letters, digits (**"0"..."9"**), and underscores
- **May** contain both upper case (**"A"..."Z"**) and lower case (**"a"..."z"**) letters
- **Is** case sensitive
- **Should** not be the same as any keyword

There is a special set of identifiers in Python called **keywords** that are predefined. Any identifiers that you define should be different from all keywords. Keywords must be spelled precisely correctly, or they will not work properly.

Table 9.1. Keywords

and	class	elif	finally	if	lambda	print	while
as	continue	else	for	import	not	raise	with
assert	def	except	from	in	or	return	yield
break	del	exec	global	is	pass	try	

You can always print out a list of the keywords in Python by typing the following in the Python console:

```
>>> import keyword
>>> print keyword.kwlist
```

Some additional forms of identifiers have special meanings and you should avoid these formats for your variables.

1. **The single underscore character**: _ is used (internally) by Python shell to store the result of the last calculation.
2. **Identifiers surrounded by double underscores**: __*__. (Here * represents a **wild card** character, which means (in this case) that it can be replaced by any valid identifier.) This format indicates that the identifier is defined by the system. The Python language reference says the following: "Any use of __*__ names, in any context, that does not follow explicitly documented use, is subject to breakage without warning."
3. **Identifiers preceded by a double underscore**: __* are private to the class in which they are defined. (Classes will be discussed in chapter 29.)

Students are often confused between **identifiers** (the names of variables) and **string literals**. Strings will be discussed in chapter 15. A string literal is a string with a specific value. You can tell the difference between the two because strings are always surrounded by quotes. Thus `'ABC'`, `"ABC"`, and `"""ABC"""` all are string literals, but `ABC` is an identifier.

Expressions

An **expression** is anything that evaluates to a **value** in Python. It may be a combination of values, operators, and variables.

```
1  >>> 5+7
2  12
3  >>> type(12)
4  <type 'int'>
5  >>> 5+7.0
6  12.0
7  >>> type(12.0)
8  <type 'float'>
```

The **types** of the variables that are combined must be compatible, and the type of the variable on the left-hand side of the assignment is determined by the result of the evaluation. The **type** function can be used to tell us the type of a variable.

In line 1, we added two integers; the result was an integer.

In line 5, we added an integer and a floating point variable (type **float**). The result was a float. Floats are used to represent real numbers (numbers with decimal points).

If the types are incompatible, an error will occur:

```
>>> 5+"fred"
Traceback (most recent call last):
  File "<stdin>", line 1, in <module>
 TypeError:unsupported operand type(s) for +: 'int' and 'str'
```

The expression `"fred"` has a **str** type, meaning it is a string. Strings are used to represent text in computer programs.

Numbers in Expressions

Python supports four types of numbers: **integers, long integers, floating point numbers,** and **complex numbers.** Long integers are integers that are not limited to machine size (e.g., 64 bits). In Python 3, all integers are long. Floating point numbers represent anything with a decimal point. Complex numbers represent numbers of the form $a + bi$, where $a, b \in \mathbb{R}$ and $i^2 = -1$. (A review of complex numbers is given in appendix A.) Note that in Python, the imaginary square root of -1 is represented by the symbol **j** and not the "expected" symbol **i**.

Integers may be expressed in decimal, octal, hexadecimal, or binary. In Python 3, the **L** is omitted.

Real numbers are represented as floating point numbers, called **float**'s in Python. Real numbers that are equal to integers are not integers, i.e., they are stored differently and may take up a different amount of space. The **e** and **E** formats are used for scientific notation, much like the $\boxed{\text{EE}}$ key on calculators. **1234.5**, **1.2345E3**, and **1.2345e3** all represent the same number 1.2345×10^3.

```
>>> x=14.0
>>> y=14
>>> z=14L
>>> (x==y, x==z, y==z)
(True, True, True)
>>> (type(x), type(y), type(z))
(<type 'float'>, <type 'int'>, <type 'long'>)
>>> (sys.getsizeof(x), sys.getsizeof(y), sys.getsizeof(z))
(24,24,28)
```

Data Types in Python

The expression **data type** refers to the way a computer language represents or stores its data in a computer. A computer language typically has several different data types that are used to represent things like integers, real numbers, and strings. Sometimes, when different data types can be used in combination with one another (like real numbers and integers) these types are sub-classified in such a way to allow either easier conversion during computer programs.

Python supports a variety of data types natively. These can be roughly classified as follows: **Numeric** types (such as integers, floats, complex numbers, and booleans (chapter 11)); **Sequential** types (particularly lists, strings, and tuples; see chapters 13, 14, and 15); **Mapping** types (dictionaries; see chapter 24); and **Sets** (chapter 16). If you need something more sophisticated, you can also define your own **class** (chapter 29).

Table 9.2. Classification of Built-in Data Types in Python

Category	Specific Types[a]
Numeric	`int, float, complex, boolean` `xrange, unicode`
Sequential	`list, str, tuple`
Sets	`set`
Mapping	`dict`
Specialized Types	`None, file, Ellipsis`
Objects	User defined classes

[a]This list is not comprehensive. In particular, the standard library has a lot of additional data types, such as **datetime**, which is used to represent (surprise) dates and times.

Integers

Integers are represented by the data type **int**. On most 32-bit machines an integer **n** may take on any value between (see page 36)

$$-2,147,483,648 = -2^{31} < n < 2^{31} - 1 = 2,147,483,647 \tag{9.1}$$

On 64-bit machines type **int** can usually fit values between

$$-9,223,372,036,854,775,808 = -2^{63} < n$$
$$< 2^{63} - 1 = 9,223,372,036,854,775,807 \tag{9.2}$$

You can always determine this value by typing in **sys.maxint**,

```
>>> import sys
>>> sys.maxint
9223372036854775807
```

If you attempt to create a larger integer, e.g., by adding one to the largest possible number, Python will automatically convert your result into a **long** integer. There is no limit to the size of **long** integers.

```
>>> x=sys.maxint
>>> y=x+1
>>> y
9223372036854775808L
>>> type(y)
<type 'long'>
>>> type(x)
<type 'int'>
>>>
```

Notice that the **long** integer has the letter L appended to the end of it. Otherwise, the conversion is completely transparent. In Python 3 this distinction is hidden and the **long** data type is removed, so that everything just looks like an **int**.

How to Write Different Integer Types

decimal	Any sequence of decimal digits such as **7351** or **129**.
long	Any sequence of decimal digits followed by an **L** or **l** such as **7351L** or **1321**. (Use of the lower case **l** is not recommended because it can be confused with the number 1.)
binary	Begin with **0b** or **0B** (number zero, followed by letter b or B), followed by any sequence of ones (**1**) and zeros (**0**), such as **0b101101**, which represents the decimal number 45.
octal	Begin with **0O** or **0o** (number zero followed by letter o or O), followed by any sequence of octal digits (**"0".."7"**), such as **0o42763**, which represent the decimal integer 17907. (The use of the upper case O is not recommended because it can be confused with the number 0).
hex	Begin with **0x** or **0X**, followed by any sequence of hexadecimal "digits", which are **"0".."9"** and **"A".."F"** (or **"a".."f"**). Hex digits are not case sensitive. An example is **0x5ab4c**, which represents the decimal integer 371532.

Floating Point Numbers

Floating Point numbers are binary approximations to real numbers. Floating point numbers are all stored using the IEEE 754 64-bit double precision standard (page 37), regardless of what type of hardware you have (even on 32-bit machines), so you can store numbers as small in magnitude as 10^{-308}, and as big as 10^{308}, each with approximately 17 digits of precision. If you need more precision than this you can use the arbitrary precision data types provided in Numpy.

How to Write Floating Point Numbers in Python

decimal notation	Must have a decimal point, such as 3.0 or 4.7
scientific notation	Use the letter **E** or **e** to specify the exponent. For example, 3E-13, 7.2E1, and 4.746e0 represent 3×10^{-13}, 7.2×10^1, and 4.746×10^0 as floating point numbers.

If you combine integer and floating point numbers together in an expression then Python will automatically do a type conversion for you. However, you should be careful about using this automatic type conversion, because it will only occur at the point where you have different types. Thus while the following two calculations both give floating point results, they are different:

```
1  >>> 3.5/2
2  1.75
3  >>> 3.5*(1/2)
4  0.0
```

On line 1, **3.5/2** is in mixed mode, so the **2** is converted to **2.0**, and the result is **1.75**. On line 3, the **(1/2)** in parenthesis is evaluated first. This sub-expression is not in mixed mode, and is entirely integer. Since **1/2** → **0** (using integer division), the expression is evaluated as follows:

$$3.5 * (1/2) \to 3.5 * 0 \to 0.0 \tag{9.3}$$

At the second stage, the **3.5*0** is mixed mode, so the result is 0.0 rather than just 0.

Type conversion can always be forced; for each type, there is a function of the same name that will attempt the conversion. Thus

```
>>> float(1)
1.0
>>> float(2)
2.0
>>> float(1/2)
0.0
>>> float(1)/float(2)
0.5
>>> 3.5*(float(1)/float(2))
1.75
>>> 3.5*float(1/2)
0.0
```

You must be careful where you make a conversion: **3.5*float(1/2)** is no better than **3.5*(1/2)** because the **1/2**→**0** is performed in integer arithmetic *before* the conversion. To get the expected answer, you may have to **float** every single number in the calculation.

Floating point numbers can also be converted to integer; in this case, the decimal part is truncated. This is like a floor function $\lfloor x \rfloor$.

```
>>> from math import pi
>>> print pi, int(pi)
3.14159265359 3
```

Complex Numbers

Complex numbers are stored using the **complex** data type, which really stores a pair of floating point numbers. For a review of the properties of complex numbers, see appendix A. The imaginary number $i = \sqrt{-1}$ is represented in Python with the letter **j**. Other imaginary numbers such as $27.5i$ are represented by ending a floating point number with the letter **j**, as in **27.5j**. No space is allowed between the number and the letter **j**. A complex number is written as the sum of a floating point number and an imaginary number. If the letter **j** is used by itself it is assumed to be a variable, so to represent the complex number i you would write **1j**.

```
1  >>> from cmath import sqrt
2  >>> x=1+2.5j
```

```
3    >>> y=3-7.2j
4    >>> z=x*y
5    >>> z
6    (21+0.2999999999999998j)
7    >>> sqrt(z)
8    (4.582692589942323+0.03273184859250788j)
```

The None Data Type

Python uses the identifier **None** to represent the absence of a value. Functions that do not have **return** statements, or have **return** statements without arguments, return the value of **None**. The argument of a function without arguments, as in **f()**, is **None**. The type of the symbol **None** is called **NoneType**, and there are no other symbols in Python with this data type.

Arithmetic expressions in Python

Arithmetic operations are summarized in table 9.3. As you might guess, the order of operations is crucial to correct evaluation of an expression. An acronym that may help you remember the default order of evaluation is **PEMDAS**:[1] **Parenthesis, Exponentiation, Multiplication/ Division, Addition/Subtraction.** Since parenthesis come first, this means you can always use parenthesis to enforce any order you like. Operators with the same precedence (table 9.4) such as addition and subtraction are evaluated left to right.

In any expression, the order of operations is important. Whenever there is any doubt, use parenthesis. If you don't, the operation may not evaluate to what you think it is going to evaluate to.

To see how operator precedence works in Python, consider the following example.

```
1    >>> 5.0/7.0/3.0/12.
2    0.019841269841269844
3    >>> 5.0/(7.0/(3.0/12.0))
4    0.17857142857142858
5    >>> ((5.0/7.)/3.)/12.0
6    0.019841269841269844
7    >>> 5/7/3/12
8    0
9    >>> (5+7)*(3*12)
10   432
11   >>> 5+7*3*12
12   257
```

---

[1] Traditionally, Please Excuse My Dear Aunt Sally. In street slang, Dear Aunt Sally has become Dope Ass Swag. In other parts of the English speaking world, alternative acronyms are used: BEDMAS (B for brackets); BODMAS (O for orders or powers); BIDMAS(I for indices); and BOMDAS. The order of MD really doesn't matter, because operations with equal precedence are evaluated left to right (see table 9.4).

In line 7, the result is 0 because 5/7 is zero using integer division, i.e., 5 divided by 7 is zero with a remainder of 5. Thus 5/7/3/12 because 0/3/12, and so forth.

If you have a mixed mode expression like 2.0/7 then Python will convert everything to floating point. But there is no guarantee that it will make the conversion in the order or way that you expect it to:

```
13   >>> (2/7)*(4.0)
14   0.0
```

Since Python evaluates the parenthesis first, the 2/7 on line 13 is evaluated in integer arithmetic and gives a zero. Then since $0 \cdot 4.0 = 0.0$, it returns 0.0.

If you had wanted the 2/7 to be evaluated as a real number, you would need to include decimal points to force conversion to floating point inside the parenthesis:

```
>>> (2./7)*(4.0)
1.1428571428571428
>>> (2/7.)*(4.0)
1.1428571428571428
>>> (2./7.)*(4.0)
1.1428571428571428
```

Some of the operators listed in table 9.4 may look a little unusual to you, because they do not apply to normal numerical quantities. For example, **is**, **and**, **or**, and **not** refer to Boolean variables (chapter 11), and the comparison operators to Boolean expressions. The assignment operators will be discussed in chapter 10.

Table 9.3. Arithmetic Operators

Operator	Description	Examples
+	Addition	3 + 7 → 10
		5+6.4 → 11.4
−	Subtraction	10−6 → 4
		10.7 − 4.3 → 6.4
*	Multiplication	5*4 → 20
		5.3*4.6 → 24.38
/	Division	12/5 → 2
		12.0/5 → 2.4
//	Floor	13 //5 → 2
		13.0 //5 → 2.0
%	Modulo	13 % 5 → 3
		13.0 % 5 → 3.0
**	Exponentiation	2**10 → 1024
		2**.5 → 1.4142135623730951
		2**(1/2) → 1

Table 9.4. Operator Precedence

Precedence rules are given from highest to lowest. Operators on the same line have equal precedence and are evaluated in an expression from left to right. Parentheses always override precedence rules.

1. `**`	(exponentiation)
2. `~,+, -`	(unary plus and minus)
3. `*, /, %, //`	(multiplication and division)
4. `+, -`	(addition and subtraction)
5. `>>, <<`	(shifting)
6. `&`	(bitwise and)
7. `|, ^`	(bitwise or, bitwise exclusive or)
8. `<, >, <=, >=`	(comparison)
9. `==, !=, <>`	(equality, inequality)
10. `=, +=, -=, %=, /=, //=, *=, **=`	(assignment)
11. `is, is not`	(identity)
12. `in, not in`	(membership)
13. `not, or, and`	(logical)

Function Calls in Expressions

Python expressions can include **function calls**. A function call in Python looks something like `somefunction(p1, p2, ..., pn)`, where `somefunction` is the name of the function and the `p1, p2, ..., pn` are parameters. Parameters contain information that is passed to the function. The function itself is another program that performs a computation and returns an answer. The answer is returned as the value of the function. For example, to calculate the cosine of an angle x, and assign the value to y, i.e., to find

$$y = \cos x$$

we could use the function call

```
y=math.cos(x)
```

In the function call we are invoking the function (asking python to execute the function) `math.cos` and passing it the value of the parameter `x`. Python passes the value of `x` to the program that has a name `math.cos`; then `math.cos` does its thing and sends back the value $\cos x$. We then extract this value by using the function call as part of an expression. In the case shown above, we assign the value of the number returned to the variable `y`.

There are a large number of built in functions in python that you may find yourself using frequently. Examples include the `len(u)` function, which returns the length of the list `u`; and `range(n)`, that returns a list of the integers `[0,1,2,...,n-1]`. Python built in functions are summarized in table 9.5. Some of the functions in table 9.5 may look a bit mysterious right now, especially if you are new to programming. Rest assured that many of them will eventually come in handy.

In addition to the built-in functions, there are even more functions available in libraries. Some of these libraries are considered standard python libraries, which means that any python distribution should have access to them. Each library can be accessed by including a single line of code in your program that tells python that you want to use it. One example of a standard library is the **math** library (table 9.6), which includes the function **math.cos**. To do mathematics in the complex plane, there is the complex math library **cmath** (table 9.7). Other standard libraries that you might find useful are **fractions** (table 9.8), **random** (table 9.9), and **operator** (table 9.10).The standard libraries are fully documented online[2] and are far too numerous to document here. Some particular ones you might want to take a look at are **csv** (read and write csv files); **os** (operating system interfaces); **time**, **datetime**, and **calendar** (for working with dates and times); and **subprocess** (execute another program). For advanced users there are also a number of markup language libraries (HTML, XML, SGML, SAX) and GUI tools (e.g., **tkinter** for using **tk**). Before you go off coding some kind of utility function on your own (or looking for an external library) you should always check to see if python already does what you need for you.

You can also define your own functions; this is the subject of chapter 18. You will probably end up writing programs in such a way that everything (or nearly everything) is a part of a function.

The Python standard **math** library

A small core of standard mathematical functions are included in the **math** library (table 9.6). These all operate nominally on **float**. For equivalent operations in the complex plane use the **cmath** library (table 9.7). Like any library, it can be included in whole or in part. To include the entire library put the statement[3]

```
from math import *
```

Then you can use the functions directly. For example, to calculate $\sqrt{x}$, type **sqrt(x)** into your code.

Sometimes you will want to have multiple libraries loaded that have functions with the same names. For example, both **math** and **numpy** have **sqrt** functions (as well as the trig functions) in common. To distinguish between these libraries, we would instead put the statement

```
import math
```

Then to calculate $\sqrt{x}$ using the **math** library you would have to put use the expression **math.sqrt(x)** instead of just **sqrt(x)**. If **cmath** and **numpy** are also loaded in this way, then you could use their square root functions as **cmath.sqrt(x)** and **numpy.sqrt(x)**.

---

[2]At https://docs.python.org/2/library/#the-python-standard-library
[3]This practice is discouraged, however, because it pollutes the name space. For example, following **from math import *** with **from numpy import *** could lead to unexpeted results as many of the functions have the same name.

Table 9.5. Python Built in Functions (1 of 3)

Function	Return Value
`abs(x)`	Absolute Value `abs(-3)→3`
`all(x)`	True if all the elements of **x** are **True**. `all([5>1, 5>99, 5<3])→False`
`any(x)`	True if any of the elements of **x** are **True**. `any([5>1, 5>99, 5<3])→True`
`bin(x)`	Converts integer **x** to a binary string. `bin(99)→'0b1100011'`
`bool(x)`	Converts **x** to **True** or **False**. `bool(5+7.5/3)→True; bool(5-50/10)→False`
`bytearry(x)`	Converts **x** to a byte array. `bytearray([1,2,3])→bytearray(b'\x01\x02\x03')`

`callable(x)`	True if **x** is callable.
	`callable(math.pi)→False`
	`callable(math.sqrt)→True`

`chr(i)`	Returns one-character string with ASCII code i.
`classmethod(f)`	A wrapper (decorator) to turn a function into a method within a class.
`cmp(x, y)`	-1, 0, or 1 depending on $x > y$, $x = y$, or $x < y$. `cmp(-5,4)→-1; cmp(9,0)→1`
`compile(s,f,m)`	Creates an object that can be executed by either **exec** or **eval**. See python web page for details.
`complex(x)`	Converts **x** into a complex number. `complex(5.7)→(5.7+0j); complex(3,4)→(3+4j)`
`delattr(obj, n)`	Delete attribute **n** from **obj**.
`dict(x)`	Create a dictionary from **x**. `dict([("a",5),("b",6)])→{'a':5,'b':6}`
`dir()`	List of names in the current scope. If called with an argument `dir(x)` returns a list of the attributes of **x**.
`divmod(a, b)`	Quotient and remainder using long division. `divmod(387,123)→(3, 18)`
`enumerate(s)`	Converts **s** into an **enumerate** object compatible with the the **next()** method.
`eval(expr)`	Evaluates **expr** as a Python expression. `eval("math.e**math.pi")→23.140692632779263`

`exec(string)`	Parses **string** to evaluate **expr**.
	`exec("x=3; y=x+7; print 'y**2=',y**2")→`
	`y**2= 100`

`execfile(fname)`	Parses the file **fname** to execute a command.

Table 9.5. Python Built in Functions (2 of 3)

`file(name, mode)`	Constructs a file object. In most cases, it is better to use `open(name,mode)` instead of `file`. See chapter 23.
`filter(f, s)`	A list of elements from iterable **s** for which **f** is true. Equivalent to `[x for x in s if f(x)]`. `filter(lambda x:x%2==0, range(10))`→ `[0,2,4,6,8]`
`float(x)`	Converts **x** to a float.
`format(value)`	Formatted string representation. `format(3, "5.3f")`→`'3.000'`
`frozenset(s)`	Converts iterable **s** into a frozen set. Chapter 16.
`getattr(x, n)`	The value of attribute **n** of **x**.
`globals()`	A dictionary of the current global symbol table.
`hasattr(x, n)`	**True** if **x** has attribute **n**.
`hash(x)`	Hash value of **x** if it exists.
`help(x)`	Invokes interactive help system.
`hex(x)`	Converts an integer to hexadecimal string. `hex(99)`→`'0x63'`
`id(x)`	A unique and persistent integer associated with **x**.
`input(prompt)`	Like `eval(raw_input(prompt))`.
`int(x)`	Converts **x** to an integer.
`isinstance(x, type)`	**True** if **x** is data type **type**. `isinstance(3.14159, float)`→**True** `isinstance("wind speed", int)`→**False**
`issubclass(A, B)`	**True** if **A** is a subclass of **B**.
`iter(x)`	Converts **x** to an iterator.
`len(s)`	Length of **s**, a string or list. `len("The life of brian")`→17
`list(x)`	Converts iterable **x** into a list. `list("monty")`→`['m', 'o', 'n', 't', 'y']`
`locals()`	Local symbol table.
`long(x)`	Converts **x** into a long integer.
`map(f,s)`	Applies function **f** to every element of **s** and returns the results. `map(math.sqrt, [1, 4, 9, 16, 25])`→ `[1.0, 2.0, 3.0, 4.0, 5.0]`
`max(arguments)`	Maximum value of arguments or iterable.
`min(arguments)`	Minimum value of arguments or iterable.
`oct(x)`	Converts integer **x** into octal.
`open(fname, mode)`	Opens file **fname** in a specified mode.
`ord(c)`	Unicode integer representing character **c**.
`pow(x,y)`	Power, x^y; same as `x**y`.
`print(x)`	Prints stuff.
`range(i, j, k)`	List `[i,i+k,i+2k,...,j-1]`. If **k** is omitted, the step size is one, `[i,i+1,i+2,...,j-1]`. `range(n)` is equivalent to `range(0,n,1)`.
`raw_input(prompt)`	Writes **prompt** to the terminal with a trailing newline, and waits for input. The input typed in is converted to a string and returned minus the trailing newline.

Table 9.5. Python Built in Functions (3 of 3)

`reduce(f, s)`	Apply function `f(x,y)` of two arguments cumulatively to the items of iterable, from left to right, so as to reduce the iterable to a single value. First computes $f(s_0 + s_1)$, then $f(f(s_0 + s_1), s_2)$, then $f(f(f(s_0 + s_1), s_2), s_3)$, and so forth. See chapter 28.
`reload(module)`	Reloads a previously imported package.
`repr(x)`	A string with a printable representation of an **x**.
`reversed(s)`	Reverses the iterator **x**.
`round(x)`	Rounds a floating point number to the nearest integer. `round(x,n)` rounds to n digits to the right of the decimal point. `round(math.pi)`$\rightarrow$`3.0` `round(math.pi,4)`$\rightarrow$`3.1416`
`setattr(X, n, val)`	Sets a value of an attribute.
`sorted(x)`	Sorts an iterable **x**. `sorted([5,8,1,7,3])`$\rightarrow$`[1, 3, 5, 7, 8]`
`staticmethod(f)`	A static method for a function **f**.
`str(x)`	Convert **x** to a string.
`sum(s)`	The sum of the elements in the iterable **x**. `sum([3.5,7.2, 9.6, -4.2,0, 3.6])`$\rightarrow$`19.7`
`tuple(s)`	Converts **s** to a tuple.
`type(x)`	The type of **x**.
`unichr(i)`	Unicode character with code given by integer i.
`unicode(x)`	Convert **x** to a unicode string.
`vars()`	Same as `locals()`. With an argument, returns the dictionary attribute.
`xrange(i,j,k)`	Same argument as `range()` but returns an **xrange** object instead of a list.
`zip(x,y,..)`	List of tuples with one element from each argument. `zip(range(5),range(100,105))`$\rightarrow$ `[(0, 100), (1, 101), (2, 102), (3, 103), (4, 104)]`

Table 9.6. Python `math` library[a] (1 of 2)

Function	Return Value
`acos(x)`	$\arccos(x)$ in radians.
	`round(pi/acos(sqrt(3)/2),10)` →`6.0`
`acosh(x)`	Hyperbolic arc cosine, $\mathrm{arccosh}(x)$.
`asin(x)`	$\arcsin(x)$ in radians.
	`round(degrees(asin(sqrt(2.0)/2))),10)` →`45.0`
`asinh(x)`	Hyperbolic arch sine, $\mathrm{arcsinh}(x)$.
`atan(x)`	$\arctan(x)$ in radians.
`atanh(x)`	Hyperbolic arc tangent, $\mathrm{arctanh}(x)$
`atan2(y,x)`	$\arctan(y, x)$ in radians, in correct quadrant, between $-\pi$ and π.
	`round(degrees(atan2(-1/2, sqrt(3))),10)` →`-30.0`
`ceil(x)`	Integer ceiling as a float: $\lceil x \rceil$.
	`ceil(4.2)` →`5.0`; `ceil(-1.9)` →`-1.0`
`copysign(x,y)`	x with the sign of y.
	`copysign(3,-42.7)` →`-.0`
`cos(x)`	$\cos x$, where x is in radians.
`cosh(x)`	Hyperbolic cosine, $\cosh x$
`degrees(x)`	Converts x from radians to degrees.
	`degrees(pi/2)` →`90.0`
`e`	e.
	`e` →`2.718281828459045`
`erf(x)`	Error function $\mathrm{erf}(x) = \dfrac{2}{\sqrt{\pi}} \displaystyle\int_0^x e^{-t^2} dt$
	`erf(sqrt(2))` →`0.9544997361036415`
`erfc(x)`	Complementary error function `erfc(x)` →`1-erf(x)`
`exp(x)`	e^x (exponential).
`expm1(x)`	$e^x - 1$ (exponential minus 1).
	`expm1(1)` →`1.718281828459045`
`fabs(x)`	Absolute value of a floating point number $|x|$.
	`fabs(-17.4)` →`17.4`
`factorial(n)`	Factorial $n!$; n must be a non-negative integer.
	`factorial(6)` →`72`
	`factorial(23)` →`25852016738884976640000L`
`floor(x)`	Integer floor as a float: $\lfloor x \rfloor$.
	`floor(37.2)` →`37.0`
`fmod(x,y)`	Floating point modulo division using the platform C library.
`frexp(x)`	Mantissa an exponent (m, e) such that $x = 2^e m$.
	`frexp(1985)` → `(0.96923828125, 11)`
	`frexp(256)` → `(0.5, 9)`
`fsum(s)`	Floating point sum of iterable **s**.
`gamma(x)`	Gamma Function
	$\Gamma(x) = \displaystyle\int_0^\infty t^{x-1} e^{-t} dt; \ \Gamma(n) = (n-1) \ n \in \mathbb{Z}^+$.
	`gamma(5)` →`24.0`; `gamma(5.001)` →`24.0361767180818`
`hypot(x,y)`	Length of hypotenuse of a right triangle. $\sqrt{x^2 + y^2}$
	`hypot(-3.4, 4.2)` →`5.403702434442518`

[a] For more details see `https://docs.python.org/2/library/math.html`

Table 9.6. Python `math` library (2 of 2)

Function	Return Value
`isinf(x)`	Checks if **x** is $\pm\infty$.
`isnan(x)`	Checks if **x** is not a number.
`ldexp(x,i)`	Returns $2^i x$; the inverse of **frexp**.
	`ldexp(.5,9)`→`256.0`
	`ldexp(.9,11)`→`1843.2`
`lgamma(x)`	$\ln|\Gamma(x)|$
`log(x,b)`	$\log_b(x)$; if **b** is omitted, returns $\ln x$.
	`log(81,3)`→`4.0`
`log1p(x)`	$\ln(1+x)$
`log10(x)`	$\log_{10}(x)$
	`log10(10000)`→4.0
`modf(x)`	Returns (f,i) where f is the fractional and i is the integer part of **x**, as floating point numbers.
	`modf(8.246)`→`(0.246, 8.0)`
`pi`	π.
`pow(x,y)`	x^y. Converts its arguments to float first.
	`pow(3,5)`→`243.0`
	`pow(2,-5)`→`0.03125`
`radians(x)`	Converts x from degrees to radians.
`sin(x)`	$\sin x$, where x is in radians.
`sinh(x)`	$\sinh x$.
`sqrt(x)`	$\sqrt{x}$
`tan(x)`	$\tan x$, where x is in radians.
`tanh(x)`	$\tanh x$.
`trunc(x)`	Truncates a real number to an integer. Returns integer.

Table 9.7. Python `cmath` (complex math) Library[a]

Function	Return Value
`acos(z)`	arccos z. Branch cuts along $(-\infty, -1)$ and $(1, \infty)$.
`acosh(z)`	arccosh z. Branch cut along $(-\infty, 1)$.
`asin(z)`	arcsin z. Branch cuts along $(-\infty, -1)$ and $(1, \infty)$.
`ainsh(z)`	arcsinh z. Branch cuts $(-j\infty, -j)$ and $(j, j\infty)$.
`atan(z)`	arctan z. Branch cuts $(-j\infty, -j)$ and $(j, j\infty)$.
`atanh(z)`	arctanh z. Branch cuts $(-\infty, -1)$ and $(1, \infty)$.
`cos(z)`	cos z
`cosh(z)`	cosh z
`e`	e
`exp(z)`	e^z
`isinf(z)`	Tests if either the real or imaginary part of z is infinite.
`isnan(z)`	Tests if either the real or imaginary part of z is not a number.
`log(z,b)`	$\log_b(z)$. b is optional. Branch cut $(-\infty, 0)$.
`log10(z)`	$\log_{10}(z)$. Branch cut $(-\infty, 0)$.
`phase(z)`	Phase of a complex number.
`pi`	π.
`polar(z)`	(r, ϕ); $r = \|z\|$ and ϕ is the phase of z.
`rect(r,phi)`	Complex number with given magnitude and phase.
`sin(z)`	sin z
`sinh(z)`	sinh z
`sqrt(z)`	$\sqrt{z}$. Branch cut on the negative real axis.
`tan(z)`	tan z
`tanh(z)`	tanh z

[a] For more details see https://docs.python.org/2/library/cmath.html

The Python standard `fractions` library

The fraction library (table 9.8) allows you to deal directly with **rational numbers** as ratios of integers. A rational number r, represented *mathematically* by the fraction $r = m/n$, where m and n are integers, can be represented by the Python expressions

```
fraction(m,n)
```

or

```
fraction(m/n)
```

Normal arithmetic operations may be performed on fractions; the computation will be performed exactly and the answer is returned as a fraction. For example

```
>>> x=Fraction(3,4)
>>> y=Fraction(7,8)
>>> x+y
Fraction(13, 8)
>>> x*y
Fraction(21, 32)
```

In mixed mode operations with integers, the integer is converted to a fraction:

```
>>> 1+Fraction("5/7")/Fraction(3,8)
Fraction(61, 21)
```

Table 9.8. Python `fractions`[a] Library

Function	Return Value
`Fraction(a,b)`	Represents a rational number a/b, where $a, b \in \mathbb{Z}$.
`Fraction("a/b")`	Same as `Fraction(a,b)`
`Fraction(x)`	Converts floating point number to Fraction.
`gcd(a,b)`	Greatest common division of $a, b \in \mathbb{Z}$.

[a] For more details see `https://docs.python.org/2/library/fractions.html`

The Python standard random library

Generation of random numbers is provided by the **random** library (table 9.9). Additional random sampling support is provided by the Numpy package **numpy.random**, and statistics support is provided by **numpy.statistics** and **statsmodels** libraries.

```
# to use without qualification:
from random import *
# or
import random
```

Table 9.9. Python random[a] library (1 of 2)

Function	Return Value[b]
`betavariate(a,b)`	A random float from a **beta distribution**
	PDF: $f(x; a, b) = \dfrac{\Gamma(a+b)}{\Gamma(a)\Gamma(b)} x^{a-1}(1-x)^{b-1}$
`choice(s)`	A random element from the sequence **s**.
`expovariate(L)`	A random float from an **exponential distribution**.
	PDF: $f(x; L) = Le^{-Lx}$.
`gammavariate(a,b)`	A random float from a **gamma distribution**.
	PDF $f(x; a, b) = \dfrac{b^a}{\Gamma(a)} x^{a-1} e^{-bx}$.
`gauss(mu,sigma)`	A random float from a **normal distribution**. A faster implementation than **normalvariate(mu,sigma)**; otherwise the two functions are the same.
`getrandbits(k)`	A long integer with k random bits.
`getstate()`	Retrieves the state set by **setstate()**.
`jumpahead(n)`	Jumps ahead in the current state. The input is used to scramble the current state.
`lognormvariate(m,s)`	A random float from a **lognormal distribution** with mean μ (**m**) and standard deviation σ (**s**).
	PDF: $f(x; \mu, \sigma) = \dfrac{1}{x\sigma\sqrt{2\pi}} e^{-\frac{(\ln x - \mu)^2}{2\sigma^2}}$.
`normalvariate(m,s)`	A random float from a **normal distribution** with mean μ (**m**) and standard deviation σ (**s**).
	PDF: $f(x; \mu, \sigma) = \dfrac{1}{\sigma\sqrt{2\pi}} e^{-\frac{(x-\mu)^2}{2\sigma^2}}$.
`paretovariate(a)`	Random float from **Pareto distribution** with shape parameter **a**.
	PDF: $f(x; a) = \dfrac{a}{x^{a+1}}$ for $x \geq 1$.
`randint(a,b)`	A random integer z such that $a \leq z \leq b$.

[a]For more details see `https://docs.python.org/2/library/random.html#random.setstate`; [b]PDF=Probability Density Function.

Table 9.9. Python random[a] library (2 of 2)

Function	Return Value[b]
`random()`	The next random floating point number in the current sequence. Will be in the range $[0, 1.0)$.
`randrange(i,j,k)`	Returns a random element from a **range**. Same arguments as **range**.
`sample(x, k)`	A random sample of size k from the population **x**.
`seed(x)`	Initializes the random number generator. If **x** is omitted, the current system time is used, unless a random seed is provided by the operating system.
`setstate()`	Sets the state (a sequence of pseudo-random numbers to be returned) of the random number generator.
`shuffle(s)`	Shuffles the sequence **s** in place.
`SystemRandom(s)`	Uses the system random number generator, if available, instead of the Python random number generator. May not be available on all operating systems. Seed **s** is optional.
`triangular(a,b,m)`	A random number from a **triangular distribution** on (a, b) with mode (vertex of triangle) m.
`uniform(a,b)`	A random floating point number x from a **uniform distribution** $a \leq x < b$. On some operating systems $a \leq x \leq b$.
`vonmisesvariate(m,k)`	A random float from a **von Mises distribution** with mean μ (**m**) and parameter κ. PDF: $f(x; \mu, \kappa) = \dfrac{e^{\kappa \cos(x-\mu)}}{2\pi I_0(\kappa)}$, where I_0 is a modified Bessel Function of order zero.
`weibullvariate(a,b)`	A random float from a **Weibull distribution** with scale parameter a and shape parameter b. PDF: $f(x; a, b) = \dfrac{b}{a}\left(\dfrac{x}{a}\right)^{b-1} e^{-(x/a)^b}$ for $x \geq 0$.
`whseed()`	Seeds the Wichmann-Hill generator.
`WichmannHill(seed)`	An alternative (older) random number generator (alternative to **random.**)

[a]For more details see `https://docs.python.org/2/library/random.html#random.setstate`; [b]PDF=Probability Density Function.

The `operator` library

All python operators are also implemented as functions in the **operator** library. For example, **operator.add(x,y)** means the same thing as **x+y**.

Table 9.10. Python standard operator library[a] (1 of 2)

Function	Return Value
add(a, b)	**a+b**
abs(x)	**abs(x)**
and_(a,b)	**a and b**
attrgetter(attr)	Returns a function that can retrieve attributes of an object.
concat(s,t)	**s+t** (concatenation)
contains(s,x)	**x in s**
countOf(a,b)	Number of times sequence **b** occurs in sequence **a**.
delitem(s, i)	Deletes item **s[i]** from **s**
div(a,b)	**a/b** when **__future__.division** is not in effect
eq(a, b)	**a==b**
floordiv(a,b)	**a//b**
ge(a, b)	**a>=b**
getitem(x,i)	**x[i]**
gt(a, b)	**a>b**
iadd(a, b)	**a=iadd(a,b)** →**a+=b** (calculation in place)
iand(a, b)	**a=iand(a,b)** →**a&=b** (calculation in place)
iconcat(p,q)	**p=iconcat(p,q)** →**p+=q** (calc. in place)
idiv(a, b)	**a=idiv(a,b)** →**a/=b** (calculation in place)
ifloordiv(a, b)	**a=ifloordiv(a,b)** →**a//=b** (in place)
ilshift(a, b)	**a=ilshift(a,b)** →**a<<=b** (calculation in place)
imod(a, b)	**a=imod(a,b)** →**a%=b** (calculation in place)
imul(a, b)	**a=imul(a,b)** →**a*=b** (calculation in place)
indexOf(a,b)	Index of first occurrence of **b** in **a**.
inv(x)	**-x**
invert(x)	Same as **inv(x)**
ior(a, b)	**a=ior(a,b)** →**a|=b** (calculation in place)
ipow(a, b)	**a=ipow(a,b)** →**a**b** (calculation in place)
irshift(a, b)	**a=irshift(a,b)** →**a>>=b** (calculation in place)
is_(a, b)	**a is b**
is_not(a, b)	**a is not b**

[a]For more details see https://docs.python.org/2/library/operator.html.

Table 9.10. Python standard `operator` library[a] (2 of 2)

Function	Return Value
`isub(a, b)`	`a=isub(a,b)`→`a-=b` (calculation in place)
`itemgetter(item)`	Returns a function that can can extract an item .
`itruediv(a, b)`	`a=itruediv(a,b)`→`/-=b` when `__future__.division` is in effect (calculation in place)
`ixor(a, b)`	`a=ixor(a,b)`→`a^=b` (calculation in place)
`le(a, b)`	`a<=b`
`lshift(a,b)`	`a<<b` (left shift b bits)
`lt(a, b)`	`a<b`
`mod(a,b)`	`a%b`
`mul(a,b)`	`a*b`
`ne(a, b)`	`a!=b`
`neg(x)`	`-x`
`not_(x)`	`not x`
`or_(a,b)`	`a or b`
`pos(x)`	`+x`
`pow(x)`	`a**b`
`rshift(a,b)`	`a>>b`
`setitem(x,i,y)`	`x[i]=y`
`sub(a,b)`	`a-b`
`truediv(a,b)`	`a/b` when `__future__.division` is in effect
`truth(x)`	`bool(x)`
`xor(a,b)`	`a^b` (bitwise exclusive or)

[a]For more details see `https://docs.python.org/2/library/operator.html`.

Exercises

1. Try to evaluate each of the following expressions by hand. Then use Python to figure out if your answers are correct. Explain why each answer comes out the way it does.

   (a) `3*4-7/9+6`

   (b) `44*(17.5/3)+6`

   (c) `3/4 + 1/4`

   (d) `99//27 + 10`

   (e) `20%7`

   (f) `2*7`

   (g) `2**7`

   (h) `2^7`

   (i) `(55|17)-55^17`

   (j) `12<<3`

   (k) `12<<3 and 3<12`

   (l) `12<<3 * 3<12`

   (m) `12<<3 * (3<12)`

   (n) `12<<3 + (3<12)`

   (o) `3^2+4^2+5^2`

2. Implement formulas for converting Farenheit to Celsius and vice-versa.

3. Find $\sqrt{3}$ both by raising the number to the 0.5 power and then by using the `math.sqrt()` function.

4. Find $\sqrt{3i}$. by raising the number to the 0.5 power. Do not use the `cmath.sqrt` function. What happens if you try `math.sqrt`?

Chapter 10

Simple Statements

Simple statements in Python are statements that can be written on a single line. The most basic of these are **assignments**, which bind values to identifiers. Other simple statements are **assert**, **pass**, **del**, **print**, **return**, **yield**, **raise**, **break**, **continue**, **import**, **global** and **exec**.

Assignment Statements

The most basic statement for scientific computation is the **assignment statement**. In an assignment statement we assign a value to a variable. Assignment statements in Python look something like equations but they are not the same thing. An assignment statement has the form

```
variable = expression
```

Here **variable** is the name of a valid Python **identifier**, and **expression** is an expression that needs to be evaluated. When the expression is evaluated, the result is assigned to the specified variable.

It is useful to think of the variable name as a pointer or an address, that points to the location of some useful information. Here are some examples in the Python shell:

```
1  >>>x = 17
2  >>>finished = True
3  >>>myname = "Monty_Python"
4  >>>grades = [98, 73.4, 26, 69.5, 76, 42]
5  >>>y = x + 3
```

In the example on line 1, the variable **x** points to a storage location in memory that contains the integer 17.

In the example on line 2, the variable **finished** points to a **boolean** variable with a value of **True**.

In the example on line 3, the variable **myname** points to a **string** that contains the text **"Monty_Python"**. The underbracket character "␣" indicates a blank space inside of a string literal.

In the example on line 4, the variable **grades** points to a list containing a sequence of numbers starting with 98.

In the example on line 5, the variable **y** points to a storage location that contains the integer 20.

The identifier on the left hand side of the assignment is called the **target**. Python handles the assignment differently depending upon the nature of the target. If the target is single item then the right hand side is assigned to the target.

```
x=7
```

If the target is a comma separated list of targets, the right hand side must be an **iterable** (something that can be iterated over, such as a list), with the same number of elements. Items are assigned successively, left to right.

```
>>> x=[1,2,3]
>>> p,q,r=x
```

If the target appears in **global** statement then its global value is changed. Otherwise, only the value in the local namespace is changed.

In an **augmented assignment**, an assignment is combined with an arithmetic operation. The arithmetic is performed first, followed by the assignment. Thus **x+=7** is equivalent to **x=x+7**. A list of augmented assignment operators is given in table 10.1.

```
>>> x=5
>>> x+=7
>>> print x
12
```

Table 10.1. Augmented Assignment Operators

Op	Description	Example	Equivalent
=	Standard asignment	x = 3+7	
+=	Add and assign	x += 3	x = x+3
-=	Subtract and assign	x -= 3	x = x-3
*=	Multiply and assign	x *= 3	x = x*3
/=	Divide and assign	x /= 3	x = x/3
//=	Floor divide and assign	x //=3	x = x//3
%=	Mod divide and assign	x %= 3	x = x % 3
**=	Exponentiate and assign	x**=3	x = x**3

The examples in the right-most column of table 10.1 illustrate how the augmented assignment statements work. Each of them combines some arithmetic operation with an assignment. Evaluation of the expression on the right-hand side of the expression is always performed first. Thus in the following code,

```
1  >>> x = 1
2  >>> y = 2
3  >>> z = 3
4  >>> z /=(x+y)
5  >>> z
6  1
```

in line 4, the expression **x+y** is evaluated first, to give **3**. Then **z**, which is already equal to **3**, is divided by **3**, giving **1**. The symbol **z** is then assigned to the result, so that it now has a value of **1**. The following code is completely equivalent:

```
>>> x = 1
>>> y = 2
>>> z = 3
>>> z = z/(x+y)
>>> z
1
```

Python allows simultaneous variable assignments in a single statement. Thus the previous code have just as easily been written as

```
>>> x,y,z=1,2,3
>>> z/=(x+y)
>>> z
1
```

The target/value associations are made left to right, as discussed above, but the variable bindings are truly simultaneous. This is particularly convenient. Consider the following algorithm for exchanging the values of two variables.

Algorithm 10.1 Exchange of Variables.

input: a, b
 1: $x \leftarrow a$
 2: $a \leftarrow b$
 3: $b \leftarrow x$
 4: **return** a, b

The intermediate variable x is used to hold the value of a so that a can be replaced with b. Then the saved value of a is put into b. A direct Python implementation follows.

```
>>> a,b=10,1
>>> print "a=",a,"b=",b
a= 10 b= 1
>>> x = a
>>> a = b
>>> b = x
```

```
>>> print "a=",a,"b=",b
a= 1 b= 10
```

If we use simultaneous assignment, we do not need to use the temporary variable:

```
>>> a,b=10,1
>>> print "a=",a,"b=",b
a= 10 b= 1
>>> a,b=b,a
>>> print "a=",a,"b=",b
a= 1 b= 10
>>>
```

Shallow and Deep Copy in Python

Assignment statements in Python do not actually copy objects, they create bindings (i.e., pointers) between an identifier (e.g., variable name) and an object (integer, list, string, etc). For example, the following result can be surprising:

```
>>> x=[1,2,3,4,5]
>>> y=x
>>> x[3]="a"
>>> print x, y
[1, 2, 3, 'a', 5] [1, 2, 3, 'a', 5]
```

When we changed the value of **x**, we also changed the value of **y**!

Both identifiers **x** and **y** point to the same list (lists are discussed in chapter 14). In most computer languages, when we change the value of **x[3]** we do not change the value of **y** at all. But in Python, both variables are pointing at the same memory location.

We can fix this with one of the **copy** statements.

```
>>> x=[1,2,3,4,5]
>>> from copy import copy
>>> y=copy(x)
>>> y
[1, 2, 3, 4, 5]
>>> x[3]="a"
>>> print x, y
[1, 2, 3, 'a', 5] [1, 2, 3, 4, 5]
```

This time **y** has not been changed.

The **copy** only works for top-level objects:

```
>>> x=[1,2,[3,4,5]]
>>> y=copy(x)
>>> x
[1, 2, [3, 4, 5]]
```

```
>>> y
[1, 2, [3, 4, 5]]
>>> x[2][0]=7
>>> print x, y
[1, 2, [7, 4, 5]] [1, 2, [7, 4, 5]]
```

Even though **y** was formed by a **copy(x)**, it only copied the top level information. The second level of **x[2]** is still a pointer to another list, which was changed in both **x** and **y** when we changed **x[2][0]**.

Here we needed to do a **deepcopy(x)** A **deep copy** of the original item constructs a new compound object and then, recursively, inserts copies into it of the objects found in the original. The **copy(x)** only returns a **shallow copy** of the original. A shallow copy constructs a new compound object and then (to the extent possible) inserts references into it to the objects found in the original.

```
>>> x=[1,2,[3,4,5]]
>>> from copy import deepcopy
>>> y=deepcopy(x)
>>> x[2][0]=7
>>> print x, y
[1, 2, [7, 4, 5]] [1, 2, [3, 4, 5]]
```

This time **y** is not affected when we change **x**.

Deep copies and shallow copies apply to all compound objects like lists, strings, and class objects.

The assert statement

The **assert** statement is used to insert debugging statements into code, for example

```
assert expression
```

is equivalent to

```
if __debug__:
    if not expression: raise AssertionError
```

The variable **__debug__** is a built in Python variable that cannot be changed. It can be turned off, however, by invoking Python with the **−o** command line option. Similarly **AssertionError** is a built in Error message that will be printed out.

```
>>> assert 3==7
Traceback (most recent call last):
  File "<stdin>", line 1, in <module>
AssertionError
```

A second form of **assert** is

```
assert expression1, expression2
```

which is equivalent to

```
if __debug__:
    if not expression1: raise AssertionError(expression2)
```

Passing the second expression to **AssertionError** allows you to print some specific information when the error flag is raised. The following assertion fails as it did before, but this time it prints out the error message that was included just in case it did fail.

```
>>> assert 3==7, "I_said_to_check_if_3==7"
Traceback (most recent call last):
  File "<stdin>", line 1, in <module>
AssertionError: I said to check if 3==7
```

Here I asserted that **3=7**, which is clearly **False**, so it raised the **AssertionError** and passed the information I requested to it, **"I said to check if 3==7"**, which was printed out with the error message **Traceback ... AssertionError:**

The pass statement

The **pass** statement does not do anything. It can be used as a placeholder when you need to put a statement some place but have nothing else to say.

The del statement

The **del** deletes items from the namespace or from a data structure. For example, you can use it to remove an item from a list (see chapter 14).

```
1  >>> x=[1,2,3]
2  >>> del x[1]
3  >>> x
4  [1, 3]
5  >>> del x
6  >>> x
7  Traceback (most recent call last):
8    File "<stdin>", line 1, in <module>
9  NameError: name 'x' is not defined
```

The second use of **del**, above, in line 5, removed the variable completely from the namespace, so that Python no longer even knew about **x** any more.

The print statement

A **print** statement is most commonly used to display the value of one or more variables on the screen. It can also be used to write a value to a file. Since **print** is a statement and not a function the sequence of things printed does not have to be enclosed in parentheses (in Python 2.7).

Python automatically prints a blank space before each item listed in a print statement.[1] The only exception is the first item printed on a line.

A newline character \n is normally written after printing, unless the print statement ends with a comma. For example, to print the numbers 1 through 9 on a single line,

```
1  >>> for i in range(1,10):
2  ...     print i,
3  ...
4  1 2 3 4 5 6 7 8 9
```

---

[1] Unlike many other languages.

If the comma at the end of line 2 is omitted, each number will be printed on a separate line. (We will discuss the **for** statement and **range** function in chapter 17. In this case, the **range(1,10)** on line 1 generated a list **[1,2,..,9]**.)

In addition, the **print** can redirect its output to a file, after that file has been opened.

```
>>> f=open("fred.txt","w")
>>> print >>f, range(10)
>>> f.close()
```

This will create a new file named **fred.txt** with a single line

```
[0, 1, 2, 3, 4, 5, 6, 7, 8, 9]
```

written in it. We will discuss file input and output in more detail in chapter 23.

The `return` statement

The **return** statement is used by a function to return a value to the calling program. Functions are discussed in chapter 28. Normally execution returns to the point where a function was invoked when the last line of the function is executed. If there is no **return** statement, or if there is a **return** statement with no value, then the returned value is **None**.

Only one "thing" may be be returned.

```
def cook_spam_and_eggs(spam,eggs,otherstuff):
        spam_omelette = spam+eggs+otherstuff
        return spam_omelette
```

If you have to return multiple items, you may enclose them in parenthesis to turn them into a tuple, or return them as a list, class, or other data objects.

```
def cook_spam_and_eggs(spam,eggs,potatoes,toast):
        spam_omelette = spam+eggs
        side_dish=[potatoes,toast]
        return (spam_omelette, side_dish)
```

The `yield` statement

The **yield** statement is discussed in chapter 18.

The `raise` statement

The **raise** statement is used to raise an exception. Details are discussed in chapter 27.

The **break** statement

The **break** statement is used inside of **while** or **for** loops (chapters 12, 17). When a **break** is encountered, flow of control exits the nearest enclosing loop without executing any optional **else** clause that may be present. See, for example, figure 17.3.

If the **break** occurs within a **try** statement, any existing **finally** clause (of the **try** statement) is executed before leaving the loop.

The **continue** statement

The **continue** statement is used inside of **while** or **for** loops (chapters 12, 17). When a **continue** is encountered, the current iteration of the nearest enclosing loop is terminated and the next iteration is begun without executing any optional **finally** clause of the loop.

If the **continue** occurs within a **try** statement, any existing **finally** clause is executed before leaving the loop iteration.

The **import** statement

The **import** statement is used to include all or part of a module (package) within a program. Packages are discussed in chapter 18.

To import a complete module such as **math** use the simplest form

```
>>> import math
```

```
>>> print math.pi
3.14159265359
```

You can import multiple modules on a single line.

```
>>> import math, random
```

To use a function from the module it must be qualified by the name. For example, the function **random.normalvariate(mu,sigma)** generates a random number with normal distribution.

```
>>> random.normalvariate(5,2)
2.409011570720191
```

You can rename a function when you import it.

```
>>> from random import normalvariate as n
>>> n(5,2)
6.69748783903759
```

You can also rename an entire package.

```
>>> import numpy as np
>>> import numpy.linalg as lin
>>> M=np.array([[1,2,3],[4,5,6],[7,8,9]])
>>> P,Q,R=lin.svd(M)
```

The singular value decomposition is discussed in chapter 40.

Finally, if you don't want to refer to a package name at all, you can just do a global import.

```
>>> from math import *
>>> print e
2.71828182846
>>>
```

The `global` statement

The **global** statement is used to define a variable in a local code block as a reference to a global variable. Consider the following code.

```
x=7                         # Set x=7
y=10                        # Set y=10
print "x, y=",x, y
def f(a, b):
    global x
    x = a                   # Set Global x to a
    y = b                   # Set Local y to a
    print "x, y=",x, y
f(200, 300)
print "x, y=",x, y
```

Here is the program output

```
x, y= 7 10
x, y= 200 300
x, y= 200 10
```

The first print statement is easy to understand. Initially the global variables are set to $x \leftarrow 7$ and $y \leftarrow 10$.

Then the function **f(200,300)** is invoked. This binds $a \leftarrow 200$ and $b \leftarrow 300$. Because of the **global** statement, the line **x=a** binds the global $x \leftarrow 200$ and the local $y \leftarrow 300$. The second print statements reflects these two values.

When flow is returned, the binding $x \leftarrow 200$ is remembered but the binding to $y \leftarrow 300$, which was local, is forgotten, in lieu of the original binding $y \leftarrow 10$. This is what is reflected by the third print statement.

The **exec** statement

The **exec** statement executes a string as if it were a line of Python code.

```
>>> y = 10
>>> z="y=y+1"
>>> exec(z)
>>> print y
11
>>> for i in range(10):
...     exec(z)
>>> print y
21
```

The main difference between **eval** and **exec** is that **eval** evaluates an expression and **exec** executes a statement.

Exercises

1. Write a program to calculate that converts a quantity **X** of currency in dollars (or your local currency) to coinage and bills. For example, $7.43 US would convert to one $5 bill, two $1 bills (or $1 coins), one quarter (25 cents), one dime (ten cents), one nickel (five cents), and three pennies (one cent each).

2. Write a program that calculates the day of the year for any integer year, month, and day.

Chapter 11

Conditional Statements

Boolean variables and expressions

Boolean variables, which have a data type **bool**, represent the values of logical expressions from Boolean Algebra in Python. They are convenient for testing if certain conditions have occurred during the execution of a program. A boolean variable can take on only two values, **True** (represented internally by a value of 1) or **False** (represented by a zero). In programs, we use the built-in identifiers **True** or **False** to represent these values.

```
>>> x,y = 7,5
>>> z=x+y
>>> w=(z==12)
>>> v=(z==11)
>>> print v,w,x,y,z
False True 7 5 12
```

Boolean comparisons are based on the standard operations of symbolic logic. Comparisons between the states of different variables (e.g., for equality or relative inequality see table 11.1) evaluate to a truth value. These may be joined by logical connectives (table 11.2) using the standard precedence rules (table 9.4).

Types of Boolean Expressions in Python	
Atomic	The values **True** or **False**.
Comparisons	See Table 11.1. Examples include: **x==y, x!=y, x>y, x<y, x>=y, x<=y** where **x** and **y** are any expression that evaluate to **True** or **False**
Logical	Logical operations (table 11.2), such as: **x and y, x or y, not x** where **x** and **y** are any expression that evaluate to **True** or **False**
Bitwise	Logical operations on individual bits (table 11.3)

The Python operators **and**, **or** and **not** correspond to the logical operators $\land$, $\lor$ and $\sim$ (table 11.2). Thus, for example, a statement such as $(x > 7) \land (y < 9)$ is written in Python as

```
x>7 and y<9
```

Since the Boolean values **True** and **False** have integer values of one and zero, respectively, it is possible to do mixed mode calculations with Boolean expressions.

```
1  >>> x=17
2  >>> (x>5)+1
3  2
```

There are also bit-by-bit versions of all of the Boolean operations (table 11.3 and their functional representations in table 9.10).

As a general rule, it is safer to test for inequality than for equality, especially between real numbers. Because of round-off and/or truncation errors, floating point numbers that you expect to be equal are very rarely actually equal.

To test if two expressions are equal, use a double equal sign:

```
>>> x=15
>>> (x*x)==(10*x+5*x)
True
```

General Rule

Never test for equality between floating point numbers.

Table 11.1. Comparison Operators

Operator[a]	Description	Example	True when:
==	Equality	x == y	$x = y$
!=	Inequality	x != y	$x \neq y$
<>	(equivalent operators)	x <> y	$x \neq y$
>	Greater than	x > y	$x > y$
<	Less than	x < y	$x < y$
>=	Greater than or equal to	x >= y	$x \geq y$
<=	Less than or equal to	x <= y	$x \leq y$

[a]Each of the comparison operators listed also has a functional representation in the Python standard **operators** package. See table 9.10.

Table 11.2. Logical Operators

Operator[a]	Description	Example	Meaning:
and	Logical and	x and y	$x \wedge y$
or	Logical or	x or y	$x \vee y$
not	Logical not	not x	$\sim x$

[a]Each of the operators listed also has a functional representation in the Python standard **operators** package. See table 9.10.

Table 11.3. Bitwise Operators

Operator[a]	Description	Example[b]
&	and	3 & 6 → 6 ($0011 \vee 0110 \rightarrow 0010$)
|	or	3|6 → 7 ($0011 \vee 0110 \rightarrow 0111$)
^	xor	3^6 → 5 (0011 xor $0110 \rightarrow 0101$)
~	ones comp.	~7 →-8 (~$000\ldots0111 \rightarrow 111\ldots1000$)
<<	shift left	3 << 2 → 12 ($0011 \rightarrow 1100$)
>>	shift right	16 >> 3 → 2 ($1\ 0000 \rightarrow 0\ 0010$)

[a] Each of the operators listed also has a functional representation in the Python standard **operators** package. See table 9.10.
[b] Using 1 for True and 0 for False.

Ternary operators

A **conditional statement** is an expression whose value depends on the value of a conditional expression. There are two types of conditional statements: **conditional assignments**, and **if** statements.

A **conditional assignment** uses a **ternary operator** to evaluate the right hand side of an assignment statement. A ternary operator has the form

```
x if P else y
```

The result of this operator is **x** if **P** is **True**, and **y** if **P** is **False**. The corresponding conditional assignment is

```
z=x if P else y
```

In the following example, **y** is assigned a value of -92.

```
>>> x=7
>>> y=(x+7) if x>99 else (x-99)
```

The if Statements

An **if** statement is a sequence of one or more tests, of the form

```
if condition:
    statements      # one or more statements
elif condition:     # zero or more elif statements
    statements      # one or more statements in each elif
else:               # the else clause is optional
    statements      # one or more statements
```

The **elif** is short for **else if**; is optional; and there may be more than one of them. The **else** is also optional. The indentation is essential.

A block of indented code is sometimes called a **suite**. The suite begins with an **INDENT** and ends with a **DEDENT**. The **DEDENT** means that the indentation level returns to where it was just before the suite begin, canceling out the corresponding **INDENT**. Each statement in the suite is separated by a newline (NL), and is indented at the same level (number of spaces).

The simplest form of the **if** statement has neither an **elif** or **else** clause, and only has a single line of code in its suite. Here are several listed back-to-back.

```
1  x,y=5,10
2  if x>y:
3      print "x is bigger"
4  if x<y:
5      print "x is smaller"
6  if x==y:
7      print "x and y are the same"
```

When this code is run, the test on line 2 will fail, so line 3 will be skipped. Since $5 < 10$, the test on line 4 is **True**, and line 5 is executed.

```
x is smaller
```

Since $5 \neq 10$, the condition on line 6 is false, and line 7 is skipped.

Figure 11.1: Flow of the **if** statement.

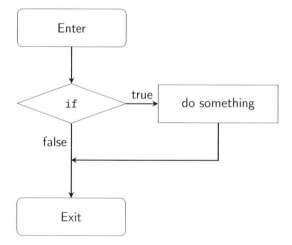

Indentation is important. This is how Python distinguishes between the consequence of the if and the remainder of the program. If it is indented, it is the consequence of the if. You can put as many lines of code as you want inside of an if statement. All of the lines must be indented the same number of spaces. (Otherwise, Python will print an error message.)

Statements within the indented blocks may be any type of python statement, including statements such as **if**, **while**, **try**, **with** statements, and function and class definitions, that may themselves require require indentation. Each time a statement is added that requires indentation, its code suite is indented to a new level.

```
x,y=5,10
if x>y:
    z = x+y
    print x, "is_bigger_than", y
    print "z=",z
if x<y:
    z = x - y
    print x, "_is_smaller_than", y
    print "z=",z
```

When this code is run, the output is

```
5 is smaller than 10
z= -5
```

The following code, on the other hand, produces a run time error, because when execution reaches line 5, the variable z has not yet been defined.

```
1  x,y=5,10
2  if x>y:
3      z = x+y
4      print x, "is_bigger_than", y
5  print "z=",z
6  if x<y:
7      z = x - y
8      print x, "is_smaller_than", y
9  print "z=",z
```

In a basic **if** with no following **else** or **elif** clause, if the condition is **True**, the suite following the **if** is executed and if the condition is **False**, the suite is skipped. In either case, the next statement executed is the first unindented statement following the **if**.

By including an **else** clause, you can divide the flow of control into two different channels (see figure 11.2). If the condition is **True**, the suite following the **if** is executed. If the condition in the **if** is **False**, then suite following the **else** is executed. After completion of the suite, flow continues with the first statement following the end of the **else** suite.

```
1   x,y=5,10
2   if x>y:
3       print "x_is_bigger"
4       print "y_is_smaller"
5   else:
6       print "x_is_not_bigger"
7       print "y_is_not_smaller"
8   if x<y:
9       print "x_is_smaller"
10      print "y_is_bigger"
11  else:
12      print "x_is_not_smaller"
13      print "y_is_not_bigger"
```

```
14  if x==y:
15      print "x_and_y_are_the_same"
16  else:
17      print "x_and_y_have_different_values"
```

Figure 11.2: Flow of the **if-else** statement. The consequence of the optional **else** clause is only executed if the original **if** test fails.

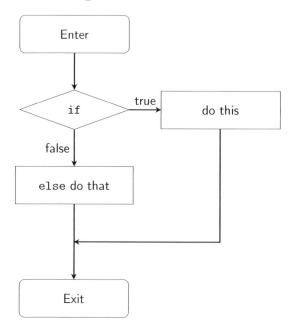

Each **if** and **else** suite in this example has two lines of code. Since $x < y$, we expect the **else** suite on line 5 to trigger (executing the two print statements on lines 6 and 7), the **if** suite on line 8 to trigger (executing the two **print** statements on lines 9 and 10), and the **else** clause on line 16 to trigger (executing the **print** on line 17):

```
x is not bigger
y is not smaller
x is smaller
y is bigger
x and y have different values
```

Finally, you can add one or more alternative conditions after the **if** and before the optional **else**, as illustrated in figure 11.3. The first condition is preceded by **if**, and all the subsequent conditions are preceded by **elif**. They may be finally followed by an **else**. There is an indented block of code after the **if**, each **elif** and the **else**. Each of the conditions is tested in succession. The block of code following the first one that evaluates to **True** is executed. If none of the conditions are **True** then the code in the **else** block is executed.

```
x,y=5,10
if x>y:
    print "x is bigger than y"
elif x==y:
    print "x equals y"
else:
    print "x is smaller than y"
```

The **if** and **elif** clauses both fail but the else succeeds.

```
x is smaller than y
```

There can be as many **elif** clauses as you like, and the **else** clause is optional.

```
1  x,y=1,3
2  if x<0 and y < 0:
3      print "both are negative"
4  elif x <0:
5      print "only x is negative"
6  elif y <0:
7      print "only y is negative"
8  elif x-y<0:
9      print "x-y=",x-y
10 else:
11     print "lah dee dah"
12 print "ta ta for now"
```

The **if** and first two **elif** tests failed but the third **elif** on line 8 is true, so in this case the output is:

```
x-y= -2
ta ta for now
```

Exercises

1. Write python code to calculate the absolute value of a real number (do no use the **abs** function). Do this in two different ways: (a) with **if** .. **elif**; and (b) with a ternary operator.

2. Without using python complex numbers, write a program to find the roots of $ax^2 + bx + c = 0$, given any real values of a, b, and c, using the quadratic formula. If the discriminant $b^2 - 4ac < 0$ the roots will be complex, and you should still solver

   for them by reversing the discriminant to $4ac - b^2$. When the solution is real, print out the real roots. When the solution is complex, print out the complex roots as a pair of real numbers, **a+bi**.

3. Write code to figure out the number of days between two dates. Remember to account for leap years. Do not use the **datetime**, **time** or any other similar python library.

4. Repeat the previous problem, but this time use the **datetime** library.

Figure 11.3: Flow of the **if–elif–else** statements. The consequence of the first **if** or **elif** that evaluates to **true** will be executed. If none of the tests are **true**, and there is an optional **else** test present, then the conseequense of the **else** will be executed.

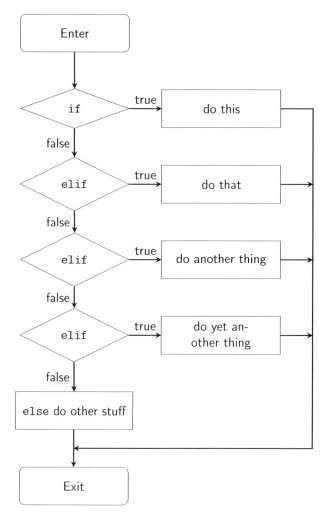

Chapter 12

While Loops

In a **while** loop, a sequence of statements is repeated over and over again while some condition is true. It looks something like this.

```
while expression:
    suite   # a suite is a sequence of indented statements
else:       # optional else clause
    suite
```

Here **expression** must evaluate to either **True** or **False**. If **expression** is never **True**, the loop will never be executed; and if it **expression** is never **False**, the loop will be repeated forever.

Figure 12.1: Flow of a generic **while** loop.

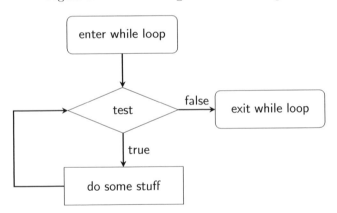

Example 12.1. Print the numbers 1 through 5 on a single line. The comma at the end of the print statement tells Python not to advance to the next line after printing (see page 80).

```
i=0
while i<5:
    i+=1
    print i,
```

Indentation is critically important in all loops. This is how Python can tell which statements are in the suite to be executed, and when the loop ends. Each statement in the suite must be indented at the same level.

Example 12.2. Find $\sqrt{5}$ using a Python while loop with the Babylonian Algorithm. (Algorithm 3.1) Print the value after each iteration.

```
1   a=5
2   x=a
3   epsilon = 0.001          # initialize termination criterion
4   delta = float("inf")     # initialize delta to infinity
5   while delta > epsilon:
6       xnew=0.5*(x+a/x)     # Babylonian algorithm
7       delta = abs(xnew-x)  # Change in estimate
8       x=xnew               # Use new estimate for next iteration
9       print x              # print each interation.
10  print "the␣square␣root␣of␣",a,"␣is␣", x
```

At line 9, the program prints the value of **x** at the current iteration, showing how far the algorithm has progressed on its road towards convergence.

```
11  3.0
12  2.33333333333
13  2.2380952381
14  2.23606889564
15  2.2360679775
16  the square root of  5  is  2.2360679775
```

The initialization of **delta** on line 4 demonstrates how we can set a variable equal to infinity. This way, no matter what value we compute subsequently, it will always be smaller.

```
>>> big=float("inf")
>>> 99<big
True
```

Greatest Common Divisor

Euclid gave an iterative algorithm for the GCD (def. 12.1) in the *Elements*, Book 7, proposition 2. Euclid's algorithm, which is generally attributed to the earlier school of Pythagoras, is expressed geometrically in terms of line segments and their corresponding lengths. A modern version of the algorithm, purely in terms of integers, can be found in most books on number theory, and is shown as algorithm 12.1 (see figure 12.2).

> **Definition 12.1. Greatest Common Divisor (GCD)**
>
> Suppose $A, B \in \mathbb{Z}^+$, with at least one of them non-zero. Then their **greatest common divisor**, denoted $\gcd(A, B)$ is the largest positive integer that divides into each of A and B without remainder.

Example 12.3. Implement Euclid's GCD algorithm in Python using a while loop. The following code implements algorithm 12.1 directly to find gcd(993,42993).

Algorithm 12.1 Euclidean Algorithm for the GCD

input: $X, Y \in \mathbb{Z}$, where $X, Y \geq 0$
1: $x \leftarrow X; y \leftarrow Y$
2: **while** $y \neq 0$ **do**
3:     $r \leftarrow x \bmod y$
4:     $x \leftarrow y$
5:     $y \leftarrow r$
6: **end while**
7: **return** x as $\mathbf{GCD}(X, Y)$

Figure 12.2: The Euclidean algorithm for the GCD (algorithm 12.1).

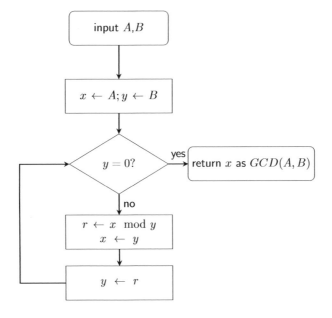

The code is on the left, and the output is on the right. The values of **x** and **y** are printed out at each step to illustrate how the algorithm is working.

```
1   X,Y = 993, 42993
2   x,y=X,Y;
3   while y!=0:
4       x, y = y, x % y
5       print x, y
6   print x
```

```
42993 993
993 294
294 111
111 72
72 39
39 33
33 6
6 3
3 0
3
```

Note how the intermediate variable r is not needed because of the use of simultaneous assignment in Python. Of course, if you just wanted to know the GCD, it is easier to use **fractions.gcd(42936,993)** (table 9.8).

Using else, break and continue in while

An **else** statement can be used at the end of a **while** loop; this has the same effect as an **else** statement in an **if** statement. The suite in the **else** is executed the first time the test in the **while** is **false** (figure 12.3).

```
while expression:
    suite    # do stuff
else:        # optional
    suite    # do other stuff
```

Both the **break** (page 82) and **continue** (page 82) statements can also be used within a **while** loop.

When the **continue** statement is reached within a loop, Python acts as if the current loop iteration is over (figure 12.3). All statements following the **continue** are skipped over and execution resumes with the next iteration of the loop. The **continue** is normally paired with an **if**; when the conditions of the test are met, the rest of the current iteration can be skipped.

For example, the following program will print the numbers 0 to 25 in increments of 5 on a single line:

```
1  i=-1
2  while i <= 25:
3      i=i+1
4      if i%5 != 0:
5          continue
6      print i,
```

At each step of the loop, i is incremented by 1. At line number 4, a test is performed to see if i is divisible by 5. If it is not divisible by 5, the program is told to **continue** with the next iteration. So execution "jumps" to the i=i+1 step. If i is divisible by 5, and only when i is divisible by 5, is the **print** statement ever reached. Here is the program output:

```
0 5 10 15 20 25
```

Of course, this example was just for illustration - an easier way to print the numbers is this:

```
1  i=0
2  while i <= 25:
3      print i,
4      i=i+5
```

When we learn about the **for** loop (chapter 17) we will see an even shorter way of doing this.

When a **break** is encountered, the current loop is assumed to be finished and flow of control is transferred to the first statement following the end of the loop (figure 12.3). This allows a loop to be exited before completion.

Figure 12.3: A **while** loop, showing the relationship between **continue**, **break**, and **else** statements to the loop.

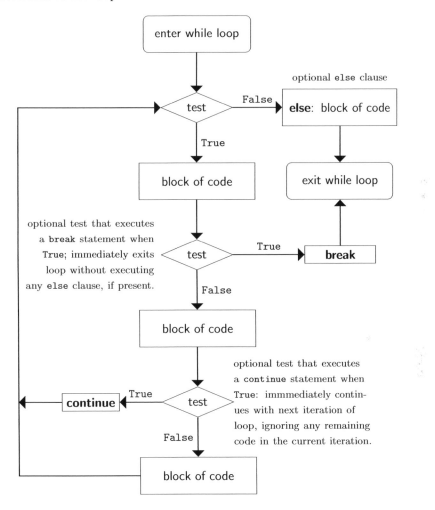

Prime Numbers

Definition 12.2. Prime Number

A positive integer $x \in \mathcal{Z}^+$, $x > 2$ is **prime** if its only factors are 1 and x.

If we are not interested in efficiency, we can figure out if a numbers is prime by brute force. Given x, go through all the numbers $j = 2, 3, 4, \ldots, x$. If j divides evenly into x, then it is not prime. If you manage to go through all the values of j without dividing evenly into x, then you have a prime number. A number j evenly divides into x if there is no remainder, i.e., $x \bmod j = 0$. This is summarized in algorithm 12.2.

Algorithm 12.2 Prime Numbers with **while**. Let **P** be the set of all primes. This algorithm determines if x is a prime.

input: $x \in \mathbb{Z}^+$, $x > 2$

1: $j \leftarrow 2$
2: **while** $x > j$ **do**
3:    **if** $x \bmod j = 0$ and $j \neq x$ **then**
4:       **return** $(x \notin \mathbf{P})$
5:    **end if**
6:    $j \leftarrow j + 1$
7: **end while**
8: **return** $x \in \mathbf{P}$

Example 12.4. Use a **while** loop with a **break** to print the prime numbers under 100.

We can implement algorithm 12.2 directly in Python as follows.

```
1  j=2
2  while x > j:
3      if x%j==0 and j != x:
4          print x, "is not prime"
5          break
6      j = j + 1
7  else:
8      print x," is prime"
```

Why do we need the **else** clause here rather than just having the **print** immediately after the **while**? Because of the **break**.

When the **break** statement executes, flow is pulled out of the entire **while** loop, which includes the contents of the **else**. If the **print** were not encapsulated within the **else**, then **x is prime** would be printed regardless of whether x is prime or not. In fact, with the **else** clause in place, that **print** statement is now only reached when $x = j$, i.e., once j has looped through all the integers from 2 to x.

The trick to get a list of all the primes from 1 to 100 now is to nest the entire **while** in another **while** loop. The flow diagram for the doubly-nested **while** loop is shown in figure 12.4.

```
a=2
while a<100:
    j=2
    x=a
    a=a+1
    while x > j:
        if x%j==0 and j != x:
            break
        j = j + 1
    else:
        print x,
```

When we run the program, this is what we see printed out:

```
2 3 5 7 11 13 17 19 23 29 31 37 41 43 47 53 59 61 67 71 73
79 83 89 97
```

Exercises

1. Suppose you want to divide up the interval (a, b) into $n+1$ sub-intervals of equal length. Using a **while** loop, write a program to determine the end points of each interval. Verify that your program works on the following: $(a, b) = (0, 10); n = 10; (a, b) = (3, 17); n = 19; (a, b) = (-4.72, 6.98); n = 12$.

2. Write a program to solve for $\sqrt{a}$ using the Babylonian algorithm with a **while** loop.

3. Write a program to find the index of a number x in a list L, assuming that $x \in L$, using a **while** loop. Do this by examining each element in the list, one at a time, and comparing it with x.

4. Use a **while** loop to explicitly calculate each of the following sums.

(a) $\displaystyle\sum_{k=1}^{n} k$

(b) $\displaystyle\sum_{k=1}^{n} k^2$

(c) $\displaystyle\sum_{k=1}^{n} k^3$

(d) $\displaystyle\sum_{k=1}^{n} k(k-1)$

(e) $\displaystyle\sum_{k=1}^{n} \frac{k^2 - k}{2k}$

(f) $\displaystyle\sum_{k=1}^{n} \frac{\pi^{-k}}{k!}$

5. Write a program to calculate $n!$, where n is an integer. Use a **while** loop. Do not use the **factorial** function in the math library or any other library.

6. Write a program to calculate the first n terms of a geometric series $a + ar + ar^2 + ar^3 + \cdots + ar^{n-1}$ by adding them up term by term.

7. Look up the Taylor series for $\cos x$. Write a program that will calculate the first n terms of the series.

Figure 12.4: Flow chart of the prime number calculation by brute force, showing the nested **while** loops. The inner loop is enclosed by a dotted line.

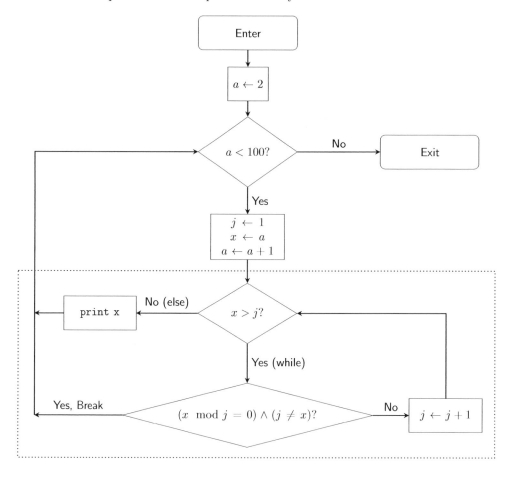

Chapter 13

Sequential Data Types

Sequential data types are **strings** (type **str**, chapter 15), **lists** (type **list**, chapter 14), and **tuples** (type **tuple**, chapter 14)). Each of these data types is really a sequence of items with an associated order. The order is referenced by an index, which starts at zero, and increases by one from left to right. The index is used to access or address an element of the sequential type. In addition, **xrange** objects are often treated as sequential data types, although they are not really a data type at all. Instead, they are objects that return a sequential data type but the data itself is not actually stored in memory.

Sequential items in python are indexed starting from zero in python. The first item in any list, string, or array is the zeroth item, e.g., **x[0]**.

To use sequential data types effectively you have to understand **slices**. A slice is a piece of a sequential data type. Let's use the string **'porcupine'** as an example. Here we label each character in the string with its index.

x[i]	p	o	r	c	u	p	i	n	e
index i	0	1	2	3	4	5	6	7	8
slice x[3:7]				✓	✓	✓	✓		

If we set **x='porcupine'** then the length of **x** is 9 because it has 9 characters in it.

```
>>> x="porcupine"
>>> len(x)
9
```

The third character (remember: we start our count at zero, not one) is **'c'** and the 7th character is an **'n'**. We can get to these directly by indexing:

```
>>> x[3]
'c'
 >>> x[7]
'n'
```

Now for slices: the slice from 3 to 7 includes **x[3]**, **x[4]**, **x[5]** and **x[6]** but not **x[7]**. We designate this as **x[3:7]**.

Think of the slice notation as **x[start_at:end_before]**. We've indicated that above with check marks.

The notation **x[i:]** means take a slice starting with index **i** to the end of the sequence.

```
>>> x[7:]
'ne'
```

Finally, the notation **x[:j]** means to take a slice of the first **j** elements.

```
>>> x[:3]
'por'
```

All sequential data types can be accessed by index and slice.

```
slicing            ::=   simple_slicing | extended_slicing
simple_slicing     ::=   primary "[" short_slice "]"
extended_slicing   ::=   primary "[" slice_list "]"
slice_list         ::=   slice_item ("," slice_item)* [","]
slice_item         ::=   expression | proper_slice | ellipsis
proper_slice       ::=   short_slice | long_slice
short_slice        ::=   [lower_bound] ":" [upper_bound]
long_slice         ::=   short_slice ":" [stride]
lower_bound        ::=   expression
upper_bound        ::=   expression
stride             ::=   expression
ellipsis           ::=   "..."
```

Additional operations common to lists and strings are summarized in table 13.1.

mutability

Python sequences can be classified according to their **mutability**. A sequence type is considered either **mutable** or **immutable**. Once an immutable sequence has been created, it cannot be changed.

Strings (type **str**), **unicode** object (single unicode character, e.g., objects created by the function **unicode**), and **tuples** (a sequence enclosed in parenthesis) are immutable (chapter 15).

Lists and **byte arrays** are mutable objects (chapter 14). Arrays are mutable sequences that are designed for fast and efficient processing of numeric values, but act very much like sequences (chapter 21). (Most numerical computations used Numpy **ndarrays** instead of the standard Python arrays, because they are more flexible.)

About **xrange** objects

The **xrange** object is used mainly for iteration. An **xrange** object is generated by the **xrange** functions, which has format

```
xrange(start, stop, increment)
```

An **xrange** object can be used in the same manner as the output of the **range** function, and both behave very similarly. The difference is that **range** has to create all of the requested values, and return them, when the function is called. The **xrange** object, on the other hand, only calculates individual values when they are needed, and so requires less memory space.

```
>>>for j in xrange(5,10): print j,
...
5 6 7 8 9
```

Table 13.1. Functions and Operations on Sequential Data Types

Operation	Description
x in y	Returns **True** if **x** is an element of **y**.
	5 in (1,3,5,7) → **True**
	34 in (1,3,5,7) → **False**
x not in y	Returns **True** if **x** is not an element of **y**.
	23 not in (1,3,5,7) → **True**
	"o" not in "Hello" → **False**
x + y	Concatenation.
	[1,3,5]+[4,9]→**'HelloWorld'**
n*x	Generates n repeats of a sequence.
	3*[1,2,3] → **[1, 2, 3, 1, 2, 3, 1, 2, 3]**
	3*'alakazam' → **'alakazamalakazamalakazam'**
x[i]	i^{th} element of **x**, starting from zero.
	"Hello"[1]→ **'e'**
x[i:j]	Slice from index **i** to just before index **j**.
	"Flying Circus"[3:11]→**'ing Circ'**
x[i:j:k]	Slice from **i** to **j** with step size **k**.
	"Monty Pythons Flying Circus"[1:15:3]→**'oyyos'**
len(x)	Number of elements in **x**.
	len("dictionary") → **10**
min(x)	Minimum value; uses alphabetical order for strings.
max(x)	Maximum value; uses alphabetical order for strings.
sum(x)	Adds up all the values in **x**.
	Only valid for numeric sequences.
	sum([1,3,-4.7, 6.2])→**5.5**
all(x)	Returns **True** if all elements are **True**.
any(x)	Returns **True** if any element is **True**.

Similar Data Types

Neither of the following are sequential data types but are collective data types that users new to programming, or who have programmed in other languages, may not be expecting.

Sets are unordered objects similar to sequences (chapter 16) and are classified into mutable **set**'s and immutable **frozenset**'s. Sets have properties similar to mathematical sets, allowing logical operations to be performed.

Dictionaries (chapter 24; also called **mapping** types) are collections of objects referenced by keys rather than numeric index. Dictionaries are mutable. Lookup by key is like looking something up in a phone book or a paper dictionary, rather than by a numerical index.

Exercises

1. Suppose that **x** is the list `[8,-3,  4,  7, 6,  12]`. Figure out what of the following should be; then verify you answers using Python.

   (a) The length of **x**

   (b) What is the Python expression to get the first element of **x**? The last? The penultimate?

   (c) `x[3]`   (f) `x[3:]`

   (d) `x[:2]`   (g) `x[-2]`

   (e) `x[-1]`   (h) `x + ["abc",7]`

2. How would you represent the matrix
$$\mathbf{A} = \begin{bmatrix} 2 & 4 & 0 & 3 \\ -7 & 3 & 6 & 0 \\ 4 & 0 & 5 & 0 \end{bmatrix} \text{ as a list?}$$

   (a) How you find the the second column of **A**?

   (b) How can you find the third row of **A**?

   (c) What is `A[1]`?

   (d) How do you find A_{12}?

   (e) What is the length of **A**?

3. Using the matrix A in the previous problem, how would you figure out if any element of the matrix is equal to 3? all the elements are positive?

4. Write a program to construct a single flat list from a 2-dimensional list.

Chapter 14

Lists and Tuples

Lists in Python are sequences of Python objects enclosed by square brackets. Any Python object can be included in a list. You can even mix types, nest lists and reference any element by an index.

```
>>> x=[3,4,5,6,7]
>>> y=["some", "day", "my","prince", "will", "come"]
>>> z=["I", "want", 7, "waffles"]
```

Implementation Note. (You can skip this paragraph if you want.) Python lists are implemented as variable length arrays. What this means is that you can access any element (even the 12 billionth) in the same amount of time. This is in contrast to some other languages (e.g., LISP), where the computer has to walk through the list to find out where the 12 billionth element is stored. However, since lists are allowed to have mixed types of elements, each element may take up a different amount of memory, and so the elements are unlikely to be contiguous. Unlike fixed size arrays (e.g., in Fortran) the address cannot be computed by multiplying the index by the size of the element. Instead, Python uses a two step process (figure 14.1). There is an array of fixed length addresses (like a Fortran array). These addresses are called pointers. If you ask for the 327th element, Python looks for the 327th pointer (which it can find by multiplying 327 times the size of the pointer) to get the memory location where X[327] is stored. And if you want to change the contents of X[327] to something that is bigger than the previous contents, Python only has to change the pointer to point to the new item. Thus while Python lists are much faster than LISP lists (if they are really long) they will be much slower than Fortran arrays. Of course all of this is completely transparent to the programmer, who just writes X[327] and wonders why it takes so much longer than Fortran or C to run through a long numerical list.[1]

Lists are **mutable**, which means you can change their contents. Items can be referenced, added, changed, and deleted by index.

```
>>> y[3]
'prince'
>>> y[3]='princess'
>>> y
['some', 'day', 'my', 'princess', 'will', 'come']
>>> z = ['I', 'want', 7, 'waffles']
>>> del[z[0]]
>>> y[5]=z
>>> y
['some','day','my','princess','will',['want',7,'waffles']]
```

---

[1]This is what Numpy is for.

Figure 14.1: Python lists are implemented as arrays of addresses. Each address has a fixed size, and can point to a different sized block of data. This way the time it takes to address any particular location in the list is fixed.

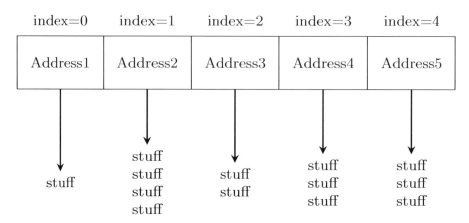

Tuples are similar to lists except that they are immutable, that is, once a tuple is defined, its contents cannot be changed. You can refer to an element by index as `x[i]` but you cannot assign a value like you can with lists. To emphasize the difference, tuples are delimited by parenthesis rather than square brackets. The following are valid examples of tuples:

```
>>> x=(3,4,5,6)
>>> y=("some","day","my","princess")
>>> z=("will", "eat",7, "waffles")
>>> w=(x,y, [x,y,z])
```

Tuples can be sliced and concatenated but to make a change you must define a new tuple:

```
>>>p= x[:2] + z[3:]
>>>p
(3, 4, 'waffles')
```

All of the sequential operations listed in table 13.1 can be used with tuples so long as you don't actually try to change the contents of an existing tuple with them, e.g., by by referring to an element or slice on the left hand side of an assignment.

Table 14.1. List Operations[a]

Operation	Result
`x[i]`=*value*	Assignment to an element of a list.
`x[i:j]`=*sequence*	Assignment to a slice.
`del(x[i])`	Element deletion.
`del(x[i:j])`	Slice deletion.
`list(x)`	Convert sequence **x** to a list.
`x.append(y)`	Adds **y** to end of **x**. No return value.
	`x=[4,5,6]; x.append(23)`
	`x→[4, 5, 6, 23]`
`x.count(y)`	Count number of times **y** occurs in **x**.
	`[1,2,5,7,3,2,4,7,9].count(7) → 2`
`x.extend(y)`	Appends list **y** to end of **x**. No return value.
	`x=[1,2];x.extend(['a','b'])`
	`x→[1, 2, 'a', 'b']`
`x.index(p)`	Returns first location of **p** in **x**.
	`[1,2,'a','b','a',3].index('a') → 2`
`x.insert(i,p)`	Inserts **p** at index **i**.
	`x=[1,2,3,4]; x.insert(1,'hi')`
	`x →[1, 'hi', 2, 3, 4]`
`x.pop(i)`	Returns element i and removes it from **x**.
`x.remove(p)`	Removes element with value **p**. Changes **x**.
`x.reverse()`	Reverses **x** (in place). No return value.
`x.sort()`	Sorts **x** in place. See page 141.

[a]Lists are mutable, so unlike strings and tuples, they can be changed by index or slice assignment.

Exercises

1. Write a program to determine if a two dimensional list is entirely numeric.

2. Write a program that returns the transpose of a two dimensional matrix represented as a list.

Chapter 15

Strings

Strings are used to represent character data, like `'Hello World'` and `"My Name is Fred"`. Strings begin and end either with an apostrophe (called a **single quote** in the Python literature) or a quote character (called a **double quote**). It doesn't matter which one you use on any given string; however, you must end the string with the same character you start with. That way you are able to embed the other character inside the string. If you need to embed both characters, you can always precede one of them with a backslash character. "Escape sequences" allow you to embed these and other special characters (string literals, table 15.2). For example, to embed a tab inside of a string, you would include the `\t` (a backslash followed by a lower case **t**).

```
>>> s="spam\teggs"
>>> print s
spam        eggs
>>>
```

There is also a special type of string called a **long string** that begins and ends with either three single-quotes or with three double quotes. In triple-quoted strings, unescaped newlines and quotes are allowed (and are retained), except that three unescaped quotes in a row terminate the string. In other words, while you would use the escape sequence `\n` to embed a newline in a normal string, in a long string you just continue writing on the next line; this automatically places a newline in the string.

On line 1 in the following example we define a normal string **x** with an embedded (escaped) newline character. String **y**, defined on line2, is a long string (using triple-quotes on either end of it) that has an embedded un-escaped newline.

```
1   >>> x="this is a string \nwith a newline in it"
2   >>> y="""this is another string
3   with a newline in it"""
4   >>> print x
5   this is a string
6   with a newline in it
7   >>> print y
8   this is another string
9   with a newline in it
10  >>>
```

Most of the operations that are performed on strings are performed by a special types of functions called **methods**. We will discuss methods in chapter 29. For now, it is easiest to think of a method as a function that operates on a variable **x** by attaching the function name to it with a period, as in the following example which returns a string in upper case

```
>>> print x
porcupine
>>> y=x.upper()
>>> print y
PORCUPINE
```

Some strings will have a **prefix** (table 15.1, such as **s=r'$I=cos y$'**. The **r** prefix
means the string is to be interpreted literally, and the escape characters should not be
interpreted as in table 15.2. This might be used, for example, to embed LATEX expression
in strings that are used to label plots.

Table 15.1. String prefixes

Prefix	Description
'r', 'R'	Raw strings (do not follow table 15.2, except for \u). Characters are embedded in the string without change. Not permitted to end in a single backslash.
'u', 'U'	Unicode string.
'b', 'B'	Byte literal (Python 3.0).

String Conversion

The special character **%** is used to insert the values of variables i A **format** instruction
can precede the **%** symbol to perform a format conversiznto strings. In general, usage is
based loosely on the `sprintf()` function from the C language.

String Conversion

For each value that is to be written to a string, the a text string with the following
format is required: **FW.PC%** where

- **F** = optional sign or left/right justification (table 15.3)
- **W**= optional minimum field width in characters
- **.P**=optional digits precision
- **C**=type of conversion (table 15.4). The conversion is always terminated by
  a percentage symbol.

Following the string, a tuple preceded by the % symbol will contain a sequence of values,
in order, that are to be matched to each format string. Thus

```
>>> from math import sin, pi, e
>>> print "pi=%7.2f,_e=%7.3f,_sin(pi/4)=%.4f" %(pi,e,sin(pi/4))
pi=   3.14, e=  2.718, sin(pi/4)=0.7071
```

Table 15.2. String Escape Sequences

Escape Sequence	Description
\newline	Ignored
\	Backslash (\)
\'	Single quote (')
\"	Double quote (")
\a	ASCII Bell $\boxed{\text{BEL}}$
\b	ASCII Backspace $\boxed{\text{BS}}$
\f	ASCII Formfeed $\boxed{\text{FF}}$
\n	ASCII Linefeed $\boxed{\text{LF}}$
\Nname	Unicode character named name
\r	ASCII Carriage Return $\boxed{\text{CR}}$
\t	ASCII Horizontal Tab $\boxed{\text{TAB}}$
\uxxxx	Unicode 16 bit hex value xxxx
\Uxxxxxxxx	Unicode 32 bit hex value xxxxxxxx
\v	ASCII Vertical Tab $\boxed{\text{VT}}$
\ooo	Character with octal value ooo
\hh	Character with hex value hh

For more detail, see `https://docs.python.org/2/reference/lexical_analysis.html#string-literals`

Table 15.3. String Conversion Flags

Flag	Description
'#'	The value conversion will use the "alternate" form.
'0'	The conversion will be zero padded for numeric values.
'-'	The converted value is left adjusted (overrides the '0' conversion if both are given).
' '	(a space) A blank should be left before a positive number (or empty string) produced by a signed conversion.
'+'	A sign character ('+' or '-') will precede the conversion (overrides a space flag).

Source: `https://docs.python.org/2/library/stdtypes.html#string-formatting-operations`

String Concatenation

Concatenation is a binary operation in which two strings are combined to form a third string. In Python the plus sign (**+**) is used for concatenation. This sometimes causes confusion with addition.

```
>>> x="Monty"
>>> y="Python"
>>> blank_space=" "
>>> z = x+blank_space+y
>>> print z
Monty Python
>>>
```

The following type of error is quite common when numbers are read from files:

```
1  >>> x="10.5 "
2  >>> y="42.3 "
3  >>> z="17.8 "
4  >>> average = (x+y+z)/3
5
6  Traceback (most recent call last):
7    File "<pyshell#31>", line 1, in <module>
8        average = (x+y+z)/3
9  TypeError: unsupported operand type(s) for /: 'str' and 'int'
```

The problem is that the numbers were stored as strings, and needed to be converted first to floats. Strings can be converted to numbers such as integers and floats if they contain values that represent such numbers. The correct code would be:

```
11  >>> average=(float(x)+float(y)+float(z))/3
12  >>> average
13  23.53333333333333
```

In fact, "summing" over a sequence of strings produces a concatenation. Thus Python didn't know what we meant when we said to divide the resulting string by 3.

```
14  >>> x+y+z
15  '10.5 42.3 17.8 '
16  >>> float(x) + float(y) + float(z)
17  70.6
18  >>>
```

Table 15.4. String Conversion Formats[a]

Conversion	Description
'd'	Signed integer decimal.
'i'	Signed integer decimal.
'o'	Signed octal value.[1]
'u'	Obsolete type it is identical to 'd'.
'x'	Signed hexadecimal (lower case).[2]
'X'	Signed hexadecimal (upper case).[2]
'e'	Floating point exponential format (lowercase).[3]
'E'	Floating point exponential format (uppercase).[3]
'f'	Floating point decimal format.[3]
'F'	Floating point decimal format.[3]
'g'	Floating point format. Uses lower case exponential format if exponent is less than -4 or not less than precision, decimal format otherwise.[4]
'G'	Floating point format. Uses upper case exponential format if exponent is less than -4 or not less than precision, decimal format otherwise.[4]
'c'	Single character (accepts integer or single character string).
'r'	String (converts any Python object using repr()).[5]
's'	String (converts any Python object using str()).[6]
'%'	No argument is converted, results in a '%' character in the result.

[1]The alternate form causes a leading zero ('0') to be inserted between left-hand padding and the formatting of the number if the leading character of the result is not already a zero.

[2]The alternate form causes a leading '0x' or '0X' (depending on whether the 'x' or 'X' format was used) to be inserted between left-hand padding and the formatting of the number if the leading character of the result is not already a zero.

[3]The alternate form causes the result to always contain a decimal point, even if no digits follow it.The precision determines the number of digits after the decimal point and defaults to 6.

[4]The alternate form causes the result to always contain a decimal point, and trailing zeroes are not removed as they would otherwise be. The precision determines the number of significant digits before and after the decimal point and defaults to 6.

[5]The precision determines the maximal number of characters used.

[6]If the object or format provided is a unicode string, the resulting string will also be unicode.

[a] For more details see https:
//docs.python.org/2/library/stdtypes.html#string-formatting-operations

Table 15.5. String Operations[a] **(1 of 2)**

Method for any **x**	Description
x.capitalize()	**"hello".capitalize()**→ **'Hello'**
x.center(n)	Centers **x** in a string of length **n**.
	"hello".center(15)→'␣␣␣␣␣hello␣␣␣␣␣'
x.count(sub)	Counts number of times **sub** occurs in **x**
	'mississippi'.count('is')→ 2
x.endswith(sub)	Returns **True** if **x** ends with **sub**.
	"Porcupine".endswith('ine')→**True**;
	"Porcupine".endswith('txt')→**False**
x.expandtabs(n)	Replaces tabs in **x** with **n** spaces.
x.find(sub)	Returns the location of **sub** in the string **x**
	"porcupine".find('cup') → 3
	"porcupine".find('fred')→ −1
x.isalnum()	**True** if all characters are alphanumeric.
	"AbcD176".isalnum() → **True**
	"Abc--176".isalnum() → **False**
x.isalpha()	**True** if all characters are alphabetic.
	"AbcD".isalpha() → **True**
	"Abc176".isalpha() → **False**
x.isdigit()	**True** if all characters are digits 0-9.
	"01997".isdigit() → **True**
	"Abc176".isdigit() → **False**
x.islower()	**True** if all alphabetic characters are in lower case **a** to **z**.
	"abc".islower() → **True**
	"aBc".islower() → **False**
	"abc-23".islower() → **True**
x.isspace()	**True** if all characters are white space (e.g., blanks, tabs, line feeds, etc.)
x.istitle()	**True** if 1st letter each word is upper case.
	"Hello World".istitle() → **True**
	"hello world".istitle() → **False**
sep.join([x,..])	Joins the strings with separator **sep**
	'-'.join(['good','morning','to','you'])
	→ **'good-morning-to-you'**
x.lstrip()	Removes leading white space.
	"␣␣␣␣fred␣␣".lstrip() → **"fred␣␣"**

[a]For more detail see https://docs.python.org/2/library/index.html.

Table 15.5. String Operations[a] **(2 of 2)**

Method for any **x**	Example
x.partition(sep)	Partitions a string into a sequence of strings at the *first* occurrence of **sep**. `"sassafras".partition("a")` → `('s', 'a', 'ssafras')`
x.replace(from, to)	Returns new string with substring replaced. `"sassafras".replace("as", "og")` → `'sogsafrog'`
x.rfind(sub)	Finds **sub** in **x**, *starting from the right*. `"sogsafrog".rfind("o")` → 7
x.rjust(n)	Right justify **x** with length **n** `"frog".rjust(8)` → `"␣␣␣␣frog"`
x.rpartition(sep)	Like **partition** but starts *from the right*. `"sassafras".rpartition("a")` → `('sassafr', 'a', 'as')`

x.rsplit(sep)	Like **split** but starts *from the right*.
	`"sassafras".rsplit("a")` →
	`['s', 'ss', 'fr', 's']`
	`"sassafras".rsplit("a",2)` →
	`['sass', 'fr', 's']`

x.rstrip()	Removes trailing white spaces. `"␣frog␣␣"` → `"␣frog"`
x.split(sep)	Splits a string on a separator. `"sassafras".split("a")` → `['s', 'ss', 'fr', 's']` `"sassafras".split("a",1)` → `['s', 'ssafras']`.
x.startswith(sub)	**True** if **x** starts with **sub**. `"sassafras".startswith("sas")` → **True**
x.strip()	Removes leading and trailing white space. `"␣␣frog␣␣".strip()` → `"frog"`
x.swapcase()	Swaps upper and lower case. `"HelloWorld".swapcase()` → `'hELLOwORLD'`
x.title()	Puts first letter of each word upper case. `"good day".title()` → `"Good Day"`
x.upper()	Converts to upper case. `"Good Day".upper()` → `"GOOD DAY"`

[a]For more detail see https://docs.python.org/2/library/index.html.

Exercises

1. Let   x="Monty Python's Flying Circus".

    (a) Convert **x** to all lower case.
    (b) Convert **x** to a list of words.
    (c) Count the number of times the letter "**y**" appears in **x**.
    (d) Convert **x** to a list of individual characters.
    (e) Convert **x** to a list of unique characters.
    (f) Replace the single quote with a double quote.
    (g) Replace every letter "**y**" with the sequence "**aieee**"

2. Let   z="You will get me",   w="A shrubbery", u="Plant Here".   Write python code to print each of the following strings only by manipulating the values of **u**, **w** and **z**.

    (a) "You will get me a shrubbery."
    (b) "you will get me a shrubbery."
    (c) "A shrubbery you will get me."
    (d) "Plant here a shrubbery."
    (e) "You will plant here a shrubbery."

    (f) "Shrubbery a me get will you?"
    (g) "Here! Plant a shrubbery."

3. Using **u**, **w**, **z** as defined in the previous problem.

    (a) What is **p=u+v+w**
    (b) Capitalize ever word in **p**. Call the result **P**
    (c) Join all the words in **P** into a single string **q** separated by dashes.
    (d) Replace the dashes in **q** with strings of length zero.
    (e) Separate **q** into a list of words without vowels.
    (f) Convert every word in **p** to lower case.
    (g) Alphabetize the results of the previous step.
    (h) Join the results of the previous step into a single sentence (first letter upper case, space between each word, period at end).

4. Write a program that takes a possibly incorrectly formatted paragraph and returns a string with all the words returned in lower case, except for the first word of each sentence.

Chapter 16

Sets

Sets are basically collections of items that (1) have no particular order and (2) no duplicate entries. There are two types: **set**, which is mutable (can be changed) and **frozenset**, which is immutable. Sets are created either using curly brackets, or by applying the function **set** to an existing list. Sets support standard mathematical set operations like union, intersection, and set difference. For example, to create a set

```
>>> s = {5, 6, 7, 12, 4, 7, 6, 3}
```

When you display a set, though, it explicitly uses the **set** notation. It also removes any duplicate items and sorts it for you.

```
>>> s
set([3, 4, 5, 6, 7, 12])
```

Table 16.1. Set Operations on mutable sets

The following may only be applied to mutable **set**'s (not to **frozenset**'s).

Method	Description
`S.update(T,...)` or `S|= T|...`	Union the elements in **T** to **S**.
`S.intersection_update(T)` or `S&=T`	Update by intersections.
`S.difference_update(T)` or `S-=T`	Update by set difference.
`S.symmetric_difference_update(T)` or `S^T`	Update by symmetric difference.
`S.add(x)`	Add **x** to **S**.
`S.remove(x)` or `S.discard(x)`	Remove **x** from **S**.
`S.clear()`	Remove everything from **S**.
`S.pop()`	Remove/return an item from **S**.

The curly bracket notation may not be used to create a new empty set because {} represents an empty dictionary (chapter 24). Empty sets may be created either by **set()** or **set([])**. The first creates an empty set directly; the second creates an empty set by conversion from an empty list. There is no distinction between the two:

```
>>> set()==set([])
True
```

Set operations are summarized in tables 16.1 and 16.2.

Table 16.2. Set Operations

The following apply to both mutable **set**'s and immutable **frozenset**'s

Method or function	Return Value
len(S)	Cardinality of **S**.
x in S	**True** if $x \in S$
x not in S	**True** if $x \notin S$
S.isdisjoint(T)	**True** if $S \cap T = \varnothing$
S.copy()	A copy of **S**.
S.issubset(T)	**True** if $S \subseteq T$
S <= T	**True** if $S \subseteq T$
S <T	**True** if $S \subset T$
S.issuperset(T)	**True** if $S \supseteq T$
S >= T	**True** if $S \supseteq T$
S > T	**True** if $S \supset T$
S.union(T)	$S \cup T$
S | T | ...	$S \cup T \cup \cdots$
S.intersection(T)	$S \cap T$
S & T & ...	$S \cap T \cap \cdots$
S.difference(T)	$S \setminus T$
S - T - ...	$S \setminus T \setminus \cdots$
S.symmetric_difference(T)	$(S \setminus T) \cup (T \setminus S)$
S^T	$(S \setminus T) \cup (T \setminus S)$

Exercises

1. Let $x = \{1, 3, 5, 9\}$ and $y = \{1, 2, 3, 4\}$. Use python to find:
   (a) $x \cap y$ (b) $x \cup y$ (c) $x - y$

2. A **panagram** is an expression that contains every letter of the alphabet. Use python to determine which letters are missing from each of the following expressions. You should be able to do each one in a single line using set expressions. Are any of them panagrams?

   (a) 'The quick brown fox jumps over the lazy dog'

   (b) 'Monty Python's flying circus'

   (c) 'Being bounced around quickly annoyed the disheveled taxi drivers.'

   (d) 'A short brimless felt hat barely blocks out the sound of a Celtic violin.'

   (e) 'Do wafting zephyrs quickly vex Jumbo?'

   (f) 'A very bad quack might jinx zippy fowls.'

   (g) 'Watch Jeopardy!, Alex Trebeks fun TV quiz game.'

   (h) 'Then a cop quizzed Mick Jaggers ex-wives briefly.'

Chapter 17

For Loops

A **for** loop repeats a statement (or collection of statements) for every element of an iterable sequence. Any iterable object, such as a **list**, **xrange**, **dict**, **file**, or **str** can be used to enumerate the loop. If you can use the **in** operator on it, chances are you can iterate over it. The suite or collection of statements is executed once for each element in the iterable. When the contents of the iterable have been exhausted control is transferred to the suite of the **else** clause, if present. If an **break** statement is encountered, control exits the loop without executing the contents of the **else**

Figure 17.1: Flow of a generic **for** loop.

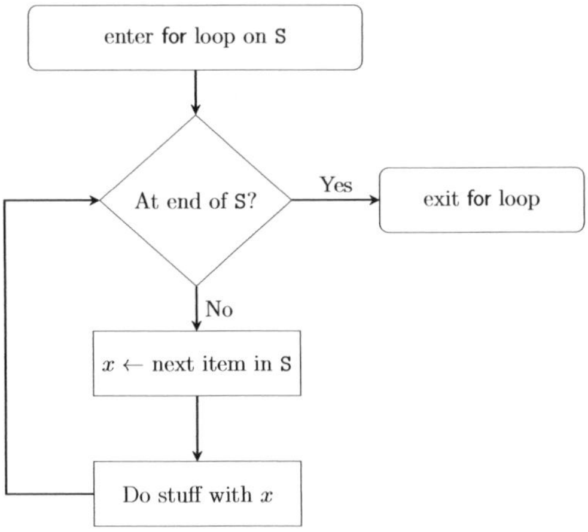

For example, you can explicitly list out every member of the iterable sequence if you want to:

```
>>> for i in 5,10,15,23:
...     print i,
...
5 10 15 23
```

Alternatively, you can assign the sequence to a variable first, and then print it.

```
>>> x=[1,2,3,4]
>>> for p in x:
...     print 5*(p+17),
...
90 95 100 105
```

The range function

The **range** function can be used to generate sequences of integers:
`range(n)` $\rightarrow$ `[0, 1, 2,..., n-1]`.
`range(p,q)` $\rightarrow$ `[p,p+1,p+2,...,q-1]`.
`range(p,q,r)` $\rightarrow$ `[p, p+r, p+2*r,..., q-1]`.

Example 17.1. Use the **range** function to generate a list of integers starting with 23, in increments of 5, that extends to at least 56.

```
>>> range(23,57,5)
[23, 28, 33, 38, 43, 48, 53]
```

Example 17.2. Print a list of the endpoints $x_0, x_1, \ldots, x_{n+1}$ of ten equally sized subintervals of an interval $[a, b]$ using a for loop.

Since there are n intervals, the width of each interval is $h = (b - a)/n$. The first interval starts at $x_0 = a$, the second at $x_1 = a + h$, the third at $x_2 = a + 2h$, and so forth, all the way to $x_{n+1} = a + nh = b$. We can generate a list of the integers $0, 1, 2, \ldots, n$ with **range(n)**, and print the endpoints (including the last one) with

```
# insert code with assignments to a, b>a, and n
h=float(b-a)/float(n)   # width of the interval
for j in range(n+1):
    print a+j*h,         # jth endpoint
```

Example 17.3. Dot products. If **v** and **w** are vectors of length n then the dot product (see, for example, eq. B.6) is the scalar x where

$$x = \sum_{i=0}^{n-1} v_i w_i \tag{17.1}$$

To calculate this, we could iterate through a list integers of $0, 1, \ldots, n-1$, calculating the product $v_i w_i$ at each index, and then accumulating the sum as we go. An algorithm for the dot product is given in algorithm 17.1.

This is how we might implement algorithm 17.1 with a Python **for** loop.

```
1  n=min(len(v), len(w))
2  product=0
3  for i in range(n):
4      product += v[i]*w[i]
```

Algorithm 17.1 The Dot Product.

---

input: v, w

  1: $n \leftarrow \min(\text{length}(v), \text{length}(w))$

  2: $s \leftarrow 0$

  3: **for all** $i=0,1,\ldots, n-1$ **do**

  4:     $s \leftarrow s + v_i w_i$

  5: **end for**

  6: **return** s

The first line ensures that we don't go out of bounds on our index counting if either vector is longer than the other.[1] The Python **min** function on line 1 returns the minimum value of its arguments. The Python **len** function returns the length of a list, so that we don't have to know in advance the dimension of a list. Of course, if the lengths of the two vectors are different, we have an input error. On line 2 we initialize the dot product to zero. That way we can refer to the variable **product** in the **for** loop. The sum is computed on lines 3 and 4.

There is a slightly more elegant way to do the dot product. The function **zip** takes two lists and pairs them up element by element. If one of the lists is longer than the other, it stops at the end of the shorter list.

```
>>> zip([1,2,3],[5,6,7])
[(1, 5), (2, 6), (3, 7)]
```

We can use the **zip** to produce our iterator:

```
>>> s=0
>>> v=[1,2,3]; w=[5,6,7]
>>> for x,y in zip(v,w):
...     s+=x*y
...
>>> s
38
```

Example 17.4. Print a multiplication table of the integers 1 through 9.

We can do this with a pair of nested **for** loops. To make the columns line up, we also use string conversion (page 110).

```
1   for j in range(1, 10):
2       for k in range(1, 10):
3           print "%2d" % (j*k),
4       print
```

The comma at the end of line 3 suppresses the line feed, so that every number is printed on the same line. At the end of a line of **k**'s, we want to go to new line, because it is time to increment **j**, and so we do this with the **print** on line 4. Here is the output:

---

[1]Typically we would also add a print statement to tell the user if the lengths are not equal.

Figure 17.2: Flow of a **for** loop with **Continue**.

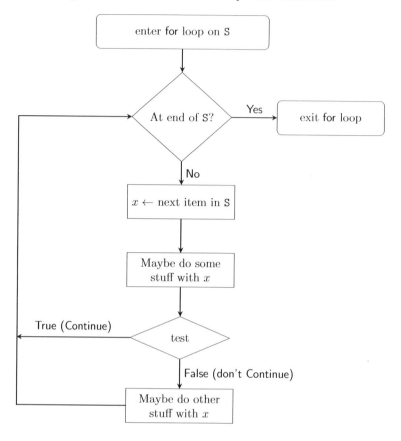

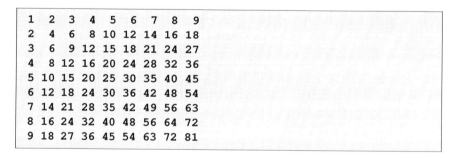

Example 17.5. Matrix of Zeros. Use nested **for** loops to initialize an $n \times m$ matrix, represented as a list, to contain all zeros.

When we represent matrices by lists, we really are using lists of lists. Each element of the list represents a row of the list. Since Python indices start at zero, the ith row is in **A[i-1]**. Thus **A[0]** is the first row, **A[1]** is the second row, and so forth. Similarly, A_{ij} is in **A[i-1][j-1]**. So to get to the fourth element of the 7th row we refer to **A[6][3]**.

Figure 17.3:   Flow of a **for** loop with **Break**.

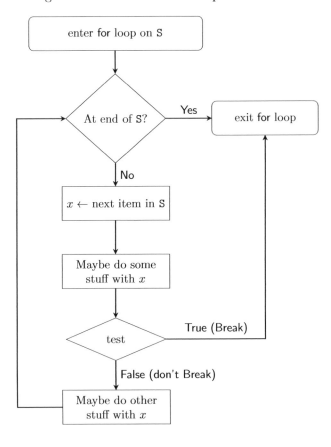

Suppose $n = 5$ and $m = 3$ (5 rows and 3 columns). Then one way to get a matrix of all zeros is to build the matrix one row at a time, and to build each row one element at a time. We add elements using the **list append** method. We grow a row until it has three zeros in it. Then we grow the matrix one row at a time, adding rows until we have enough of them.

```
>>> c=[]
>>> for i in range(5):
...     row=[]
...     for j in range(3):
...         row.append(0)
...     c.append(row)
...
>>> c
[[0, 0, 0], [0, 0, 0], [0, 0, 0], [0, 0, 0], [0, 0, 0]]
```

Normally one would not initialize a matrix with all zeros in this manner, because of functions like **numpy.zeros** and **numpy.zeros_like**. The first function, **numpy.zeros(n)**, returns a one-dimensional ndarray of length **n**. The second one, **numpy.zeros(n,m)** returns a two dimensional $n \times m$ ndarray. Similarly, the function **numpy.zeros_like(A)** returns a matrix of all zeros that is the same size as **A**.

Example 17.6. Matrix multiplication. Let **A** be an $n \times p$ matrix and **B** a $p \times m$ matrix. Then the matrix product **C** is defined as the $m \times n$ matrix with ij element given by (see definition B.9)

$$c_{ij} = \sum_{k=0}^{p-1} a_{ik} b_{kj} \qquad (17.2)$$

A brute force approach is shown in algorithm 17.2. The triple-nested for loop is illustrated by the flow chart in figure 17.4.

Algorithm 17.2 Matrix Multiplication.

---

input: a $(n \times p)$ and b $(p \times n)$ matrices

1: **for all** $i=0,1,\ldots,n-1$ **do**
2:     **for all** $j=0,1,\ldots,m-1$ **do**
3:         $c_{ij} \leftarrow 0$
4:         **for all** $k=0,1,\ldots,p-1$ **do**
5:             $c_{ij} \leftarrow c_{ij} + a_{ik} b_{kj}$
6:         **end for**
7:     **end for**
8: **end for**
9: **return** c

Lets assume that **C** has already been initialized to a matrix of all zeros. Then we can implement this directly in Python as follows:

```
for i in range(n):
    for j in range(m):
        for k in range(p):
            C[i][j]+=A[i][k]*B[k][j]
```

Both the matrix initialization and matrix multiplication can be implemented more elegantly with list comprehension. (However, this is normally not necessary as Numpy contains an extensive library for matrix manipulation, including matrix multiplication.)

Figure 17.4: Triply nested for loop for brute force matrix multiplication shown in algorithm 17.2. The middle and innermost loops are enclosed in the dashed and dotted boxes, respectively.

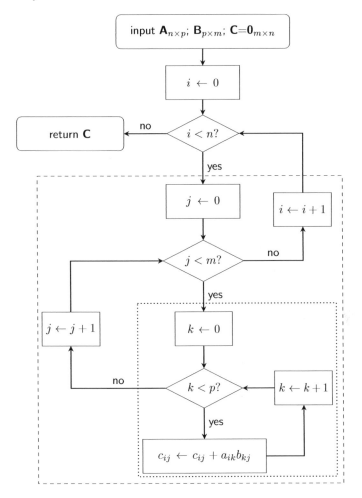

Exercises

1. Suppose you want to divide up the interval (a, b) into $n+1$ sub-intervals of equal length. Using a **for** loop, write a program to determine the end points of each interval. Verify that your program works on the following: $(a, b) = (0, 10)$; $n = 10$; $(a, b) = (3, 17)$; $n = 19$; $(a, b) = (-4.72, 6.98)$; $n = 12$.

2. The standard formula used to compute the wind-chill temperature **WC** is

$$\textbf{WC} = a + bT + (c + dT)W^n$$

in degrees F and where $a = 35.74$, $b = 0.6215$, $c = -35.75$, $d = 0.4275$, and $n = 0.16$ are fixed constants; T is the Fahrenheit temperature; and W is the wind speed in miles per hour. Write a python program to generate a neatly aligned table of wind-chill temperatures rounded to the nearest degree, for $-45 \leq T \leq 40$ and $5 \leq W \leq 60$, at 5 degree and 5 MPH increments.

3. Write a program to find the k unique k^{th} roots of a complex number $z = a + bi$. They can be determined as follows.

   (a) Write $z = a + bi$ in its polar form, as $z = re^{i\theta}$ (see chapter 18 exercise 11), where r is a non-negative real number and θ is between zero and 2π.

   (b) Observe that $z = re^{i(\theta + 2p\pi)}$ for all integers p. Thus $z^{1/k} =$

$r^{1/k}e^{i(\theta + 2p\pi)/k}$, also for all integers p.

   (c) Use Euler's formula, $e^{iz} = \cos z + i \sin z$ to write the roots as

$$z^{1/k} = r^{1/k}\left[\sin \frac{\theta + 2p\pi}{k} + \cos \frac{\theta + 2p\pi}{k}\right]$$

   This will give unique roots for $p = 0, 1, 2, \ldots, k - 1$.

4. Write your own implementation of a **factorial** function using a **for** loop.

5. Write your own implementation of **combinations(n,k)** which should calculate

$$\binom{n}{k} = \frac{n!}{n!(n - k)!}$$

without using any factorials. Use a **for** loop. Assume $n \geq k \geq 0$ are integers.

6. Using a **for** loop, implement a program that calculates $(1 + x)^n$ where x is any real number and n is any positive integer.

7. Using a **for** loop and the binomal theorem, write a program that calculates the coefficients of the expansion $(x + y)^n$ where x and y are unknown and n is any positive integer.

8. Write a program to print out Pascal's triangle.

Chapter 18

Python Functions

A **function** encapsulates a sequence of statements so that it can be invoked by a single line of code with clearly defined input and output. There are many built in functions in Python, such as `len(u)` (which returns the length of the list **u**). We say that we are **calling** or **invoking** the function when we use it in our program, e.g., with a statement like `y=sin(theta)`.

A Python function is very much analogous to a mathematical function: it maps values from an input domain to an output domain (figure 18.1), but with its implementation (the way the function is coded) hidden. The calling program should know nothing about the code inside the function. The input values are specified as **arguments** when we call the function, and the output values are called **return values**. Within the function

Figure 18.1: A function as a machine with its insides hidden. All that the calling program sees is its interfaces: the input arguments and the returned values.

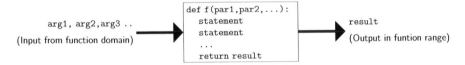

(inside its code) the arguments are referred to as **parameters**. Each argument in a call is mapped to a function parameter. The function performs a calculation, and then may (or in some cases may not) return a result. If we define a function but do not specify a return value in the function, then the return value defaults to the special Python symbol **None**.

To use our own functions in a program requires two steps: (1) defining the function; (2) invoking (or calling) the function.

In a **function definition** we tell the computer how to convert the input parameters into the desired results by performing a sequence of calculations. This is analogous to defining a mathematical function, e.g., by saying "Let $f : \mathbb{R} \mapsto \mathbb{R}$ be defined by $f(x) = 3x^2 - 4x + 7$." In Python, the corresponding function definition is

```
1  def f(x):                    # function definition
2      return 3*x**2-4*x+7
```

In a **function invocation** we actually use the function. In math this is expressed by something like "let $y = f(x + 7) + f(f(x))$ where $x = 3$." Here we are referring to a previously defined function $f(x)$. We do the same thing with our function in Python. The corresponding function call is

```
3   x=3
4   y=f(x+7)+f(f(x))                    # function call
```

The two function calls on line 4 refer to the function defined on lines 1 and 2.

A function definition is not limited to a single line of code; you can have as many lines of code as you like, and may call other previously defined functions, or may even call itself. The general rule of thumb for good programming style, however, is that your function should fit on one printed page (or on a single screen without scrolling, depending on who you ask). Otherwise, the function is too long, and should be broken down into smaller functions.

A function definition looks something like this:

```
def MyFunctionsName(sequence_of_parameters):
    ...
    statement
    statement
    ...
    return          # usually (not always) ends with return
```

The sequence of parameters is a comma-separated sequence that defines the names of the variables that are supplied to the function, as they are known to the code inside the function. There are four general types of parameters; beginners usually only come into contact with the first two. These are **named positional parameters** (referenced by position), **keyword** expressions (referenced by keyword), ***expression**'s (variable number of parameters), and ****expression**'s (unspecified keyword sequences).

When the function is called, the assignment of function **arguments** (in the call) to function **parameters** (in the definition) is made as follows.

a) **Positional parameters** must be invoked in the same order as in the function definition. A function definition with only positional parameters looks like this:

```
def f(x,y,z):   # function defintion
    ...          # contents omitted
    return
```

If **A**, **B** and **C** are any identifiers in the calling program, then the corresponding function invocation is

```
f(A,B,C)        # function invocation
```

In the invocation, arguments **A**, **B** and **C** in the calling code are mapped to parameters **x**, **y** and **z** in the function definition, respectively: $x \leftarrow A$, $y \leftarrow B$, $z \leftarrow C$. based on the position in the definition. The arguments in the function invocation are applied in the order as the function definition.

b) **Keyword parameters** are specified by name and are given default values. For example, we could define the same function as

```
def f(x=10, y=20, z=30):   # function defintion
    ...                    # contents omitted
    return
```

The function call specifies each parameter by name, and in any order:

```
A=0
f(x=5, z=7, y=A)   # x<--5,  y<--0,  z<--7
```

In this case, the values are applied as specified in the invocation. If we do not specify a value, the default, as given in the definition, takes over:

```
A=17
f(y=A)   # x<--10,  y<--17,  z<--30
```

If positional parameters are combined with keyword parameters in the same function definition, then the positional parameters must come first:

```
def f(x, y=20, z=30):   # function defintion
    ...                 # contents omitted
    return
```

In this case, a value must always be given for the variable **x**, and it must be specified in the first position. The values for **y** and **z** are optional.

```
f(1)          # x<--1, y<--10, z<--20
f(1,z=5)      # x<--1, y<--10, z<--5
f(1,z=5,y=3)  # x<--1, y<--3,  z<--5
```

c) ***parameter**: **Variable number of parameters** - all additional positional parameters are treated as a tuple.

```
>>> def myfunc(A, B=10, *C):
...      print "A=",A, "B=",B, "C=",C
>>> myfunc(5, 10, 15, 20, 25)
A= 5 B= 10 C= (15, 20, 25)
```

Thus if a function is called with too many parameters, the extras are assigned to the parameter with the *****. This parameter must follow any unstarred parameters.

d) ****parameters**: **Additional named parameters** - if the function is called with additional named parameters not listed in the **def** statement, these are specified with the double-star syntax. These parameters are put into a dictionary (chapter 24) that can be accessed by the function.

```
>>> def myfunc(A, B=10, *C, **D):
... print "A=",A, "B=",B, "C=",C, "D=",D
>>> myfunc(5, 10, 15, 20, 25,x=99,y=66)
A= 5 B= 10 C= (15, 20, 25) D= {'y': 66, 'x': 99}
```

Example 18.1. Babylonian Square Root. Recall the Babylonian square root algorithm (algorithm 3.1) to find $\sqrt{a}$. The update formula is 3.9:

$$x_{n+1} = \frac{1}{2}\left(x_n + \frac{a}{x_n}\right) \tag{18.1}$$

We can define a function **next_iteration(x, a)** to implement equation 18.1,

```
def next_iteration(x, a):
    return 0.5 * (x + a/x)
```

The parameters of **next_iteration** are **x** and **a**. The **return value** of **next_iteration** is the expression **0.5 * (x + a/x)**. To use the function in the Babylonian algorithm we would enclose it in a **while** loop. At each step we invoke **next_iteration** with arguments **xold** and **a** where **x** is the return value of the previous iteration. We stop when we reach a desired tolerance, in this case 10^{-10}.

```
1  a = 4.0
2  xold = a
3  error = float("inf")
4  while error > 10**-10:
5      x=next_iteration(xold, a)
6      error = abs(x-xold)
7      xold = x
8      print x, error
```

When we print the values of **x** and **error** at each step of the iteration (line 8), we get the following output.

```
2.5 1.5
2.05 0.45
2.0006097561 0.0493902439024
2.00000009292 0.000609663175266
2.0 9.29222925272e-08
2.0 2.22044604925e-15
```

We can now put this all together in a single function, e.g. by writing a function **find_root(a,err)**. When we call **find_root(a,err)**, it will use the our code to print the iterations of the Babylonian algorithm to find $\sqrt{a}$ with a tolerance **err**.

```
def find_root(a, err):
    xold = a
    error = float("inf")
    while error > err:
        x=next_iteration(xold, a)
        error = abs(x-xold)
        xold = x
        print x, error
    return x
```

When we run this to find $\sqrt{9}$, it takes 7 iterations to converge.

```
>>> a=9.0
>>> s=find_root(a,10**-10)
5.0 4.0
3.4 1.6
3.02352941176 0.376470588235
3.00009155413 0.0234378576333
3.0000000014 9.15527343963e-05
```

```
3.0 1.39698386192e-09
3.0 0.0
>>> print "the_square_root_of",a,"is",s
the square root of 9.0 is 3.0
```

Now that we are confident that our program works, it is time to remove the **print** statement. But we might want to leave it in for later. One way to do this to include a debug flag as a parameter, with a default value set to **False**. Default values are set in the **def** statement with an equal sign.

```
def find_root(a, err=10**-10, debug=False):
    xold = a
    error = float("inf")
    while error > err:
        x=next_iteration(xold, a)
        error = abs(x-xold)
        xold = x
        if debug: print x, error
    return x
```

Here both **err** and **debug** are optional arguments. With a function call, such as **find_root(17)**, Python sets **err** $\leftarrow 10^{-10}$ and **debug**$\leftarrow$**False** immediately upon entering the function.

```
>>> find_root(17.0)
4.123105625617661
```

Example 18.2. Print a table of the square roots of the integers from 1 to 25 to five digits using the Babylonian algorithm function.
We can do this with a simple **for** loop using format strings (see chapter 15).

```
>>> for i in range(1,26):
...     print "%2d_%7.5f" % (i, find_root(float(i)))
1 1.00000
2 1.41421
3 1.73205
...             # lines omitted
23 4.79583
24 4.89898
25 5.00000
```

Packages

Suppose we have a function we've written before and would like to use it again. We could copy it from our old program file into our new file. But then we would end up with lots of copies of the same function, and if we later find a way to improve the function, we have to fix it in lots of different places. Packages give us a way to put the function in only one location, but in such a way that every program (that we want to do this with) can call it directly.

To create a package with **find_root** and **next_iteration**, type the following into in a text editor, and then save it as a file, e.g., as **babyl.py**.

```
# Babylonian Root Finding Package
#    created by Ima Somma Hacka 23 Feb 2007
#    revised by Heeza Betah Codah 15 Mar 2007
#
def next_iteration(x, a):
    xnew = 0.5 * (x + a/x)
    return xnew

def find_root(a, err=10**-10, debug=False):
    xold = a
    error = float("inf")
    while error > err:
        x=next_iteration(xold, a)
        error = abs(x-xold)
        xold = x
        if debug: print x, error
    return x
```

Then the next time you want to use the function **find_root**, **import** it from **babyl.py** in any of the same ways discussed on page 82. There are several different ways to do this, and the format of invocation of your function varies. First, you can import only the specific function needed:

```
>>> from babyl import find_root
>>> find_root(24)
4.898979485566356
```

This allows you to use **find_root**, but hides everything else in **babyl.py**:

```
>>> next_iteration(5.0, 3.0)
Traceback (most recent call last):
  File "<stdin>", line 1, in <module>
NameError: name 'next_iteration' is not defined
```

Second, you can import everything in the package using the "wild card" *.

```
1  >>> from babyl import *
2  >>> next_iteration(5.0, 3.0)
3  2.8
```

```
4  >>> find_root(99.5)
5  9.974968671630002
```

Next, you can just import the package itself, not referring to the specific function. This also lets you access everything, but you must qualify it by the package name. If you don't specify the name of the package, Python won't be able to find your function:

```
>>> import babyl
>>> babyl.find_root(36.0)
6.0
>>> find_root(36.0)
Traceback (most recent call last):
  File "<stdin>", line 1, in <module>
NameError: name 'find_root' is not defined
>>>
```

Finally, you can import the package, but give it a new name using the **import as** command.

```
>>> import babyl as bigB
>>> bigB.find_root(76.76)
8.761278445523804
>>>
```

The new name **bigB** replaces the actual package name **babyl**. Your program will only know about **bigB**, and not about **babyl**.

Exercises

1. Write a function **normal(x, mu, sigma)** that returns the value of the normal probability density function,

$$y = \frac{1}{\sigma\sqrt{2\pi}} \exp\left[-\frac{1}{2}\left(\frac{x-\mu}{\sigma}\right)^2\right]$$

2. Modify the function in exercise 1 so that the default value of the mean is zero and the standard deviation is zero.

3. Write a function **my_linspace[a,b,n]** that implements either chapter 12 exercise 1or chapter 17 exercise 1.

4. Write a function to print out values of the normal probability function (exercise 1) at n equally spaced points on an interval (a, b). Verify that it works for each of the following cases:
   (a) $(\mu, \sigma) = (0, 1)$; $(a, b) = (-3, 3)$; $n = 10$
   (b) $(\mu, \sigma) = (3, 1)$; $(a, b) = (3, 6)$; $n = 25$
   (b) $(\mu, \sigma) = (3, .5)$; $(a, b) = (0, 6)$; $n = 20$

5. Write a function that implements the Babylonian square root algorithm to find $\sqrt{a}$.

Terminate the iteration when you reach machine accuracy or an optional tolerance.

6. Suppose you know the values of a function $f(x)$ only at some discrete values $x_0, x_1, \ldots, x_n$. The values of $f(x_i)$ are stored in an array **y** and the corresponding x values are stored in an array **x**. If the data points are sufficiently close together, it is possible to approximate the derivative y' at each point with either the forward difference formula,

$$y'_i \approx \frac{y_{i+1} - y_i}{x_{i+1} - x_i}$$

or the backward difference formula,

$$y'_{i+1} \approx \frac{y_{i+1} - y_i}{x_{i+1} - x_i}$$

Write a function **diff(x,y)** that takes as input the two arrays and returns a third array with the values of $y'_0, y'_1, \ldots, y'_n$.

7. Suppose you know the values of a function $f(x)$ only at some discrete values

$x_0, x_1, \ldots, x_n$. The values of $f(x_i)$ are stored in an array **y** and the corresponding x values are stored in an array **x**. If the data points are sufficiently close together, it is possible to approximate the second derivative y' at each point $x_1, x_2, \ldots, x_{n-1}$ with the following centered difference formula:

$$y'' \approx \frac{y_{i+1} - 2y_i + y_{i-1}}{(x_{i+1} - x_i)(x_i - x_{i-1})}$$

Write a function **diff2(x,y)** that takes as input the two arrays and returns a third array with the values of $y'_0, y'_1, \ldots, y'_n$.

8. Explore numerical integration. The package **scipy.integrate** proves a number of functions that allow you find the definite integral of a mathematical function that you have defined in Python. Look up the package pm the SciPy.org web site and use **quad** find the following definite integrals.

   (a) $\int_{-1}^{1} \frac{x^2}{1 + x^2}$

   (b) $\int_{2}^{3} f(x)\,dx$ where $f(x) = x^2 e^{-x}$

   (c) $\int_{1}^{2} \frac{e^x}{x}\,dx$

9. Read exercise 8. Then use **dblquad**, **tplquad**, or **nquad** to find the following integrals.

   (a) $\int_{-\pi}^{\pi} \int_{-\pi}^{\pi} f(x)g(y)\,dy\,dx$, where $f(x) = x$ and $g(y) = y$

   (b) $\int_{-\pi}^{\pi} \int_{-\pi}^{\pi} f(x)g(y)\,dy\,dx$, where $f(x) = e^x$ and $g(y) = e^{-y^2/\pi}$

   (c) $\int_{0}^{1} \int_{0}^{1} \int_{0}^{1} xy^2 z^3 \, dx\,dy\,dz$

   (d) $\int_{0}^{1} \int_{0}^{1} \int_{0}^{1} \int_{0}^{\pi} w^2 y^{0.1} z \cos x \\ dx\,dy\,dz\,dw$

10. The **Fourier Cosine Coefficients** $a_0, a_1, \ldots$ and **Fourier Sine Coefficients** $b_0, b_1, \ldots$ for an integrable function $f(x) : (0, P) \mapsto \mathbb{R}$ are given by

$$a_0 = \frac{2}{P} \int_{0}^{P} f(x)\,dx$$

$$a_k = \frac{2}{P} \int_{0}^{P} f(x) \cos\left(\frac{2\pi k x}{P}\right) dx, \; k \geq 1$$

$$b_k = \frac{2}{P} \int_{0}^{P} f(x) \sin\left(\frac{2\pi k x}{P}\right) dx$$

Write functions **FourierA(f, P, k)** and **FourierB(f, P, k)** to find the Fourier cosine and sine coefficients of degree k for a function **f(x)** that is defined on the interval $(0, P)$. Hint: use **scipy.integrate.quad** to do the numerical integration.

11. Any complex number $z = a + bi$, where $a, b \in \mathbb{R}$, can be written in a **polar form**, as $z = re^{i\theta}$, where $r = \sqrt{a^2 + b^2}$ and $\tan\theta = b/a$. The choice of θ (or $\theta + \pi$) is determined by the quadrant of the point (a, b). Write a function **PolarForm(z)** to convert a complex number $z = a + ib$ from standard from to polar form. It should return a tuple **(r, θ)**.

Chapter 19

Sorting

Sorting was one of the first major problems in computer science extensively studied. We now turn to it because it provides some examples of how, by doing something a little more intelligently, you can significantly improve performance. Turning things around the other way, it shows how you can end up writing very slow and inefficient programs if you approach them by brute force. We will cover these techniques to help you understand some concepts of the study of algorithms, not to help you write proFgrams on sorting. You will most likely never need to do that, since highly efficient sort functions are built into most programming languages, including Python.

The twin problem to sorting is **searching**, finding an item in a list or array. There is a similar literature on searching, but we will not cover it here. There is ample support for both searching and sorting lists built into Python, so you are not likely to have to actually implement any of these algorithms.

Insertion Sort

Insertion sort is perhaps the simplest algorithm for sorting. Imagine you are playing cards, and you are dealt a hand of n cards (say 5 in poker or 13 in bridge). Start with the first card. For the sake of simplicity, forget about the different suits; assume we only care about the card number or value. When you pick up the second card, if it is smaller than the one in your hand, put on the left; if it is larger, put it on the right. Then pick up card three. If it is smaller than both cards, put in on the far left. If its value is between the values of the two cards in your hand, put it in the middle; if it is larger than both put it on the right. If it is equal to one of the cards in your hand, put it next to that card. Keep doing this with each successive card, putting the card into its correct "slot."

A similar problem is alphabetizing student papers. I can pick up one paper, then pick up the second one. If it comes later in the alphabet put it after the first paper; if it comes before, put it first. Then, as I pick up each successive unsorted paper, I go through the alphabetized pile, starting from the beginning, until I get to the spot where the new paper belongs, and **insert** it into that location. I continue with this process until I am completely finished with all of the unsorted papers.

How complicated is this, measured in terms of the number of operations? Lets count the operations to see.

For the first paper, I didn't have to do any comparison.

For the second paper, I have to do one comparison.

For the third paper, I have to do between one and two comparisons.

For the fourth paper, I have to do somewhere between one and three comparisons.

For the nth paper, I have to do somewhere between one and $n - 1$ comparisons.

So the total number of comparisons is, worst case,

$$\sum_{k=0}^{n-1} k = \frac{n(n-1)}{2} = O(n^2) \tag{19.1}$$

The worst case would be if the papers were already sorted, so that I have to go through every paper every time. In the best case, the papers are already sorted, but sorted backwards, and I stop after the first comparison, so there are a total of $n-1$ comparisons for the whole sort. In general, if the papers are randomly sorted, I will have to go through about half the papers each time, and the number of comparisons will be

$$\sum_{k=0}^{n-1} \frac{k}{2} = \frac{1}{2} \sum_{k=0}^{n-1} k = \frac{n(n-1)}{4} = O(n^2) \tag{19.2}$$

There are really two operations here: **insert** and **insertionsort**. The **insert** operations involves picking up a single item and putting it in its proper place. It adds a new item to the list, and returns the modified list.

insert(list, item)→longer list with item inserted

The **insertionsort** then involves cycling through all data with **insert**.

Algorithm 19.1 Insert.

---

input: y (sorted list); x item to be inserted.

1: **for** $y_i \in$ **y do**
2:            Entire loop is skipped if **y** is $\varnothing$; in this case a one item list is returned.
3:    **if** $x < y_i$ **then**
4:                        if $x < y_0$ then x will be first item in returned list here
5:        **return** $(y_0, \ldots, y_{i-1}, x, y_i, \ldots, y_n)$ as **insert(y**, $x)$
6:    **end if**
7: **end for**
8: **return** $(y_0, \ldots, y_n, x)$ as **insert(y**, $x)$

Algorithm 19.2 Insertion Sort

---

input: x list to be sorted.

1: **y** $\leftarrow \varnothing$
2: **for** $z \in$ **x do**
3:    **y** $\leftarrow$ **insert(y**, $z)$
4: **end for**
5: **return y** as **InsertionSort(x)**

Insertion sort is $O(n^2)$ for most situations, including the worst case. The difference between the worst case and a typical case is a factor of 2. In the best case situation it is $O(n)$.

To see how the algorithm works, suppose we want to sort the list

$$[477, 788, 26, 16, 305, 699]$$

using insertion sort. We pick up the first number, and place that at the front of our list. The we pick up the second number, 788. It is larger than 477, so we put it to the right of 477. Then we pick up the third number, 26. It is smaller than 477 so we put it at the far left. We continue through our data one item at a time. In the following illustration, the boxes indicate which items have already been sorted.

477	788	26	16	305	699
477	788	26	16	305	699
477	788	26	16	305	699
26	477	788	16	305	699
16	26	477	788	305	699
16	26	305	477	788	699
16	26	305	477	699	788

Selection Sort

Instead of picking the elements one at a time and growing a sorted list out of unsorted items as we did with insertion sort, we can look at our collection as a whole. We can go through the entire set, and pick out the smallest (or first, or alphabetical) item. Then we go through the remaining $n - 1$ items, and pick out the second smallest item, and put it after the first one. Then we pick out the third smallest item, and so forth.

Algorithm 19.3 Selection Sort

input: x list to be sorted.

1: $n \leftarrow \text{length}(\mathbf{x})$
2: **for** $i \leftarrow 1, \dots, n$ **do**
3:   $k \leftarrow i$ Check all unsorted items to see if any $x_j < x_k$
4:   **for** $j \leftarrow i + 1, \dots, n$ **do**
5:     **if** $x_j < x_k$ **then**
6:       $k \leftarrow j$ Found one, so its the new next smallest
7:     **end if**
8:   **end for**
9:   $x_i \leftrightarrow x_k$ Swap x_i and x_k because x_k is the smallest unsorted item.
10: **end for**
11: **return x** as **SelectionSort(x)**

The selection process is illustrated in the following diagram, with the same list we simulated for insertion sort.

477	788	26	[16]	305	699
[16]	788	[26]	477	305	699
16	[26]	788	477	[305]	699
16	26	[305]	[477]	788	699
16	26	305	[477]	788	[699]
16	26	305	477	[699]	788
16	26	305	477	699	[788]

The selection sort has the interesting property that it takes the same number of steps regardless of how the data is sorted. Counting each if and swap as a line of code, the number of operations is

$$\overbrace{1}^{\text{line 1}} + \sum_{i=1}^{n}\left(\overbrace{1}^{\text{line 3}} + \underbrace{\sum_{j=i+1}^{n} \overbrace{(1)}^{\text{line 6}} + \overbrace{1}^{\text{line 9}}}_{\text{for:lines 4-8}} \right)$$

$$\text{for loop lines 2-10}$$

$$= 1 + \sum_{i=1}^{n} 1 + \left(\sum_{i=1}^{n}(n - (i+1) + 1) \right) + \sum_{i=1}^{n} 1 \tag{19.3}$$

$$= 1 + n + \left(\sum_{i=1}^{n}(n - i) \right) + n \tag{19.4}$$

$$= 1 + 2n + n^2 - \sum_{i=1}^{n} i \tag{19.5}$$

$$= 1 + 2n + n^2 - \frac{n(n+1)}{2} = \frac{n^2}{2} + \frac{3n}{2} + 1 = O(n^2) \tag{19.6}$$

On the average, the insertion sort will run about twice as fast than the selection sort, even though, they are both $O(n^2)$.

Bubble Sort

In a bubble sort, you go through the entire list start to finish comparing two items at a time. If any pair are out of order, you swap them, "bubbling" the elements one step in the correct direction. You keep doing this until you can step through the entire set without making any swaps.

Here is the trace of the bubble sort on the same data set.

Algorithm 19.4 Bubble Sort

input: x list to be sorted.

  1: $n \leftarrow$ **length(x)**
  2: flag $\leftarrow$ True
  3: **while** flag **do**
  4:     flag $\leftarrow$ False
  5:     **for** $i \leftarrow i, \ldots, n-1$ **do**
  6:        **if** $x_{i+1} < x_i$ **then**
  7:           $x_i \leftrightarrow x_{i+1}$
  8:           flag $\leftarrow$ True
  9:        **end if**
10:     **end for**
11: **end while**
12: **return x** as **BubbleSort(x)**

477	**788**	26	16	305	699
477	26	**788**	16	305	699
477	26	16	**788**	305	699
477	26	16	305	**788**	699
477	26	16	305	699	**788**
26	**477**	16	305	699	788
26	16	**477**	305	699	788
26	16	305	**477**	699	788
16	**26**	305	477	699	788

The bubble sort has a complexity of $O(n^2)$ and does not buy us anything over either insertion or selection sort.

Merge Sort

In the **Merge Sort**, our list is repeatedly broken down into two lists of approximately[1] half the length of the original list. In at most $\log_2 n$ steps the list will be broken down into lists of at most length 2. Each of these length 2 lists can be sorted by a simple comparison. The short lists are merged back together in pairs to build the long list up again. Merging two lists of length k can be done in k steps, by walking down the two lists simultaneously and picking out whichever element should come next.

Here is an illsutration of the merge sort:

477, 788, 26, 16, 305, 699, 183, 219, 7					
477, 788, 26, 16		305, 699, 183, 219, 7			
477, 788	26, 16	305, 699	183, 219, 7		
477, 788	16, 26	305, 699	183	219,7	

---

[1]Not exactly because the list may have an odd number of elements in it.

Algorithm 19.5 MergeSort. The algorithm for **Merge** is left as an exercise.

input: x list to be sorted.

1:	$n \leftarrow \mathbf{length}(\mathbf{x})$	
2:	**if** $n = 1$ **then**	
3:	**return x** as **MergeSort(x)**	Length 1 list already sorted
4:	**else if** $n = 2$ **then**	
5:	**if** $x_1 \leq x_2$ **then**	
6:	**return x** as **MergeSort(x)**	The Length 2 list came in sorted
7:	**else**	
8:	**return** $[x_2, x_1]$ as **MergeSort(x)**	The Length 2 list was backwards
9:	**end if**	
10:	**end if**	
11:	$m \leftarrow \lfloor n/2 \rfloor$	Split the list in half
12:	$A \leftarrow \mathbf{MergeSort}([x_1, \ldots, x_m])$	Sort the first half-list
13:	$B \leftarrow \mathbf{MergeSort}([x_{m+1}, \ldots, x_n])$	Sort the second half-list
14:	**return Merge(A,B)** as **MergeSort(x)**	Merge the two lists

---

16, 26, 477, 788	305, 699	183	7, 219

16, 26, 477, 788	305, 699	7, 183, 219

16, 26, 477, 788	7, 183, 219, 305, 699

7, 16, 26, 183, 219, 305, 477, 699, 788

Splitting the list into two parts significantly improves the speed of the sort; the merge sort has a complexity of $O(n \log n)$.

To see why this is true, first consider the merge step. In merging, we go through both lists simultaneously, comparing the first element of each list. Whichever element is smaller goes into the new list. Assuming the two sub-lists have the same length $n/2$, there are at most $n/2$ comparisons in this step.

The previous merge had lists that were half as long as this, of length $n/4$, so they required $n/4$ comparisons, but you have to do twice as many, so there are also $n/2$ steps.

The step before that has lists of length $n/8$, so each merge takes $n/8$ comparisons, but since there are four sets, the total is also $n/2$.

This keeps repeating; each merge requires $n/2$ comparisons. The most number of merges we have to do is the largest number of k such that $2^k \leq n$, because that is the furthest we could have split things. Thus there are $k = \log_2 n$ merges, and since each merge requires $n/2$ comparisons, the merge step requires

$$\text{merge} \sim \frac{n}{2} + 2 \times \frac{n}{4} + 2^2 \times \frac{n}{8} + \cdots + 2^k \frac{n}{2^{k+1}} \tag{19.7}$$

$$\sim k \times \frac{n}{2} \sim \frac{n}{2} \log_2 n \tag{19.8}$$

What about the sorting part? Since the list keeps getting split in half, we can keep doing that until we have either 1 or 2 elements. If there is one element, its already sorted. If there are two elements they can be sorted with at most 1 comparisons. So the number of comparisons in the sorting is at most one when you get to the bottom of the splitting. There can be at most $n/2$ of these. So the total algorithmic complexity is

$$f(n) \sim \frac{n}{2} + \frac{n}{2} \log_2 n \sim O(n \log_2 n) \tag{19.9}$$

This technique of splitting and merging is an example of the **Divide and Conquer** heuristic. The idea behind divide and conquer is to split a problem up into two smaller problems, and solve each one separately. Then the solutions are stitched back together again. This idea is usually much easier to implement recursively (i.e., with functions that can call themselves), and is usually much more difficult to use in a purely iterative environment. The "divide and conquer" heuristic and recursion almost always go together in an implementation. An algorithm like the merge sort, for example, is trivially easy to implement in a purely recursive language like Haskell, while it is extraordinarily difficult in a purely iterative environment like FORTRAN.

Sorting in Python

The main functions for sorting in Python are **sort** and **sorted**.

If **list** is any mutable sequence type (like a list) then **list.sort()** can be used. It has three options and sorts the list **in place**. The three options are **cmp**, **key**, and **reverse**.

```
list.sort([cmp[, key[, reverse]]])
```

Unlike **sort**, the function **sorted(list)** returns a new list and leaves the original unchanged. It has the same parameters as **sort**

Normally **list.sort()** will sort the list in increasing order. If the first option is specified it should be a function of two variables that redefines the comparison function. It will define a function **cmp(x,y)** that tells Python whether $x < y$ (**cmp(x,y)** $\rightarrow -1$); $x = y$ (**cmp(x,y)** $\rightarrow 0$); or $x > y$ (**cmp(x,y)** $\rightarrow 1$). For example, the following code illustrates how to sort a list of numbers in order of their magnitude, regardless of sign:

```
1  >>> y = [57, 91, -50, 79, 63, 94, 44, -67, 44, -12]
2  >>> y.sort(cmp=lambda x,y: cmp(abs(x), abs(y)))
3  >>> y
4  [-12, 44, 44, -50, 57, 63, -67, 79, 91, 94]
```

The argument **key** is used to process one of the arguments before doing the comparison; it is a function. Another way to sort a list of numbers by magnitude uses **key=abs**.

```
5  >>> y = [57, 91, -50, 79, 63, 94, 44, -67, 44, -12]
6  >>> y.sort(key=abs)
7  >>> y
8  [-12, 44, 44, -50, 57, 63, -67, 79, 91, 94]
```

The **key** is useful when sorting multidimensional lists. For example, you may have a list of names in one column, ages in another, and birth month in the third.

```
>>> data=[("tom", 23, 8), ("Dick", 21, 12), ("Harry", 19, 6)]
```

If you want to sort them by month,

```
>>> sorted(data, key=lambda triple:triple[2])
[('Harry', 19, 6), ('tom', 23, 8), ('Dick', 21, 12)]
```

and to sort them by age,

```
>>> sorted(data, key=lambda triple:triple[1])
[('Harry', 19, 6), ('Dick', 21, 12), ('tom', 23, 8)]
```

The **reverse** argument reverses the sorting test.

```
3   >>> y = [57, 91, -50, 79, 63, 94, 44, -67, 44, -12]
4   >>> y.sort(reverse=True)
5   >>> y
6   [94, 91, 79, 63, 57, 44, 44, -12, -50, -67]
```

Additionally, Numpy provides a number of sorting and searching functions for numpy arrays (tables 19.2 and 19.1).

Table 19.1. Sorting in Numpy

Function[a]	Return Value
sort(a)	Sorted copy of an array.
lexsort(keys)	Indirect sort using a sequence of keys.
argsort(a)	Indices that would sort an array.
ndarray.sort()	Sort an array, in-place.
msort(a)	A copy of an array sorted along the first axis.
sort_complex(a)	Sorts a complex array.
partition(a, kth)	Return a partitioned copy of an array.
argpartition(a, kth)	Indirect partition along an axis

[a]For a complete list of parameters and details see http://docs.scipy.
org/doc/numpy/reference/routines.sort.html#sorting

Table 19.2. Searching in Numpy

Function[a]	Return Value
`argmax(a)`	Indices of maximums along an axis.
`nanargmax(a)`	Indices of maximums ignoring NaNs.
`argmin(a)`	Indices of minimums along an axis.
`nanargmin(a)`	Indices of minimums ignoring NaNs.
`argwhere(a)`	Indices of non-zero elements, grouped by element.
`nonzero(a)`	Indices of non-zero elements.
`flatnonzero(a)`	Indices of non-zero elements in the flattened version of **a**.
`where(condition)`	Condition dependent elements.
`searchsorted(a, v)`	Indices where elements should be inserted to maintain order.
`extract(condition, arr)`	Elements of an array that satisfy some condition.

[a] For a complete list of parameters and details see `http://docs.scipy.org/doc/numpy/reference/routines.sort.html#searching`

Exercises

1. Write a function **SelSort(x)** that performs a selection sort on a list of of numbers. Then generate random lists of numbers of lengths 10, 50, 100, 500, 1000, 5000, 10,000, and 50,000. Measure the time it takes to perform a sort, and make a table of sorting time as a function of list length. You can determine your computation time as follows:

```
from time import time
...
tstart = time()
... # do your computation
tend = time()
computation_time = tstart - tend
```

2. Repeat exercise 1, but this time write a function **MergeSort** that implements Merge Sort instead of selection sort.

3. Repeat exercise 1, but this time use the built in Python function **sort**.

4. Download the Consumer Financial Protection Bureau **consumer complaint database** in comma separate value (**csv**) format from data.gov (direct link at https://catalog.data.gov/dataset/consumer-complaint-database).
   Make sure to save the file as comma-separated value. Your browser will probably offer to open it directly for you in Excel, LibreOffice, or OpenOffice, if you have one of the programs installed; this is not recommended as the file has over 300,000 records and is updated daily.

(a) Write a program to read the file into a large list of lists, one list for each row of the data file. Separate the items at commas; some of the cells will be empty, but there will still be commas separating the empty cells. The names of the fields are in the first record. If your computer does not have enough memory to handle the entire file, stop after reading 1000 records. Use **readlines()** to read the file (if you can read the whole file or **readline()** to read one line at a time instead.

(b) Sort the data by Complaint ID. Print out the first 10 records.

(c) Sort the data by Product. Print out the first 10 records.

(d) Find all items in the database for which the **"Product"** is **"Debt Collection"** and which the **"Sub-product"** is **"Medical"**. Count the number of occurrences.

(e) Count the items in the database by State and make a histogram of items per state.

5. Repeat the previous problem, but this time use **pandas**. Read the file as a data frame. Use **DataFrame.from_csv()** to read the file, **DataFrame.sort()** to do the sorting, **DataFrame.query()** to do the searching, etc. The **pandas** package is described at http://pandas.pydata.org/pandas-docs/stable/.

Chapter 20

List Comprehension

List comprehension is the simplest and shortest of loop operations. It is defined in analogy to mathematical set definitions. Suppose that

$$S = \{y = f(x) | x \in Q\} \tag{20.1}$$

We would normally read equation 20.1 as "S is the set of all $y = f(x)$ such that x is taken from the set Q."

In Python, if we have a function **f** and some enumerable object **Q** such as a set, list, or dictionary, then we can define a new list **S** in the same way:

```
S = [f(x) for x in Q]
```

Thus if **Q** is the list **[1, 2, 3, 4, 5]** and **f** is a function that multiplies **x** by 2 and adds 7:

```
def f(x):
    return(2*x+7)
```

Then **[f(x) for x in [1,2,3,4,5]]** → **[9, 11, 13, 15, 17]**.

Example 20.1. Create a list of zeros.

To create a list of n zeros we can use **range** to create a list of integers of length n and then replace each one with zero:

```
v = [0 for j in range(n)]
```

An easier way to create a list of zeros is this:

```
>>> 5*[0]
[0, 0, 0, 0, 0]
```

Example 20.2. Create an $m \times n$ matrix of zeros represented as a list.

```
>>> m=3
>>> n=2
>>> [[0 for i in range(n)] for j in range(m)]
[[0, 0], [0, 0], [0, 0]]
```

Again, this is not the best way to do things in Python; it is better to use Numpy.

Example 20.3. Dot product. If **v** and **w** are vectors of length n then the dot product (see equation B.6 or example 17.3) is the scalar x given by

$$x = \sum_{i=0}^{n-1} v_i w_i \qquad (20.2)$$

For example if $\mathbf{v} = [5, 6, 7]$ and $\mathbf{w} = [1, 2, 3]$ then

$$\mathbf{v} \cdot \mathbf{w} = 5 \cdot 1 + 6 \cdot 2 + 7 \cdot 3 = 38 \qquad (20.3)$$

If we represent the vectors $\mathbf{v}$ and $\mathbf{w}$ by the Python lists $\mathbf{v}$ and $\mathbf{w}$ then we can find the dot product using list comprehension,

```
>>> v=[5,6,7]
>>> w=[1,2,3]
>>> sum([x*y for (x,y) in zip(v,w)])
38
```

Example 20.4. Calcluate the mean and standard deviation of a list of numbers using list comprehension.

Suppose we need to find the **mean** $\bar{x}$ and **standard deviation** σ of the list a $[4.7, 25.7, 1.8, 1.5, 56.9, 92.6, 36., 85., 79.6, 52.5]$. These are commonly used statistical measures defined by

$$\bar{x} = \frac{1}{n} \sum_{i=1}^{n} x_i \text{ and } \sigma^2 = \frac{1}{n-1} \sum_{i=1}^{n} (x_i - \bar{x})^2 \qquad (20.4)$$

We can begin by typing the data into a list:

```
>>> x=[4.7, 25.7, 1.8, 1.5, 56.9, 92.6, 36., 85., 79.6, 52.5]
```

Then the mean is

```
>>> mean =  sum(x)/(len(x))
>>> mean
43.629999999999995
```

Since we have already determined the mean, we can calculate the list

$$y = \{(x_i - \bar{x})^2 | x_i \in x\} \qquad (20.5)$$

by using list comprehension:

```
>>> y = [(z-mean)**2 for z in x]
```

This is useful because $\sigma^2 = (1/(n-1)) \sum y_i$:

```
>>> sigma = (sum(y)/(n-1))**0.5
```

Of course, we could have combined the last two statements together into a single statement and eliminated the need for the dummy variable y.

```
>>> sigma = (sum(  [(z-mean)**2 for z in x] )/(n-1))**0.5
```

Finally, we note that we could have implemented the standard deviation completely independently of both **n** and **mean**

```
>>> (sum([(z-sum(x)/len(x))**2 for z in x] )/(len(x)-1))**0.5
35.0841543846918
```

As an afterthought to example 20.4, we note that these particular calculations (mean and standard deviations) are built in to Numpy.

```
>>> np.std(x,ddof=1)
35.0841543846918
```

The parameter **ddof** specifies the statistical degrees of freedom. It tells Numpy to use $n - 1$ in the denominator of the standard deviation calculation. If you do not specify **ddof**, it will divide by n:

```
>>> np.std(x)
33.283751290982806
>>> (sum([(z-sum(x)/len(x))**2 for z in x] )/(len(x)))**0.5
33.283751290982806
```

Exercises

1. Use list comprehension to define each of the following lists:

   (a) The list of all even numbers between 175 and 225.

   (b) The list of all perfect square integers under 1000.

   (c) The list of all square roots of positive integers from 1 to 20.

2. Suppose you want to divide up the interval (a, b) into $n + 1$ sub-intervals of equal length. Using a list comprehension only, but not using either a **For** or **while** loop, write a program to determine the end points of each interval. Verify that your program works on the following: $(a, b) = (0, 10); n = 10;$ $(a, b) = (3, 17); n = 19;$ $(a, b) = (-4.72, 6.98); n = 12$.

3. Write a function **mymax(f, a, b, precision)** that calculates the maximum value of a function **f(x)** on the interval (a, b). Here **precision** is the precision in the value of x where the maximum occurs. Hint: generate a list of values of x at equally spaced intervals of width **precision**, and calculate **f(x)** and each of these numbers.

4. The trapezoidal rule can be used to approx-imate the area under the curve of $f(x)$ as

$$\int_a^b f(x)dx \approx \frac{1}{2}h(f(a)+f(b))+h\sum_{i=1}^{n-1} f(x_i)$$

Write a function **trap(f,a,b,n)** that approximates $\int_a^b f(x)\,dx$ with the trapezoidal rule. Implement your function using list comprehension. Calculate each of the following with your function. Compare each value you calculate with the exact value that you can determine by solving the integral analytically.

   (a) $\int_0^\pi \cos x \, dx$ with $n = 100$

   (b) $\int_1^5 (x^3 - x^2) \, dx$ with $n = 50$

   (c) $\int_0^3 e^{-x^2} \, dx$ with $n = 100$ (this integral cannot be solved analytically; to find the exact value look up a table of the error function **erf(x)**)

   (d) $\int_{-\pi}^\pi \sin x \, dx$ with $n = 25$

Chapter 21

Numpy Arrays

Arrays are indexed data structures where each element has a fixed size.[1] Arrays may be single or multi-dimensional. The data is stored sequentially within the array. Programmers access each data element by the index or indices of the data element, and the compiler can figure out the address of each array element by applying an appropriate formula to the index number, the size and number of dimensions of the array, and the size of each data element. It is convenient to visualize one dimensional arrays as linear

Figure 21.1: A one-dimensional array.

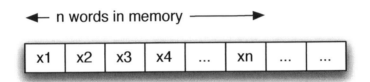

sequences (figure 21.1), two dimensional arrays as rectangular arrangements of memory elements (figure 21.2), and so forth (figure 21.3). While this visualization may be correct in some languages, it is not universal; the actual implementation depends on the computer language. One dimensional arrays are analogous to vectors, two dimensional arrays are analogous to matrices, and higher dimensional arrays are analogous to tensors. In principal, there is no limit to the number of dimensions that an array can have, though some languages limit the number.

Python implements one-dimensional arrays in the class **array**. However, there is a more general class of arrays in Numpy, and for most applications, you are better off just using the Numpy classes instead of the built in classes. Numpy's array class is called both **array** or **ndarray**. These terms may be used interchangeably. Performing calculations with numpy arrays is significantly faster than with Python lists, so if you are doing any seriously large amount of iteration you should use numpy arrays instead of lists or Python arrays. Numpy also provides some support for structured records and character data types. All of the array functions that we discuss here refer to Numpy arrays in package **numpy** and not to the built in python package **array**.

Array variables must be declared by using one of the array create functions, either as an uninitialized array, or one filled with zero's or ones of a given shape, or by conversion from a list (see tables 21.1, 21.2).

---

[1]The fixed size requirement is true in most languages; a notable exception is Perl.

Figure 21.2: Abstract representation of a two dimensional array.

x11
x12
x13
x14
...
x1q
x21
x22
x23
x24
x2q
xp1
xp2
xp3
xp4
xpq

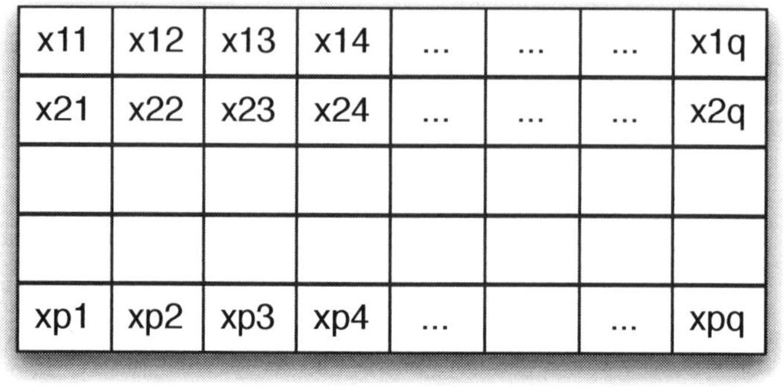

Figure 21.3: Abstract representation of a three dimensional array.

x11
x12
x13
x14
...
x1q
x21
x22
x23
x24
x2q
xp1
xp2
xp3
xp4
xpq

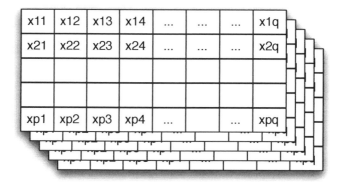

For example, to create an array from a one or two dimensional list,

```
>>> import numpy as np
>>> x=np.array([1,2,3])
>>> x
array([1,2,3])
>>> y=np.array([[1,2],[3,4]])
>>> y
array([[1, 2],
       [3, 4]])
>>>
```

As you can see, when Python prints out a two-dimensional array, it tries to align the elements so that it looks like a matrix.

The most important attributes of the array class are its dimensions, shape, size, data type, item size, and data buffer.

The **shape** of an array, `A.shape`, gives its dimensions as a tuple (rows, columns):

```
1  >>> A=np.array([[1,2,3],[4,5,6]])
2  >>> A.shape
3  (2,3)
```

Table 21.1. Numpy Array Creation: Empty, Ones, Zeros

Function[a]	Return Value
`empty(shape)`	Empty array of given shape (values not initialized).
`empty_like(a)`	Empty array, same shape as **a**.
`eye(N)`	Identity matrix (more options than `identity(n)`.
	`np.eye(2)`→ `array([[ 1., 0.], [ 0., 1.]])`
`identity(n)`	Identity matrix.
`ones(shape)`	An array of 1's of the given shape.
	`np.ones([2,3])`→
	`array([[ 1., 1., 1.],[ 1., 1., 1.]])`
`ones_like(a)`	An array of 1's of the same shape as **a**.
	`x=np.array([[1,2,3],[4,5,6]]);`
	`np.ones_like(x)`→
	`array([[1, 1, 1], [1, 1, 1]])`
`zeros(shape)`	An array of 0's of the given shape.
	`np.zeros([2,3])`→
	`array([[ 0., 0., 0.],[ 0., 0., 0.]])`
`zeros_like(a)`	An array of 0's of the same shape as **a**.
`full(shape, fill)`	An array of given shape, filled with **fill**
	`np.full([2,2],7.4)`→
	`array([[ 7.4, 7.4],[ 7.4, 7.4]])`
`full_like(a, fill)`	An array the same shape as **a** but filled with **fill**

[a]For more details and complete lists of options see http://docs.scipy.org/doc/numpy/reference/routines.array-creation.html

The **dimension** of an array, `A.ndim`, gives the number of dimensions (number of indices) in the shape (1 for a vector, 2 for a $p \times q$ matrix, etc).

```
1  >>> A=np.array([[1,2,3],[4,5,6]])
2  >>> A.ndim
3  2
```

The **data type** (`A.dtype`), **size** (`A.size`) and **item size** (`A.itemsize`) attributes give the data type, total number of elements in the array, and size in bytes:

```
4  >>> (A.dtype,A.size,A.itemsize)
5  (dtype('int64'), 6, 8)
```

Table 21.2. Numpy Array Creation: From Existing Data

Funtion[a]	Return Value
`array(a)`	Create an array.
`asarray(a)`	Convert the input to an array.
`asanyarray(a)`	Convert the input to an **ndarray**
`ascontiguousarray(a)`	Return a contiguous array in memory.
`asmatrix(data)`	Interpret the input as a matrix.
`copy(a)`	Return an array copy of the given object.
`frombuffer(b)`	Interpret a buffer as a one dimensional array.
`fromfile(fname)`	Construct an array from file.
`fromfunction(f, shape)`	Constructs an array by executing the function f over each coordinate.
`fromiter(r, dtype)`	Create a new one dimensional array from an iterable object r such as a **range**
`fromstring(string)`	A new one dimensional array from a string.
`loadtxt(fname)`	An array from a text file.

[a]For a complete list of arguments and options see `http://docs.scipy.org/doc/numpy/reference/routines.array-creation.html`

In addition to providing support for a large number of mathematical functionality in linear algebra, Numpy arrays support vectorization. In most cases, a function can be applied to a full array.

```
>>> def f(x):
...     return(x*x)
...
>>> u=np.array([5,10,25])
>>> f(u)
array([ 25, 100, 625])
>>>
```

If **u** were a list in the above code snippet, you would have to loop through the elements, e.g,. with list comprehension or a for loop, to apply **f** to every element of the list.

Array indexing is simpler with numpy arrays than with lists. Suppose you represent the matrix

$$\mathbf{M} = \begin{bmatrix} 1 & 2 & 3 \\ 4 & 5 & 6 \\ 7 & 8 & 9 \\ 10 & 11 & 12 \end{bmatrix} \tag{21.1}$$

as both a Python list **M** and a numpy array **A**:

```
>>> M=[[1,2,3],[4,5,6],[7,8,9],[10,11,12]]
>>> A=np.array(M)
>>> A
array([[ 1,  2,  3],
       [ 4,  5,  6],
       [ 7,  8,  9],
       [10, 11, 12]])
```

To access element $\mathbf{M}_{12} \to 6$ of the matrix using the Python list, we must refer to each list element as a separate integer index:

```
>>> M[1][2]
6
```

We can also do that in the array:

```
>>> A[1][2]
6
```

However in the array, we can now refer to the list index (1,2) as a tuple:

```
>>> A[1,2]
6
```

In the list, that produces an error:

```
>>> M[1,2]
Traceback (most recent call last):
  File "<stdin>", line 1, in <module>
TypeError: list indices must be integers, not tuple
>>>
```

This gives us an added bonus: **column slicing!** We can extract the columns of an array as a slice:

```
>>> A[:,0]
array([ 1,  4,  7, 10])
>>> A[:,1]
array([ 2,  5,  8, 11])
>>> A[:,2]
array([ 3,  6,  9, 12])
```

If we were to try to do column slicing with the list syntax, the slice is ignored, and it still returns the rows and not the columns:

```
>>> M[:][0]
[1, 2, 3]
>>> M[:][1]
[4, 5, 6]
```

Table 21.3. Numpy Array Manipulation (1 of 2)

Basic Operation[a]	Description
`copyto(B,A)`	Copies values from **B** to **A**.

Changing Shape	Description or Example
`A.reshape(new)`	Reshapes the array **A**.
`reshape(A,new)`	Reshapes the array **A**.
	`A=np.array([1,2,3,4,5,6,7,8,9,10])`
	`A.reshape(2,5)`
	`→ array([[1, 2, 3, 4, 5],`
	`          [6, 7, 8, 9,10]])`
`ravel(A)`	Returns a flattened array.
`A.flat`	Iterator object over array **A**
	`for j in B.flat ...`
`A.flatten()`	Returns flattened copy of **A**.
	`(np.array([[1,2],[3,4]]).flatten())`
	`→ array([1, 2, 3, 4])`

Transposes	Description or Example
`rollaxis(A,ax,n)`	Change the shape of the array by "rolling" axis **ax** back by **n** spaces (the default number is zero.) If **A** has a shape $3 \times 4 \times 5 \times 6$ then a rollback of axis 3 by 1 results in a reshaping to new dimensions of $3 \times 6 \times 5$.
`swapaxis(A,x1,x2)`	Swaps the two designated axis of the array.
	`A=array([[[1,2,3],[4,5,6],`
	`           [7,8,9]], [[10,11,12],`
	`           [13,14,15], [16,17,18]]])`
	`np.swapaxes(A,0,2) →`
	`array([[[1,10],[4,13],[7,16]],`
	`  [[ 2, 11], [ 5, 14], [ 8, 17]],`
	`  [[ 3, 12], [ 6, 15], [ 9, 18]]])`
`A.T`	Flips rows and columns of **A**
`transpose(A)`	Transpose along specific axes

Adding or Removing Elements	Description or Example
`delete(A, index)`	Removes the sub-array at the given **index**
`insert(A, index, x)`	Inserts **x** after given **index**.
`append(A, x)`	Appends to the end of an array.
`trim_zeros(A)`	Returns a new 1D array with leading or trailing zeros removed.

[a]For a complete list of arguments and options see http://docs.scipy.org/doc/numpy/
reference/routines.array-manipulation.html

Table 21.3. Numpy Array Manipulation (2 of 2)

Changing Kind of Array	Description or Example
`asarray(A)`	Convert input to an array.
`asanyarray(A)`	Convert to array but pass through arrays.
`asmatrix(A)`	Convert to a matrix.
`asfortranarray(A)`	Arrange in memory like a Fortran array.
`ascontiguousarray(A)`	Organize elements in memory like a C array.
`asarray_chkfinite(A)`	Convert to an array but returns an error if any nan or inf is found.
`asscalar(A)`	Convert a 1×1 array to its scalar equivalent

Joining and Tiling Arrays	Description of Example
`column_stack((A,B,..))`	Stacks 1D arrays as columns.
`concatenate((A,B,..))`	Concatenates arrays.
`dstack((A,B,..))`	Stacks arrays along 3rd axis.
`hstack((A,B,..))`	Stacks arrays column-wise.
`tile(A, n)`	Repeats **A** by tiling it **n** times.
`vstack((A,B,..))`	Stacks arrays vertically (row-wise).

Splitting Arrays	Description of Example
`array_split(A, n)`	Indices do not have to equally divide the axis.
`dsplit(A, n)`	Splits along the 3rd axis as per **split**.
`hsplit(A, n)`	Splits along the 2nd axis as per **split**.
`split(A, n)`	Splits array in **n** equal sized sub arrays. If **n** is a sequence, it is treated as a slice location.
`vsplit(A, n)`	Splits row-wise. **n** is as per **split**.

Table 21.4. Sorting Numpy Arrays

Function[a]	Description
`A.sort()`	Sorts **A** in place.
`argpartition(A, k [, axis, kind, order])`	Performs an indirect partition along a specified axis.
`argsort(A, [,axis, kind, order])`	Returns indices to sort **A**; **axis** is **int** or **None**; **kind** is **"quicksort"**, **"mergesort"**, **"heapsort"**
`lexsort(keys [,axis])`	Indirect sort using sequence of keys.
`msort(A)`	Returns copy of **A** sorted along first axis.
`partition(A, k [, axis, kind, order])`	Returns a partitioned copy of an array. The element in position **K** is in the position it would be in a sorted array. All smaller elements will be moved before it and all greater elements behind it.
`sort(A)`	Returns sorted copy of **A**.
`sort_complex(A)`	Like **sort** but sorts first along the real part, then the imaginary part.

[a]See http://docs.scipy.org/doc/numpy/reference/routines.sort.html for full details.

Table 21.5. Numpy Array Functions: Grids and Ranges

Function[a]	Return Value
`arange(start, stop, step)`	Evenly spaced values within a given interval. Similar to **range** but real valued.
`linspace(start, stop, num)`	Evenly spaced numbers over a specified interval. Similar to **range** but real valued and specifies number of points rather than step size.
`logspace(start, stop)`	Numbers spaced evenly on a log scale. Similar to **arange** except logarithmically spaced.
`meshgrid(x1,x2,..)`	Coordinate matrices from coordinate vectors.
`mgrid`	Dense multi-dimensional meshgrid.
`ogrid`	Open multi-dimensional meshgrid.

[a]For a complete list of arguments and options see `http://docs.scipy.org/doc/numpy/reference/routines.array-creation.html`

Table 21.6. Numpy Searching

Function[a]	Description
`argmax(A [,axis])`	Returns indices of max values along **axis**.
`argmin(A [,axis]))`	Returns indices of min values along **axis**.
`argwhere(A)`	Indices of nonzero elements, grouped by element.
`extract(cond,A)`	Extract elements from **A** according to boolean array **cond**, which must be the same length as **A**.
`flatnonzero(A)`	Returns indices of nonzero elements in a flattened version of **A**.
`nanargmax(A, [axis]))`	Like **argmax** but ignores **NaN**'s.
`nanargmin(A, [axis]))`	Like **argmin** bug ignores **NaN**'s.
`nonzero(A)`	Returns indices of nonzero elements.
`searchsorted(A, v)`	Find indices where elements should be inserted to maintain order.
	`np.searchsorted(range(5), 2.7)`→3
`where(cond, [x,y])`	Returns elements either from **x** or **y** depending on the boolean values in the array **cond**. The arrays **x**, **y** and **cond** must be the same length.
	`np.where([True, False, True], [5,10,15], [1,2,3])`→ `array([ 5, 2, 15])`

[a]See `http://docs.scipy.org/doc/numpy/reference/routines.sort.html` for complete descriptions.

Table 21.7. Numpy Miscellaneous and Statistical Functions

Function[a]	Description
`amax(A[,axis])`	Maximum value [along an axis].
`amin(A[,axis])`	Minimum value [along an axis].
`average(A[,axis, weights])`	[Weighted] average [along an axis].
`correlate(u, v)`	Cross correlation between two sequences $c_k = \sum_n u_{n+k} v_n^*$
`corrcof(A)`	Correlation coefficients of observations. Each column represents a single observations, each row a variable. The relationship between between correlation and covariance used is $P_{ij} = C_{ij}/\sqrt{C_{ii}C_{jj}}$.
`cov(A)`	Covariance matrix of data in **A**.
`count_nonzero(A)`	Number of nonzero elements in **A**.
`digitize(x, bins)`	Return indices of the bins to which each value of the input array belongs.
`histogram(A)`	Computes histogram of a data set.
`mean(A[[axis])`	Mean [along an axis].
`median(A[,axis])`	Median [along an axis].
`nanmax(A[,axis])`	Like **amax**, bug ignores **NaN**'s.
`nanmean(A[,axis])`	Like **mean**, but ignores **NaN**'s.
`nanstd(A[,axis])`	Like **std**, but ignores **NaN**'s.
`nanvar(A[,axis])`	Like **var**, but ignroes **NaN**'s.
`nanmin(A[,axis])`	Like **amin**, but ignores **NaN**'s.
`percentile(A,q[,axis])`	Returns q^{th} percentile [along an axis].
`ptp(A[,axis])`	Peak to peak (min/max) values [along axis].
`std(A[,axis])`	Standard Deviation [along an axis].
`var(A[,axis])`	Variance [along an axis].

[a]See http://docs.scipy.org/doc/numpy/reference/routines.sort.html and http://docs.scipy.org/doc/numpy/reference/routines.statistics.html for complete descriptions.

Table 21.8. Numpy Random Sampling (1 of 4)

Function[a]	Return value
rand(d0, d1, ..., dn)	Random values in a given shape.
randn(d0, d1, ..., dn)	Sample (or samples) from the 'standard normal dist.
randint(low[,high,size])	Random integers on $[\text{low}, \text{high})$.
random_integers(low[, high, size])	Random integers on $[\text{low}, \text{high}]$.
random_sample([size])	Random floats in $[0, 1)$.
random([size])	Random floats in $[0, 1)$.
ranf([size])	Random floats in $[0, 1)$.
sample([size])	Random floats in $[0, 1)$.
choice(a[, size, replace, p])	Random sample from a given 1D array
bytes(length)	Random bytes.

Permutations

shuffle(x)	Modifies a sequence in-place by shuffling.
permutation(x)	Randomly permute a sequence.

Random Numbers from Distributions

Distribution Name	Density Function
beta(a, b[, size])	Beta distribution over $[0, 1]$. $$f(x; \alpha, \beta) = \frac{1}{B(\alpha, \beta)} x^{\alpha-1} (1-x)^{\beta-1} \text{ where}$$ $$B(x, y) = \Gamma(x)\Gamma(y)/\Gamma(x+y)$$
binomial(n, p[, size])	Binomial distribution. $$P(N) = \binom{m}{N} p^N (1-p)^{m-N}$$
chisquare(df[, size])	Chi-squared. $$f(x; k) = \frac{(1/2)^{k/2}}{\Gamma(k/2)} x^{k/2-1} e^{-x/2}$$ $$\text{where } \Gamma(x) = \int_0^{-\infty} t^{n-1} e^{-t} dt$$
dirichlet(alpha[, size])	Dirichlet distribution. $$f(x) = \frac{1}{B(\alpha)} \prod_i x_i^{\alpha_i - 1}, \; B(\alpha) = \frac{\prod_i \Gamma(\alpha_i)}{\Gamma(\sum_i \alpha_i)}$$
exponential([scale, size])	Exponential distribution. The scale parameter is $1/\lambda$. $$f(x, \lambda) = \lambda e^{-\lambda x}$$
f(dfnum, dfden[, size])	F distribution. **dfnum** and **dfden** are the degrees of freedom in the numerator and denominator. $$f(x; d_1, d_2) = \frac{1}{xB\left(\frac{d_1}{2}, \frac{d_2}{2}\right)} \sqrt{\frac{(d_1 x)^{d_1} d_2^{d_2}}{(d_1 x + d_2)^{d_1 + d_2}}}$$ $$\text{where } B(x, y) = \Gamma(x)\Gamma(y)/\Gamma(x+y)$$

[a]See http://docs.scipy.org/doc/numpy/reference/routines.random.html.

Table 21.8. Numpy Random Sampling (2 of 4)

Function[a]	Density Function (continued)
`gamma(shape[, scale, size])`	Gamma distribution. Let $\theta=$**scale** and $k=$**shape** $$f(x) = x^{k-1}\frac{e^{-x/\theta}}{\theta^k\Gamma(k)}$$
`geometric(p[, size])`	Geometric distribution. $$f(k) = (1-p)^{k-1}p$$
`gumbel([loc, scale, size])`	Gumbel distribution. **mode**$=\mu$, **scale**$=\beta$. $$p(x;\mu,\beta) = \frac{e^{(-x-\mu)/\beta}}{\beta}e^{-e^{-(x-\mu)/\beta}}$$
`hypergeometric(ngood, nbad, nsample[, size])`	Hypergeometric distribution. $$P(x;n,m,N) = \binom{m}{n}\binom{N-m}{n-x}\bigg/\binom{N}{n}$$ where **ngood**$=n$; **nbad**$=m$; **nsample**$=N$
`laplace([loc, scale, size])`	Laplace distribution. **loc**$=\mu$, **scale**$=\lambda$. $$f(x;\mu,\lambda) = \frac{1}{2\lambda}\exp\left(-\frac{|x-\mu|}{\lambda}\right)$$
`logistic([loc, scale, size])`	Logistic distribution. **location**$=\mu$, **scale**$=s$ $$f(x;\mu,s) = \frac{e^{-(x-\mu)/s}}{s(1+e^{-(x-\mu)/s})^2}$$
`lognormal([mean, sigma, size])`	Log-normal distribution. $$f(x;\mu,\sigma) = \frac{1}{\sigma x\sqrt{2\pi}}e^{-\frac{(\log(x)-\mu)^2}{2\sigma^2}}$$
`logseries(p[, size])`	Logarithmic Series distribution. $$P(k;p) = -p^k/(k\log(1-p))$$
`multinomial(n, pvals[, size])`	Multinomial distribution.
`multivariate_normal(mean, cov[, size])`	Multivariate normal distribution.
`negative_binomial(n, p[, size])`	Negative binomial distribution. $$P(N;n,p) = \binom{N+n-1}{n-1}p^n(1-p)^N$$
`noncentral_chisquare(df, nonc[, size])`	Noncentral chi-square distribution. $$P(x;d,n) = \sum_{i=0}^{\infty}\frac{1}{i!}e^{n/2}\left(\frac{n}{2}\right)^i P_{\chi^2}(x;d+2i)$$ where $d=$**df**, $n=$**nonc**

[a]See http://docs.scipy.org/doc/numpy/reference/routines.random.html for complete descriptions.

Table 21.8. Numpy Random Sampling (3 of 4)

Function[a]	Density Function (continued)
`noncentral_f(dfnum, dfden, nonc[, size])`	Non-central F distribution.

$$f(x) = \sum_{k=0}^{\infty} \frac{e^{-\lambda/2}(\lambda/2)^k (d_1/d_2)^{k+d_1/2}}{k! B(d_2/2, d_1/2 + k)} \left(\frac{d_2}{d_2 + d_1 x}\right)^{k+(d_1+d_2)/2} x^{k-1+d_1/2}$$

Function[a]	Density Function (continued)
`normal([loc, scale, size])`	Normal (Gaussian) distribution. $f(x; \mu, \sigma) = \dfrac{1}{2\pi\sigma^2} e^{-(x-\mu)^2/(2\sigma^2)}$
`pareto(a[, size])`	Pareto II (Lomax) distributon. $P(x; a, m) = am^a/x^{a+1}$
`poisson([lam, size])`	Poisson distribution. $P(k; \lambda) = \lambda^k e^{-\lambda}/k!$
`power(a[, size])`	Power distribution. $P(x; a) = ax^{a-1}$
`rayleigh([scale, size])`	Rayleigh distribution. $P(x; \sigma) = \dfrac{x}{\sigma^2} e^{-x^2/(2\sigma^2)}$
`standard_cauchy([size])`	Cauchy distribution with mode = 0. $P(x; x_0, \gamma) = \dfrac{1}{\pi\gamma\left[1 + ((x-x_0)/\gamma)^2\right]}$ with $x_0 = 0$ and $\gamma = 1$
`standard_exponential([size])`	Exponential distribution. An exponential distribution with $\lambda = 1$.
`standard_gamma(shape[, size])`	Gamma distribution. Same as a gamma distribution, but with a scale of 1. $f(x) = x^{k-1}e^{-x}/\Gamma(k)$
`standard_normal([size])`	Standard Normal distribution (mean=0, stdev=1). $f(x) = \dfrac{1}{2\pi} e^{-x^2/2}$
`standard_t(df[, size])`	Standard Students t distribution. $f(x; d) = \dfrac{\Gamma((1+d)/2)}{\Gamma(d/2)\sqrt{\pi d}}(1 + x^2/d)^{-(1+d)/2}$
`triangular(left, mode, right[, size])`	Triangular distribution.
`uniform([low, high, size])`	Uniform distribution.
`vonmises(mu, kappa[, size])`	von Mises distribution. $f(x; \kappa, \mu) = \dfrac{e^{\kappa \cos(x-\mu)}}{2\pi I_0(\kappa)}$ where I_0 is the modified Bessel function of order zero.

[a]See http://docs.scipy.org/doc/numpy/reference/routines.random.html for complete descriptions.

Table 21.8. Numpy Random Sampling (4 of 4)

Function[a]	Density Function (continued)
`wald(mean, scale[, size])`	Wald distribution. $f(x; \mu, \sigma) = \sqrt{\dfrac{\sigma}{2\pi x^3}}\, e^{-\sigma(x-\mu)^2/(2\mu^2 x)}$ where $\mu=$**mean** and $\sigma=$**scale**.
`weibull(a[, size])`	Weibull distribution with one parameter.
`zipf(a[, size])`	Zipf distribution. $f(x; a) = x^{-a}/\zeta(a)$ where ζ is the Riemann Zeta function.

Control of Random Number Generator	Description
`RandomState`	Exposes a number of methods for the random number generator.[b]
`seed([seed])`	Re-seeds the random number generator.
`get_state()`	Gets the current state of the random number generator.
`set_state(state)`	Sets the current state of the random number generator. You should normally not need to change the internal state.

[a]See `http://docs.scipy.org/doc/numpy/reference/routines.random.html` for complete descriptions.
[b]See `http://docs.scipy.org/doc/numpy/reference/generated/numpy.random.RandomState.html#numpy-random-randomstate` for more details.

Table 21.9. Numpy Boolean Functions

Function	Description

`in1D(A, B)`	Tests whether each element of **A** is in **B**
	`np.in1d(range(3,7),range(5))` $\rightarrow$
	`array([ True, True, False,`
	`False], dtype=bool)`

`intersect1d(A, B)`	Set intersection of **A** and **B**
`setdiff1d(A, B)`	Set difference of **A** and **B**
`setxor1d(A,B)`	Set exclusive or of **A** and **B**

`union1d(A,B)`	Set union of **A** and **B**
	`A=np.array([[1,2],[3,4]])`
	`B=np.array([[6,8],[3,7]])`
	`np.union1d(A,B)` $\rightarrow$
	`array([1, 2, 3, 4, 6, 7, 8])`

`unique(A)`	Returns a sorted, flattened array with the unique elements.

Numpy Matrices

A Numpy **matrix** is a special class of numpy arrays. It has a collection of special operations that are related to matrices. Matrices may be created from arrays. Methods that can be applied to Numpy matrices are summarized in table 21.10. Linear algebra support (matrix and vector products, solution of linear systems, singuar value decompositions, norms) is provided by **numpy.linalg** (table 30.1). The interface to **numpy.matrix** is somewhat easier to use than the interface to numpy arrays and has a syntax that is similar to Matlab. However, there is no particular advantage numerically in using matrices over array and the array support is more extensive.

Table 21.10. Numpy Matrices

Function[a]	Return Value
bmat(a)	A matrix built from **a**.
diag(a)	If **a** is a matrix, returns its diagonal. If **a** is a vector, returns a matrix with **a** on the diagonal.
diagflat(v)	Like **diag**, but flattens **a** first.
mat(data)	Interpret the input as a matrix. Equivalent to **matrix(data, copy=False)**.
matrix(a)	returns a matrix from an array or array like object.
tri(size)	An array with ones at and below the given diagonal and zeros elsewhere.
tril(m)	Lower triangle of an array.
triu(m)	Upper triangle of an array.
vander(x)	Vandermonde matrix of **x**: $\left[\ \mathbf{x}^{n-1}\ \middle|\ \mathbf{x}^{n-2}\ \middle|\ \cdots\ \middle|\ \mathbf{x}\ \middle|\ \mathbf{1}\ \right]$: where $\mathbf{x}^k$ is the column matrix of of all the elements of **x** raised to the integer k power.

---

[a]For a complete list of arguments and options see http://docs.scipy.org/doc/numpy/reference/routines.array-creation.html

Table 21.11. Operations on Numpy Matrices (1 of 2)

Method[a]	Return Value of `a.method(arguments)`
`all(axis)`	**True**/**False** whether all elements along a given axis are **True**
`any(axis)`	Does any array element along a given axis evaluates to True.
`argmax(axis)`	Indices of the maximum values along an axis.
`argmin(axis)`	Indices of the minimum values along an axis.
`argpartition(k)`	Indices that would partition this array.
`argsort(axis)`	Indices that would sort this array.
`astype(t)`	Copy of the array, cast to type **t**.
`byteswap(k)`	Swap the bytes of the array elements
`choose(choices)`	New array from a set of choices.
`clip(a,b)`	Array whose values are limited to **[a, b]**.
`compress(c)`	Selected slices of array along an axis.
`conj()`	Complex-conjugate all elements.
`conjugate()`	Complex conjugate, element-wise.
`copy()`	A copy of the array.
`cumprod(axis)`	Cumulative product along an axis.
`cumsum(axis)`	Cumulative sum along an axis.
`diagonal()`	Specified diagonals.
`dot(b)`	Dot product of two arrays.
`dump(file)`	Dump a pickle of the array to the specified file.
`dumps()`	Pickle of the array as a string.
`fill(value)`	Fill the array with a scalar value.
`flatten()`	A copy of the array collapsed into one dimension.
`getA()`	Self as an ndarray object.
`getA1()`	Self as a flattened ndarray.
`getH()`	The (complex) conjugate transpose.
`getI()`	The (multiplicative) inverse.
`getT()`	Matrix transpose.
`getfield(t)`	A field of the given array as type **t**
`item(*args)`	Copy an element of an array to a standard Python scalar and return it.
`itemset(*args)`	Insert scalar into an array.
`max(axis)`	Maximum value along an axis.
`mean()`	Mean of matrix elements along given axis.
`min(axis)`	Minimum value along an axis.
`nonzero()`	Indices of non-zero elements.
`partition(kth)`	Rearranges array so that kth element is at position it would be in a sorted array.
`prod(axis)`	Product of elements over an axis.
`ptp(axis)`	Peak-to-peak (max - min) value along an axis.
`put(j, values)`	Set `a.flat[i] = values[i]` $\forall i \in j$.
`ravel()`	Flattens array.
`repeat(x)`	Repeats elements.

[a]For a complete list of arguments and options see http://docs.scipy.org/doc/numpy/reference/generated/numpy.matrix.html

Table 21.11. Operations on Numpy Matrices (2 of 2)

Method[a]	Return Value of `a.method(arguments)`
`reshape(shape)`	Reshapes array.
`resize(new_shape)`	Change shape and size of array in-place.
`round()`	Rounds array values.
`searchsorted(x)`	Find indices where elements of **x** should be inserted in **a** to maintain order.
`sort()`	Sort an array, in-place.
`squeeze()`	Remove single-dimensional entries.
`std()`	Standard deviation along an axis.
`sum(axis)`	Sum along an axis.
`swapaxes(ax1, ax2)`	View an array with axes swapped.
`take(indices)`	Sub-array at **indices**.
`tofile(fid)`	Write array to a file.
`tolist()`	Return the matrix as a (possibly nested) list.
`tostring()`	Construct to a byte string.
`trace()`	Sum along diagonals of the array.
`transpose(*axes)`	View of the array with axes transposed.
`var(axis)`	Variance along a given axis.
`view()`	View of array with the same data.

[a]For a complete list of arguments and options see `http://docs.scipy.org/doc/numpy/reference/generated/numpy.matrix.html`

Exercises

1. Let **A** represent the matrix $\begin{bmatrix} 1 & 2 & 3 \\ 0 & -4 & 6 \\ 3 & 7 & 5 \end{bmatrix}$.

   Find or show that:

   (a) Represent A as a numpy array **A**.
   (b) The first row of **A**.
   (c) The second column of **A**.
   (d) The matrix inverse of **A**.
   (e) The matrix inverse of **A** rounded to 10 significant digits.
   (f) Show $\mathbf{AA}^{-1} = \mathbf{I}$.
   (g) Find the determinant of **A**.
   (h) Find the eigenvectors and eigenvalues of **A**.

2. Create an array of ones that has the same dimensions as **A** in the previous problem.

3. Represent $\mathbf{A} = \begin{bmatrix} 1 & 2 & 3 \\ -1 & 0 & 5 \end{bmatrix}$ and

   $\mathbf{B} = \begin{bmatrix} 0 & 1 \\ 1 & 0 \\ 2 & 3 \end{bmatrix}$ as numpy arrays.

   (a) Find **AB** and **BA**.
   (b) Find $\mathbf{M} = \mathbf{B}^{\mathrm{T}}\mathbf{B}$
   (c) Find $\mathbf{M}^{-1} = (\mathbf{B}^{\mathrm{T}}\mathbf{B})^{-1}$
   (d) Find $\mathbf{J} = \mathbf{M}^{-1}\mathbf{B}^{\mathrm{T}} = (\mathbf{B}^{\mathrm{T}}\mathbf{B})^{-1}\mathbf{B}^{\mathrm{T}}$
   (e) Prove analytically, based on the definition of **J**, that $\mathbf{JB} = \mathbf{I}$. The matrix **J** is called the **pseudo inverse** because it gives the identity matrix **I** when **B** is left-multiplied by **J**. What are the dimensions of **I**
   (f) Derive an equivalent right-inverse for **B**. What are the dimensions of the corresponding identity matrices for both left and right inverses? Are they the same or are they different?
   (g) Show that $\mathbf{JB} = \mathbf{I}$ (use 5-digit rounding) but $\mathbf{BJ} \neq \mathbf{I}$,

Chapter 22

Plotting with pyplot

The standard plotting package for Python is called **matplotlib**. Portions of it were based on a similar plotting package in Matlab, and if you already know Matlab, it may look somewhat familiar. However, much of it is different.

While you can use the **matplotlib** library directly for all of your plots, you don't have to, because there are higher level interfaces that make it easier to use. We will cover **pyplot** here. The capabilities of **pyplot** and **matplotlib** are so extensive that whole books have been written about them.[1] The code is extensively documented online, but so much material is available that it is fairly difficult for a beginner to wade through. The best place to start is at the image gallery on the official matplotlib documentation page at http://matplotlib.org. Just look for an graph in the gallery that sort-of like what you want, download the code, and start hacking from that.

This chapter is much longer than the others in this book because it tries to convey to the student something of the vast capability of this library. Even more is left out than what is shown, and much of of what is shown is limited to short summaries of functions in long tables. Every single one of these functions is documented extensively online. If anything, the list of names of functions will give you a starting point for you web search. Perhaps by having the tables in front of you on the bus ride to school will inspire you when you get to the campus computer lab.

A Note About Scope

Through most of this chapter, the examples begin with the nonstandard inclusion of the entire **pyplot** library via

```
from matplotlib.pyplot import *
```

While this is perfectly legal python it is not recommended as it clutters up the namespace. We do this to simplify the code. The standard code would be

```
import matplotlib.pyplot as plt
```

Then functions like **plot**, **scatter**, **xlabel**, etc., would be explicitly preceded by the prefix **plt** as in **plt.plot**, **plt.scatter**, or **plt.xlabel**. This is done to make the code simple as possible for beginning students.

---

[1]A. Devert (2014) *Matplotlib Plotting Cookbook*; D. McGreggor (2015) *Mastering MatPlotlib*; S. Tosi (2009)*Matplotlib for Python Developers*

Advanced Plotting Options

Pyplot is a basic two-dimensional plotting package. It has only rudimentary interactive capability[2] and you must save static files as images (e.g. jpg files) if you want to post them on web page. There is a matplotlib toolkit designed for three-dimensional plotting called **mpl_toolkits.mplot3d**.[3] However, **mplot3d** is itself somewhat buggy and it is difficult to extract high-quality (e.g., publishable) two dimensional projections of the kind you can get from other mathematical software. Other packages that are available for plotting and data visualization in python include: **bokeh** (interactive web visualizations)[4]; **MPLD3**(interactive web visualizations merging **matplotlib** with D3)[5]; mayavi(a VTK-based package)[6]; **seaborn** (a matplotlib extension for statistical visualization)[7]; visvis (an OpenGL based package for images, volumes and meshes)[8]; ivupy (an interface to COIN)[9]; gnuplotpy (an interface to gnuplot)[10] and chaco[11] among others. A list of data plotting and data visualization packages for python is maintained by the scipy project.[12]

Plotting in iPython notebooks

If you are writing in an iPython notebook, you should always include the line

```
%matplotlib inline
```

before your first plotting command. This will force the plots to automatically display (and be saved) inside your notebook and not in pop-up windows. Furthermore, the **show()** function is unnecessary.

Using plot

Consider the following simple example: plot the trigonometric functions $y = \sin x$ and $y = \cos x$ on the interval $(0, 2\pi)$. We will need to import both **numpy** and **pyplot** for our example. Numpy is not needed for plotting per se, but in this example we will be using **numpy.linspace** to generate a list of x values, and to generate the trig functions.

```
1  from matplotlib.pyplot import *
2  import numpy as np
```

---

[2]These are not discussed in this text.
[3]http://matplotlib.org/mpl_toolkits/mplot3d/tutorial.html
[4]http://bokeh.pydata.org/en/latest/
[5]http://mpld3.github.io/
[6]http://code.enthought.com/projects/mayavi/
[7]http://stanford.edu/~mwaskom/software/seaborn/
[8]https://github.com/almarklein/visvis
[9]http://ivupy.sourceforge.net/
[10]http://gnuplot-py.sourceforge.net/
[11]http://code.enthought.com/projects/chaco/
[12]http://www.scipy.org/topical-software.html#plotting-data-visualization-3-d-programming

To make our plots we need to generate a set of (x, y) data points, and then connect the dots. When we tell **pyplot** what to plot, however, we do not give it a list of (x, y) pairs; instead, we give it lists of x-values and a separate list of y-values. It might help to visualize your data as being listed in a table or spreadsheet, with each (x, y) pair on a different line.

Then the rows correspond to points. The first column of the spreadsheet or table has all the x-values, and the second column has all the y-values. Suppose we represent the values of these columns by the numpy arrays **x** and **y**. For our plots of the $\sin x$ and $\cos x$, we need to generate these arrays.

```
3  x=np.linspace(0,2*np.pi,200)
4  y1=np.cos(x)
5  y2=np.sin(x)
```

Here in lines 4 and 5 have used array math to apply the **np.cos** and **np.sin** to every element of **x**. This is more efficient (though functionally equivalent) to

```
y1=[np.cos(u) for u in x]
```

or

```
import math
y1=[math.cos(u) for u in x]
```

However, **math.cos** does not allow array calculations so a loop is required.

To get the plot, all we have left is the following:

```
6  plot(x,y1)   # Make a plot of cos(x) vs x but don't show it
7  plot(x,y2)   # Make a plot of sin(x) vs x but don't show it
8  show()       # Show the plots
```

A figure that looks something like this pops up on our screen.

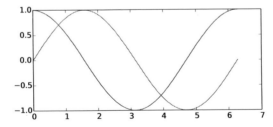

Had we wanted instead to display the curves on two *different* plots, we would insert a call to **figure()** before each **plot()**.

```
figure()
plot(x,y1)   # Make a plot of cos(x) vs x but don't show it
figure()
plot(x,y2)   # Make a plot of sin(x) vs x but don't show it
show()       # Show the plots
```

The x and y axis aren't to the same scale. The y axis is significantly stretched out. If we want to make them equal, we can change the aspect ratio.

```
6  plot(x,y1)   # Make a plot of cos(x) vs x but don't show it
7  plot(x,y2)   # Make a plot of sin(x) vs x but don't show it
8  axes().set_aspect("equal")   # equal aspects on each axis
9  show()         # Show the plots
```

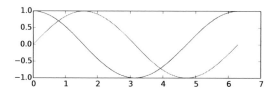

Now we want to change the x-axis to only go to π, and not 7, and renumber the tick marks to something involving π.

```
6   plot(x,y1)   # Make a plot of cos(x) vs x but don't show it
7   plot(x,y2)   # Make a plot of sin(x) vs x but don't show it
8   axes().set_aspect("equal")
9   xlim(0, 2*np.pi)        # upper and lower limits of x axis
10  yticks([-1,0,1], ["-1", "0", "1"]) # tick marks and labels
11  xticks([x for x in np.arange(0,2.5*np.pi, np.pi/2)],
12        [0, r"$\pi$/2", r"$\pi$", r"3$\pi$/2", r"2$\pi$"])
13  show()         # Show the plots
```

We've also inserted the π into the label using the string `"r"` math escape. To label the curves, and add colors and lines styles, we can change lines 6 and 7

```
6  plot(x,y1, ls="-", color="k", label="cosine")
7  plot(x,y2, ls="--",color="k", label="sine")
8  legend(loc=(.55,.65), fontsize="small")
```

The `legend` function places the legend on the plot (table 22.19). To add labels to the axis and plot itself, we use `xlabel`, `ylabel` and `title` before `show`.

```
xlabel("angle_in_radians")
ylabel("function_value")
title("Plots_of_the_Sine_and_Cosine")
```

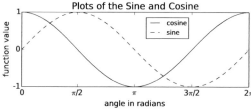

To save your plot to a 300 dpi png file myplot.png,

```
fig=gcf()                         # get current figure
fig.set_size_inches(6,4)          # optional size
fig.savefig("myplot.png", dpi=300)
```

Scatter plots

Scatter plots are xy plots in which each point is represented by a marker. The points may or may not be joined by a connected line. Scatter plots are useful for representing observed or experimental data and are often used in combination with line plots (the plots we make with **plot**) on the same figure to compare a model with observations.

Here we generate random points about the parabola $y = 10x - x^2$ (shifted only in the y direction). We then plot both the random points with small diamonds, and the original parabola as a solid line.

```python
from matplotlib.pyplot import *
import numpy as np
xvals = np.linspace(0,10,25)     # x grid
y =  10*xvals - xvals**2         # y points on parabola
                                 # uses vector arithmetic
plot(xvals, y, c="black")        # plot parabola
# generate noisy data
noise = 10*(np.random.rand(25)-.5)
ynoise = y + noise
# plot markers for each noisy data point
scatter(xvals, ynoise, marker="D", c="black")
show()
```

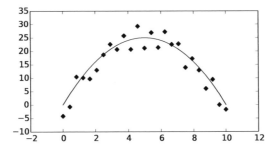

The different types of markers that can be used are summarized in table 22.6. Some of them are illustrated here. By default, or if you use the **color** option, the markers are filled. To get hollow markers set **facecolor** and **edgecolor** to different colors.

'+'	'*'	','	'.'	'1'	'3'	'2'	'4'	'8'	'<'	'>'	'D'	'H'	'_'	'^'	'd'	'h'	'o'	'p'	's'	'v'	'x'	'|'
+	★	■	●	Y	◄	►	⅄	●	◀	▶	◆	⬢	–	▲	◆	⬡	●	⬠	■	▼	✕	❙
+	☆	□	○	Y	◁	▷	⅄	○	◁	▷	◇	⬡	–	△	◇	○	○	⬠	□	▽	✕	❙

Summary of basic plotting functions

Table 22.1. Some pyplot functions (1 of 3)	
Function[a]	Description
`acorr(x)`	Plots the autocorrelation of **x**.
`angle_spectrum(x)`	Plots the angle spectrum of array **x**.
`annotate()`	Annotates the plot. Tables 22.4 ,22.5
`arrow(x,y,dx,dy)`	Put arrows on the axes. Table 22.8.
`autoscale()`	Controls autoscaling of axes. Keywords are:
	enable Boolean value **True** or **False**.
	axis Select **"x"**, **"y**, or **"both"**
	tight Boolean value **True** or **False**.
`axes()`	Create an **Axes** instance. Table 22.2.
`axhline()`	Draw a horizontal line. Table 22.9.
`axhspan()`	**axhspan(ymin,ymax,xmin=0,xmax=1)** draws a horizontal rectangle from **ymin** to **ymax**. Units are axis fractions. Table 22.10.
`axis()`	Set values for the axis. Table 22.3.
`axvline()`	Draw a vertical line. Table 22.9.
`axvspan()`	**axvspan(xmin,xmax,ymin=0,ymax=1)** draws a vertical rectangle from **xmin** to **xmax**. Units are axis fractions. Table 22.10.
`bar()`	Draw a bar plot. Tables 22.11 and 22.10.
`barh()`	Draw a horizontal bar plot. Tables 22.11 and 22.10.
`box()`	Turns the axes box on or off.
`boxplot()`	Draws a boxplot. Table 22.13.
`broken_barh()`	Draws horizontal bar plots that have multiple bars at the same y value so that they look like broken bars. Table 22.12.
`cla()`	Clears the current axes.
`clabel(CS)`	Labels a contour plot. Table 22.15
`clf()`	Clears the current figure.
`clim(a,b)`	Limits to colors to the range (a, b).
`close()`	Closes current figure. **close(f)** closes **f**.
`cohere(x,y)`	Coherence plot of normalized cross spectral density
`colorbar()`	Adds a color bar to a plot.
`contour()`	Plot a contour plot. Table 22.14
`contourf()`	Draw a filled contour plot. Table 22.14
`csd(x,y)`	Plots the cross-spectral density of the data.

[a]For a complete list of all functions and their capabilities see http://matplotlib.org/api/pyplot_api.html

Table 22.1. Some pyplot functions (2 of 3)

Function	Description
`delaxes()`	Removes an axes from current figure.
`draw()`	Redraws the current figure.
`errorbar(x,y))`	Plots a graph with error bars. Table 22.16
`eventplot(x)`	Plots a sequence of vertical lines representing events. Table 22.18.
`figlegend()`	Adds a legend to a **figure**
`figtext()`	Adds text to a **figure**. `figtext(x, y, **kwargs)`. Standard text keywords.
`figure()`	Creates a new **figure**.
`fill()`	Plots filled polygons. `fill(x,y)`, where **x** and **y** are arrays of the vertices. Standard polygon properties.
`fill_between(x,y1,y2)`	Fills between two curves. Standard polygon properties.
`gca()`	Gets current **Axes** instance.
`gcf()`	Gets a reference to the current **figure** instance.
`grid()`	Turns grid on or off. `grid(flag, which, axis, **kwargs)` `which ← "major", "minor", "both"` `axis ← "x", "y",` or `"both"` `flag←True` or `False` Typical line keywords apply.
`hexbin(x,y)`	Hexagonal binning plot.
`hist(x)`	Plots a histogram. See page 195.
`hist2d(x)`	Plots a histogram on a 2D plot.
`hlines(y, a, b)`	Plots horizontal lines at y from a to b
`legend()`	Print a legend on a plot.
`loglog()`	Like **plot** but with logarithmic scaling on both axes.
`magnitude_spectrum(x)`	Plots the magnitude spectrum.
`margins(x,y)`	Sets or retrieves the current margins.
`matshow(A)`	Displays a matrix as an image. The origin is put at the upper left hand corner of the matrix and the rows are displayed horizontally.
`minorticks_off()`	Turns off minor ticks.
`minorticks_on()`	Turns on minor ticks.
`phase_spectrum(x)`	Plot a phase spectrum.
`pie(x)`	Pie chart. See page 196
`plot(x,y)`	Make an xy plot.
`plot_date(x, y)`	Plot where one or both of the axes is dates.
`plotfile(name)`	Plots data from a column delimited file.
`polar(theta, r)`	Plot in polar coordinates.
`psd(x)`	Plots the power spectral density.

[a]For a complete list of all functions and their capabilities see http:// matplotlib.org/api/pyplot_api.html

Table 22.1. Some pyplot functions (3 of 3)

Function	Description
`quiver()`	Plots a field of 2D arrows.
`quiverkey()`	Add a key to a quiver plot.
`rc()`	Set the current rc parameters.
`savefig(f)`	Saves the current figure to the specified file.
`sca(ax)`	Sets the current **Axes** instance to **x**
`scatter(x, y)`	Scatter plot.
`semilogx()`	Like **plot** but with a logarithmic x axis.
`semilogy()`	Like **plot** but with a logarithmic y axis.
`setp()`	Set a property.
`show()`	Show current figure.
`specgram(x)`	Plots a spectogram.
`spy(A)`	Plots the sparsity pattern of a two dimensional array.
`stackplot(x)`	Stacked area plot.
`stem(x)`	Makes a stem plot.
`step(x,y)`	Makes a step plot.
`streamplot(x,y,u,v)`	Plots a vector flow's streamlines.
`subplot()`	**subplot(nrows, ncols, plot_number)**
`tick_params`	Sets the properties of the ticks .
`ticklabel_format()`	Format of the tick label.
`title(s)`	Adds a title to the plot.
`tricontour()`	Contours on a triangular grid.
`tripcolor()`	Contours on an unstructured triangular grid such as a delaunay triangulation.
`triplot()`	Triangular grid.
`twinx(ax)`	Share the x axis.
`twiny(ax)`	Share the y axis.
`vlines(x, a, b)`	Plots vertical lines at x from a to b
`violinplot(data)`	Makes a violin plot, a box plot with a rotated kernel density plot on each side that shows the probability density.
`xcorr(x,y)`	Plots cross correlation.
`xkcd()`	Changes display to make plots look like they were drawn by the artist of the comic strip xkcd.
`xlabel(s)`	Sets the x axis label.
`xlim()`	Set or retrieve the x axis limits. Table 22.3.
`xscale()`	See table 22.3.
`xticks()`	Sets the current x ticks.
`ylabel(s)`	Sets the y axis label.
`ylim()`	Set or retrieve the y axis limits. Table 22.3.
`yscale()`	See table 22.3.
`yticks()`	Sets the y axis ticks.

Axes

Table 22.2. pyplot.axes

`axes()` returns a full `subplot(111)`.
`axes(rect)` returns an axis, where
`rect=[left, bottom, width, height]`, all values between 0 and 1.

Keyword	Description
`axisbg`	Background color
`frameon`	Boolean value `True` or `False`.
`sharex`	Share attributes of another `axes` instance.
`sharey`	Share attributes of another `axes` instance.
`polar`	Use polar coordinates. Boolean value `True` or `False`.
`aspect`	Aspect ratio as a number, or `"equal"`, or `"auto"`

Table 22.3. Axis scales in pyplot

both	`axis()` → current axis `[xmin, xmax, ymin,ymax]`
	`axis([xmin, xmax, ymin, ymax])` sets axis limits
	`axis("off")` turns off the axis.
	`axis("equal")` changes axes so a circle is circular.
	`axis("scaled")` changes plot box so a circle is circular.
	`axis("tight")` fits all data.
x only	`xlim(xmin, xmax)` sets the x axis limits.
	`xlim( (xmin, xmax))` sets the x axis limits.
	`xlim()` → `(xmin, xmax)`, gets current x axis limits.
	`xscale("log")`, `xscale("linear")`
y only	`ylim(ymin, ymax)` sets the y axis limits.
	`ylim( (ymin, ymax))` sets the y axis limits.
	`ylim()` → `(ymin, ymax)`, gets current y axis limits.
	`yscale("log")`, `yscale("linear")`

Texts and Annotations

Table 22.4. `pyplot.annotate` parameters

`pyplot.annotate(*args,**kwargs)`

Parameter	Description
`s`	The string to print.
`xy`	(x,y) location on item being annotated.
`xytext`	Optional (x,y) tuple, where to put the annotation (optional).
`xycoords`	Optional (string) units include:
	`"data"` `"figure points"`
	`"figure pixels"` `"figure fraction"`
	`"axes points"` `"axis fraction"`
	`"axis pixels"` `"offset points"`
	`"polar"`
`textcoords`	Optional units for the text. See `xycoords`.
`arrowprops`	Optional properties for arrow that connects the annotation to the data object being annotated. Possible values include:
	`width` Arrow width in points
	`frac` Fraction of arrow used up by head
	`headwidth` Width of the arrow base in points
	`shrink` Shrinkage factor

Table 22.5. `pyplot.annotate` keywords (1 of 2)

Keyword	Description
`alpha`	0=transparent; 1=opaque
`animated`	**True** or **False**
`axes`	see table 22.2
`backgroundcolor`	Sets background colors.
`bbox`	rectangle properties
`clip_box`	a mutable bounding box
`clip_on`	**True** or **False**
`color`	Arrow color
`contains`	A function, e.g., for mouse clicks.
`family`	Font family.
`figure`	A matplotlib **Figure**
`fontproperties`	Sets Font Properties.
`horizontalalignment`	`"center"`, `"right"`, or `"left"`
`label`	String %s conversion

Table 22.5. `pyplot.annotate` keywords (2 of 2)

Keyword	Description
`linespacing`	Numerical multiple of font size.
`position`	(x,y)
`rasterized`	Values are **True**, **False** or **None**
`rotation`	Angle in degrees, **"horizontal"** or **"vertical"**
`size`	Alternative is **fontsize** Possible values are the numerical size in points or any of the following: `"xx-small"` `"x-small"` `"small"` `"medium"` `"large"` `"x-large"` `"xx-large"`
`stretch`	Alternative is **fontstretch**. A numerical value in the range 0 to 1000 or: `"ultra-condensed"` `"extra-condensed"` `"condensed"` `"semi-condensed"` `"normal"` `"semi-expanded"` `"expanded"` `"extra-expanded"` `"ultra-expanded"`
`style`	Alternative is **fontstyle**. Options are `"normal"`, `"italic`, and `"oblique"`.
`text`	Anything that can be printed with % string conversion (table 15.4)
`transform`	A **Transform** instance.
`url`	A URL string.
`variant`	Alternative is **fontvariant**. Possible values are `"normal"` or `"small-caps"`
`verticalalignment`	Alterantives are **va** and **ma**. Possible values are `"center"`, `"top"`, `"bottom"`, and `"baseline"`
`visible`	Is the text visible. **True** or **False**.
`weight`	Alternative: **fontweight**. May be a numerical value between 0 and 1000, or any of the following strings: `ultralight` `light` `normal` `regular` `book` `medium` `roman` `semibold` `demibold` `demi` `bold` `heavy` `extra bold` `black`
`x`	x position of text
`y`	y position of text
`zorder`	Items with lower z order are drawn first.

markers, lines and arrows

Table 22.6. `pyplot` markers

Marker	Name	Marker	Name	Marker	Name
0	`tickleft`	7	`caretdown`	`"^"`	`triangle_up`
1	`tickright`	8	`octagon`	`"|"`	`vline`
`"1"`	`tri_down`	`"D"`	`diamond`	`","`	`pixel`
2	`tickup`	`"h"`	`hexagon1`	`"+"`	`plus`
`"2"`	`tri_up`	`"H"`	`hexagon2`	`"*"`	`star`
3	`tickdown`	`"o"`	`circle`	`"."`	`point`
`"3"`	`tri_left`	`"p"`	`pentagon`	`"_"`	`hline`
4	`caretleft`	`"S"`	`square`	`""`	nothing
`"4"`	`tri_right`	`"v"`	`triangle_down`	`" "`	nothing
5	`caretright`	`"x"`	`x`	`None`	nothing
6	`caretup`	`"<"`	`triangle_left`	`"None"`	nothing
		`">"`	`triangle_right`		

Table 22.7. Common keywords in line-related functions

Many line drawing functions have similar parameters. These include **arrow**, **axhline**, **axvline**, **errorbar**, **eventplot**, **plot**.

Keyword	Description
`alpha`	Opaqueness (0 is transparent, 1 is opaque).
`animated`	Boolean value **True** or **False**.
`antialiased`	**True** or **False**. Alternative is **aa**
`axes`	An **Axes** instance.
`capstyle`	"butt", "round", "projecting"
`clip_box`	A bounding box
`clip_on`	Boolean value **True** or **False**.
`color`	Color of object
`contains`	A callable function.
`edgecolor`	Alternative is **ec**, color of edge
`facecolor`	Alternative is **fc**, color of face
`figure`	A Matplotlib **Figure** instance.
`hatch`	Possible values are "\", "/", "|", "+", "o", "O", ".", "*"
`joinstyle`	"miter", "round", "bevel"
`label`	Any string label.
`linestyle`	Alternative is **ls**. Short or long forms:

	Short	Long	Drawn
	`"-"`	`"solid"`	Solid line
	`"--"`	`"dashed"`	Dashed line
	`"-."`	`"dashdot"`	Dash-dot line
	`":"`	`"dotted"`	Dotted line
	`" "` or `""`	`"None"`	Nothing.

Keyword	Description
`linewidth`	Alternative is **lw**. Numerical value.
`rasterized`	Boolean value **True** or **False**.
`url`	A URL string.
`visible`	Show or not show. **True** or **False**.
`zorder`	Items with lower z order are drawn first.

Table 22.8. `pyplot.arrow` parameters

`arrow(x, y, dx, dy, **kwargs)` will draw an arrow from (x, y) to $(x + dx, y + dy)$. Keywords in table 22.7 may also be used.

Keyword	Description
`width`	Width of tail, default is 0.001
`length_includes_head`	`True` or `False`
`head_width`	Width of arrowhead.
`head_length`	Length of arrowhead.
`shape`	`"full"` draws full arrowhead
	`"left"` or `"right"` draws only one half of the arrowhead
`head_starts_at_zero`	Normally the head ends at coordinate zero. Set this to `True` to reverse this.
`fill`	Boolean value `True` or `False`.

Table 22.9. `pyplot.axhline` and `pyplot.axvline`

`axhline(y, xmin, xmax, **kwargs)` draws a horizontal line at `y` (Default: 0) from `xmin` (default: far left) to `xmax` (default: far right).
`axvline(x, ymin, ymax, **kwargs)` draws a vertical line at `x` (default: 0) from `ymin` (default:bottom) to `ymax` (default: top).
Keywords in table 22.7 may also be used.

Keyword	Description
`dash_capstyle`	`"butt"`, `"round"`, or `"projecting"`
`dash_joinstyle`	`"butt"`, `"round"`, or `"bevel"`
`dashes`	A sequence of on/off numbers, in points.
`fillstyle`	How much of each marker to fill. Values are: `"full"` `"left"` `"right"` `"bottom"` `"top"` `"none"`
`label`	String to print.
`markeredgecolor`	Alternative `mec`. Any color.
`markeredgewidth`	Alternative `mew`. Marker width in points.
`markerfacecolor`	Alternative `mfc`. Any color.
`markerfacecoloralt`	Alternative `mfcalt`. Any color.
`markersize`	Marker size in points. Alternative is `ms`
`picker`	Distance in points or pick function.
`pickradius`	Distance in points using in picking.
`solid_capstyle`	`"butt"`, `"round"`, or `"projecting"`
`solid_joinstyle`	`"miter"`, `"round"`, or `"bevel"`
`xdata`	x-values, data array.
`ydata`	y-values, data array.

Rectangles and Patches

Table 22.10. Keywords in pyplot rectangle functions

These keywords are common to most rectangle functions, such as **axhspan**, **axvspan**, **bar**, **barh**, **broken_barh**

Keyword	Description
alpha	Opaqueness. 0 is transparent, 1 is opaque.
animated	Boolean value **True** or **False**.
antialiased	**True** or **False**. Alternative is **aa**
axes	An **Axes** instance.
capstyle	"butt", "round", or "projecting"
clip_box	A bounding box.
clip_on	Boolean value **True** or **False**.
clip_path	Clipping path. If used, may be a **Path**, **Transform**, or a **Patch**.
color	Color of line. Alternative is **c**.
contains	A callable function.
edgecolor	Alternative is **ec**. Color of edge of rectangle.
facecolor	Alternative is **fc**. Color of inside of rectangle.
figure	A Matplotlib **Figure** instance.
fill	Fill the rectangle: **True** or **False**.
hatch	Possible values are "\", "/", "|", "+", "o", "O", ".", "*"
joinstyle	"miter", "round", "bevel"
label	Any string label.
linestyle	Alternative is **ls**. "solid", "dashed", "dashdot, "dotted"
linewidth	Alternative is **lw**. Numerical value.
picker	Distance in points or pick function.
rasterized	Boolean value **True** or **False**.
transform	A **Transform** instance
url	A URL string.
visible	Line visibility. **True** or **False**.
zorder	Items with lower z order are drawn first.

Subplots

Subplots are used to display multiple plots in a single figure. The function **subplots** returns a figure instance and a tuple containing an array of axis objects. The general form is

```
fig, ax = subplots(nrows=1, ncols=1, sharex=False,
        sharey=False)
```

The returned value of **ax** is an array that contains the same number of rows as the value of **nrows**, and the same number of columns as the value of **ncols**. If either (or both) or **sharex** or **sharey** are set to **True** then the corresponding axes are shared. When an axis is shared, then only the bottom (x axis) or left (y axis) is annotated with tick marks.

The following code will plot the Airy Ai and Bi functions on two plots in a single figure, with the Ai function on the top row, and the Bi function on the bottom row.

```
 1  from scipy.special import *
 2  from matplotlib.pyplot import *
 3  import numpy as np
 4
 5  xvals=np.linspace(-15,3.0,200)
 6  airyvals=np.array([airy(x) for x in xvals])
 7  ai = (airyvals.T)[0]
 8  bi = (airyvals.T)[2]
 9
10  fig, (ax1 ax2) = subplots(nrows=2,ncols=1,sharex=True)
11
12  ax1.plot(xvals, ai, color="black")
13  ax1.set_ylim(-.75, .75)
14  ax1.set_title("Airy Ai Function")
15  ax1.axhline(0.0,color="black")
16  ax1.axvline(0.0,color="black")
17
18  ax2.plot(xvals, bi, color="black")
19  ax2.set_ylim(-.75, .75)
20  ax2.set_title("Airy Bi Function")
21  ax2.axhline(0.0,color="black")
22  ax2.axvline(0.0,color="black")
23  show()
```

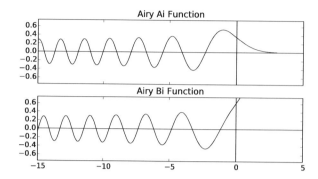

The function **airy(X)** used on line 6 (from **scipy.special**) returns a tuple with (Ai, Ai′, Bi,Bi′). We calculate all of these 4-tuples on line 6. To extract the Ai and Bi values only, we take the transpose of the matrix **airyvals**. This transpose has Ai in the first row, Ai′ in the second row, Bi the third row, and Bi′ in the fourth row.

The **axhline** and **axvline** functions were used on lines 15-16 and 21-21 to draw horizontal and vertical lines to represent the x and y axes. Observe in the figure how the x axis is shared by both plots.

To demonstrate the use of both rows and columns, we plot the first six Legendre polynomials $P_1(x)$ through $P_6(x)$ with the following code. The first three are plotted on the top row, and the second three are plotted in separate plots on the second row.

```
1    from scipy.special import *
2    from matplotlib.pyplot import *
3    import numpy as np
4
5    xvals=np.linspace(-1, 1, 200)
6
7    fig,AX = subplots(nrows=2,ncols=3,sharey=True,sharex=True)
8    i=1
9
10   legendre=np.array([list(lpn(6,x)[0]) for x in xvals]).T
11
12   for row in AX:
13       for ax in row:
14           yvals=legendre[i]
15           ax.plot(xvals,yvals, color="black")
16           ax.axhline(0.0, color="black")
17           ax.axvline(0.0, color="black")
18           ax.set_title("Legendre_P"+str(i))
19           i+=1
20
21   show()
```

The function **lpn(m,x)** in **scipy.special** returns two arrays which. The first array contains the values of $P_1(x), \ldots, P_m(x)$; the second array contains the derivatives at the same points. We are not interested in the derivatives, which is why we select the **[0]**'th element of the return value in line 10. When we evaluate **lpn(m,x)** at every value in our domain we get a 200 tuples of y values. We place these in an array and then take the transpose, so that the first element will have all the P_1 values, the second element all the P_2 values, etc.

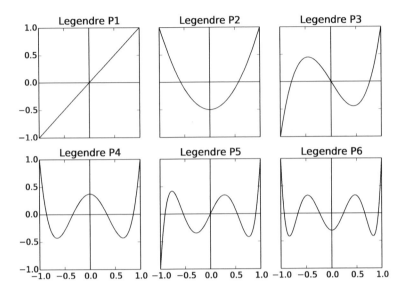

In this figurre we share both the x axes and the y axes by setting both the **sharex=True** and **sharey=TRUE** in the call to **subplots** on line 7 of the code. The call to **subplots** is a tuple **(fig, AX)**:

```
>>> fig, AX = subplots(nrows=2, ncols=3)
>>> AX
array([[<matplotlib.axes.AxesSubplot object at 0x7fc1dd6ea650>,
        <matplotlib.axes.AxesSubplot object at 0x7fc1de080390>,
        <matplotlib.axes.AxesSubplot object at 0x7fc1dd768ed0>],
       [<matplotlib.axes.AxesSubplot object at 0x7fc1d989be10>,
        <matplotlib.axes.AxesSubplot object at 0x7fc1d97cd750>,
        <matplotlib.axes.AxesSubplot object at 0x7fc1d974e410>]],
      dtype=object)
>>>
```

We assign values to the top row in the first iteration through the outer **for** loop, and to the bottom row in the second iteration through the outer **for** loop starting on line 12. The inner **for** loop starting on line 12 processes the columns left to right.

Bar Plots

Bar plots represent categorical data quantitatively as either horizontal or vertical bars. The data is broken down into a collection of categories, and the number of items in each categories is represented by a bar of a given length. The length of each bar is proportional to the number of items in the category. For example, the following dictionary gives the breakdown by declared major of students in the California State University System in the fall term of 2013.

```
 1  majors={
 2      "Agriculture":6887,
 3      "Architecture":2457,
 4      "Area\nStudies":373,
 5      "Biological\nSciences":25594,
 6      "Business&\nManagement":66525,
 7      "Communications":15347,
 8      "Education":26986,
 9      "Engineering":33045,
10      "Fine_&\nApplied_Arts":19275,
11      "Foreign\nLanguages":2290,
12      "Health":20460,
13      "HomeEconomics":5869,
14      "Information\nScience":12204,
15      "Interdisciplinary":16406,
16      "Letters":14757,
17      "Mathematics":4673,
18      "Physical\nScience":6797,
19      "Psychology":25979,
20      "Public\nAffairs":20668,
21      "Social\nSciences":33256,
22      "Undeclared":33103}
```

The data was given in alphabetical order, and we left it that way for easy reading. The newlines were added later because we are going to use the keys as labels on our plot. First, we will make a horizontal bar plot of the top seven declared majors, ordered by number of students. In the following, we convert the data into an array **xy** containing (*major, number*). Then we sort the data by major using **sorted**. Since **sorted** sorts from low to high, we use the **reverse** keyword, and sort by the second element in the tuple using the **key** and a **lambda** function that picks out the last item.

```
23  x=list(majors)
24  y=[majors[j] for j in x]
25  xy=zip(x,y)
26  xy=sorted(xy,key=lambda z:z[-1],reverse=True)
```

The seven most popular majors are the first tuples in the list **xy**. We now unzip them into the arrays **majors** and **numbers**

```
27  big=xy[:7]
28  majors,numbers=zip(*big)
```

Now we can show the plot. We plot the bars in the color **"burlywood"**, which is one
of the 140 standard colors, and is chosen because it appears frequently as an example
color in the official Pyplot documentation.

```
29  import numpy as np
30  from matplotlib.pyplot import *
31
32  yvals=np.arange(len(majors), 0, -1)   # put longest bar on top
33  title("Top_Declared_Majors_in_the_CSU,_2013")
34  barh(yvals, numbers, align="center", color="burlywood")
35  yticks(yvals, majors)
36  xticks(rotation="45")
37  show()
```

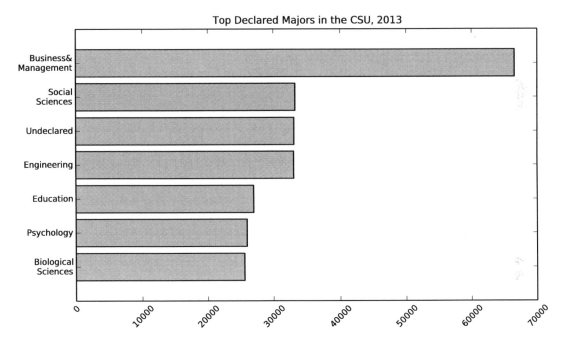

Here we repeat the plot as a vertical bar chart, using all of the data, rather than just
the top majors. Note that the html compliant colors must be specified in lower case.

```
38  majors,numbers=zip(*xy)
39  xvals=np.arange(len(majors))
40  axis([-1,len(majors), 0, 70000])
41  title("Top_Declared_Majors_in_the_CSU,_2013")
42  bar(xvals, numbers,  align="center", color="lightgreen")
43  xticks(xvals, majors, rotation="45")
44  show()
```

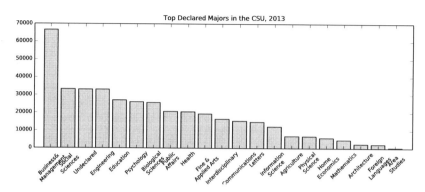

The parameters and keywords that can be used for bar graphs are summarized in table 22.11. Many bar parameters can also be configured according to the rectangle parameters as summarized in table 22.10.

Table 22.11. pyplot bar plots

`bar(left, height, width=0.8, bottom=None, **kwargs)` makes a barplot.
`hbar(bottom, width, height=0.8, left=None)` makes a horizontal barplot.

These functions return Matplotlib **rectangle** objects and most options for rectangles as given in table 22.10 can also be used.

Parameter	Description
`bottom`	Optional single number or array. y-coordinates of bar bottoms.
`align`	`"edge"` aligns left edge (or bottom edge for horizontal bars). `"center"` uses the values of `"left"` as the centers of the bars rather than the left edges.
`capsize=3`	Integer size in points of the caps of the optional error bars.
`color`	Optional single color or array of colors.
`ecolor`	Optional single color or array of colors to be used to display the optional error bars.
`edgecolor`	Optional single color or array of colors.
`error_kw`	Optional dictionary of keyword arguments to be passed to the **errorbar** method.
`height`	Sequence of numbers, the heights of the bars.
`left`	Sequence of numbers, the left sides of the bars.
`linewidth`	Optional thickness of bar edges.
`log`	If **True** use a logarithmic scale.
`orientation`	Direction of bars: `"vertical"` or `"horizontal"`
`xerr`	Optional single or array of numbers to use for horizontal error bars.
`width=8`	Single number or an array. Width of the bars.
`yerr`	Optional single or array of numbers to use for vertical error bars.

broken bar plots

Broken bar plots are like bar plots but the bars may have breaks in them. The bars can be either horizontal or vertical. For example, suppose you are the manager of a round-the-clock organization scheduling employee shifts. You want to make a plot showing when each employee is scheduled to work. Each horizontal bar represents one employee in the following example.

```
from matplotlib.pyplot import *
#
# draw each bar separately
broken_barh([(0,8), (24,8), (48,8)], (1,1), facecolor="r")
broken_barh([(8,8), (32,8), (56,8)], (2,1), facecolor="g")
broken_barh([(16,8),(40,8), (64,8)], (3,1), facecolor="y")
# x and y tick marks
yticks([1.5,2.5,3.5],["Curly", "Moe", "Larry"])
xticks([4,12,20,28,36,44,52,60,68],
   ["Mon_12-8", "Mon_8-4", "Mon_4-12", "Tue_12-8",
    "Tue_8-4", "Tue_4-12", "Wed_12-8", "Wed_8-4",
    "Wed_4-12"], rotation=45)
rc("font", size=9)      # set font size
axis([0,72,1,4])        # set axes
axes().set_aspect(3.5)  # set aspect ratio
show()
```

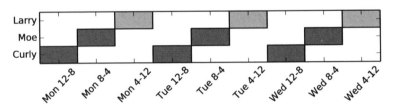

The usual options for bar plots shown in table 22.11 can be used in broken bar plots.

Table 22.12. Broken bar plots		
broken_barh(xrange, yrange, **kwargs)** returns a bar plot with gaps. The usual keyword arguments for rectangles (table 22.10) may be used.		
parameter	Description	
xrange	Sequence of (xmin, xwidth) pairs.	
yrange	sequence of (ymin, ywidth) pairs.	

Box Plots

Box plots display the spread of data for collections of samples. For each sample, a rectangle is drawn. The top of the rectangle falls at the third quartile (Q_3 or 75th percentile); the bottom of the rectangle falls at the first quartile (Q_1 or 25th percentile) (figure 22.1). A horizontal line is drawn across the rectangle at the sample median (50th percentile). **Whiskers** extend above and below each rectangle, showing the **extent** of the data. The whiskers do not necessarily show all the data points, as **outliers** are defined to be points that fall above $Q_3 + 1.5I$ or below $Q_1 - 1.5I$, where $I = Q_3 - Q_1$ is the **Interquartile Range, IQR**. Outliers, if any exist are plotted as lone symbols above or below the whiskers. Table 22.13 summarizes the parameters that can be used in `boxplot`. In the following example we generate ten random samples from a uniform distribution, each with 100 data points.

Figure 22.1: Plotting of each sample in a box and whisker plot.

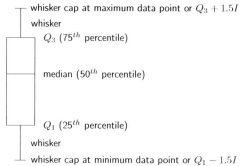

```
import numpy as np
from matplotlib.pyplot import *
dataset = np.random.random([100,10])
boxplot(dataset)
xticks(range(1,11), list("ABCDEFGHIJ"))
show()
```

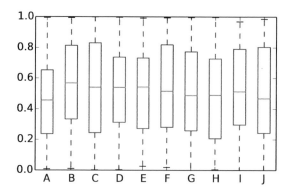

Table 22.13. `pyplot.boxplot` parameters

`boxplot(x,**kwargs)` makes a box and whisker plot. **x** is a sequence of vectors. Makes a box and whisker for each vector in **x**, with the box extending from Q1 to Q3, the whiskers extending further, and a horizontal line at the median.

Keyword[a]	Description
bootstrap	Integer or **None** (default). If specified, gives the number of times to bootstrap the median to determine 95% confindence intervals.
boxprops	Optional dictionary of plotting styles for boxes.
capprops	Optional dictionary of plotting styles for caps.
conf_intervals	Optional array of confidence intervals.
flierprops	Optional dictionary of plotting styles for outliers.
labels	Optional sequence of labels for the data.
meanline	If **True** and **showmeans** is also **True** then will render the means as a box-spanning line, if possible.
meanprops	Optional dictionary of plotting styles for means.
medianprops	Optional dictionary of plotting styles for medians.
notch	If **True**, the boxes will be notched.
positions	Optional sequence of box positions.
showbox	Normally **True**. If **False** will hide the box.
showfliers	Normally **True**. If **False** will hide outliers.
showmeans	Normally **False**. If **True**, will display the means in addition to the medians.
sym	String or symbol to use to plot outliers, or "" to not plot them. The default is "b+".
usermedians	Sequence of numbers or **None** default of user supplied values that override the medians computed by matplotlib.
vert	If **True** (default), boxes are vertical.
whis	Single number of sequence to determine the reach of whiskers beyond the first and third quartiles. Default is 1.5. Units are IQR (Inter-quartile range). 1.5 IQR means extend 1.5(Q3-Q1) beyond the box.
whiskerprops	Optional dictionary of plotting styles for whiskers.
widths	Optional number or sequence of widths for each box. Default = 0.5, based on distance between extreme positions.

[a]Unfortunately due to a bug in Matplotlib 1.4.1, the version used in Python 2.7.6, most of these keywords will either cause errors or be ignored. For a few of them some workarounds have been documented, but the errors were reported fixed in 1.4.2/2.7.8.

Contour Plots

Contour plots can be drawn with the **contour()**. If the values are stored in an array, then a simple call to the function with the array as a single argument is sufficient. Here is a short example with contour labels.

```
1  from matplotlib.pyplot import *
2  import numpy as np
3  from math import *
4  A = [[x + cos(.5*x*y) + cos(.5*y)*cos(.5*x)
5       for y in np.linspace(0,6,100)]
6       for x in np.linspace(0,6,100)]
7  axis("equal")
8  axis([0,100,0,100])
9  xticks([])
10 yticks([])
11 cp=contour(A, colors="k", levels=np.linspace(0,6,7))
12 clabel(cp, fontsize=9, fmt="%.f")
```

This produces the figure on the left. Replacing lines 11 and 12 as shown in lines 13 and 14 below produces the filled contour on the right.

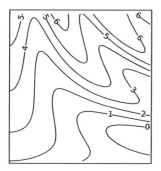
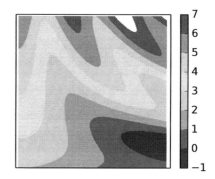

```
13 cp=contourf(A, levels=np.linspace(-1,7,9))
14 colorbar(cp)
```

The function **contourf()** works pretty much the same as **contour** except that it produces filled contours, so you need a color bar to read it. Parameters for **contour** are given in table 22.14. Details on contour labeling with **clabel** are given in table 22.15, and details on color bars can be found in table 22.17.

Table 22.14. Contour plots with `pyplot.contour()`

Keyword	Description
`alpha`	Blending value.
`antialiased`	Boolean value.
`cmap`	The color map used.
`colors`	Single color or array of colors.
`extend`	Contours to add to either end of range so that all data are included. Values are `"neither"`, `"both"`, `"min"`, `"max"`
`extent`	Optional outer pixel boundaries.
`hatches`	Optional cross hatches for filled contours.
`linestyles`	`None`, `"solid"`, `"dashed"`, `"dashdot"`, `"dotted"`
`linewidths`	`None`, a number, or a tuple.
`origin`	Optional location of origin.
`vmax`	Max to use to override default color scaling.
`vmin`	Min to use to override default color scaling.

Table 22.15. Contour Plot Labels with `clabel`

`clabel(CS)` labels a contour plot `CS`.

Keyword	Description
`colors`	Single color or array of colors.
`fmt`	Format string for the labels. Default is `"%1.3f"`
`fontsize`	Size in points or relative size.
`inline`	If `True` the underlying contour is not removed.
`inline_spacing`	Space in pixels between underlying contours (default = 5).
`manual`	If `True` labels can be placed by mouse click. Button 1: add a label Button 2: finished adding labels. Button 3: remove a label Can also be an iterable object of (x,y) tuples giving positions.
`rightside_up`	If `True` labels are rotated orthogonal to contours.

errorbar plots

Plots can be generated with vertical and/or horizontal error bars using **pyplot. errorbar**. It works in a manner similar to **pyplot.plot**. The x values must be in one array, and the corresponding y values in a second array of the same length.

To add error bars, use the keyword arguments **yerr** (for vertical error bars) or **xerr** (for horizontal error bars). If neither keyword is specified, no error bars will be drawn. If either parameter is set to a constant, the same value will be used for all points. Otherwise, each parameter should be passed as an array of the same length as the x and y values. Visual properties of the error bars such as colors and line widths can be set as summarized in table 22.16.

The following example uses Numpy's **random** module to produced a simulated set of errors to use for the lengths of the error bars, and then demonstrates the use of vertical error bars.

```python
import numpy as np
from matplotlib.pyplot import *
from math import *

# produce simulated x and y values:
xvals=np.linspace(0, 6,60) # simulated x values
yvals=[3*(x+2)/(2+(x+2)*cos(x+2)*cos(x+2)) for x in xvals]

errs=np.random.rand(60)      # produce simulated errors
rc("font", size=12)          # changes font size

# this line produces the plot with the error bars
errorbar(xvals, yvals, yerr=errs, c="k", ecolor="r")

show() # display current figure on the screen
```

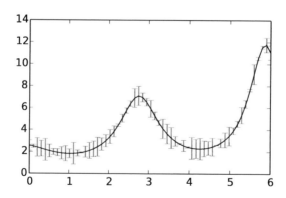

Table 22.16. `pyplot errorbar` plots

`errorbar(x,y, yerr=None, xerr=None, *kwargs)` generates a plot with error bars.

Where appropriate (e.g., in plotting lines), many of the keywords in table 22.7 may also be used.

Keyword	Description
`xerr`	Single number or array of horizontal error bars.
`yerr`	Single number or array of vertical error bars.
`alpha`	0 to 1 for transparent to opaque.
`axes`	An axes instance.
`barsabove`	If **True**, plots bars above plot symbols.
`capsize`	Single number, size of error bar caps in points.
`dash_capstyle`	**"butt"**, **"round"**, or **"projecting"**
`dash_joinstyle`	**"butt"**, **"round"**, or **"bevel"**
`data`	A two dimensional array of data for **x** and **y**
`dashes`	A sequence of on/off numbers, in points.
`ecolor`	Error bar color, or **None** to use the marker color.
`elinewidth`	Error bar line width, or **None** to use the line width.
`errorevery`	Positive integer to use for subsampling the error.
`figure`	A Matplotlib **Figure** instance.

`fillstyle`	How much of each marker to fill. Values are:
	  "full" **"left"** **"right"**
	  "bottom" **"top"** **"none"**

`fmt`	Symbol for points or **None** (only plot bars).
`label`	String to print.
`lolims`	Boolean, indicates a value only gives lower limits.
`marker`	Marker to use. Table 22.6
`markeredgecolor`	Alternative **mec**. Any color.
`markeredgewidth`	Alternative **mew**. Marker width in points.
`markerfacecolor`	Alternative **mfc**. Any color.
`markerfacecoloralt`	Alternative **mfcalt**. Any color.
`markersize`	Marker size in points. Alternative is **ms**
`picker`	Distance in points or pick function.
`pickradius`	Distance in points using in picking.
`solid_capstyle`	**"butt"**, **"round"**, or **"projecting"**
`solid_joinstyle`	**"miter"**, **"round"**, or **"bevel"**
`uplims`	Boolean, indicates a value only gives upper limits.
`xdata`	x-values, data array.
`xlolims`	Boolean, for an x value only gives lower limits.
`xuplims`	Boolean, for an x value only gives upper limits.
`ydata`	y-values, data array.

Color Bars

A color bar is a graduated bar showing the range of colors or gray levels used in a plot such as **imshow** or a contour plot. On can be generated with the **colorbar** function.

```
import numpy as np, matplotlib.cm as cm
from matplotlib.pyplot import *
A = np.random.rand(5,5)
imshow(A, interpolation="nearest", cmap=cm.Greys_r)
colorbar(ticks=(0,.25,.5,.75), shrink=.77)
xticks([])
yticks([])
show()
```

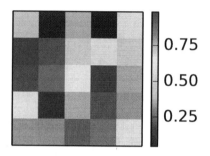

Table 22.17. `pyplot.colorbar` parameters

`colorbar(mappable=None, cax=None, ax=None, **kwarg)`

Keyword	Description
anchor	Anchor point. Default (0, 0.5) if vertical; (.5, 1) if horizontal.
aspect	Aspect ratio of bar (default = 20).
ax	**None** or parent axes.
cax	**None** or axes object to use.
drawedges	Boolean to draw edges of the bar.
format	Format string or **None** for the labels. Default `"%.3f"`
fraction	Default is 0.15; fraction of original axis to use for bar.
orientation	`"vertical"`, `"horizontal"`
pad	Fraction of original axis between color bar and new axis. Default is 0.05 if vertical, 0.15 if horizontal.
shrink	Fraction to shrink the color bar; default is 1.0
ticks	List of ticks or **None** for the bar.

event plots

<table>
<tr><td colspan="2">Table 22.18. <code>eventplot</code></td></tr>
<tr><td colspan="2">

<code>eventplot(events, *args, **kwargs)</code> plots a spike plot or sequence of parallel lines representing events. All of the lines in a single data series have the same length. Many of line related keywords listed in table 22.7 can also be used, where appropriate.

</td></tr>
</table>

Keyword	Description
axes	An **Axes** instance.
clim	A pair of numbers for image scaling.
colors	Single color or list of colors, one for each data series.
cmap	A color map.
linelengths	Single number of array. If array, lengths of each data series.
linewidths	Single number or array.
lineoffsets	Single number or array. If array, offset in dependent axis for each data series.
linestyles	Single value or array of typical **linestyle** values.
offset	Single number or array.
orientation	**"horizontal"** or **"vertical"**

To illustrate how **eventplot** works, consider the tube line departures from the Victoria Station underground during a four hour period on a typical Friday afternoon. These have been tabulated in four lists **g**, **h**, **j**, **u**, corresponding to four train lines G to Battersea and Sloan Square; H to Marble Arch and Nightsbridge; J to Westminster and Trafalger Square; and U to Pimlico, in minutes past noon. For example, **u**, which represents line U, has the fewest trains.[13]

```
>>> u
[15.0, 22.0, 45.0, 52.0, 75.0, 82.0, 105.0, 112.0, 135.0,
142.0, 165.0, 172.0, 195.0, 202.0, 225.0, 232.0, 255.0,
262.0, 285.0, 292.0]
```

Once we have the four lists set up (each one has a different length), we can make an event plot. We just have to decide what color we want each data series to be, and how much space each one takes up. By default, the first series will be plotted at $y = 0$, the second series at $y = 1$, and so on, and each one will have vertical lines of length 1. In the following, we shorten the lines to 0.75 to give a little space between them.

---

[13]You can view the current schedule for the next hour online at `http://www.tfl.gov.uk/bus/stop/HUBVIC/victoria-station/`

```
clrs=(["blue","red","green","magenta"])
eventplot([g,h,j,u], colors=clrs, linelengths=.75)
axis([0,300,-.5,3.5])
yticks([0,1,2,3],["(G)Battersea\nSloan_Square",
                  "(H)Marble_Arch\nNightsbridge",
                  "(J)Westminster\nTrafalger_Square",
                  "(U)Pimlico"])
show()
```

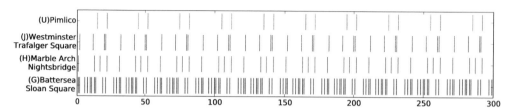

We can also plot all of the lines on a single axis, but then we need a color or different line style to tell them apart.

```
eventplot([g,h,j,u], colors=clrs, linelengths=.75, lineoffsets=4*[0],
          linestyles=["solid", "dashed", "dashdot", "dotted"])
axis([0,100,-.5,.5])
yticks([])
show()
```

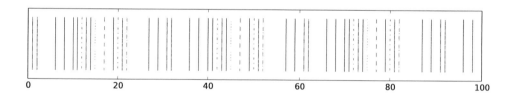

While in most other plotting functions, you can use the label option to label each series and then invoke **legend()** to print a legend of the bars, that particular connection is currently broken in Matplotlib. If you want to identify each spike in this format, you will have to build the legend yourself.

Histograms

In a **histogram** measurements are divided up equally into bins, and the number of items in each bin is plotted with a bar.[14] A histogram looks somewhat like a barplot with vertical bars, except that the bars in a histogram touch each other, while the bars in a bar plot do not. The reason for this is that if the data is normalized by dividing the height of each bar by the total number of measurements, and the number of measurements is very, very large, then the histogram should resemble the probability density function for the distribution that the data was sampled from.

In the following example a histogram is generated from a collection of simulated test data, with grades ranging between 0 and 100. The data is collected into 10 bins and then plotted on the histogram.

```
import numpy as np
from matplotlib.pyplot import *

scores=[
13, 26, 49, 52, 57, 59, 59, 65, 65, 66, 68, 70, 73, 74, 75,
76, 77, 77, 77, 78, 78, 81, 82, 83, 83, 87, 88, 90, 91, 91,
92, 92, 93, 95, 95, 95, 100]

hist(scores, 10, range=(0,100), facecolor="salmon",
     align="mid")
xlabel("Score")
ylabel("Number_of_Students")
title("Grade_Distribution")
fig=gcf()
axes().set_aspect(2)
fig.set_size_inches(8,3)
savefig("a-histogram.pdf", dpi=600)
```

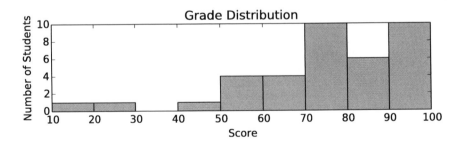

---

[14]More detail on histograms is given at http://matplotlib.org/api/pyplot_api.html?highlight=pyplot.hist#matplotlib.pyplot.hist

Pie Charts

Pie charts illustrate how a data set is broken down into parts.[15] The following example illustrates how full time equivalent student population was distributed among the 23 California State University campuses in the fall term of 2013.

```
from matplotlib.pyplot import *
# data from http://www.calstate.edu/AS/stats.shtml
CampusNames=["Bakersfield", "Channel_Islands", "Chico",
  "Dominguez_Hills", "East_Bay", "Fresno", "Fullerton",
  "Humboldt", "Long_Beach", "Los_Angeles", "Maritime",
  "Monterey_Bay", "Northridge", "Pomona", "Sacramento",
  "San_Bernardino", "San_Diego", "San_Francisco", "San_Jose",
  "San_Luis_Obispo", "San_Marcos", "Sonoma", "Stanislaus"]
CampusFTE=[7550.7, 4476.7, 15120, 10377.6,
          13395.2, 19441.3, 29892.5, 7559.7,
          28806.5, 18219.9, 1269.4, 5315.1,
          29893.6, 18824.6, 23062.1, 15672,
          29091.1, 24332.2, 24548.5,
          18259.9, 8937.6, 7990.8, 7246]
pie(CampusFTE, explode=23*[.25], labels=CampusNames)
axis("equal")
show()
```

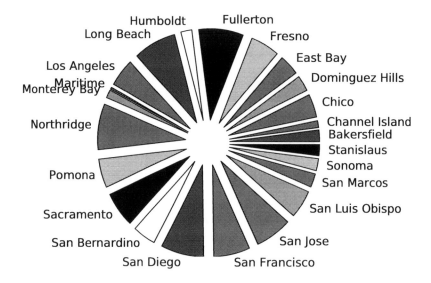

---

[15]For more details see http://matplotlib.org/api/pyplot_api.html?highlight=pyplot. pie#matplotlib.pyplot.pie

adding legends to plots

Legends can be easily added to your plots. You just have to add a label to each plot curve and then invoke the function **legend**. See pages 168 for an example.

Table 22.19. `pyplot.legend` parameters[a]

`pyplot.legend(*args, **kwargs)`

Keyword	Description
loc	String, integer code, or pair of numbers describing the location of the legend. Codes and strings are:

Code	String
0	"best"
1	"upper right"
2	"upper left"
3	"lower left"
4	"lower right"
5	"right"
6	"center left"
7	"center right"
8	"lower center"
9	"upper center"
10	"center"

Keyword	Description
borderpad	Additional white space to add inside the legend. Measured in font-size units.
columnspacing	Spacing between columns.
fontsize	An integer or a string as in **"small"**, **"medium"**, **"large"**, **"x-large"**, **"xx-large"**, **"x-small"**, **"xx-small"**
framealpha	Transparency of the frame.
frameon	Set to **False** to turn off the box around the legend.
labelspace	Vertical spacing between legend entries in font-size units.
markerscale	Relative size of markers in legend wrt markers in figure.
ncol	Number of columns (default 1)
numpoints	Number of markers to show when a marker used on line.
prop	A dictionary of font properties
scatterpoints	Number of markers to show if scatter plot.
scatteryoffset	Vertical offset for marker points in legend.
shadow	Turn on a shadow.
title	Title of the legend. Default is no title.

[a]For a complete list of parameters and keywords and more details see `http://matplotlib.org/api/pyplot_api.html#matplotlib.pyplot.legend`

Colors

Colors can be specified as hexadecimal 32 bit RGB descriptors, e.g., **"#32AAEA"**; as RGB tuple **(.7, .3, .8)**, where each value of the RGB is in the range $[0, 1]$; or by name for known named colors. A collection of eight basic colors also can be referenced by one-character short names (table 22.20). Shades of gray can be specified as a string representing a float between zero and 1, as in **"0.77"**.

Table 22.20. Pyplot basic built in color codes			
Code	Name	Code	Name
"b"	"blue"	"g"	"green"
"r"	"red"	"c"	"cyan"
"m"	"magenta"	"y"	"yellow"
"k"	"black"	"w"	"white"

In python you can also refer to a large number of colors by their standard html color name in the W3C extended color set, as summarized in table 22.21. The way each color looks will vary with your hardware. Therefore it is best to preview it on the system that you will be displaying the figures on, or to print on the printer that you will be using for your final copy. The following code can be used to build a table of named colors on your system. See figure 22.6. You can use it to either display the colors on your screen or save them to a graphics file – by changing the pdf extension in the **savefig** on line 42, for example, to any other file type supported by your system, such as **.png**.

```
 1  from matplotlib.pyplot import *
 2  import matplotlib.patches as patches
 3  import matplotlib.colors as colors
 4  #
 5  # get a list of the colors in alphabetical order
 6  #
 7  allcolors=list(colors.cnames)
 8  allcolors.sort()
 9  #
10  # ncolors = 147
11  #
12  ncolors = len(allcolors)
13  #
14  rows = ncolors/3
15  i=0
16  fig,ax=subplots(1,1)
17  #
18  # There are 147 colors, which is divisible by 3
19  # so we don't have to worry about the remainder
20  #
21  # for each named color, draw a small rectangle
22  # and put its name in the center
23  #
```

```
24   for c in allcolors:
25       y = rows- (i % rows) - 1
26       x = i / rows
27       ax.add_patch(patches.Rectangle((x,y), 1, 1, color=c))
28       annotate(c, xy=(x+.5,y+.5), ha="center", va="center",
29       fontsize=8)
30       i+=1
31
32   # turn off the ticks
33
34   xticks([])
35   yticks([])
36   axis([0,3,0,rows])
37
38   # save to a pdf file
39
40   tight_layout()
41   fig.set_size_inches(6,9)
42   fig.savefig("html-named-colors.pdf",dpi=300)
43
44   # display on the screen
45
46   show()
```

Specific color maps can be used in most two-dimensional plots such as **contourf** and **imshow** using the **cmap** keyword.[16] There are four different types of color maps that are built into python: sequential, diverging, qualitative, and miscellaneous. In a **sequential color map**, the colors vary continuously between two colors (figure 22.3). This type of color mapping is most frequently used to display scientific data, because the colors can used to illustrate clear gradations in quantitative values. In a **diverging color map**, a light color is used to represent the median value and two contrasting colors are used to represent extreme values (figure 22.2). Color gradation moves smoothly from each extreme to the median, which appears like a bright light appearing in the middle of the map separating the two extremes. These maps are useful for illustrating data that have a clear median and specific extremes that need to be highlighted. In a **qualitative color map**, specific combinations of colors are used and the transitions may appear to be either gradual or quite rapid, depended on the choice of colors (figure 22.4). These may be useful for illustrating data that contain a discrete collection of values. A **miscellaneous color map** is a color map that does not fit in to one of the above categories (figure 22.5).[17]

The following code defines the function **plotColorMap()** which can be used to display all of the color maps on your hardware.

---

[16]See http://matplotlib.org/examples/color/colormaps_reference.html for complete details.

[17]Additional advice on chooosing a proper color map for your data is given in the user's guide at http://matplotlib.org/1.4.1/users/colormaps.html

```
1    import numpy as np
2    from matplotlib.pyplot import *
3    cmaps = ['Blues', 'BuGn', 'BuPu', 'GnBu', 'Greens', 'Greys',
4             'Oranges', 'OrRd','PuBu','PuBuGn','PuRd','Purples',
5             'RdPu','Reds', 'YlGn', 'YlGnBu', 'YlOrBr', 'YlOrRd',
6             'afmhot', 'autumn', 'bone', 'cool', 'copper',
7             'gist_heat',  'gray', 'hot', 'pink', 'spring',
8             'summer','winter','BrBG', 'bwr', 'coolwarm','PiYG',
9             'PRGn', 'PuOr', 'RdBu', 'RdGy', 'RdYlBu', 'RdYlGn',
10            'Spectral', 'seismic','Accent', 'Dark2', 'Paired',
11            'Pastel1','Pastel2', 'Set1', 'Set2', 'Set3',
12            'gist_earth','terrain','ocean','gist_stern','brg',
13            'CMRmap', 'cubehelix','gnuplot', 'gnuplot2',
14            'gist_ncar','nipy_spectral', 'jet', 'rainbow',
15            'gist_rainbow', 'hsv','flag', 'prism']
16   gradient = np.linspace(0, 1, 256)
17   gradient = np.vstack((gradient, gradient))
18
19   def plotColorMap():
20       fig, axes = subplots(nrows=len(cmaps))
21       fig.subplots_adjust(top=0.95, bottom=0.01,
22                           left=0.2, right=0.99)
23
24       for ax, name in zip(axes, cmaps):
25           ax.imshow(gradient, aspect='auto',
26               cmap=get_cmap(name))
27           pos = list(ax.get_position().bounds)
28           x = pos[0] - 0.01
29           y = pos[1] + pos[3]/2.
30           fig.text(x, y,  name, va='center', ha='right',
31                   fontsize=10)
32       for ax in axes:
33           ax.set_axis_off()
34
35       show()
36
37   plotColorMap()
```

Table 22.21. W3C Extended Color Set (1 of 2)

Color Name	Hex RGB	Decimal RGB	Color Name	Hex RGB	Decimal RGB
aliceblue	#f0f8ff	240,248,255	ivory	#fffff0	255,255,240
antiquewhite	#faebd7	250,235,215	khaki	#f0e68c	240,230,140
aqua	#00ffff	0,255,255	lavender	#e6e6fa	230,230,250
aquamarine	#7fffd4	127,255,212	lavenderblush	#fff0f5	255,240,245
azure	#f0ffff	240,255,255	lawngreen	#7cfc00	124,252,0
beige	#f5f5dc	245,245,220	lemonchiffon	#fffacd	255,250,205
bisque	#ffe4c4	255,228,196	lightblue	#add8e6	173,216,230
black	#000000	0,0,0	lightcoral	#f08080	240,128,128
blanchedalmond	#ffebcd	255,235,205	lightcyan	#e0ffff	224,255,255
blue	#0000ff	0,0,255	lightgoldenrodyellow		
blueviolet	#8a2be2	138,43,226		#fafad2	250,250,210
brown	#a52a2a	165,42,42	lightgray	#d3d3d3	211,211,211
burlywood	#deb887	222,184,135	lightgreen	#90ee90	144,238,144
cadetblue	#5f9ea0	95,158,160	lightgrey	#d3d3d3	211,211,211
chartreuse	#7fff00	127,255,0	lightpink	#ffb6c1	255,182,193
chocolate	#d2691e	210,105,30	lightsalmon	#ffa07a	255,160,122
coral	#ff7f50	255,127,80	lightseagreen	#20b2aa	32,178,170
cornflowerblue	#6495ed	100,149,237	lightskyblue	#87cefa	135,206,250
cornsilk	#fff8dc	255,248,220	lightslategray	#778899	119,136,153
crimson	#dc143c	220,20,60	lightslategrey	#778899	119,136,153
cyan	#00ffff	0,255,255	lightsteelblue	#b0c4de	176,196,222
darkblue	#00008b	0,0,139	lightyellow	#ffffe0	255,255,224
darkcyan	#008b8b	0,139,139	lime	#00ff00	0,255,0
darkgoldenrod	#b8860b	184,134,11	limegreen	#32cd32	50,205,50
darkgray	#a9a9a9	169,169,169	linen	#faf0e6	250,240,230
darkgreen	#006400	0,100,0	magenta	#ff00ff	255,0,255
darkgrey	#a9a9a9	169,169,169	maroon	#800000	128,0,0
darkkhaki	#bdb76b	189,183,107	mediumaquamarine	#66cdaa	102,205,170
darkmagenta	#8b008b	139,0,139	mediumblue	#0000cd	0,0,205
darkolivegreen	#556b2f	85,107,47	mediumorchid	#ba55d3	186,85,211
darkorange	#ff8c00	255,140,0	mediumpurple	#9370db	147,112,219
darkorchid	#9932cc	153,50,204	mediumseagreen	#3cb371	60,179,113
darkred	#8b0000	139,0,0	mediumslateblue	#7b68ee	123,104,238
darksalmon	#e9967a	233,150,122	mediumspringgreen		
darkseagreen	#8fbc8f	143,188,143		#00fa9a	0,250,154
darkslateblue	#483d8b	72,61,139	mediumturquoise	#48d1cc	72,209,204
darkslategray	#2f4f4f	47,79,79	mediumvioletred	#c71585	199,21,133
darkslategrey	#2f4f4f	47,79,79	midnightblue	#191970	25,25,112
darkturquoise	#00ced1	0,206,209	mintcream	#f5fffa	245,255,250
darkviolet	#9400d3	148,0,211	mistyrose	#ffe4e1	255,228,225
deeppink	#ff1493	255,20,147	moccasin	#ffe4b5	255,228,181
deepskyblue	#00bfff	0,191,255	navajowhite	#ffdead	255,222,173
dimgray	#696969	105,105,105	navy	#000080	0,0,128
dimgrey	#696969	105,105,105	oldlace	#fdf5e6	253,245,230
dodgerblue	#1e90ff	30,144,255	olive	#808000	128,128,0
firebrick	#b22222	178,34,34	olivedrab	#6b8e23	107,142,35
floralwhite	#fffaf0	255,250,240	orange	#ffa500	255,165,0
forestgreen	#228b22	34,139,34	orangered	#ff4500	255,69,0
fuchsia	#ff00ff	255,0,255	orchid	#da70d6	218,112,214
gainsboro	#dcdcdc	220,220,220	palegoldenrod	#eee8aa	238,232,170
ghostwhite	#f8f8ff	248,248,255	palegreen	#98fb98	152,251,152
gold	#ffd700	255,215,0	paleturquoise	#afeeee	175,238,238
goldenrod	#daa520	218,165,32	palevioletred	#db7093	219,112,147
gray	#808080	128,128,128	papayawhip	#ffefd5	255,239,213
green	#008000	0,128,0	peachpuff	#ffdab9	255,218,185
greenyellow	#adff2f	173,255,47	peru	#cd853f	205,133,63
grey	#808080	128,128,128	pink	#ffc0cb	255,192,203
honeydew	#f0fff0	240,255,240	plum	#dda0dd	221,160,221
hotpink	#ff69b4	255,105,180	powderblue	#b0e0e6	176,224,230
indianred	#cd5c5c	205,92,92	purple	#800080	128,0,128
indigo	#4b0082	75,0,130	red	#ff0000	255,0,0

Figure 22.2: Diverging color maps

Table 22.22. W3C Extended Color Set (2 of 2)

Color Name	Hex RGB	Decimal RGB	Color Name	Hex RGB	Decimal RGB
rosybrown	#bc8f8f	188,143,143	springgreen	#00ff7f	0,255,127
royalblue	#4169e1	65,105,225	steelblue	#4682b4	70,130,180
saddlebrown	#8b4513	139,69,19	tan	#d2b48c	210,180,140
salmon	#fa8072	250,128,114	teal	#008080	0,128,128
sandybrown	#f4a460	244,164,96	thistle	#d8bfd8	216,191,216
seagreen	#2e8b57	46,139,87	tomato	#ff6347	255,99,71
seashell	#fff5ee	255,245,238	turquoise	#40e0d0	64,224,208
sienna	#a0522d	160,82,45	violet	#ee82ee	238,130,238
silver	#c0c0c0	192,192,192	wheat	#f5deb3	245,222,179
skyblue	#87ceeb	135,206,235	white	#ffffff	255,255,255
slateblue	#6a5acd	106,90,205	whitesmoke	#f5f5f5	245,245,245
slategray	#708090	112,128,144	yellow	#ffff00	255,255,0
slategrey	#708090	112,128,144	yellowgreen	#9acd32	154,205,50
snow	#fffafa	255,250,250			

Figure 22.3: Sequential color maps

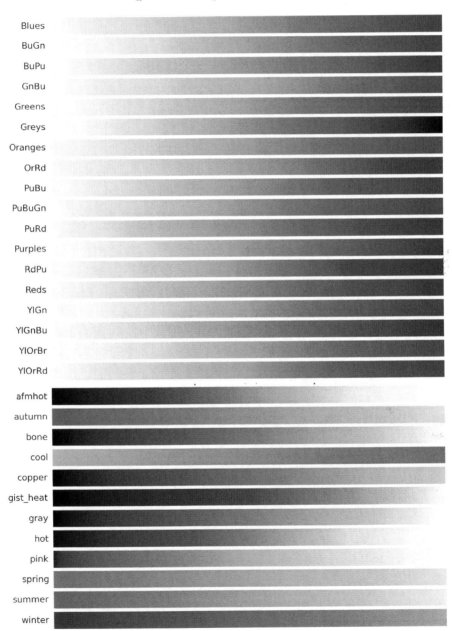

Figure 22.4: Qualitative color maps

Figure 22.5: Miscellaneous color maps

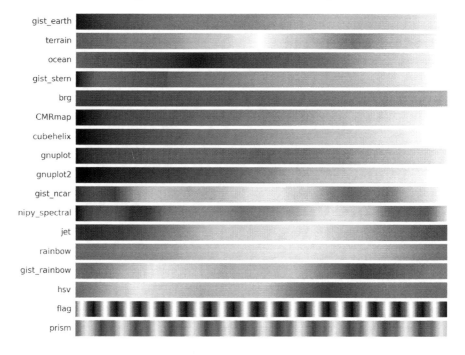

Figure 22.6: Named html colors that may be used in Python.

aliceblue	gainsboro	mistyrose
antiquewhite	ghostwhite	moccasin
aqua	gold	navajowhite
aquamarine	goldenrod	navy
azure	gray	oldlace
beige	green	olive
bisque	greenyellow	olivedrab
	grey	orange
blanchedalmond	honeydew	orangered
blue	hotpink	orchid
blueviolet	indianred	palegoldenrod
brown	indigo	palegreen
burlywood	ivory	paleturquoise
cadetblue	khaki	palevioletred
chartreuse	lavender	papayawhip
chocolate	lavenderblush	peachpuff
coral	lawngreen	peru
cornflowerblue	lemonchiffon	pink
cornsilk	lightblue	plum
crimson	lightcoral	powderblue
cyan	lightcyan	purple
darkblue	lightgoldenrodyellow	red
darkcyan	lightgray	rosybrown
darkgoldenrod	lightgreen	royalblue
darkgray	lightgrey	saddlebrown
darkgreen	lightpink	salmon
darkgrey	lightsalmon	sandybrown
darkkhaki	lightseagreen	seagreen
darkmagenta	lightskyblue	seashell
darkolivegreen	lightslategray	sienna
darkorange	lightslategrey	silver
darkorchid	lightsteelblue	skyblue
darkred	lightyellow	slateblue
darksalmon	lime	slategray
darkseagreen	limegreen	slategrey
darkslateblue	linen	snow
darkslategray	magenta	springgreen
darkslategrey	maroon	steelblue
darkturquoise	mediumaquamarine	tan
darkviolet	mediumblue	teal
deeppink	mediumorchid	thistle
deepskyblue	mediumpurple	tomato
dimgray	mediumseagreen	turquoise
dimgrey	mediumslateblue	violet
dodgerblue	mediumspringgreen	wheat
firebrick	mediumturquoise	white
floralwhite	mediumvioletred	whitesmoke
forestgreen	midnightblue	yellow
fuchsia	mintcream	yellowgreen

Exercises

1. Use Python to plot the functions $y = \sin x$ and $y = \cos x$ on $(-2\pi, 2\pi)$ on a single plot.

2. Use Python to plot the Bessel functions $J_0(x)$, $J_1(x)$, $J_2(x)$ on a single figure (same axes) in different colors (or different line styles), incorporating a legend. Scale the figure so that the the the x axis ranges from 0 to 20 and the y axis ranges from -1 to 1.1. Label the x and y axes as "x" and "y", and label the plot "Bessel Functions." You may use the functions **numpy.linspace** and **scipy.special.jn**.

3. Write a python function **plotme(f, a, b)** that takes as input a function that you can calculate analytically (via a python function call) and returns a plot of the function on the interval (a, b), in the following manner:

    (a) Use **np.linspace** to generate a table of 500 equally spaced x values in (a, b).

    (b) Use a function call to the argument **f** to get 500 y values.

    (c) Calculate the y' and y'' values using divided differences (see exercises 6 and 7 of chapter 18).

    (d) Return a **pyplot.axis** instance so that further modifications of the plot can be made outside the function **plotme**

    (e) Verify with the following functions:

    i. $f(x) = 4x^3 - 3x^2 + 2$ on $[0, 1]$
    ii. $f(x) = \cos x$ on $[0, 2\pi]$

4. The **Fourier Trigonometric Series** of an integrable function $f(x)$ on $(0, P)$ is written as

$$f(x) \sim \frac{a_0}{2} + \sum_{k=1}^{n}\left[a_k \cos\left(\frac{2\pi kx}{P}\right) + b_k \sin\left(\frac{2\pi kx}{P}\right)\right]$$

where a_k and b_k are given by the formulas in chapter 18 exercise 10. Write a Python function **FourierSeries(f, P, x)** that returns the values of the Fourier Series of the function **f(x)** at the point x. Plot the Fourier Series of each of the following functions using $P = 1$, but calculate the series on the interval $(-2P, 2P)$. Repeat each plot using $n = 5, 10, 25, 100$.

    (a) $f(x) = 1 - x$

    (b) $f(x) = \begin{cases} 1, & \text{if } x < P/2 \\ 0, & \text{if } x \geq P/2 \end{cases}$

    (c) $f(x) = x^2$

What do you observe as n becomes larger?

5. The central limit theorem says that if N samples of size p are taken from any random distribution with mean μ and standard deviation σ, then the distribution of the means $\bar{x}_1, \bar{x}_2, \ldots$ of the samples will approach a normal distribution with mean μ and standard deviation $s(p) = \sigma/\sqrt{p}$. In this exercise you will demonstrate the central limit theorem.

    (a) Using **np.random.rand** to generate 1,000,000 random numbers uniformly distributed on $(a, b) = (0,1)$. Calculate their mean $\bar{x}$ and standard deviation s using **np.mean** and **np.std**. Compare with the theoretical values of $\mu = \frac{1}{2}(b - a)$ and $\sigma = \frac{1}{\sqrt{12}}(b - a)$. Plot a histogram of the data.

    (b) Write a function **samples(p,N)** that will:

        i. Generate N lists of random numbers, each list consisting of p random numbers in the interval $(0, 1)$.

        ii. Calculate the mean x_i of each sample, $i = 1, 2, ..., N$

        iii. Plot a histogram of the means (the list of length N different $\bar{x}_i$ values $\bar{x}_1, \bar{x}_2, \ldots$), with x axis the entire interval $(0,1)$ and labeled in some way with the size of the sample

        iv. Calculates the standard deviation $s(p)$ of the means $\bar{x}_1, \bar{x}_2, \ldots$

        v. Returns the value of the standard deviation.

    (c) Using the function your wrote in part(b), display the histograms for sample sizes p=2, 3, 5, 7, 10, 20, 30,50, 100. There should be 9 histograms. Use $N = 10,000$.

    (d) Using the output of the function from part(b) draw a scatter plot of the standard deviations $s_1, s_2, s_3, \ldots$, of the samples as a function of sample size. On the same figure, draw a line plot of the predicted values using $s(p) = \sigma/\sqrt{p}$

Chapter 23

Input and Output

File input and output

File input or output is a three-step process:(1) open the file; (2) process the file; and (3) close the file.

To open a file you use the open statement. To open a file for **reading**, you use either

```
f=open("filename.txt")
```

or

```
f=open("filename.txt","r")
```

If you are going to write to the file, by adding data at the end of an existing file, you open in **append mode**:

```
f=open("filename.txt","a")
```

If you plan on creating a new file, even if the file already exists, open it in **write mode**,

```
f=open("filename.txt","w")
```

Each line is called a **record**. Records are separated by a **newline** character, which is different on each operating system. By default, Python will translate the newline character to the current operating system you are working on so that this process should be transparent to you. You can change or modify this translation with additional options when you open the file. More details are given in the Python library reference.[1].

When you read a text file, you have the option of reading it one line at a time, or reading in the entire file all at once. You can read it in one line at a time with a loop, for example, using the file variable as an iterator. The following will read the contents of a file into a list **data**.

```
f = open("filename.txt","r")
data=[]
for line in f:
  data.append(line)
f.close()
```

The following code is completely equivalent.

---

[1]See https://docs.python.org/2/library/functions.html#open

```
f = open("filename.txt","r")
data=f.readlines()
f.close()
```

When you read your data file this way it is input as a lists of strings. This means you may need to strip and convert the data to some other format. For example, if the file contains three comma-separated numerical values you can process it line by line with

```
results=[]
for line in data:
    nextline = line.strip().split(",")
    x, y, z = map(float, nextline)
    results.append([x,y,z])
```

This will fail miserably if there are either a variable number of cells in each row (common in many spread sheets), or if some cells are left blank. To fix this,

```
results=[]
for line in data:
    nextline=[]
    cells = line.strip().split(",")   # split data by commas
    for cell in cells:
        try:                          # convert to float
            value=float(cell.strip())
        except:    # if it doesn't work, use the original
            value=cell
        nextline.append(value)
    results.append(nextline)
```

When you write to a file you need to remember to include the newline character at the end of each line, as Python will not do this automatically for you. The newline character in Python is \n.

```
x=["Tom","Dick","Harry"]
f=open("tdh.txt","w")
f.write("\n".join(x))
f.close()
```

This creates a new file with three lines in it.

Command line parameters

When you execute a program from the command line, as in

```
$ python myprogram.py
```

you can also pass in parameters. For example, you could write a program that calculates the square root of a sequence of numbers by passing them in the command line:

```
$ python squareroots.py 5 15 23
```

You would like the program to return to you, in sequence, the square roots of 5, 15, and 23. The variable **sys.argv** will give you the contents of the command line, starting with the name of your program. If all your program contains is this:

```
import sys
print sys.argv
```

Then the command line dialogue will look like this:

```
$ python squareroots.py 5 15 23
['squareroots.py', '5', '15', '23']
```

This makes the square root program look like this:

```
import sys
queries = sys.argv
for x in queries[1:]:
    print float(x)**.5,
```

If there are no queries, then the **for** loop is skipped.

```
$ python squareroots.py 5 15 23
2.2360679775 3.87298334621 4.79583152331
```

Note that the data read from the command line is a string, so it has to be converted to a floating point number before any numerical computation can be performed on it.

The **with** Statement

The with statement is used to wrap the execution of a block with methods defined by a context manager. Context managers handle the allocation and release of resources. For example:

```
with file("stuff.txt","w") as f:
    print >>f, "Hello,_World!"
```

This will create a file called **stuff.txt** in the current working directory, open the file, write the string **"Hello,_World!"** to the file, and then close the file.

The **with** may be used in conjunction with the **try** for error checking:

```
try:
    with open("datafile.txt", "r") as f:
        data = f.readlines()
        print data
except IOError:
    print "Unable_to_read_data_file."
```

The **with** gives you better error handling – especially for file operations, since it always remembers to close files for you, even if you forget to.

Exercises

1. Type or copy the following two columns of data into a file, exactly as shown (including the commas):

```
1,0.9984489205
2,0.9752788428
3,0.8769402712
4,0.6284264418
5,0.1772490897
6,-0.4210076698
7,-0.9162875775
8,-0.9116652003
9,-0.1990087588
10,0.7565584253
11,0.8973685995
12,-0.1666463731
13,-0.9999420786
14,-0.0774674983
15,0.9994582237
```

Write a function **readxy(filename)** that will (a) open the file; (b) read the data and convert it into two arrays of **float**'s (one for each column); (c) close the file; and (d) return a tuple **(x,y)** that contains each data array. You may want to use the **readlines()**, **strip()**, and **split()** functions.

2. Write a command line program **Degrees** that will convert a temperature from both Celsius to Farenheit, if the command is like this:

> $ **Degrees 37 C**

and from Farenheit to Celsius if the command is like this:

> $ **Degrees 72 F**

The program should print an error message indicating the correct format and then terminate if invalid input is detected.

Chapter 24

Dictionaries

A **mapping data type** is a like a phone directory. It is a collection of values (like phone numbers) that are indexed by keys (like names). The mapping data type in Python is called a **dictionary**. You look things up, add them, and remove them by **key** rather than by index.

Suppose we have short list of college mascots:

College	Mascot
CSUN	Matty Matador
Florida	Gators
Irvine	Anteater
Maryland	Terrapin
MIT	Beaver
Purdue	Purdue Pete
UCLA	Bruins
USC	Tommy Trojan

A Python dictionary **mascots** for this data is defined as follows:

```
1   mascots={'CSUN'      : 'Matty_Matador',
2            'Florida'   : 'Gators' ,
3            'Irvine'    : 'Anteater',
4            'Maryland'  : 'Terrapin' ,
5            'MIT'       : 'Beaver' ,
6            'Purdue'    : 'Purdue_Pete',
7            'UCLA'      : 'Bruins',
8            'USC'       : 'Tommy_Trojan'}
```

Because the contents of the dictionary are defined within curly braces the indentation and white space do not matter. You could type the whole thing on a single line with no blank spaces at all; the following is also perfectly valid:

```
9    mascots={'CSUN':'Matty_Matador','Florida':'Gators',
10    'Irvine':'Anteater','Maryland':'Terrapin',
11    'MIT':'Beaver','Purdue':'Purdue_Pete',
12    'UCLA':'Bruins','USC':'Tommy_Trojan'}
```

Standard practice (for code readability) is to line things up into columns like the code in lines 1-8 and not the code in lines 9-12. To find the mascot for, say MIT, type

```
print mascots['MIT']
'Beaver'
```

211

If you look for **"Caltech"**, wich is not listed, an error will occur. For example,

```
print mascots["Caltech"]
Traceback (most recent call last):
File "<stdin>", line 1, in <module>
KeyError: 'Caltech'
```

You could fix this with a ternary operator, an if test, or a **try** /**except** construction; see chapter 27.

```
s=(mascots["Caltech"] if "Caltech" in mascots else "not␣listed")
```

Finding the school whose mascot is a Beaver is somewhat more complicated. First you have to find out if **Beaver** is even in the dictionary. The method **x.values()** returns a list of all the values in the dictionary **x**, that is everything in column 2 of the table.

```
1  if "Beaver" in mascots.values():
2      i=mascots.values().index("Beaver")
3      print mascots.keys()[i]
4  else:
5      print "not␣listed"
```

On line 1, we test to see if there is an entry with value **"Beaver"**. If the entry exists, we determine the integer index of that entry and save it as **i** on line 2, and then print the key value on line 3. The key value is the corresponding school in the **key:value** pair **"MIT"**:**"Beaver"** in **mascots**.

Table 24.1. Dictionary Operations

Operation	Description
`len(d)`	Returns the length of the dictionary.
`d[key]`	Returns the entry with entry with key **key**.
`d[key]=value`	Adds a new entry, or updates existing entry.
`del d[key]`	Delete an element from **d** by **key**.
`key in d`	Returns **True** if **key** is in list of keys of **d**.
`d.clear()`	Deletes everything from a dictionary.
`d.copy()`	Copies a dictionary.
`d.fromkeys(s, value)`	Creates a new dictionary. All the keys are taken from the sequence **s**. All of the entries are set equal to **value**. If **value** is not specified, **None** is used.
`d.get(key)`	Returns the dictionary entry associated with **key**. Same as **d[key]**.
`d.has_key(key)`	Returns **True** if **key** is a key in **d**.
`d.items()`	Returns a list of **(key, value)** pairs in **d**.
`d.keys()`	Returns a list of all the keys in **d**.
`d.pop(key)`	Returns **d[key]** and removes it from **d**.
`d.popitem()`	Returns a random **(key, value)** pair and removes it from **d**.
`d.values()`	Returns a list of all the values in **d**.

Chapter 25

Recursion

A **recursive function** is a function that calls itself. Python allows recursion, which makes some types of software implementations very elegant.

You've probably seen recursive mathematics lots of times without even thinking twice about it.

A classic example is the definition of the Fibonacci numbers:

$$F_1 = 0 \tag{25.1}$$
$$F_2 = 1 \tag{25.2}$$
$$F_n = F_{n-1} + F_{n-2} \text{ for integers } n > 1 \tag{25.3}$$

The *mathematical function* F_n is a recursive function definition because it depends on F_{n-1} and F_{n-2}.

Example 25.1. Write a Python function **Fibonacci(n)** to find the nth Fibonacci number F_n.

Directly implementing the definition,

```
def Fibonacci(n):
    if n<= 0:
        return 0
    elif n==1:
        return 1
    else:
        return Fibonacci(n-1)+Fibonacci(n-2)
```

The trick with recursion is to always take care of the stopping case. If we had just written a function such as

```
def Fib(n):
        return Fib(n-1)+Fib(n-2)
```

then the screen would just freeze whenever we called it. Depending upon the implementation we might eventually get a stack overflow message like this:

```
File "<stdin>", line 2, in Fib
    ... repeated a whole lot of times ...
File "<stdin>", line 2, in Fib
RuntimeError: maximum recursion depth exceeded
```

The problem is that **Fib** does not stop calling itself when it gets to F_1 and F_2. You have to tell it that with the first two lines of the **if..elif** clause.

213

Furthermore, this program does not do any error checking for non-integer input. So if somebody types in **Fibonacci(3.7)**, it will also get caught in a loop and crash. One way to fix this is to add a type check using the built-in **isinstance** function.

```
def Fibonacci(n):
        if not isinstance(n, int):
        print "Error: Invalid input"
        exit()
    elif n<= 0:
        return 0
    elif n==1:
        return 1
    else:
        return Fibonacci(n-1)+Fibonacci(n-2)
```

To get, e.g., F_{20} then we would type in.

```
>>> Fibonacci(20)
6765
```

Example 25.2. Print the first 20 Fibonacci numbers (i.e., through F_{19}).

One way to do this is to put **Fibonacci in a while loop.**

```
>>> for i in range(20):
...         print Fibonacci(i),
...
0 1 1 2 3 5 8 13 21 34 55 89 144 233 377 610 987 1597 2584
  4181
>>>
```

The comma at the end of the line means to suppress the line feed, so that all the numbers are printed on the same line.

Unfortunately this code is very inefficient because it duplicates effort. To print each F_j, it calculates each of the earlier $F_1, F_2, \ldots, F_{j-1}$. To print F_5, it needs to calculate F_4 and F_3; the recursive call for F_4 requires F_3 and F_2 and the call for F_3 requires F_2 and F_1. Then to calculate F_6, it begins again, by calling for F_5 and F_4. To get F_5, it calls for F_4 and F_3. To get each F_4, it calls for F_3 and F_2. Thus to calculate F_6, a total of 13 recursive function calls are made (figure 25.1). An efficient implementation should only require six. The solution is to build up and save the sequence as you go along. For a more efficient program, you could implement the Fibonacci sequence using a while loop.[1]

Example 25.3. List Flattening. A flattened listed is a list with all of the sub-lists moved to the top. Diagrammatically, if we write down the list and erase all of the brackets except for the very first and very last, we have a flattened list.

For example, the flattened version of

```
[[1,2,3],[4,[5,6,7]],[8,9]]
```

---

[1]See, for example, the Python Tutorial at https://docs.python.org/2/tutorial/controlflow.html#defining-functions.

Figure 25.1: Recursive calls for function `Fibonacci` to find F_6.

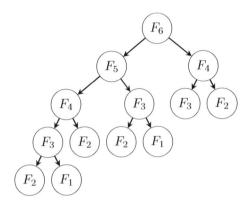

is

```
[1, 2, 3, 4, 5, 6, 7, 8, 9]
```

Recursion is perfect for this type of task. The basic idea is to define a function with two arguments, an input list an output list. We initialize the output list with `[]`, an empty list. Then we go through the input list from left to right, looking at each element. If the first element is a list, we call **Flatten** recursively on the first element, passing the output list we have built so far. If the first element is not a list, we append it to the end of the output list we have built so far, and continue with the rest of the list.

```
def Flatten(inputlist, outputlist):
    for x in inputlist:
        if isinstance(x, list):
            Flatten(x, outputlist)
        else:
            outputlist.append(x)
```

To make this work, we initialize the output list with a variable that points to the null list. We can do this by defining a new function **flatten**

```
def flatten(list):
    result=[]
    Flatten(list,result)
    return result
```

The second function **flatten** is a **wrapper function** for our recursive function, so that we never actually have to call **Flatten** directly. Instead we always call `flatten`, something like this:

```
>>> a = [[1,2,3],[4,[5,6,7]], [8,9]]
>>> b = flatten(a)
>>> print(b)
[1, 2, 3, 4, 5, 6, 7, 8, 9]
```

Another way of looking at list flattening is given in example 26.3.

Example 25.4. Implement the Babylonian algorithm using recursion.
We define two functions: the recursive function, and a wrapper.

```
def rooter(a, x, tol=10**-10):
    return rooter(a, 0.5*(x+a/x)) if abs(a-x*x)>tol else x
def root(a):
    return rooter(a,a)
```

You would call the program as, e.g., `root(5)`; this is a wrapper for the recursive function `rooter(a,x)`. If $|x^2 - a| > $`tol`, then `rooter(a,x)` is called recursively until the error is sufficiently small. Instead of the ternary operator within the `return` statement, you could also use an `if` statement with a `return`.

```
if abs(a-x*x)>tol:
    return rooter(a, 0.5*(x+a/x))
return x
```

Exercises

1. Write a recursive function that sums up the first n terms of the Taylor series for $\cos x$.

2. Write a recursive implementation of $n!$.

3. Write a function to completely flatten a list.

4. Write a recursive function to calculate the length of a list.

5. Write a recursive function to find the maximum element of a list.

Chapter 26

Lambda Functions

Lambda functions are anonymous (sometimes) in the sense that they don't always have to have names – you can define them in a single statement where you are using them and then forget about them.

Small anonymous functions can be defined using the **lambda** function in Python. Lambda functions were originally invented as a part of the **lambda calculus** in the 1930's by Alonzo Church as a mathematical representation of computation. It was proven in 1937 by none other than Alan Turing that the Lambda calculus is equivalent to the concept of an **algorithm** implemented on a **Turing Machine**. Some commonly used functional programming languages such as Haskell, Lisp, Erlang, R and Mathematica are heavily based on concepts derived from the Lambda Calculus. Other more general languages such as Python include Lambda expressions, and allow programmers to use them, but deeply entrenched functional programming can be less efficient in these languages.

A lambda expression has the form

```
lambda arguments: expression
```

and behaves in the same manner as a function defined by

```
def name(arguments):
    return expression
```

except that function defined in the **lambda** expression, does not have a name. While it is possible to bind a name to a lambda expression, as in

```
>>> AddTwoNumbers = lambda x, y: x+y
>>> AddTwoNumbers(5,2)
7
```

this is not often done. Lambda functions are more often used when a short function can be defined inside another function, such as the **map** statement:

```
>>> map(lambda x:x**2+3, range(10))
[3, 4, 7, 12, 19, 28, 39, 52, 67, 84]
```

This particular example is similar to list comprehension, in that it defines a function "on the fly." Here **lambda x:x**2+3** defines a function of a single variable $f(x) = x^2 + 3$. Thus the particular example we have shown is functionally identical to the list comprehension

```
>>>[x**2+3 for x in range(10)]
```

Using `lambda` with `filter` and `reduce`

A `lambda` can be used within a `filter`. This is useful because `filter` returns a list of elements in a list that satisfy a given condition, and it requires a function as one of its argument to defined the condition. Without the `lambda` it would be necessary to define a function that is only used once and never used again.

```
>>> y=[x**2+3 for x in range(10)]
>>> y
[3, 4, 7, 12, 19, 28, 39, 52, 67, 84]
>>> filter(lambda x:10<x<25, y)
[12, 19]
```

Thus in one line of code we can pick out the numbers that satisfy $10 < x < 25$ in the set $\{x^2 + 3 | x = 0, 1, \ldots, 9\}$

The `reduce` statement applies a function repeatedly to a list. The function must have two arguments, and it is repeated until there are no more elements left in the list. The general form is

```
reduce(g, list)
```

Suppose `list` contains the numbers `w,x,y,z`. Then the `reduce` statement calculates each of the following numbers in sequence and returns the last of the them:

```
g(w,x)
g(g(w,x),y)
g(g(g(w,x) y),z)
```

Example 26.1. Sum the squares of the numbers in a list using `reduce`.

```
reduce(lambda x, y:x+y*y, list)
```

will calculate the sum of the squares of all the numbers in a list.

Example 26.2. Fibonacci numbers. A function to list out all the Fibonacci numbers[1] up to n is given by the following code.

```
def fib(n):
    fibs=[0,1]
    for i in range(1,n):
        fibs.append(
            reduce(lambda x,y:x+y,
                    (fibs[-1], fibs[-2])))
    return(fibs)
```

Example 26.3. List Flattening. In example 25.3 we saw a recursive algorithm to completely flatten a list. The following example, using `reduce` and `lambda` will flatten a list by one level.

---

[1] Based on a program posted on "Peter's Website" at http://www.petercollingridge.co.uk/blog/python-fibonacci-generator-using-reduce.

```
>>> a= [[1, 2, 3], [4, [5, 6, 7]], [8, 9]]
>>> reduce(lambda x,y: x+y, a)
[1, 2, 3, 4, [5, 6, 7], 8, 9]
```

It is left as an exercise to figure out a way to flatten the list all the way using **reduce**.

Example 26.4. Babylonian algorithm using **reduce** and a **lambda** function.

Usually fixed point will converge within, say, around 5 to 10 iterations, so if we generate a list of length 10, e.g., **[a,a,a,a,a,a,a,a,a,a]**, and then apply the update formula to it using **reduce**, we should get fixed point iteration.

```
def SquareRoot(a,n=10):
    return reduce(lambda x, a: .5 *(x + a/x), n*[a])
```

The sequence of evaluations by the **reduce** here is illustrated in figure 26.1. The input list to **reduce** is drawn across the top, and the sequence of outputs down the left. The first calculation uses the first two arguments of the list in f, to return $f(5,5) \to 3$. Then this result becomes the first argument, and the next element in the list is the second argument, to return $f(3,5) \to 2.333$. In each step, the output of the previous calculation goes into the first slot of f, and the next element of the list goes into the second slot of f.

Figure 26.1: Illustration of how the **reduce** function works in the implementation of the Bablylonian algorithm in example 26.4. In the flow diagram, it is assumed that $f(x,a) = .5(x + a/x)$.

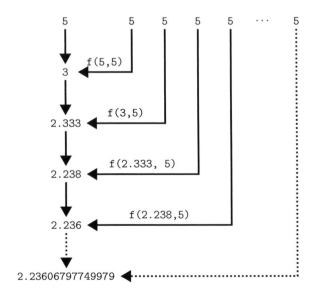

Exercises

1. Use **map** and a **lambda** to returns a list of 1's and 0's, corresponding to a list of integers, where 1 is returned for each even integer and 0 for each odd. For example, given **[3,4,6,9,2]**, you should return **[0,1,1,0,1]**.

2. Use **map** and a **lambda** function to write a program that finds the p-norm of a list of numbers.

3. Use **lambda** and **filter** to extract the even numbers from a list of integers.

Chapter 27

Exceptions

The **try** statement says what to do when something goes wrong. It is a special case of a something called an **exception handler**. An exception is an out-of-the ordinary condition, like dividing by zero, or attempting to convert a list to an integer, that Python does not know how to handle.

> **Definition 27.1. Exception**
>
> An **exception** is an unexpected condition that occurs during the course of a computer program.

> **Definition 27.2. Exception Handler**
>
> An **exception handler** tells a computer program what to do when an exception occurs. Exception handlers may be hard-wired (hardware), built into a compiler, or special sections of code added to computer programs.

There are exception handlers built into Python that will tell you when an exception occurs, but sometimes you will expect that an exception may occur and will want to write some code to handle it.

The **try** statements allow you to write your own exception handlers. The simplest way to do this is with **try** and **except**:

```
try:
    statements
except:
    statements
```

Example 27.1. Use **try** and **except** to implement a function **IsAFloat(x)** that determines if a string represents a real number.

We will implement **IsAFloat(x)** as follows: first, we attempt (try) to convert **x** to a float. If we are successful (including when the number is actually either an integer or a real number), then we return **True**. If we get an error, then we return **False**.

```
def IsAFloat(some_string):
# Returns True if some_string represents a
# floating point number and False otherwise.
    try:
        float(some_string)
    except:
        return False
    return True
```

The **try**/ **except** pair can optionally be followed by either an **else** or a **finally** clause, or both:

```
try:
    statements
except:
    statements
else:      # the else is optional if you use except
    statements
finally:   # the finally is optional if you use except
    statements
```

Flow of control continues with the contents of the **else** after all of the statements in the **try** have been executed without an exception. If an exception occurs then the **else** is not executed. When the **try** is left, regardless of whether there is an exception or not, the contents of the **finally** are executed.

For example:

```
def IsAFloat(some_string):
    try:
        float(some_string)
    except:
        return False
    else:
        print "yada_yada_yada"
    finally:
        print "Yo_Ho_Ho"
    return True
```

When we run the program in the Python shell this is what we see:

```
>>> IsAFloat('fred')
Yo Ho Ho
False
>>> IsAFloat("98.6")
yada yada yada
Yo Ho Ho
True
```

The **try**/**finally** may also be used together without the **except** clause. This is sometimes used if you want to force some code to always be executed in the **finally** clause,

Figure 27.1: Flow diagram of the basic **try**..**except**..**finally** statement.

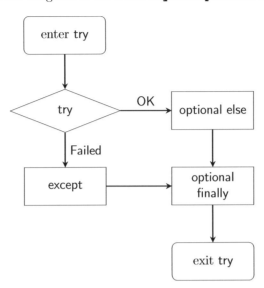

regardless of whether or not the exception is triggered, but you don't particularly care what exception, if any, gets triggered.

```
try:
    statements
finally:
    statements
```

When a **return**, **break** or **continue** statement is executed in the **try**, the **finally** clause is also executed "on the way out."

A **continue** statement is not allowed in the finally **finally**.

The **except** clause(s) specify one or more exception handlers. When no exception occurs in the try clause, no exception handler is executed.

If no **except** clause matches the exception, the search for an exception handler continues in the surrounding code and on the invocation stack.

Multiple exception handlers can also be specified.

```
try:
    statements
except expression:
    statements
except expression:    #optional excepts
    statements
except:
    statements
```

or

```
try:
    statements
except expression as identifier:
    statements
except expression as identifier:   # optional except
    statements
except:            # optional
    statements
```

Figure 27.2: Flow diagram of the basic **try** statement with multiple exception handlers.

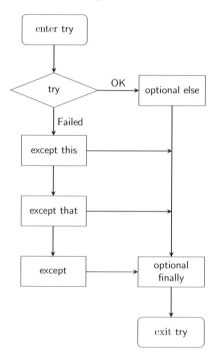

The **expression as identifier** is analogous to the **with** statement (See chapter 23).

Python has a large number of built in exceptions.

For example, the exception **ZeroDivisionError** will occur if you divide by zero.

You can also define your own exceptions. You may invoke any exception, either a built-in exception, or a user-defined exception, with a **raise** statement.

```
>>> raise ZeroDivisionError
Traceback (most recent call last):
  File "<pyshell#5>", line 1, in <module>
    raise ZeroDivisionError
ZeroDivisionError
```

If you need to determine whether an exception was raised but dont intend to handle it, a simpler form of the raise statement allows you to re-raise the exception (this example is from the Python tutorial):[1].

```
>>> try:
...     raise NameError('HiThere')
... except NameError:
...     print 'An_exception_flew_by!'
...     raise
...
An exception flew by!
Traceback (most recent call last):
  File "<stdin>", line 2, in ?
NameError: HiThere
```

To define your own exceptions you have to create a subclass of the **exception** class. The following example is given in the Python tutorial.[2]

```
>>> class MyError(Exception):
...     def __init__(self, value):
...         self.value = value
...     def __str__(self):
...         return repr(self.value)
...
>>> try:
...     raise MyError(2*2)
... except MyError as e:
...     print 'My_exception_occurred,_value:', e.value
...
My exception occurred, value: 4
>>> raise MyError('oops!')
Traceback (most recent call last):
  File "<stdin>", line 1, in ?
__main__.MyError: 'oops!'
```

Exception classes are just like any other class and can contain any kind of code and do anything that any other class can do. See chapter 29 for more detail on classes.

Exercises

1. Using **try .. except**, write a function that will convert a string to an integer if possible; else to a floating point number if not; otherwise, will return the original string as a sting if neither is possible.

2. Using **try .. except**, write a function will open a file and return the contents as a list of strings, or will print a message **'Unable to open file'** and return an empty list if the file does not exist or can't be found.

---

[1]https://docs.python.org/2/tutorial/errors.html#raising-exceptions
[2] See https://docs.python.org/2/tutorial/errors.html#user-defined-exceptions

Chapter 28

Functional Programming

Functional Programming in Python

The hallmarks of functional programming include, among other things, immutable data, iterators, lazy evaluation (don't do it till you need it), recursive function calls, anonymous functions (e.g., lambda functions), pure functions (functions without side effects), and being able to pass and return functions as parameters and return values (called higher order functions). These are all implemented in Python. Since Python includes support for other paradigms as well and does not force you to use only these methods to program, it is not considered a functional programming language.

The typical style[1] of a functional program consists of transformations and compositions rather than assignments and loops. State changes must be avoided altogether. For example, suppose we read in a string of numbers that we want to add together, such as **"3+7+4++9+6"**. We want to allow for double **+** signs with missing numbers. An imperative implementation might look like this:

```python
def adder(input):
    total = 0
    for number in input.split("+"):
        try:
            total += int(number)
        except:
            pass
    return(total)
```

(See chapter 27 for more detail on the **try**/**except** statement.)

```python
>>> adder("1+2+++3+4+5")
15
```

In a functional implementation we would only use function calls.

```python
from operator import add
def addf(input):
    return reduce(add,
        map(int, filter(bool,input.split("+"))))
```

This particular implementation works with strings like **"1+2++3+4"** but fails when there are blanks between the plus signs. To fix that would require an additional mapping of the **strip()** method; this is left as an exercise.

---

[1]see http://kachayev.github.io/talks/uapycon2012

227

Recursion in Functional Programming

Recursion is required for many functional programming implementations. For example, a basic implementation (without idiot-proofing) for $n!$ would be

```
def factorial(n):
    return (1 if n==0 else n*factorial(n-1))
```

This will cause recursive overload if **n** is either negative or not an integer, so we can add some error checking to make it work:

```
def factorial(n):
    return (1 if n==0 else n*factorial(n-1)) \
        if (isinstance(n,int) and n >= 0) \
        else None
```

In **tail recursion** a recursive function call is made as the final call of a function. When this happens, every recursive call has to be completed before the final calculation is performed, and this can be very demanding on computational resources. For example,[2] the following function inputs a number **n** and recursively adds up the integers $1 + 2 + 3 + \cdots + n$. To illustrate what is going on, a **print** statement is used to echo each recursive call.

```
def mysum(n):
    if n == 1:
        print n
        return n
    else:
        print n,"+mysum(",n-1,")"
        return n + mysum(n-1)
```

Then if we call the function to get the sum $1 + 2 + 3 + 4 + 5$,

```
>>> print mysum(5)
5 +mysum( 4 )
4 +mysum( 3 )    mysum(4) call = 5+(4+mysum(3))
3 +mysum( 2 )    mysum(3) call = 5+(4+(3+mysum(2)))
2 +mysum( 1 )    mysum(2) call = 5+(4+(3+(2+mysum(1))))
1                mysum(1) call = 5+(4+(3+(2+1)))
15
```

In a tail recursive language, the compiler recognizes that tail recursion is taking place and updates the calculation automatically to save space. Python does not implement tail recursion, but you can simulate it yourself. In this case, the trick is to keep a running total.

```
1  def tailsum(n, total=0):
2    if n == 0:
3      print total
4      return total
```

---

[2] see http://stackoverflow.com/questions/33923/what-is-tail-recursion

```
5     else:
6        print "tailsum(",n-1,",",total+n,")"
7        return tailsum(n - 1, total + n)
```

Here is the tail recursive trace of the same operation.

```
>>>tailsum(5)
tailsum( 4 , 5 )
tailsum( 3 , 9 )
tailsum( 2 , 12 )
tailsum( 1 , 14 )
tailsum( 0 , 15 )
15
```

Anonymous functions

Anonymous functions are functions that are not bound to any identifier, i.e., they do not have a name. They are usually used to pass arguments to higher order functions or to construct the result of a higher order function. They are typically only used once. Anonymous functions are implemented with the **lambda** construct in Python as described in chapter 26.

Higher order functions

Higher order functions are function that allow passing functions as arguments, returning them as values, and storing them in data structures. Other functions are called **first order functions**. Higher order functions are sometimes called **first class functions** in the sense of not being second class citizens.

Python functions are, by default, higher order. For example, the following imperative function finds the integral

$$\int_a^b f(x)\,dx \tag{28.1}$$

using the trapezoidal rule with a step size of $\Delta x = (b-a)/n$.

```
1   def trapezint(f, a, b, n=10):
2       h=(float(b)-float(a))/float(n)
3       xvals = [a+i*h for i in range(n+1)]
4       fvals = [f(x) for x in xvals]
5       integral=0.5*h*sum( [a+b for a,b in \
6                           zip(fvals[1:], fvals[:-1])] )
7       return integral
```

The function f is an argument; to find $\int_0^\pi \sin x\,dx$ with a step size of 0.001π we would type

```
>>> from math import sin, pi
>>> trapezint(sin, 0, pi, 1000)
1.9999983550656635
```

A more functional implementation would be this:

```
def trap(f,a,b,n):
    return 0.5*((b-a)/float(n))*(f(a)+f(a+(b-a)/float(n)))+\
            trap(f,a+(b-a)/float(n),b,n-1) if n>0 else 0.0
```

If we prefer, we could use the step size, rather than the number of intervals as an argument; this makes the program more readable, and more efficient, because it does not have to compute the number `a+(b-a)/float(n)` multiple times at each iteration (although the compiler might take care of that for us).

```
def trap(f,a,b,h):
    return 0.5*h*(f(a)+f(a+h)+\
            trap(f,a+h,b,h) if a<b else 0.0
```

Here is an even more concise functional implementation of the same trapezoidal function in Python.

```
trp = lambda f, a, b, h: (
    0.5*h*(f(a)+f(a+h))+trp(f,a+h,b,h) \
                            if a<b else 0.0)
```

The danger here is the default stack depth in Python. In purely functional programming languages such as Haskell, the recursive calls can go infinitely deep. Here, if we make a call such as

```
>>> trp(sin, 0, pi, 0.001*pi)
 (a lot of noise gets printed out here )
RuntimeError: maximum recursion depth exceeded in cmp
```

This is because the number of recursive calls are nested 1000 levels deep, which is just a tad too large for the system, so we get an overflow error. To fix this we must increase the recursion limit.

```
>>> import sys
>>> sys.setrecursionlimit(2000)
>>> trp(sin, 0, pi, 0.001*pi)
1.9999934202716034
```

To find out the currently allowed recursion depth use

```
>>> import sys
>>> sys.getrecursionlimit()
1000
```

We can also return a function from a function. The following function uses `trp` to figure out which of two functions has a larger integral on $[0, x]$.

```
maxint = lambda f1,f2,h,x: \
    (f1 if trp(f1,0,x,h) >= trp(f2,0,x,h) else f2)
```

For example, if we define two function $f_1(x) = x$ and $f_2(x) = 1 - x$ (not shown) then

```
>>>from numpy import linspace
>>>for x in linspace(0,2, 11):
...    print x, maxint(f1, f2, .01, x)
0.0 <function f1 at 0x7f43dbc36500>
0.2 <function f2 at 0x7f43dbc36578>
0.4 <function f2 at 0x7f43dbc36578>
0.6 <function f2 at 0x7f43dbc36578>
0.8 <function f2 at 0x7f43dbc36578>
1.0 <function f1 at 0x7f43dbc36500>
1.2 <function f1 at 0x7f43dbc36500>
1.4 <function f1 at 0x7f43dbc36500>
1.6 <function f1 at 0x7f43dbc36500>
1.8 <function f1 at 0x7f43dbc36500>
2.0 <function f1 at 0x7f43dbc36500>
>>>
```

The function **numpy.linspace(a,b,n)** returns a list of n floating point numbers evenly spaced between a and b. The implementation correctly determines that on $[1, 2]$

$$\int_0^x t \, dt > \int_0^x (1 - t) \, dt \tag{28.2}$$

while on $[0, 1]$, the inequality is reversed.

Additional support for higher order functions is provided in the built in library **functools**[3] which provides tools for functions that act on functions or return other functions.

Pure functions

Pure functions are functions that do not have any side effects. For example, in the following code, the value of **x** is changed by the call to the **append** function.

```
>>> x=[1,2,3,4]
>>> x.append(5)
>>> x
[1, 2, 3, 4, 5]
>>>
```

Even though the **append** is tagged on to the end of the **x** this is considered a **side effect** and is not allowed in functional programming. A pure function would not be permitted to change the state of the variable **x**. A pure version of appending an element might look like this (without error checking!)

---

[3]For more details on the **functools** library see https://docs.python.org/2/library/functools.html#module-functools

```
>>> x=[1,2,3,4]
>>> def appendto(x,y):
...    return x+[y]
...
>>> appendto(x,5)
[1,2,3,4,5]
>>> x
[1,2,3,4]
```

To actually change the state of x we would need to type

```
>>> x = appendto(x,5)
```

Lazy evaluation and generators

Lazy evaluation is a compiler implementation strategy in which expressions are not actually evaluated until they are actually needed, and when they are evaluated, their results are stored in case the same calculation is needed again later. It is sometimes called **call by need**. An example in Python is the **iterator** data structure, which stores the result of a list for later use.

```
1  >>> i = iter(range(10))
2  >>> print i
3  <listiterator object at 0x7f88f160fbd0>
4  >>> i.next()
5  0
6  >>> i.next()
7  1
```

```
8   >>> i.next()
9   2
10  >>> for j in i:
11  ...    print j,
12  ...
13  3 4 5 6 7 8 9
14  >>>
```

Lazy evaluation can be used similarly to list comprehension. For example, the expression

```
A=[x*x for x in range(1000000)]
```

will generate a list that contains the squares of the first one-million integers (starting from zero). The entire list is generated, and stored, at once. Alternatively, the iterator

```
B=(x*x for x in range(1000000))
```

stores the information that is needed to generate the sequence. It is only generated when needed.

Another way that Python implements lazy evaluation is with the **yield** statement. A **yield** is like a **return**, except that the code inside the function that uses it is not executed when you call the function. Instead, the code returns a generator.

```
def fred():
    stuff=range(10)
    for i in stuff:
        yield i*i
```

Each time the generator is called by the **for** loop, it picks up where it left off and stops when it hits the **yield** statement.

```
>>> x=fred()
<generator object fred at 0x7f88f161c0a0>
>>> for i in x: print i,
...
0 1 4 9 16 25 36 49 64 81
>>>
```

Iterators and the `itertools` library

An **iterator** is an object that represents a steady stream of data. You access this stream one item at a time using the **next()** method of the iterator object. Once an item is accessed it is removed from the stream (you don't go backwards). When you reach the end of the iterator, further calls to **next()** return a **StopIteration** exception. Programmers experienced with functional languages like Haskell or APL will probably be familiar with iterators.

For example, the function **itertools.combinations(s,n)** returns an iterator with all the possible lists of length n that can be formed by combinations of elements of the list **s**. It is returned as an iterator, not as a list.

```
1  >>> from itertools import *
2  >>> r=range(4)
3  >>> combos=combinations(r,3)
4  >>> print combos
5  <itertools.combinations object at 0x7fecded7bf18>
6  >>>
```

We may access the first couple of elements manually, e.g,

```
7   >>> next(combos)
8   (0, 1, 2)
9   >>> next(combos)
10  (0, 1, 3)
11  >>>
```

The tuples (0,1,2) and (0,1,3) are no longer in the iterator:

```
12  >>> [x for x in combos]
13  [(0, 2, 3), (1, 2, 3)]
14  >>>
```

The iterator **combos** is now empty:

```
15  >>> [x for x in combos]
16  []
17  >>>
```

To see the entire iterator as a list at this point, we need to start over:

```
18  >>> [x for x in combinations(r,3)]
19  [(0, 1, 2), (0, 1, 3), (0, 2, 3), (1, 2, 3)]
20  >>>
```

Table 28.1. Python standard `itertools` library[a] (1 of 2)

Function	Return Value
`chain(i)`	Chains sequence of iterables into a single iterator. `[x for x in chain(range(3), range(25,28))]`$\rightarrow$`[0,1,2,25,26,27]`
`combinations(i,k)`	Combinations of length k from iterable `i`. `combinations_with_replacement(i,k)` replaces elements after selection so some combinations may occur more than once.
`compress(data,sel)`	Filters `data` if elements of `sel` are **True**. Like `(d for d,s in izip(data,sel) if s)`.
`count(start,step)`	An (infinite) iterator with evenly space values.
`cycle(i)`	An iterator that cycles through an iterable.
`dropwhile(p, i)`	An iterator that drops elements from `i` while `p` is **True**; subsequently returns all elements. `>>>q=[9,5,2,10,1,10,1,2,2,2]` `>>>A=dropwhile(lambda x:x<10,q)` `>>> [x for x in A]` `[10,1,10,1,2,2,2]`
`from_iterable(i)`	Like `chain` but for a single iterable.
`groupby(i, key)`	An iterator that returns keys and groups from iterable `i` like the Unix **uniq** filter. `>>>[x for x, y in groupby("heeeellllooo")]` $\rightarrow$ `['h', 'e', 'l', 'o']`
`ifilter(p,i)`	An interator based on the iterable `i` for which those elements in `p` are **True**. Compare: `ifilterfalse(p,i)` does same thing but for elements that are **False**.
`imap(f,i)`	Like **map** but returns an iterator.
`islice(i, stop)`	A slice of iterator `i`. May also specify start and stop: `islice(i, start,stop,step)`.
`izip(i,..)`	Like **zip** but returns an iterator. For iterables of unequal length, returns shortest. To fill to length of the longest use `izip_longest(i,j,..,value)`.
`permutations(i, k)`	Successive permutations of length k from `i`.
`product(i,j,..)`	Cartesian product of iterables as an iterator.
`repeat(x, times)`	Iterator with same item `x` repeated. If the number of repeats `times` is omitted, emits a steady stream of repeats.

[a]For a complete listing and more details see `https://docs.python.org/2/library/itertools.html`.

Function	Return Value
starmap(f,i)	Like **imap** but when arguments to function are themselves pre-grouped lists. **starmap(f, [1,2,3,4,5,6])** → **f(1,2),f(3,4),f(5,6)**.
takewhile(p,i)	An iterator that takes elements from the iterable **i** while the elements in **p** are **True**.
tee(i, n)	Returns **n** iterators from a single iterable.

Table 28.1. Python standard **itertools** library[a] (2 of 2)

[a]For a complete listing and more details see https://docs.python.org/2/ library/itertools.html.

Exercises

1. Write a function that raises a number to an integer power using recursion.

2. Write a function to find the trace of a square matrix represented as a list using recursion (not using a trace function).

3. Implement dot product recursively.

4. Implement a function to find the determinant of a matrix, represented as a list, recursively.

5. Write a function that finds the first n terms of the Taylor series for sin x recursively.

Chapter 29

Classes

Python classes provide you a way to define your own **objects**. Objects are new data types that are created by the programmer that represent *things*. You can change these things with special functions called **methods**. Programmers like to use objects because with objects you can separate the **implementation** (the code that implements the object) from the **application** (the code that uses the object). This is done by only allowing the two to interface in specifically delineated ways. In addition, many programming problems can be tackled much more easily by first describing the *things*, and then describing how the things can be changed. In **object oriented programming** the *things* become the **classes**, and *how things change* become the **methods**.

For example, suppose you are writing a computer program that performs operations on 2-dimensional vectors. One operation you might want to perform on a vector is take its norm. Mathematically, there are lots of different norms, such as the L^1 or taxicab norm (the sum of the absolute values); the usual L^2 or Euclidean norm (the square root of the sum of the squares); the L^∞ or sup-norm (the absolute value of the largest element); and the L^p norm for any positive integer p. You want to be completely general. First, you would **define a class** which you **initialize** with the values of x and y. Then, within this class, you would define a function **norm** that tells the program the type of norm to use. If no norm is specified, you decide to use the Euclidean norm. When you want to use a vector in a program, you **instantiate** your class.

To instantiate your vector class (create a new vector), you would invoke the code **vector**. Inside the class definition, you should have created a special method called **__init__** method.This method is invoked when you create a new vector.

To create the vector $\mathbf{u} = (5, 10)$,

```
1  >>> u=MyVectorType(5,10)
2  >>> print u
3  <__main__.MyVectorType instance at 0x7fa560a76638>
```

The whole point of the class is that you can't see inside the vector, except by any special methods you might have written. This prevents you from "cheating." For example, if you know the class is defined as a list, you might to to find x and y by using list indices. This is not permitted unless you say so in the class definition. Here we allow the user to peek into the contents with special methods call **x** and **y**.

```
4  >>> (u.x, u.y)
5  (5, 10)
6  >>> (u.norm(), u.norm("Taxicab"), u.norm("Sup"), u.norm(3))
7  (11.180339887498949, 15, 10, 10.400419115259519)
```

Here is an implementation of the entire class that includes the vector norm function

```
1   class MyVectorType():
2       def __init__(self, x,y):
3           self.x = x
4           self.y = y
5       def norm(self, how="Euclidean"):
6           X=self.x
7           Y=self.y
8           if how=="Euclidean":
9               return (X*X+Y*Y)**.5
10          elif how=="Taxicab":
11              return abs(X) + abs(Y)
12          elif how=="Sup":
13              return max(abs(X), abs(Y))
14          elif isinstance(how, int) and (how>0):
15              return (X**how + Y**how)**(1.0/float(how))
16          else:
17              return self.norm()
```

Notice how each function in the implementation has as its first argument **self**. This is because each method in the class refers to an instantiation of the class. *You do not specifically refer to* **self** *when you call a method.*

Each class should have a special method called **__init__(self, arguments)** which returns a new instantiation of the class as a python object. When you call your class (in this case, **MyVectorType(x,y)**, the return value is a new object. The only arguments to the call are the input to the init function; for the vector they were **x** and **y**.

Exercises

1. Define a class **vector** that represents a three dimensional vector. Implement the following:

   (a) A **length** class that gives the length of vector.

   (b) A **dotproduct** method that returns a number.

   (c) A **crossproduct** method that returns a new vector.

2. Define a **rotation** class that represents a rotation matrix in 3 dimensions. As input,

you give it a direction vector, represented by the **vector** class defined in exercise 1, and an angle. Then implement

   (a) A **rotate** method that inputs a **rotation** and a **vector** and returns a new vector.

   (b) A **multiply** method that inputs two **rotation** objects and returns a new **rotation** object.

   (c) A **matrix** method that returns the 3×3 matrix corresponding to the **rotation**.

Part III

Scientific Computa-
tion

Chapter 30

Linear Systems

A linear system of n equations with n unknowns $x_1, x_2, \ldots, x_n$

$$a_{11}x_1 + a_{12}x_2 + \cdots + a_{1n}x_n = b_1 \qquad (30.1\text{a})$$

$$a_{21}x_1 + a_{22}x_2 + \cdots + a_{2n}x_n = b_2 \qquad (30.1\text{b})$$

$$\vdots \qquad (30.1\text{c})$$

$$a_{n1}x_1 + a_{n2}x_2 + \cdots + a_{nn}x_n = b_n \qquad (30.1\text{d})$$

where the a_{ij} and b_k are all known constants, can be written more compactly in matrix form

$$\begin{bmatrix} a_{11} & \cdots & a_{1n} \\ \vdots & & \vdots \\ a_{n1} & \cdots & a_{nn} \end{bmatrix} \begin{bmatrix} x_1 \\ \vdots \\ x_n \end{bmatrix} = \begin{bmatrix} b_1 \\ \vdots \\ b_n \end{bmatrix} \qquad (30.2)$$

Designating the square matrix as **A** and the column vectors as **x** and **b**, respectively, this becomes the problem of solving the matrix equation

$$\mathbf{Ax} = \mathbf{b} \qquad (30.3)$$

for **x**. Mathematically, the solution is "simple:" if the matrix **A** is non-singular then

$$\mathbf{x} = \mathbf{A}^{-1}\mathbf{b} \qquad (30.4)$$

However, because calculation of the inverse is computationally inefficient, linear systems are generally not solved this way.

There are several methods that are derived from **Gaussian elimination** which you probably studied in a basic linear algebra class. We will discuss the basic method here. We begin by observing that if we can transform equation 30.3 into the form

$$\mathbf{Tx} = \mathbf{b}' \qquad (30.5)$$

where **T** is an upper triangular matrix, and **b**$'$ is some column vector (most likely different from **b**), then the solution for the x_i can be read off by **back-substitution**, that is, by starting at the bottom of the matrix and working backwards. To see this, write out the matrix equations:

$$
\begin{bmatrix}
T_{11} & T_{12} & T_{13} & \cdots & T_{1n} \\
0 & T_{22} & T_{23} & & T_{2n} \\
0 & 0 & T_{33} & & T_{3n} \\
\vdots & & & \ddots & \vdots \\
0 & \cdots & & 0 & T_{nn}
\end{bmatrix}
\begin{bmatrix}
x_1 \\ x_2 \\ x_3 \\ \vdots \\ x_n
\end{bmatrix}
=
\begin{bmatrix}
b_1' \\ b_2' \\ b_3' \\ \vdots \\ b_n'
\end{bmatrix}
\tag{30.6}
$$

This is exactly the matrix equation for the linear system

$$T_{11}x_1 + T_{12}x_2 + T_{13}x_3 + \cdots + T_{1n}x_n = b_1' \tag{30.7a}$$
$$T_{22}x_2 + T_{23}x_3 + \cdots + T_{2n}x_n = b_2' \tag{30.7b}$$
$$T_{33}x_3 + \cdots + T_{3n}x_n = b_3' \tag{30.7c}$$
$$\vdots \tag{30.7d}$$
$$T_{n-1,n-1}x_{n-1} + T_{n-1,n}x_n = b_{n-1}' \tag{30.7e}$$
$$T_{nn}x_n = b_n' \tag{30.7f}$$

We can solve for x_n from equation 30.7f; then we substitute this into equation 30.7e to get x_{n-1}; and so forth, all the way back to x_1. This process is called **back-substitution**.

To get the equations for implementation, we start with equations 30.1.

Solving equation 30.1a for x_1 in terms of $x_2, \ldots, x_n$,

$$x_1 = (b_1 - a_{12}x_2 - a_{13}x_3 - \cdots - a_{1n}x_n)/a_{11} \tag{30.8}$$

Thus if we already know $x_2, \ldots, x_n$ we can solve for x_1.

If we can instead somehow first eliminate x_1 from each of the remaining equations, we have a system of $n - 1$ equations in the $n - 1$ variables $x_2, \ldots, x_n$. A smaller system is always easier to solve than a larger system.

We can get this smaller system by subtracting an appropriate multiple of the first equation from each of the remaining equations. Specifically, if we multiply equation 30.1a by a_{i1}/a_{11} then the resulting equation will have $a_{i1}x$ in the first term:

$$(a_{i1}/a_{11}) \times (a_{11}x_1 + a_{12}x_2 + \cdots + a_{1n}x_n = b_1) \tag{30.9}$$

or equivalently

$$a_{i1}x_1 + (a_{i1}a_{12}/a_{11})x_2 + \cdots + (a_{i1}a_{1n}/a_{11})x_n) = a_{i1}b_1/a_{11} \tag{30.10}$$

If we subtract equation 30.10 from the ith equation in the system 30.1,

$$a_{i1}x_1 + a_{i2}x_2 + \cdots a_{in}x_n = b_i \tag{30.11}$$

then the term in x_1 precisely cancels out:

$$(a_{i2} - a_{i1}a_{12}/a_{11})x_2 + \cdots + (a_{in} - a_{i1}a_{1n}/a_{11})x_n = b_i - a_{i1}b_1/a_{11} \tag{30.12}$$

If we do this for $i = 2, 3, \ldots, n$ then we have a system in $n - 1$ equations and $n - 1$ unknowns,

$$(a_{22} - a_{21}a_{12}/a_{11})x_2 + \cdots + (a_{2n} - a_{21}a_{1n}/a_{11})x_n = b_2 - a_{21}b_1/a_{11} \qquad (30.13\text{a})$$
$$(a_{32} - a_{31}a_{12}/a_{11})x_2 + \cdots + (a_{3n} - a_{31}a_{1n}/a_{11})x_n = b_3 - a_{31}b_1/a_{11} \qquad (30.13\text{b})$$

$$\vdots$$

$$(a_{n2} - a_{n1}a_{12}/a_{11})x_2 + \cdots + (a_{nn} - a_{n1}a_{1n}/a_{11})x_n = b_n - a_{n1}b_1/a_{11} \qquad (30.13\text{c})$$

Algorithm 30.1 Algorithm **LinearSolve(A, b)**. Gaussian reduction algorithm to solve the linear system $\mathbf{Ax} = \mathbf{b}$.

---

input: **A,b**
1: **if** $n > 1$ **then**
2:     $(\mathbf{T}, \mathbf{b}') \leftarrow$ reduce(**A, b**)
3:     $(x_2, x_3, \ldots, x_n) \leftarrow$ **LinearSolve(T, b')**
4: **end if**
5: $x_1 \leftarrow (b_1 - a_{12}x_2 - \cdots - a_{1n}x_n)/a_{11}$
6: **return** $(x_1, x_2, \ldots x_n)$ as **LinearSolve(A, b)**

Algorithm 30.2 Algorithm **reduce(A, b)**. Row reduction on the linear system $\mathbf{Ax} = \mathbf{b}$.

---

input: **A,b**
1: $n \leftarrow \dim(\mathbf{b})$
2: **for** $k \in 2, 3, \ldots, n$ **do**
3:     $m \leftarrow a_{k1}/a_{11}$
4:     **for** $j \in 2, 3, \ldots, n$ **do**
5:        $T_{k-1,j-1} \leftarrow a_{kj} - ma_{1j}$
6:     **end for**
7:     $b'_{k-1} \leftarrow b_k - mb_1$
8: **end for**
9: **return** $(\mathbf{T}, \mathbf{b}')$ as **reduce(A, b)**

If we repeat this process with the $n - 1 \times n - 1$ system, we end up with an $n - 2 \times n - 2$ system, and so forth. If we keep doing this until we run out of rows, we have an upper triangular system.

This process is called **Gaussian Reduction**. We then solve for the $x_1, \ldots, x_n$ by starting on the bottom and working our way upwards, as previously described. This second step is called **back substitution** (algorithms 30.1 and 30.2).

Example 30.1. Use Gaussian reduction and back substitution to solve the linear system

$$\begin{bmatrix} 1 & 2 & 3 \\ 4 & 5 & 2 \\ 2 & 8 & 5 \end{bmatrix} \begin{bmatrix} x \\ y \\ z \end{bmatrix} = \begin{bmatrix} 5 \\ 10 \\ 15 \end{bmatrix} \qquad (30.14)$$

The first step towards triangularization is to subtract multiples of row 1 of the matrix

$$\begin{bmatrix} 1 & 2 & 3 \end{bmatrix} \tag{30.15}$$

from the remainder of the matrix with a goal of making the rest of the first column 0. Since we need to subtract the same multiple of the first element of the column vector **b**, it is convenient to rewrite the system (diagrammatically) in the following format

$$\begin{bmatrix} 1 & 2 & 3 & 5 \\ 4 & 5 & 2 & 10 \\ 2 & 8 & 5 & 15 \end{bmatrix} \tag{30.16}$$

We can zero-out the 4 by subtracting $4 \times$ (row 1), and we can zero out the 2 by subtracting $2 \times$ (row 1)

$$\begin{bmatrix} 1 & 2 & 3 & 5 \\ 4 & 5 & 2 & 10 \\ 2 & 8 & 5 & 15 \end{bmatrix} \begin{array}{l} \leftarrow \text{Subtract } 4 \times \text{(row 1)} \\ \leftarrow \text{Subtract } 2 \times \text{(row 1)} \end{array} \tag{30.17}$$

The result is

$$\begin{bmatrix} 1 & 2 & 3 & 5 \\ 0 & -3 & -10 & -10 \\ 0 & 4 & -1 & 5 \end{bmatrix} \tag{30.18}$$

Now we need to repeat the process on the second column. To remove the 4 in the bottom of the second column, without changing the zero in the first column, we can add $(4/3) \times$ (row 2).

$$\begin{bmatrix} 1 & 2 & 3 & 5 \\ 0 & -3 & -10 & -10 \\ 0 & 4 & -1 & 5 \end{bmatrix} \begin{array}{l} \\ \\ \leftarrow \text{add } (4/3) \times \text{(row 2)} \end{array} \tag{30.19}$$

The result is

$$\begin{bmatrix} 1 & 2 & 3 & 5 \\ 0 & -3 & -10 & -10 \\ 0 & 0 & -43/3 & -25/3 \end{bmatrix} \tag{30.20}$$

Now we can read of the solution by back-substitution, because (30.20) is equivalent to

$$\begin{bmatrix} 1 & 2 & 3 \\ 0 & -3 & -10 \\ 0 & 0 & -43/3 \end{bmatrix} \begin{bmatrix} x \\ y \\ z \end{bmatrix} = \begin{bmatrix} 5 \\ -10 \\ -25/3 \end{bmatrix} \tag{30.21}$$

The equivalent linear system is thus

$$x + 2y + 3z = 5 \tag{30.22a}$$

$$-3y - 10z = -10 \tag{30.22b}$$

$$-\frac{43}{3}z = -\frac{25}{3} \tag{30.22c}$$

From (30.22c)

$$z = \frac{25}{43} \tag{30.23}$$

From (30.22b)

$$y = \frac{1}{3}(10 - 10z) = \frac{60}{43} \tag{30.24}$$

Finally, from (30.22a),

$$x = 5 - 2y - 3z = \frac{20}{43} \tag{30.25}$$

Normally we don't have to solve a linear system this way because extensive linear system support is already built into Numpy. We can use the package **np.linalg.solve** instead, which solves the systems $\mathbf{Ax} = \mathbf{b}$ for $\mathbf{x}$, where $\mathbf{A}$, $\mathbf{b}$, and $\mathbf{x}$ are all represented as Numpy arrays.

In the following code we solve the system

$$\begin{bmatrix} 1 & 2 & 3 \\ 4 & 5 & 2 \\ 2 & 8 & 5 \end{bmatrix} \mathbf{x} = \begin{bmatrix} 5 \\ 10 \\ 15 \end{bmatrix} \tag{30.26}$$

for the vector $\mathbf{x}$.

```
1  >>> import numpy as np
2  >>> A=np.array([[1,2,3],[4,5,2],[2,8,5]])
3  >>> b=np.array([5,10,15])
4  >>> np.linalg.solve(A,b)
5  array([ 0.46511628,  1.39534884,  0.58139535])
6  >>> 25./43
7  0.5813953488372093
8  >>> 60/43.
9  1.3953488372093024
10 >>> 20/43.
11 0.46511627906976744
12 >>>
```

We could also solve the problem directly as $\mathbf{x} = \mathbf{A}^{-1}\mathbf{b}$, using the matrix inversion function **np.linalg.inv**, as in the following example.

```
13 >>> AINV=np.linalg.inv(A)
14 >>> AINV.dot(b)
15 array([ 0.46511628,  1.39534884,  0.58139535])
16 >>>
```

Exercises

1. Solve the linear systems $\mathbf{Ax} = \mathbf{b}$ where

   (a) $A = \begin{bmatrix} 1 & 3 \\ 4 & 5 \end{bmatrix}$ and $b = \begin{bmatrix} -1 \\ 2 \end{bmatrix}$

   (b) $A = \begin{bmatrix} 4 & 0 & -1 \\ 0 & 2 & 0 \\ 5 & 6 & 7 \end{bmatrix}$ and $b = \begin{bmatrix} 0 \\ 1 \\ 2 \end{bmatrix}$

2. Find the eigenvalues and eigenvectors of the matrix $\mathbf{A}$ in each of the parts of exercise 1.

Table 30.1. Linear Algebra in `numpy.linalg`

Matrix and vector products

`dot(a, b)`	Dot product of two arrays.
`vdot(a, b)`	Dot product of two vectors.
`inner(a, b)`	Inner product of two arrays.
`outer(a, b)`	Outer product of two vectors.
`tensordot(a, b)`	Tensor dot product along specified axes.
`einsum(subscripts)`	Einstein summation convention on the operands.
`matrix_power(M, n)`	Raise square matrix to an (integer) power.
`kron(a, b)`	Kronecker product of two arrays.

Decompositions

`cholesky(a)`	Cholesky decomposition $\mathbf{A}=\mathbf{LL}^{\dagger}$ where $\mathbf{L}$ is lower triangular and $\mathbf{L}^{\dagger}$ is its conjugate transpose.
`qr(a)`	$\mathbf{A}=\mathbf{QR}$ factorization, where $\mathbf{Q}$ has orthonormal columns and $\mathbf{R}$ is upper triangular.
`svd(a)`	Singular Value Decomposition $\mathbf{A}=\mathbf{USV}^{\dagger}$ where $\mathbf{S}$ is diagonal and $\mathbf{U}$ and $\mathbf{V}$ are unitary (orthonormal if real). See chapter 40.

Matrix eigenvalues

`eig(a)`	Eigenvalues and right eigenvectors of a square array.
`eigh(a)`	Eigenvalues and eigenvectors of a Hermitian or symmetric matrix.
`eigvals(a)`	Eigenvalues of a general matrix.
`eigvalsh(a)`	Eigenvalues of a Hermitian or real symmetric mat.

Norms and other numbers

`norm(x)`	Matrix or vector norm.
`cond(x)`	Matrix condition number.
`det(a)`	Determinant.
`matrix_rank(M)`	Matrix rank.
`slogdet(a)`	Sign and natural logarithm.
`trace(a)`	Sum along diagonals of the array.

Solving equations and inverting matrices

`solve(a, b)`	Solve a linear matrix equation $\mathbf{Ax}=\mathbf{b}$.
`tensorsolve(a, b)`	Solve the tensor equation $\mathbf{Ax}=\mathbf{b}$ for $\mathbf{x}$.
`lstsq(a, b)`	Return the least-squares solution to $\mathbf{Ax}=\mathbf{b}$.
`inv(a)`	Matrix inverse.
`pinv(a)`	Moore-Penrose pseudo-inverse of a matrix.
`tensorinv(a)`	Inverse of a multi-dimensional array.

*For additional details and complete list of options see
http://docs.scipy.org/doc/numpy/reference/routines.linalg.html.

Chapter 31

Computational Geometry

In **computational geometry** we solve some basic problems in geometry numerically. Computational geometry provides an excellent opportunity to demonstrate the use of classes in Python. Suppose we define a class called a `point`.

```
class point():
    def __init__(self, x, y):
        self.x = x
        self.y = y
```

We will also define a line segment class consisting of two points. If we try to initialize it with anything besides points, it will give us an error. We will add methods that give us the length and the horizontal and vertical extent of the line segment.

```
class lineseg():
    def __init__(self, p1, p2):
        if not isinstance(p1,point):
            print p1, "is_not_a_point!"
            exit()
        if not isinstance(p2, point):
            print p2, "is_not_a_point!"
            exit()
        self.point1=p1
        self.point2=p2

    def dx(self):
        return (self.point2.x - self.point1.x)
    def dy(self):
        return ( self.point2.y - self.point1.y)
    def length(self):
        return (self.dx()**2 + self.dy()**2)**0.5
```

Are two points on the same side of a line?

Given a line $\overleftrightarrow{AB}$ and two points **C** and **D**, how do we determine if the points fall on the same side or on different sides of the line? Define the following three vectors:

$$\left.\begin{array}{l} \overrightarrow{AB} = B - A \\ \overrightarrow{AC} = C - A \\ \overrightarrow{AD} = D - A \end{array}\right\} \tag{31.1}$$

247

The vector cross product $\overrightarrow{AC} \times \overrightarrow{AB}$ will be out of the paper if **C** is on one side of $\overleftrightarrow{AB}$, and will be into the paper if it is on the other side of the line (figure 31.1). These two cases correspond to the z-component of the cross product being positive (one side) or negative (other side). If the z-component is zero, the point lies on the line.

The same argument holds for point **D**.

Thus both points **C** and **D** will be on the same side of the line $\overleftrightarrow{AB}$ if the z component of their cross product is the same, i.e., if

$$\left[(\mathbf{k} \cdot (\overrightarrow{AC} \times \overrightarrow{AB}))\right]\left[\mathbf{k} \cdot (\overrightarrow{AD} \times \overrightarrow{AB})\right] > 0 \tag{31.2}$$

Figure 31.1: Left: Are **C** and **D** on the same side of the line defined by **A** and **B** or different sides? Right: Construction of vectors used to determine the answer to the question posed on the left.

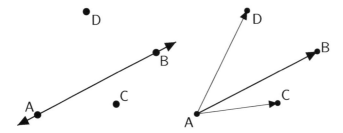

From the definition of the cross and dot products, this means

$$\begin{vmatrix} 0 & 0 & 1 \\ AC.x & AC.y & 0 \\ AB.x & AB.y & 0 \end{vmatrix}\begin{vmatrix} 0 & 0 & 1 \\ AD.x & AD.y & 0 \\ AB.x & AB.y & 0 \end{vmatrix} > 0 \tag{31.3}$$

where the notation vec.x and vec.y refers to the x and y component of the vector. These components would correspond to the **dx** and **dy** extent methods of the **lineseg** class that we defined on page 247. Since the determinant calculation drops down to two dimensions, we can explicitly write the formula as

$$((AC.x)(AB.y) - (AB.x)(AC.y))((AD.x)(AB.y) - (AB.x)(AD.y)) > 0 \tag{31.4}$$

A Python implementation that would return **True** only when the points are on the same side can be built from our class definitions, for example,

```python
def SameSide(A,B,C,D):
# Return True only if C and D are on the same side of AB
    AB=lineseg(A,B)
    AC=lineseg(A,C)
    AD=lineseg(A,D)
    M1 = (AC.dx() * AB.dy() - AB.dx()* AC.dy())
    M2 = (AD.dx() * AB.dy() - AB.dx()* AD.dy())
    return(M1*M2>0)
```

Algorithm 31.1 Algorithm **SameSide** to determine if points **C** and **D** are on the same of the line **AB**.

---

input: **A**, **B**, representing line segments; points **C**, **D**

1: $\mathbf{AB} \leftarrow \mathbf{B} - \mathbf{A}$
2: $\mathbf{AC} \leftarrow \mathbf{A} - \mathbf{C}$
3: $\mathbf{AD} \leftarrow \mathbf{A} - \mathbf{D}$
4: $M_1 \leftarrow (AC.x)(AB.y) - (AB.x)(AC.y)$
5: $M_2 \leftarrow (AD.x)(AB.y) - (AB.x)(AD.y)$
6: **if** $M_1 M_2 > 0$ **then**
7:     **return** True as **SameSide**($\overleftrightarrow{\mathbf{AB}}, \mathbf{C}, \mathbf{D}$)
8: **else if** $M_2 M_2 < 0$ **then**
9:     **return** False as **SameSide**($\overleftrightarrow{\mathbf{AB}}, \mathbf{C}, \mathbf{D}$)
10: **end if**
11: **return** Indeterminate as **SameSide**($\overleftrightarrow{\mathbf{AB}}, \mathbf{C}, \mathbf{D}$)   One Point is on line

---

Is a point on a line?

A point **C** is on the line $\overleftrightarrow{\mathbf{AB}}$ if the vectors

$$\left.\begin{array}{l} \overrightarrow{\mathbf{AB}} = \mathbf{B} - \mathbf{A} \\ \overrightarrow{\mathbf{AC}} = \mathbf{C} - \mathbf{A} \end{array}\right\} \tag{31.5}$$

are collinear. When this occurs, their cross product will be zero. The method is summarized in algorithm 31.2

Algorithm 31.2 Algorithm **OnLine** to determine if point **C** is on the line **AB** (in two dimensions).

---

input: **A**, **B**, **C**

1: **if** $C = A$ or $C = B$ **then**
2:     **return** True as **OnLine**($\overleftrightarrow{\mathbf{AB}}, \mathbf{C}$)
3: **end if**
4: $\mathbf{AB} \leftarrow \mathbf{B} - \mathbf{A}$
5: $\mathbf{AC} \leftarrow \mathbf{A} - \mathbf{C}$
6: **if** $(AC.x)(AB.y) = (AB.x)(AC.y)$ **then**
7:     **return** True as **OnLine**($\overleftrightarrow{\mathbf{AB}}, \mathbf{C}$)
8: **end if**
9: **return** False as **OnLine**($\overleftrightarrow{\mathbf{AB}}, \mathbf{C}$)

For numerical stability it is best not to check for equality. When implementing the algorithm on line 6, rather than testing for equality, the algorithm will be more stable numerically if you check

$$|(AC.x)(AB.y) - (AB.x)(AC.y)| < \epsilon \tag{31.6}$$

where $\epsilon \approx 0$ is a small number that represents numerical errors that should be rounded to zero. The actual value will be problem dependent, but ϵ should be many orders of magnitude (say 10) smaller than the typical vector length.

```
def OnLine(A, B, C):
    AB = lineseg(A, B)
    AC = lineseg(A, C)
    if abs(AC.dx()*AB.dy()-AB.dx()*AC.dy()) < 1.0E-10:
        return True
    return False
```

Betweenness of Points

We say that a point C is **between** A and B if it lies on the line segment $\overline{AB}$ (inclusive of the endpoints, for our purposes). This means that C lies on the line $\overleftrightarrow{AB}$ and falls between the endpoints of the line segment,

$$AB.x_{min} \le C.x \le AB.x_{max} \tag{31.7}$$

$$AB.y_{min} \le C.y \le AB.y_{max} \tag{31.8}$$

We summarize this in algorithm 31.3.   When we implement this in Python, it is

---

Algorithm 31.3 Algorithm **Between** to determine if point C is between the points A and B (in two dimensions).

---

input: A, B, C

1: **if** $C = A$ or $C = B$ **then**
2:     **return** True as **Between**(A, B, C)
3: **end if**
4: **if** **OnLine**($\overleftrightarrow{AB}$, C) **then**
5:     **if** $(\min(A.x, B.x) \le C.x \le \max(A.x, B.x))$ **then**
6:         **if** $(\min(A.y, B.y) \le C.y \le \max(A.y, B.y))$ **then**
7:             **return** True as **Between**(A, B, C)
8:         **end if**
9:     **end if**
10: **end if**
11: **return** False as **Between**(A, B, C)

---

convenient to make use of the double comparison operator in line 6 of the following code that implements each of the comparisons from the algorithm lines 5 and 6.

```
1  def Between(A, B, C):
2      if C==A or C==B:  return True
3      if OnLine(A, B, C):
4          minx=min(A.x, B.x); maxx=max(A.x, B.x);
5          miny=min(A.y, B.y); maxy=max(A.y, B.y);
6          if (minx <= C.x <= maxx) and (miny <= C.y <= maxy):
7              return True
8      return False
```

Do two line segments intersect?

Given two line segments $\overline{AB}$ and $\overline{CD}$, how do we know whether or not they intersect?

If we are only checking if the lines $\overleftrightarrow{AB}$ and $\overleftrightarrow{CD}$ (and not the line segments $\overline{AB}$ and $\overline{CD}$) intersect, the problem is much simpler, because we do not have to check the endpoints. There are only two tests that we need to implement. Either of the following conditions are sufficient to ensure that the lines intersect.

1. **C** and **D** are on opposite sides of $\overleftrightarrow{AB}$; or
2. **A** and **B** are on opposite sides of $\overleftrightarrow{CD}$.

This is expressed in algorithm 31.4.

Algorithm 31.4 Algorithm **LineIntersect** to determine if lines **AB** and **CD** intersect.

input: **A, B, C, D**

1: if not$\left(\text{SameSide}(\overleftrightarrow{AB}, \text{ C, D})\right)$ then
2:     return True as **LineIntersect**$\left(\overleftrightarrow{AB}, \overleftrightarrow{CD}\right)$
3: else if not$\left(\text{SameSide}(\overleftrightarrow{CD}, \text{ A, B})\right)$ then
4:     return True as **LineIntersect**$\left(\overleftrightarrow{AB}, \overleftrightarrow{CD}\right)$
5: else
6:     return False as **LineIntersect**$\left(\overleftrightarrow{AB}, \overleftrightarrow{CD}\right)$
7: end if

Line segments are more difficult. If the line segments are non-collinear, then they intersect if any of the following are true:

1. **C** and **D** are on opposite sides of $\overline{AB}$, and **A** and **B** are on opposite sides of $\overline{CD}$, and the intersection point is between the endpoints; or
2. **A** is between **C** and **D**; or
3. **B** is between **C** and **D**; or
4. **C** is between **A** and **B**; or
5. **D** is between **A** and **B**.

If the line segments are collinear, then they intersect if at least one of items 2 through 5 is true in the above list.

In order to solve this problem we need a formula for the intersection point of the two lines (assuming that they do intersect). We can do this by expressing the lines parametrically. Then a general point (AB.x, AB.y) on the line $\overleftrightarrow{AB}$ is given by

$$AB.x = A.x + t(B.x - A.x) \tag{31.9a}$$
$$AB.y = A.y + t(B.y - A.y) \tag{31.9b}$$

for $\infty < t < \infty$. At $t = 0$, the point is **A** and at $t = 1$, the point is **B**. Similarly, the line $\overleftrightarrow{CD}$ can be parametrized by

$$CD.x = C.x + s(D.x - C.x) \tag{31.10a}$$

$$CD.y = C.y + s(D.y - C.y) \qquad\qquad (31.10b)$$

for $\infty < s < \infty$. At $s = 0$, the parameterization returns $\mathbf{C}$ and at $s = 1$, it returns $\mathbf{D}$. The intersection occurs when the equations for x are equal and the equations for y are equal.

$$A.x + t(B.x - A.x) = C.x + s(D.x - C.x) \qquad\qquad (31.11)$$
$$A.y + t(B.y - A.y) = C.y + s(D.y - C.y) \qquad\qquad (31.12)$$

Rearrangement gives two equations in two unknowns s and t.

$$t(B.x - A.x) + s(C.x - D.x) = C.x - A.x \qquad\qquad (31.13a)$$
$$t(B.y - A.y) + s(C.y - D.y) = C.y - A.y \qquad\qquad (31.13b)$$

In matrix form,

$$\begin{bmatrix} B.x - A.x & C.x - D.x \\ B.y - A.y & C.y - D.y \end{bmatrix} \begin{bmatrix} t \\ s \end{bmatrix} = \begin{bmatrix} C.x - A.x \\ C.y - A.y \end{bmatrix} \qquad\qquad (31.14)$$

In fact, we do not need to know both s and t; knowledge of either one is sufficient to give us the intersection point from either of equations 31.9 or 31.10. We can solve for t directly (either user Cramer's rule, or by multiplying the first of (31.13) by $C.y - D.y$ and the second by $C.x$-$D.x$, and subtracting. The result is

$$\begin{vmatrix} B.x - A.x & C.x - D.x \\ B.y - A.y & C.y - D.y \end{vmatrix} t = \begin{vmatrix} C.x - A.x & C.x - D.x \\ C.y - A.y & C.y - D.y \end{vmatrix} \qquad\qquad (31.15)$$

As long as the lines are non-collinear, the determinant is non-singular, and it is possible to solve for t. The result is given in algorithm 31.5.

By combining algorithm 31.5 for the location of the intersection point and algorithm 31.3 for the betweenness of points, we are now able to determine if two line segments intersect.

Algorithm 31.5 Algorithm **LineIntersectionPoint** to determine coordinates of intersection point of non-collinear lines **AB** and **CD**.

input: A, B, C, D
1: **if** **LineIntersect**$(\overleftrightarrow{AB}, \overleftrightarrow{CD})$ **then**
2:     $t \leftarrow$ equation (31.15)
3:     $(x, y) \leftarrow$ equation (31.9)
4:     **return** (x, y) as **LineIntersectionPoint(AB, CD)**
5: **end if**
6: **return** None as **LineIntersectionPoint(AB, CD)**

Is a point inside a polygon?

Here we pose the following question: given a point **P**, is it inside or outside of a given polygon?

Algorithm 31.6 Algorithm **LineSegIntersect** to determine if line segments **AB** and **CD** intersect.

---

input: **A**, **B**, **C**, **D**

1: if LineIntersect$\left(\overleftrightarrow{\textbf{AB}}, \overleftrightarrow{\textbf{CD}}\right)$ then

2:     **Q** ← LineIntersectionPoint$\left(\overleftrightarrow{\textbf{AB}}, \overleftrightarrow{\textbf{CD}}\right)$

3:     if (Between(**A**,**B**,**Q**) and Between(**C**,**D**,**Q**)) then

4:         return True as **LineSegIntersect**(**AB**, **CD**)

5:     end if

6: else if (Between(**A**,**B**,**C**) or
             (Between(**A**,**B**,**D**) or
             (Between(**C**,**D**,**A**) or
             (Between(**C**,**D**,**B**) then

7:     return True as **LineSegIntersect**(**AB**, **CD**)

8: end if

9: return False as **LineSegIntersect**(**AB**, **CD**)

We will describe the polygon as an ordered sequence of vertices $\mathbf{P}_1, \mathbf{P}_2, \ldots, \mathbf{P}_n$, where the edges are assumed to be the line segments

$$\overline{\mathbf{P}_1\mathbf{P}_2}, \overline{\mathbf{P}_2\mathbf{P}_3}, \ldots, \overline{\mathbf{P}_{n-1}\mathbf{P}_n}, \overline{\mathbf{P}_n\mathbf{P}_1} \qquad (31.16)$$

It does not matter if the points are arranged clockwise or counterclockwise.

Figure 31.2: Several cases to consider in the algorithm for determining if a point is inside a polygon.

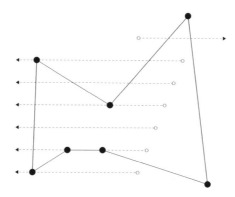

One algorithm is illustrated in figure 31.2. First (not shown) we check to see if **P** matches any of the vertices $\mathbf{P}_i$ and return `False` if we find a match.

If **P** does not match any of the vertices, then we construct a ray in any direction from **P** and count the number of edges it intersects. For simplicity, we make our ray horizontal (it does not have to, but its easier to implement that way). If the ray does not intersect a vertex, then we the point is inside if the ray crosses an odd number of edges and outside if it crosses an even number of edges.

Complications arise when the ray passes through vertices. A vertex could possibly count as two edge crossings. The number of crossings should not change if we perturb the location of **P** slightly in such a way that the ray still crosses the edge. There are two situations we need to consider, as illustrated in figure 31.3. In both cases we can fix the count by only including in the count the number of edges that contain a second vertex that is lower than the intersecting vertex.

Figure 31.3: If the ray passes through a vertex, only count the edge crossing that includes a second vertex that is lower than the intersecting vertex. In case (a), the ray only passes through one vertex; in case (b), it passes through two vertices.

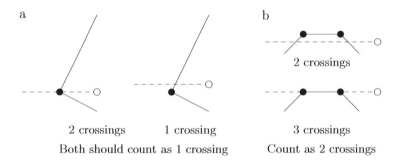

Algorithm 31.7 Algorithm **LineSegIntAbove**[a] to determine if a horizontal line segment at y intersects **AB** in such a way that at least one end point falls above the intersection.

input: A, **B**, $x_1, x_2 = \infty, y$
1: **P** $\leftarrow (x_1, y)$
2: **Q** $\leftarrow (x_2, y)$
3: **if LineSegIntersect(AB, PQ) then**
4:      **return** $(A.y < y) \vee (B.y < y)$ as **LineSegIntAbove(AB**, $x_1, x_2, y)$
5: **end if**
6: **return** False as **LineSegIntAbove(AB**, $x_1, x_2, y)$

[a] It is sufficient to default x_2 to be larger than any *expected* input value such as `float(sys.maxint)`.

An alternative method to determine if a point is inside a polygon is to project line segments from **P** to each vertex of the polygon, and then add up the angles between each successive pair of segments. If the angles sum to 2π, then **P** is inside; otherwise, **P** is outside.

Area of a Polygon

We can calculate the area of a polygon by breaking it up into triangles, calculating the area of each triangle, and then adding up all the areas to get the total area.

Consider first the area of a single triangle formed by vertices **A**, **B** and **C**. We define

---

Algorithm 31.8 Algorithm **InsidePolygon** to determine if a point **A** is inside a polygon $\mathbf{P}_1, \ldots, \mathbf{P}_n$. The 0.1 in the third argument to **LineSegIntAbove** can be replaced with any small positive number.

---

input: $\mathbf{A}, \mathbf{P}_1, \ldots, \mathbf{P}_n$

1: $k \leftarrow 0$
2: $u \leftarrow \min(\mathbf{P}_1.\mathsf{x}, \ldots, \mathbf{P}_n.\mathsf{x}) - 1$
3: $v \leftarrow \max(\mathbf{P}_1.\mathsf{x}, \ldots, \mathbf{P}_n.\mathsf{x}) - 1$
4: **for** $i \in 1, 2 \ldots, n$ **do**
5:     **if** **LineSegIntAbove**$(\mathbf{P}_i\mathbf{P}_{i+1}, \mathsf{A}.\mathsf{x}, v + 0.1(v - u), \mathsf{A}.\mathsf{y})^a$ **then**
6:         $k \leftarrow k + 1$
7:     **end if**
8: **end for**
9: **if** k is even **then**
10:     **return** False
11: **end if**
12: **return** True

---

^{a}Points are indexed cyclically, so $\mathbf{P}_n\mathbf{P}_{n+1}$ is to be interpreted here as $\mathbf{P}_n\mathbf{P}_0$.

---

the vectors

$$\mathbf{v} = \mathbf{B} - \mathbf{A} \tag{31.17}$$
$$\mathbf{w} = \mathbf{C} - \mathbf{A} \tag{31.18}$$

Then the area of the triangle formed by the vectors $\mathbf{v}$ and $\mathbf{w}$ is (see figure 31.4)

Figure 31.4: The area of a triangle formed by vectors $\mathbf{v}$ and $\mathbf{w}$ is $(1/2)|\mathbf{v}||\mathbf{w}|\sin\theta$.

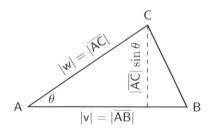

$$A(\mathbf{A}, \mathbf{B}, \mathbf{C}) = \frac{1}{2}|\overline{\mathbf{AB}}||\overline{\mathbf{AC}}|\sin\theta \tag{31.19}$$

The expression on the right is identical to the magnitude of the cross product; therefore

$$A = \frac{1}{2}|\mathbf{v} \times \mathbf{w}| \tag{31.20}$$

Using the standard basis vectors $\mathbf{i}$, $\mathbf{j}$, and $\mathbf{k}$, in terms of the usual matrix expression for a cross product the area becomes

$$A = \frac{1}{2} \begin{vmatrix} \mathbf{i} & \mathbf{j} & \mathbf{k} \\ \mathsf{B.x} - \mathsf{A.x} & \mathsf{B.y} - \mathsf{A.y} & 0 \\ \mathsf{C.x} - \mathsf{A.x} & \mathsf{C.y} - \mathsf{A.y} & 0 \end{vmatrix} \tag{31.21}$$

$$= \frac{1}{2} (\mathsf{B.x} - \mathsf{A.x})(\mathsf{C.y} - \mathsf{A.y}) - (\mathsf{B.y} - \mathsf{A.y})(\mathsf{C.x} - \mathsf{A.x})) \tag{31.22}$$

In the last step, use the fact that $|\mathbf{k}| = 1$.

Generalizing to a convex polygon, denote the vertices by $\mathbf{P}_0, \mathbf{P}_1, \ldots, \mathbf{P}_{n-1}$, in sequence around the edge of the polygon counter-clockwise (figure 31.5). Using the triangulation

Figure 31.5: Triangulation of a convex polygon.

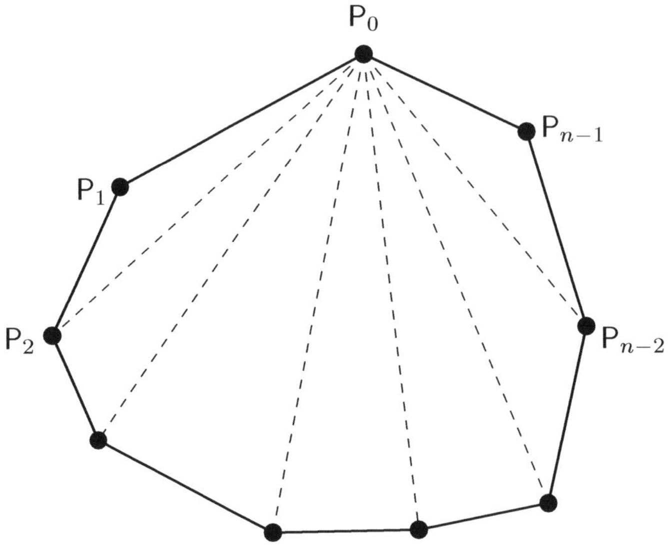

shown,

$$A(\mathbf{P}_0, \ldots, \mathbf{P}_{n-1}) = A(\mathbf{P}_0, \mathbf{P}_1, \mathbf{P}_2) + A(\mathbf{P}_0, \mathbf{P}_2, \mathbf{P}_3) +$$
$$A(\mathbf{P}_0, \mathbf{P}_3, \mathbf{P}_4) + \cdots + A(\mathbf{P}_0, \mathbf{P}_{n-2}, \mathbf{P}_{n-1}) \tag{31.23}$$

$$= \sum_{i=1}^{n-2} A(\mathbf{P}_0, \mathbf{P}_i, \mathbf{P}_{i+1}) \tag{31.24}$$

Generalizing equation 31.22,

$$2A(\mathbf{P}_0, \mathbf{P}_i, \mathbf{P}_{i+1}) = (\mathbf{P}_i.\mathsf{x} - \mathbf{P}_0.\mathsf{x})(\mathbf{P}_{i+1}.\mathsf{y} - \mathbf{P}_0.\mathsf{y})$$
$$- (\mathbf{P}_i.\mathsf{y} - \mathbf{P}_0.\mathsf{y})(\mathbf{P}_{i+1}.\mathsf{x} - \mathbf{P}_0.\mathsf{x}) \tag{31.25}$$
$$= [(\mathbf{P}_i.\mathsf{x})(\mathbf{P}_{i+1}.y) - (\mathbf{P}_0.\mathsf{x})(\mathbf{P}_{i+1}.\mathsf{y}) - (\mathbf{P}_i.\mathsf{x})(\mathbf{P}_0.\mathsf{y}) + (\mathbf{P}_0.\mathsf{x})(\mathbf{P}_0.\mathsf{y})]$$
$$- [(\mathbf{P}_{i+1}.\mathsf{x})(\mathbf{P}_i.y) - (\mathbf{P}_0.\mathsf{x})(\mathbf{P}_i.\mathsf{y}) - (\mathbf{P}_{i+1}.\mathsf{x})(\mathbf{P}_0.\mathsf{y}) + (\mathbf{P}_0.\mathsf{x})(\mathbf{P}_0.\mathsf{y})] \tag{31.26}$$

$$= [(\mathbf{P}_i.\mathsf{x})(\mathbf{P}_{i+1}.\mathsf{y}) - (\mathbf{P}_i.\mathsf{y})(\mathbf{P}_{i+1}.\mathsf{x})] + (\mathbf{P}_0.\mathsf{x})(\mathbf{P}_i.\mathsf{y} - \mathbf{P}_{i+1}.\mathsf{y})$$
$$+ (\mathbf{P}_0.\mathsf{y})(\mathbf{P}_{i+1}.\mathsf{x} - \mathbf{P}_i.\mathsf{x}) \tag{31.27}$$

Substituting (31.27) into (31.24),

$$2A(\mathbf{P}_0, \ldots, \mathbf{P}_{n-1}) = 2 \sum_{i=1}^{n-2} A(\mathbf{P}_0, \mathbf{P}_i, \mathbf{P}_{i+1}) \tag{31.28}$$

$$= \sum_{i=1}^{n-2} [(\mathbf{P}_i.\mathsf{x})(\mathbf{P}_{i+1}.\mathsf{y}) - (\mathbf{P}_i.\mathsf{y})(\mathbf{P}_{i+1}.\mathsf{x})]$$

$$+ (\mathbf{P}_0.\mathsf{x}) \sum_{i=1}^{n-2} (\mathbf{P}_i.\mathsf{y} - \mathbf{P}_{i+1}.\mathsf{y}) + (\mathbf{P}_0.\mathsf{y}) \sum_{i=1}^{n-2} (\mathbf{P}_{i+1}.\mathsf{x} - \mathbf{P}_i.\mathsf{x}) \tag{31.29}$$

The second sum in equation 31.29 telescopes to

$$\sum_{i=1}^{n-2} (\mathbf{P}_i.\mathsf{y} - \mathbf{P}_{i+1}.\mathsf{y}) = (\mathbf{P}_1.\mathsf{y} - \mathbf{P}_2.\mathsf{y}) + (\mathbf{P}_2.\mathsf{y} - \mathbf{P}_3.\mathsf{y}) + \cdots$$

$$+ (\mathbf{P}_{n-2}.\mathsf{y} - \mathbf{P}_{n-1}.\mathsf{y}) = \mathbf{P}_1.\mathsf{y} - \mathbf{P}_{n-1}.\mathsf{y} \tag{31.30}$$

Similarly, the third sum in equation 31.29 telescopes to

$$\sum_{i=1}^{n-2} (\mathbf{P}_{i+1}.\mathsf{x} - \mathbf{P}_i.\mathsf{x}) = (\mathbf{P}_2.\mathsf{x} - \mathbf{P}_1.\mathsf{x}) + (\mathbf{P}_3.\mathsf{x} - \mathbf{P}_2.\mathsf{x}) + \cdots$$

$$+ (\mathbf{P}_{n-1}.\mathsf{x} - \mathbf{P}_{n-2}.\mathsf{x}) = \mathbf{P}_{n-1}.\mathsf{x} - \mathbf{P}_1.\mathsf{x} \tag{31.31}$$

Algorithm 31.9 Algorithm for the area of a convex polygon.

input: Distinct ordered vertices $\mathbf{P}_0, \ldots, \mathbf{P}_{n-1}$ (counter-clockwise)

1: $\mathbf{P}_n \leftarrow \mathbf{P}_0$
2: $A \leftarrow 0$
3: **for** $i \in 1, 2, \ldots, n-1$ **do**
4:     $A \leftarrow A + (\mathbf{P}_i.\mathsf{x})(\mathbf{P}_{i+1}.\mathsf{y}) - (\mathbf{P}_i.\mathsf{y})(\mathbf{P}_{i+1}.\mathsf{x})$
5: **end for**
6: **return** $(A/2)$

Thus equation 31.29 simplifies to

$$2A(\mathbf{P}_0, \ldots, \mathbf{P}_{n-1})$$

$$= \sum_{i=1}^{n-2} [(\mathbf{P}_i.\mathsf{x})(\mathbf{P}_{i+1}.\mathsf{y}) - (\mathbf{P}_i.\mathsf{y})(\mathbf{P}_{i+1}.\mathsf{x})]$$

$$+ (\mathbf{P}_0.\mathsf{x})(\mathbf{P}_1.\mathsf{y} - \mathbf{P}_{n-1}.\mathsf{y}) + (\mathbf{P}_0.\mathsf{y})(\mathbf{P}_{n-1}.\mathsf{x} - \mathbf{P}_1.\mathsf{x}) \tag{31.32}$$

$$= \sum_{i=1}^{n-2} [(\mathbf{P}_i.\mathsf{x})(\mathbf{P}_{i+1}.\mathsf{y}) - (\mathbf{P}_i.\mathsf{y})(\mathbf{P}_{i+1}.\mathsf{x})]$$

$$+ [(\mathbf{P}_0.\mathsf{x})(\mathbf{P}_1.\mathsf{y}) - (\mathbf{P}_0.\mathsf{y})(\mathbf{P}_1.\mathsf{x})] + [(\mathbf{P}_{n-1}.\mathsf{x})(\mathbf{P}_0.\mathsf{y}) - (\mathbf{P}_{n-1}.\mathsf{y})(\mathbf{P}_0.\mathsf{x})] \quad (31.33)$$

Now we use the following notational trick: let the sum go to $n-1$ instead of $n-2$, and define $\mathbf{P}_n$ to be $\mathbf{P}_0$. Then the entire sum collapses to

$$A = \frac{1}{2} \sum_{i=1}^{n-1} [(\mathbf{P}_i.\mathsf{x})(\mathbf{P}_{i+1}.\mathsf{y}) - (\mathbf{P}_i.\mathsf{y})(\mathbf{P}_{i+1}.\mathsf{x})] \qquad (31.34)$$

Convex Hull

The **convex hull** of a discrete set X of points in $\mathbb{R}^2$ is the smallest convex polygon that contains X (fig 31.6).

The simplest algorithm to find the convex hull is called **package wrapping**. To visualize the concept of package wrapping, imagine that all the points are represented by nails sticking out of piece of wood. Bring a straight-edge up to one of the nails $\mathbf{P}_0$ on the edge of the set. This nail is guaranteed to be on the hull, because the first point in X that any line swept across the plane intersects will be on the hull. Tie a string to $\mathbf{P}_0$, wrap it around the outside of all the nails, bring it back to $\mathbf{P}_0$, and pull it tight. The set of nails it touches comprises the convex hull.

Figure 31.6: The convex hull.

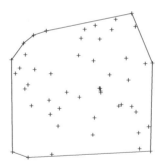

To implement this algorithm, we start by finding the point $\mathbf{P}$ with the smallest y coordinate. This point is guaranteed to be on the hull. Then we attach a line to $\mathbf{P}$ and rotate it counter-clockwise until it hits a point. This is the next point on the hull. We repeat this process until we come back to $\mathbf{P}$.

To "attach and rotate" a line to $\mathbf{P}$, we consider every other point $\mathbf{Q}$ in the set of points that remain. We construct the vector $\mathbf{PQ}$ and find the angle it makes with the x axis. The point that makes the smallest angle is the next point.

Meanwhile, at each step, we can test the remaining points during the "attach and rotate" step to see if they are inside the partial-hull that we have already built. If they are, we can eliminate them from the set of points that we need to check. We are done

---

Algorithm 31.10 Algorithm to find the convex hull.

---

input: Set of distinct points $X = \{\mathbf{P}_0, \ldots, \mathbf{P}_{n-1}\}$

1: Find $\mathbf{P}_j$ such that $\mathbf{P}_j.y = \min(\mathbf{P}_0.y, \ldots, \mathbf{P}_n.y)$

2: $\mathbf{A} \leftarrow \mathbf{P}_j$

3: $H \leftarrow \{\mathbf{A}\}$ Initialize hull with lowest - y point

4: $X \leftarrow X - \mathbf{P}_j$ Remove that point from the points to be checked

5: $\mathbf{A}_{first} = \mathbf{A}$

6: $\mathbf{A}_{new} = \varnothing$

7: $\theta_{old} \leftarrow 0$

8: **while** $\mathbf{A}_{new} \neq \mathbf{A}_{first}$ **do**

9:     $\theta \leftarrow 2\pi$ Find heading from $\mathbf{A}$ to all other points

10:    **for** $\mathbf{P} \in X$ **do**

11:      **if** InsidePolygon($\mathbf{P}, H$) **then**

12:        $X \leftarrow X - \mathbf{P}$ $\mathbf{P}$ can't be on convex hull

13:      **else**

14:        $\phi \leftarrow \mathrm{angle}(\mathbf{AP} \cdot \mathbf{i})$ Use atan2 to ensure quadrant

15:        **if** $\theta_{old} \leq \phi \leq \theta$ **then**

16:          $\mathbf{A}_{new} \leftarrow \mathbf{P}$ Pick as next point with smallest heading

17:          $\theta \leftarrow \phi$

18:        **end if**

19:      **end if**

20:    **end for**

21:    $\mathbf{A} \leftarrow \mathbf{A}_{new}$

22:    $\theta_{old} \leftarrow \theta$

23:    $H \leftarrow H \cup \{\mathbf{A}\}$ Add to Hull

24:    $X \leftarrow X - \{\mathbf{A}\}$ Remove from points to check

25: **end while**

---

when we have returned to our starting point.

The convex hull can be generated with the functions **ConvexHull** and plotted with **convex_hull_plot2d** in the library **scipy.spatial**.

```
>>> from scipy.spatial  import *
>>> from matplotlib.pyplot import *
>>> pts=np.random.rand(50,2)   # generate 50 random points
>>> H=ConvexHull(pts)
>>> p=convex_hull_plot_2d(H); show()
```

The convex hull is produced by Scipy using the Qhull[1] library. Qhull includes efficient implementations of several functions, including the convex hull, and is the de-facto industry standard for two-dimensional computational geometry.

It is possible to access the contents of the Convex Hull produced by **ConvexHull** using the **vertices** and **simplices** methods of the ConvexHull class.

The **vertices** gives the indices, amongst the original vertices, of the points that are in the convex hull:

---

[1]Barber, C.B., Dobkin, D.P., and Huhdanpaa, H.T., "The Quickhull algorithm for convex hulls," *ACM Trans. on Mathematical Software*, **22**(4):469-483, Dec 1996, http://www.qhull.org

```
 6  >>> H.vertices
 7  array([43, 42, 40, 34, 14, 12,  4, 27, 39], dtype=int32)
```

In this examples, the convex hull is comprised of `pts[43]`, `pts[42]`,...,`pts[39]` that were generated on line 3. To obtain the coordinates of the points,

```
 8  >>> pts[H.vertices]
 9  array([[  9.86357589e-01,    5.69105935e-02],
10         [  9.62730958e-01,    8.50639247e-01],
```

```
11         ...   # intermediate points omitted
12         [  2.84295551e-04,    2.38240905e-02],
13         [  7.55807063e-01,    3.86330015e-03]])
```

The **simplices** method will return convex hull vertex indices as pairs that describe the line segments:

```
14  >>> H.simplices
15  array([[42, 43],
16         [39, 27],
17         [39, 43],
18         [ 4, 27],
19         [40, 42],
20         [12, 14],
21         [12,  4],
22         [34, 14],
23         [34, 40]], dtype=int32)
```

A **simplex** is a generalization of a triangle (or **2-simplex**) to n-dimensions that is used in computational geometry. Previously we used triangles to fill up a polygon in two dimensions. In three dimensions, a triangles is replaced with a tetrahedron (or **3-simplex**); in one dimensions, the triangle becomes a line segment (a **1-simplex**). We can extract the vertices corresponding to these simplexes directly as follows:

```
24  >>> pts[H.simplices]
25  array([[[  9.62730958e-01,    8.50639247e-01],
26          [  9.86357589e-01,    5.69105935e-02]],
27
28         [[  7.55807063e-01,    3.86330015e-03],
29          [  2.84295551e-04,    2.38240905e-02]],
30
31          ...  # intermediate points omitted
32
33         [[  5.29291066e-01,    9.58768089e-01],
34          [  8.49272016e-01,    9.26997334e-01]]])
```

Voronoi Diagram

Given any discrete set S of points in $\mathbb{R}^2$, a **Voronoi Diagram** is a tessellation of the plane, one tile T_i per point P_i, such that every point $P \in T_i$ is closer to P_i than to any other point in S (figure 31.7). The original points are referred to as the **Voronoi Centers** and the tiles are **Voronoi Cells**.

Figure 31.7: Voronoi Diagram (left) and Delaunay Triangulation (right). The visualization of the Voronoi Diagram is truncated to include all the cell centers, but cells around the edge either extend to infinity or edges join at some point off the edge of the figure.

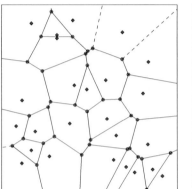 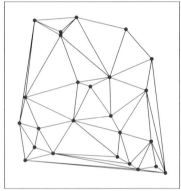

Voronoi diagrams are named after Georgy Voronoi[2] who described them in detail in 1907. They were first mentioned in the scientific literature by René Descartes in the 17th century in a discussion on the influences of the planets.[3] In 1854, the physician John Snow analyzed outbreaks of cholera in London by comparing the locations of individual deaths to the locations of water pumps. He determined that nearly all deaths occurred in the same Voronoi cell, meaning that they were tied to a common water pump. (Snow used pipe length rather than Euclidean distance as his metric.[4]) About the same time they were also studied by Dirichlet.[5] In two dimensions individual Voronoi cells are sometimes also called **Voronoi-Dirichlet polygons** or **Thiessen polygons**.[6]

Since the Voronoi Diagram is a tessellation of the *entire* plane, in any visualization, some cells must be cut off, as the boundary cells will extend to infinity.

The corresponding **Delaunay Triangulation** is found by constructing segments joining

---

[2]G. Voronoi, ["Nouvelles applications des paramètres continus à la théorie des formes quadratiques." (in French)] *Journal für die Reine und Angewandte Mathematik*, **133**:97-178 (1907)

[3]R.Descartes. [*Le Monde, ou Traite de la Lumiere* (in French)] (1644).

[4]J.Snow. *On the mode of communication of cholera.* London: John Churchill. (1855).

[5]Gustav Lejeune Dirichlet. [" Uber die Reduktion der positiven quadratischen Formen mit drei unbestimmten ganzen Zahlen." (in German)] *Journal für die Reine und Angewandte Mathematik*, **40**:209-227 (1850).

[6]Ater meteorologist After Alfred Thiessen (1872-1965) who used them in his analysis of the effects of weather on different land areas. See A. Thiessen, "Precipitation Averages for Large Areas." *Monthly Weather Review*, **39**(7):1082-1098 (1911).

Figure 31.8: Early applications of Voronoi diagrams. Left: Descartes' analysis of distribution of matter in the solar system. Right: John Snow's map of the 1854 cholera outbreak in central London. Snow labeled the water pumps and marked the deaths by each block by a bar plot. Superimposed on this are larger markers indicating the coordinates of the water pumps, the address of each death, and the Voronoi cells of the water pumps using a Euclidean metric.

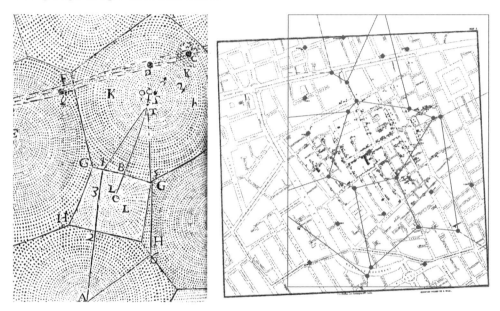

Voronoi Centers in adjacent cells such by line segments, such that each line segment is perpendicular to the edge of the Voronoi cell between them. These definitions can all be extended to higher dimensions.

A brute force calculation of the Voronoi diagram requires finding the intersection of $n-1$ half planes for each cell. Construction the intersections takes $O(n \log n)$ calculations and hence repeating this n times takes $O(n^2 \log n)$. This can be quite computationally intensive. Fortunately, much more efficient algorithms have been found.

The most common one is known as Fortune's algorithm.[7] Fortune observed the following tidbit from high school algebra: a parabola is the locus of points equidistant from a line (the **directrix**) and a point (the **focus**). In Fortune's algorithm, a horizontal **sweep line** moves upward through the diagram starting from the bottom. As the line sweeps up through the diagram, construct a parabola using each point below it as a focus and the sweep line as a directrix. The envelope of this collection of parabolas is called the **beach line**. As the sweep line moves up, the beach line follows it.

---

[7]Steven Fortune. "A sweep-line algorithm for Voronoi diagrams." *Proceedings of the second annual symposium on Computational geometry*, pp. 313-322 (1986), http://portal.acm.org/citation.cfm?id=10549; A good description of this algorithm and Voronoi diagrams in general is given by David Austen, "Voronoi Diagrams and a Day at the Beach" *AMS Monthly Essays on Mathematical Topics*, August 2006, http://www.ams.org/featurecolumn/archive/voronoi.html.

Figure 31.9: Fortune's Algorithm. Left: directrix and focus of a parabola. Right: Implementation of the algorithm. The thin horizontal line across the diagram is the sweep line; the beach line is shaded. Voronoi edges that have already been identified are shown in thicker lines; those that have not yet been discovered are thinner. The vertical line segments connect the directrix to the points required to define the current beach line.

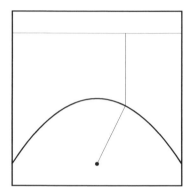
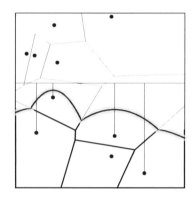

The important observation is that the intersections between different parabolas in the beach line are equidistant between two focii, because they are also the same distance from the sweep line. *Hence the cusps of the beach line sweep out the edges of Voronoi cells. The vertices of the cells will be located at points where precisely three parabolas come together.*

The diagram is found by observing the **events** where three parabolas come together as the line moves through the diagram. Overall the calculation of the entire Voronoi diagram requires $O(n \ln n)$ calculations, compared to the $O(n^2 \log n)$ required by a brute force method.

In higher dimensions, the following observation (stated here without proof) is used to calculate the Voronoi diagram.

1. Given a set of points in $\mathbb{R}^n$, project to the points orthogonally to a paraboloid in $\mathbb{R}^{n+1}$

2. Calculate the convex hull of the points in $\mathbb{R}^{n+1}$

3. Project the lower side of the convex hull back down to $\mathbb{R}^n$

4. The resulting projection in $\mathbb{R}^n$ is the Delaunay Triangulation of the original data in $\mathbb{R}^n$.

Both Voronoi diagrams and Delaunay triangulations are implemented in the scipy **spatial** package. The plots in figure 31.7 were generated with the following code.

```
1  import numpy as np
2  from matplotlib.pyplot import *
3  from scipy.spatial import *
4  pts = np.random.rand(25,2)    # generate random points
5  DT=Delaunay(pts)              # find the Delaunay triangulation
6  V=Voronoi(pts)                # find the Voronoi diagram
7  #--------------------------- all the rest is plotting
8  F,(axV,axD)=subplots(nrows=1,ncols=2) # 2-column plot
9  #--------------------------- first plot
10 VP=voronoi_plot_2d(V,axV)     # Voronoi on left plot
11 axV.set_aspect("equal")
12 axV.set_xticks([])            # turn off tick marks
13 axV.set_yticks([])
14 #--------------------------- second plot
15 DP=delaunay_plot_2d(DT,axD)   # Delaunay on right plot
16 axD.set_aspect("equal")
17 axD.set_xticks([])
18 axD.set_yticks([])
19 show()                        # display on screen
```

Table 31.1. Scipy Spatial Geometry[a]

Function	Return Value
`ConvexHull(points)`	Convex hull.
`convex_hull_plot_2d(CH)`	Plot of the convex hull using matplotlib (only in 2 dimensions). **CH** is the output of **ConvexHull**.
`Delaunay(points)`	Delaunay triangulation.
`delaunay_plot_2d(DT)`	Plot Delaunay triangulation using matplotlib (only in 2 dimensions). **DT** is the return value from **Delaunay**.
`KDTree(data)`	Quick nearest-neighbor lookup.
`Voronoi(points))`	Voronoi diagrams.
`voronoi_plot_2d(V)`	Plot of the voronoi diagram using matplotlib (only in 2 dimensions). **V** is the output of **Voronoi**.
`distance_matrix(x,y,p)`	Computes L-p distance matrix between two arrays.
`minkowski_distance(x,y,p)`	Minkowski L-p distance between two arrays.
`minkowski_distance_p(x,y,p)`	Miknowski L-p distsance raised to the pth power.

[a]For more details see http://docs.scipy.org/doc/scipy-dev/reference/tutorial/spatial.html#qhulltutorial

Input to **Delaunay**, **Voronoi**, and **ConvexHull** is given as a Numpy array of **points**. The simplices and near neighbors in the n-dimensional Delaunay triangulation are given by

```
DT = Delaunay(points)
DT.points[DT.simplices[i, j], :]
DT.neighbors[i,j]
```

The facets of the n-dimensional convex hull are

```
CH = ConvexHull(points)
CH.points[CH.simplices[i, j], :]
```

The ridges of the n-dimensional Voronoi diagram are represented according to

```
VD = Voronoi(points)
VD.vertices[VD.ridge_vertices[i, j], :]
```

Table 31.2. Distance Calculations in `scipy.spatial.distance`[a]

Function	Distance Measure	Input[b]
`braycurtis(u, v)`	Bray-Curtis distance	numeric
`canberra(u, v)`	Canberra distance	numeric
`chebyshev(u, v)`	Chebyshev distance.	numeric
`cityblock(u, v)`	City Block (Manhattan) distance	numeric
`correlation(u, v)`	Correlation distance	numeric
`cosine(u, v)`	Cosine distance	numeric
`dice(u, v)`	Dice dissimilarity	boolean
`euclidean(u, v)`	Euclidean distance	numeric
`hamming(u, v)`	Hamming distance	numeric
`jaccard(u, v)`	Jaccard-Needham dissimilarity	boolean
`kulsinski(u, v)`	Kulsinski dissimilarity	boolean
`mahalanobis(u, v, VI)`	Mahalanobis distance	numeric
`matching(u, v)`	Matching dissimilarity	boolean
`minkowski(u, v, p)`	Minkowski distance	numeric
`rogerstanimoto(u, v)`	Rogers-Tanimoto dissimilarity	boolean
`russellrao(u, v)`	Russell-Rao dissimilarity	boolean
`seuclidean(u, v, V)`	Standardized Euclidean distance	numeric
`sokalmichener(u, v)`	Sokal-Michener dissimilarity	boolean
`sokalsneath(u, v)`	Sokal-Sneath dissimilarity	numeric
`sqeuclidean(u, v)`	Squared Euclidean distance	numeric
`wminkowski(u, v, p, w)`	Weighted Minkowski distance	numeric
`yule(u, v)`	Yule dissimilarity	boolean

[a]For complete listing and additional details see http://docs.scipy.org/doc/scipy-dev/reference/spatial.distance.html#module-scipy.spatial.distance

[b]**u** and **v** are one-dimensional arrays.

Exercises

1. Implement a function to determine if two points are on the same side of a line. Test it out with the following points.

   (a) $y = x$, $(1,0)$ and $(3,7)$; $(1,0)$ and $(3,19)$; $(1,0)$ and $(1,1)$

   (b) $y = -2x - 3$, $(0,0)$ and $(3,0)$; $(0,0)$ and $(-10, -10)$

2. Implement a function to determine if a point is on a given line. Test it out with the following lines and points.

   (a) $y = 3x + 7$, $(x, y) = (5, 22)$, $(x, y) = (1, 11)$, $(x, y) = (0, 0)$

   (b) $y = -4x + 12$, $(x, y) = (2, 2)$, $(x, y) = (0, 0)$, $(x, y) = (1, 8)$

3. Geometricians use the notation **A*B*C** to indicate that **B** is between points **A** and **C**. Implement a function for betweeness and use to test of **A*B*C** when

   (a) **A**=(0,1), **B**=(1,2), **C**=(3,3)

   (b) **A**=(0,1), **B**=(1,2), **C**=(2,3)

   (c) **A**=(0,1), **B**=(1,2), **C**=(1,2)

   (d) **A**=(0,1), **B**=(2,3), **C**=(1,2)

4. Write a function to determine if two line segments intersect. Then use it to determine if the following segments intersect.

   (a) The segment from $(0,1)$ to $(2,2)$ and the segment from $(1,0)$ to $(2,2)$

   (b) The segment from $(0,1)$ to $(2,2)$ and the segment from $(0,2)$ to $(2,2)$

   (c) The segment from $(0,1)$ to $(2,2)$ and the segment from $(1,2)$ to $(3,3)$

   (d) The segment from $(0,0)$ to $(3,0)$ and the segment from $(1,0)$ to $(1,1)$

5. Let P be the polygon with the following vertices: $(1, 1)$, $(2, 1)$, $(2, 1.5)$, $(2.5, 2)$, $(1.5, 3)$, $(1, 1)$. Write a function to determine if a point is inside a polygon. Use it on the polygon P and each of the following points: $(2,1)$, $(0,1)$, $(2,2)$, $(3,3)$. Plot the polygon and the points to verify your results.

6. Write a function to find the area of a polygon. Use it on the polygon P defined in the previous exercise.

7. John Snow's data for the locations of the pumps and the coordinates of the deaths are given in tabular format at http://www.math.uah.edu/stat/data/Snow.html. Download the data and generate the Voronoi cells shown in figure 31.8. Locate Snow's map on the internet and see if you can resize your plot to combine it with the map as shown in the figure.

8. Search the internet for a table of the latitudes and longitudes of the major cites in North America. Your table should contain at least 50 cities.

   (a) Find their convex hull and plot it.

   (b) Plot a Voronoi diagram of the cities.

   (c) Excluding the cities in Alaska, plot the Delaunay Triangulation. Label the cities.

   (d) Use **basemap** (chapter 45) to plot either the Voronoi or Delauny diagram of the cities in the contiguous 48 states in the same figure as a map of the United States.

Chapter 32

Interpolation

Representing Continuous Functions Numerically

A **numerical representation** of a function $f(x)$ is a collection of points

$$\{(x_0, y_0), (x_1, y_1), (x_2, y_2), \ldots, (x_n, y_n)\} \tag{32.1}$$

where each $y_i = f(x_i)$. We do not know the value of the function except at these points. The numbers

$$a = x_0 < x_1 < x_2 < \cdots < x_n = b \tag{32.2}$$

are called **grid points**. Usually when we represent a function this way it is because the data has been obtained empirically, e.g., by a survey or an experiment, and we do not have any exact model for the data. For example, the U.S. Census Bureau tabulates values of the population on July 1 of each year. For the 1900's, it gives the following data[1] for the population in millions.

Year	Population
1900	76.094
1910	92.407
1920	106.461
1930	123.077
1940	132.122
1950	152.271
1960	180.671
1970	205.052
1980	227.224
1990	249.464

It is convenient, though not necessary, for the grid points to be separated by a fixed interval. In the population data, the grid points are separated by a fixed interval of 10 years, and are given by

$$x_0 = 1900, x_1 = 1910, x_2 = 1920, \ldots, x_9 = 1990 \tag{32.3}$$

The data is plotted in figure 32.1. Suppose we were to define a function $f(t)$ that represents the population of the United States at any year t. Intuitively, we could "eyeball" the value of the population in-between the dots, if we wanted to know $f(t)$ at

---

[1]From   https://www.census.gov/popest/data/national/totals/pre-1980/tables/
popclockest.txt

Figure 32.1: US population during the 1900s.

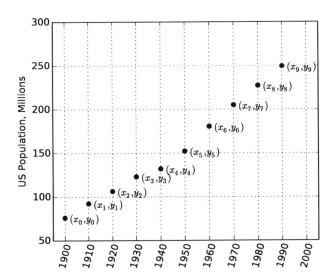

some number t that was not among the grid points, such as 1995 or 1937. This process is called **interpolation**.

Interpolation

Suppose we know the values of some function $f(x)$ at $n+1$ distinct **grid points** $a = x_0, x_1, x_2, ..., x_n = b$. Denote the values of the function at each of these points as $f_k = f(x_k), k = 0, 1, 2, ..., n$. Then the problem of **interpolation** is to find an approximate (numerical) value for $f(x)$ at any point $x \in [a, b]$ that does not necessarily correspond to one of the grid points (figure 32.2).

In **linear interpolation** we draw line segments connecting each pair of consecutive grid points (x_k, f_k) and (x_{k+1}, f_{k+1}). Then

$$y = f_k + m(x - x_k) = f_k + \frac{f_{k+1} - f_k}{x_{k+1} - x_k}(x - x_k), \quad x_k \le x \le x_{k+1} \tag{32.4}$$

Linear interpolation can be performed using `interp1d` in scipy. For example, to find an **interpolation function** – a function that will give a linear interpolation between the grid points – on the population data, we can write the following code.

```
1  import numpy as np
2  from scipy.interpolate import *
3  years=range(1900,2000,10)
4  population=[76.094,92.407,106.461,123.077,132.122, 152.271,
5     180.671,205.052,227.224,249.464]
```

Figure 32.2: The problem of interpolation is to find the value of a function between its known values at a sequence of grid points.

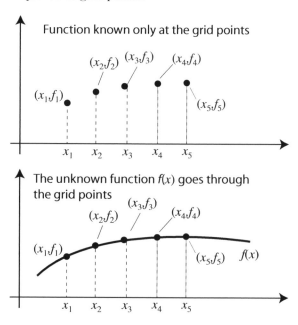

```
 6  import matplotlib.pyplot as plt
 7  f=interp1d(years, population)
 8  x=np.linspace(1900,1990,100)
 9  y=f(x)
10  plt.plot(x,y,color="Red")
11  plt.scatter(years, population, color="Black")
12  plt.xlim(1895,1995)
13  plt.ylim(50,275)
14  plt.xticks(range(1900,1995,10), rotation=75)
15  plt.ylabel("US_Population,_Millions")
16  plt.show()
```

The resulting plot is shown in figure 32.3.

The usage of **interp1d** is summarized in table 32.1.

Figure 32.3: Linear interpolation of US Population data.

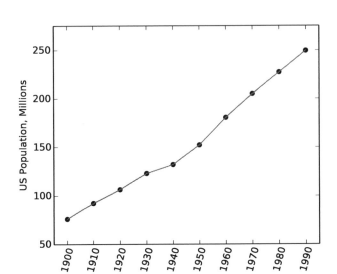

Table 32.1. Interpolation with `scipy.interpolate.interp1d`

`interp1d(x,y,**kwargs)` returns a function that can be used to interpolate at any value of x.

keyword	description
assume_sorted	If **"False"** the data can be in any order. Otherwise the x values should be monotonically increasing.
axis	Axis to use for interpolation.
bounds_error	**"True"** (default) if an attempt is made to interpolate outside the original data range.
copy	**"True"** (default) for doing calculations on a internal copy of the array.
fill_value	**NaN** (default) or value to use when attempting to interpolate outside the original data range.
kind	**"linear"**, **"quadratic"** (quadratic spline), **"cubic"** (cubic spline), **"nearest"**, **"zero"**, **"slinear"** (linear spline). See figure 32.4.

Figure 32.4: Different kinds of interpolation options using `interp1d`

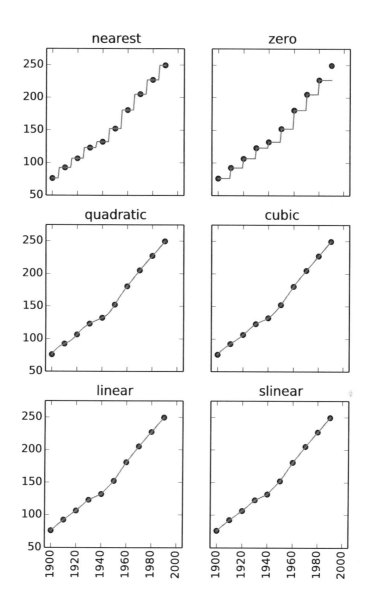

Polynomial Interpolation

Unless the grid points are very close, linear interpolation does not usually give very accurate results. Sometimes a better approximation is given by a polynomial. In this chapter we are assuming that all of the data is exact, so we will require our interpolating function to go through every data point precisely.

Given any set of n data points (at distinct x values) it is always possible to find a polynomial of degree at most $n + 1$ that goes through all the data points. It is also sometimes possible to find higher degree polynomials than $n + 1$ that go through all the data points, but because of their extra turning points, these are usually worse choices. Furthermore, a single polynomial that goes through every data point might not be the best choice, especially if the underlying data source is not polynomial.

Often it is better to fit lower degree polynomials to subsets of the data. For example, in linear interpolation, we fit a line to each pair of points. We could also fit a parabola or a cubic to successive tuples.

Denote the $n + 1$ unique points by

$$(x_0, f_0), (x_1, f_1), \ldots, (x_n, f_n) \tag{32.5}$$

where

$$x_0 < x_1 < \cdots < x_n \tag{32.6}$$

Our goal is find the coefficients $a_0, a_1, \ldots, a_n$, of the degree n polynomial

$$P(x) = a_0 + a_1 x + a_2 x^2 + \cdots + a_n x^n \tag{32.7}$$

such that $P(x)$ passes through every data point (x_i, f_i) exactly:

$$P(x_i) = f_i, \quad i = 0, \ldots, n \tag{32.8}$$

Then

$$\left.\begin{aligned}
f_0 &= a_0 + a_1 x_0 + a_2 x_0^2 + \cdots + a_n x_0^n \\
f_1 &= a_0 + a_1 x_1 + a_2 x_1^2 + \cdots + a_n x_n^n \\
&\;\;\vdots \\
f_n &= a_0 + a_1 x_n + a_2 x_n^2 + \cdots + a_n x_n^n
\end{aligned}\right\} \tag{32.9}$$

In matrix form

$$\begin{bmatrix} 1 & x_0 & x_0^2 & \cdots & x_0^n \\ 1 & x_1 & x_1^2 & \cdots & x_1^n \\ \vdots & & & & \vdots \\ 1 & x_n & x_n^2 & \cdots & x_n^n \end{bmatrix} \begin{bmatrix} a_0 \\ a_1 \\ \vdots \\ a_n \end{bmatrix} = \begin{bmatrix} f_0 \\ f_1 \\ \vdots \\ f_n \end{bmatrix} \tag{32.10}$$

Because the points are distinct, the rows of the matrix are linearly independent. Thus the matrix is non-singular and invertible. In principal we could solve this equation precisely as $\mathbf{a} = \mathbf{M}^{-1}\mathbf{f}$, where $\mathbf{a}$ and $\mathbf{f}$ are the column vectors of the a_i and f_i, and $\mathbf{M}$ is the matrix of constants in equation 32.10.

Rather the solving the system directly, Lagrange made the following observation. For $n = 1$, we are merely fitting a line to the two points (x_0, f_0), (x_1, f_1). If we define the functions

$$L_0(x) = \frac{x - x_1}{x_0 - x_1}, \quad L_1(x) = \frac{x - x_0}{x_1 - x_0} \tag{32.11}$$

Then

$$P(x) = \sum_{k=0}^{1} L_i(x) f_i = L_0(x) f_0 + L_1(x) f_1 = \frac{x - x_1}{x_0 - x_1} f_0 + \frac{x - x_0}{x_1 - x_0} f_1 \tag{32.12}$$

is a line that goes through both points. This is because[2]

$$\left. \begin{array}{ll} L_0(x_0) = 1 & L_0(x_1) = 0 \\ L_1(x_0) = 0 & L_1(x_1) = 1 \end{array} \right\} \implies L_i(x_j) = \delta_{ij} = \begin{cases} 1, & i = j, \\ 0, & i \neq j \end{cases} \tag{32.13}$$

By uniqueness, this is the only line that goes through both points.

For $n = 2$ we have 3 points: (x_0, f_0), (x_1, f_1), and (x_2, f_2). Define

$$L_0(x) = \frac{(x - x_1)(x - x_2)}{(x_0 - x_1)(x_0 - x_2)} \tag{32.14}$$

$$L_1(x) = \frac{(x - x_0)(x - x_2)}{(x_1 - x_0)(x_1 - x_2)} \tag{32.15}$$

$$L_2(x) = \frac{(x - x_0)(x - x_1)}{(x_2 - x_0)(x_2 - x_1)} \tag{32.16}$$

Therefore $L_i(x_j) = \delta_{ij}$. Next we define the parabola

$$P(x) = L_0(x) f_0 + L_1(x) f_1 + L_2(x) f_2 = \sum_{k=0}^{2} L_i(x) f_i \tag{32.17}$$

which goes through all three points. By uniqueness it is the only parabola that goes through all three points. This method can be generalized to higher order by adding one more factor per term and one more term per equation for each degree.

Theorem 32.1. Lagrange Interpolation

Suppose that $f(x)$ is known precisely at $n + 1$ distinct points $x_0, \ldots, x_n$, given by $f_0, \ldots, f_n$. Then the nth **Lagrange interpolating polynomial**

$$P(x) = \sum_{k=0}^{n} L_{nk}(x) f_k = \sum_{k=0}^{n} f_k \prod_{j=0, j \neq k}^{n} \frac{x - x_j}{x_k - x_j} \tag{32.18}$$

where $L_{nk}(x) = \prod_{j=0, j \neq k}^{n} \frac{x - x_j}{x_k - x_j}$ is the unique polynomial of degree at most n such that $P(x_i) = f_i$.

---

[2]The function δ_{ij} is called the **Kronecker delta function**, for the German mathematician Leopold Kronecker (1823-1891).

Algorithm 32.1 Lagrange Interpolation

---

input: $x_0, \ldots, x_n$, $f_0, \ldots, f_n$, x

1: $P \leftarrow 0$
2: **for** $i \leftarrow 0, \ldots n$ **do**
3:     $U \leftarrow \{x_0, \ldots, x_n\} \setminus \{x_i\}$ Set difference
4:     $L \leftarrow \left(\prod_{u \in U} (x - u) \right) \Big/ \left(\prod_{u \in U} (x_i - u) \right)$
5:     $P \leftarrow P + f_i L_i^n$
6: **end for**
7: **return** P

Theorem 32.2. Error Bounds for Lagrange Interpolation

Suppose that $f(x)$ is $n + 1$ times continuously differentiable, and that the points $x_0, \ldots, x_n$ are distinct. Then for any $x \in [a, b]$ there exists a number $c \in [a, b]$ such that

$$f(x) = P(x) + \frac{f^{n+1}(c)(x - x_0)(x - x_1) \cdots (x - x_n)}{(n + 1)!} \tag{32.19}$$

where

$$P(x) = \sum_{k=0}^{n} f_k L_{nk}(x) = \sum_{k=0}^{n} f_k \prod_{j=0, j \neq k}^{n} \frac{x - x_j}{x_k - x_j} \tag{32.20}$$

Cubic Splines

In this method, instead of trying to fit a single polynomial to all of our data points, we use a **patched** approach, in which we fit a **different cubic polynomial** $S_i(x)$ to each successive interval $[x_i, x_{i+1}]$, in such a way that that the first and second derivatives (slopes and curvature) of the fits on adjacent polynomials are continuous. This gives us four conditions at each point:

$$S_i(x_i) = f_i \tag{32.21}$$
$$S_i(x_{i+1}) = S_{i+1}(x_{i+1}) \tag{32.22}$$
$$S_i'(x_{i+1}) = S_{i+1}'(x_{i+1}) \tag{32.23}$$
$$S_i''(x_{i+1}) = S_{i+1}''(x_{i+1}) \tag{32.24}$$

The functions $S_0(x), \ldots, S_{n-1}(x)$ are called **Spline functions**. At the endpoints there are no derivatives to match, so we can only apply equations 32.22 through 32.24 to the $n - 1$ internal points. This gives a total of $4(n - 1) = 4n - 4$ conditions. At the end points, only condition (32.21) can be applied. Thus we have set a total of $4n - 2$ conditions.

Since each cubic $S_i(x)$ has four undetermined coefficients, and there are n intervals, we will need to find $4n$ coefficients. Since the problem is under-determined by two

Figure 32.5: Cubic spline interpolation.

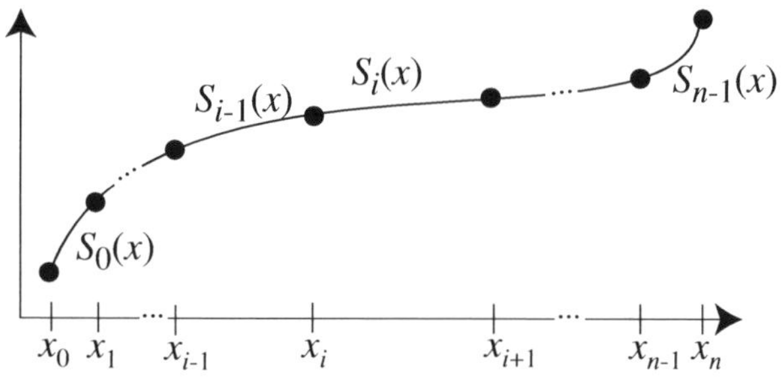

conditions two different methods are usually used.

1. **free (natural) boundary conditions**: set the curvature to zero at the end points.

$$S_0''(x_0) = S_{n-1}''(x_n) = 0 \tag{32.25}$$

2. **clamped boundary conditions**: - if we somehow have knowledge of the slope at the end points, use that information.

$$S_0'(x_0) = f'(x_0) \tag{32.26}$$
$$S_{n-1}'(x_n) = f'(x_n) \tag{32.27}$$

Denote the splines by

$$S_i(x) = a_i + b_i(x - x_i) + c_i(x - x_i)^2 + d_i(x - x_i)^3 \tag{32.28}$$

If we assume that the grid points are equally spaced with separation h (this is not required, but it makes the equations simpler), it is possible to show that[3] for free splines

$$a_i = f_i \tag{32.29}$$
$$b_i = \frac{1}{h}(a_{i+1} - a_i) - \frac{h^2}{2}(2c_i + c_{i+1}) \tag{32.30}$$
$$d_i = \frac{1}{3h}(c_{i+1} - c_i) \tag{32.31}$$

---

[3]The derivation is given in any introductory book on numerical analysis; see, for example, pp 146-148 of Burden R.L. and Faires J.D. (2011) **Numerical Analysis**, 9th Ed, Boston:Brooks/Cole.

$$
\begin{bmatrix}
1 & 0 & \cdots & & & 0 \\
h & 4h & h & 0 & & \vdots \\
0 & h & 4h & h & 0 & \\
\vdots & & \ddots & \ddots & \ddots & \\
0 & & 0 & h & 4h & h \\
0 & & & & 0 & 1
\end{bmatrix}
\begin{bmatrix}
c_0 \\ c_1 \\ c_2 \\ \vdots \\ \\ c_n
\end{bmatrix}
= \frac{3}{h}
\begin{bmatrix}
0 \\
a_0 - 2a_1 + a_2 \\
\vdots \\
a_{n-2} - 2a_{n-1} + a_n \\
0
\end{bmatrix}
\tag{32.32}
$$

Thus the a_i are determined by the f_i, the c_i are determined by the a_i, the b_i are determined by the a_i and the c_i, and the d_i are determined by the c_i. The only potential difficulty is the linear system (32.32), which can be solving using the methods of chapter 30.

For clamped cubic splines, (32.32) is replaced by

$$
\begin{bmatrix}
2h & h & \cdots & & & 0 \\
h & 4h & h & & & \vdots \\
0 & h & 4h & h & & \\
\vdots & & \ddots & \ddots & \ddots & 0 \\
0 & & 0 & h & 4h & h \\
0 & & & 0 & h & 2h
\end{bmatrix}
\begin{bmatrix}
c_0 \\ c_1 \\ c_2 \\ \vdots \\ \\ c_n
\end{bmatrix}
\frac{3}{h}
\begin{bmatrix}
(a_1 - a_0) - hf'(a) \\
a_2 - 2a_1 + a_0 \\
\vdots \\
a_n - 2a_{n-1} + a_{n-2} \\
hf'(b) - (a_n - a_{n-1})
\end{bmatrix}
\tag{32.33}
$$

Python's Scipy package provides support for splines. Splines can be represented either directly or parametrically.

Example 32.1. Fit a Cubic Spline to the US Population Data.

> **scipy.interpolate.splrep(x, y)** returns a direct representation of the curve of two dimensional spline as tuple **t, c, k** where **t** are **knot points** (the points where the different splines connect together), **c** is the set of **coefficients**, and **k** is the spline **order**. The keyword **k** can be used to change the order from its default value of 3.[4] The function **splev** can be used to evaluate the spline. The implementation for the US population data is thus (see figure 32.6).

```
1  x=np.linspace(1900,1990,100)
2  f=splrep(years,population)
3  y=splev(x,f)
4  plt.plot(x,y,color="Red")
5  plt.scatter(years,popopulation,color="Black")
6  plt.xlim(1895,1995)
7  plt.ylim(50,275)
8  plt.xticks(range(1900,1995,10), rotation=75)
9  plt.ylabel("US_Population,_Millions")
```

In higher dimensions than the plane, the function **splprep(data)** returns a parametric representation, where **data** is a list of n dimensional points representing the data.[5]

---

[4]Details on **splrep** are given at http://docs.scipy.org/doc/scipy-0.14.0/reference/generated/scipy.interpolate.splrep.html#scipy.interpolate.splrep

[5]See http://docs.scipy.org/doc/scipy-0.14.0/reference/generated/scipy.interpolate.splprep.html#scipy.interpolate.splprep for more detail.

Figure 32.6: US population data, using a cubic spline interpolation.

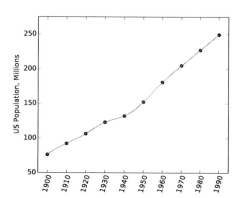

Multivariate Interpolation

Multivariate interpolation generalizes the concept of interpolation to functions of multiple variables. For example, if you know a function $f(x, y)$ at a **grid** of points $z_{ij} = (x_i, y_j)$ for $i = 0, \ldots, n; j = 0, \ldots, n$, the goal is to find the value of $f(x, y)$ at points that are not represented by the grid. Multivariate interpolation can be performed with the function **griddata**. The following code illustrates its use for the function $f(x, y) = \cos x + \sin y$ on the region $[\pi, 3\pi] \times [\pi, 3\pi]$ using 100 interpolation points.

This defines the original function and plots it as an image:

```
import numpy as np
from matplotlib.pyplot import *
from scipy.interpolate import griddata

# original function
def f(x,y):
    return np.cos(x) + np.sin(y)
# define a full grid
xg,yg=np.mgrid[np.pi:3*np.pi:100j, np.pi:3*np.pi:100j]

# plot original function for comparison
fig, (ax1, ax2, ax3) =subplots(1,3)
p1=ax1.imshow(f(xg,yg).T,
    extent=[np.pi, 3*np.pi, np.pi, 3*np.pi], origin="lower")
ax1.set_title("Original_Function")
```

Now we set up a grid of interpolation points

```
1  # define interpolation grid
2  xpts = np.linspace(np.pi, 3*np.pi,10)
3  ypts = np.linspace(np.pi, 3*np.pi,10)
4  pts=[]
```

```
5   for x in xpts:
6       for y in ypts:
7           pts.append([x,y])
8   pts = np.array(pts)
9   fpts = f(pts[:,0], pts[:,1])
```

Next, we do two different interpolations: cubic, and nearest point.

We plot the results of each on the middle and right subplot.

```
# do a cubic interpolation
fit = griddata(pts, fpts, (xg,yg), method="cubic")
c2=ax2.imshow(fit.T, extent=[np.pi, 3*np.pi, np.pi, 3*np.pi],
              origin="lower")
ax2.set_title("Cubic Interpolation")

# do a nearest interpolation
fitn = griddata(pts, fpts, (xg,yg), method="nearest")
c3=ax3.imshow(fitn.T, extent=[np.pi, 3*np.pi, np.pi, 3*np.pi],
              origin="lower")
ax3.set_title("Nearest Interpolation")

show()
```

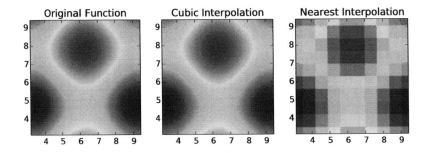

We could also plot the functions with contour plots (**contour** or **contourf**) instead of
imshow().

Bezier Splines

Bezier curves, commonly used in computer graphics, are related to interpolation, but
the functions do not actually match all of the points. Instead, some of the points are
used for control, to pull the curve in different directions, like a string pulling on a piece
of fabric. They are named for Piere Bézier (1910-1999) who created them to model
automobile surfaces in the early 1960's. He worked for Renault for virtually his entire
career.

Bezier curves are used by many interactive graphics programs to draw smooth curves. One typically marks the end points of the curve by clicking a mouse, then then drags a mouse to define the handles, which can be used interactively to pull the curve in different directions. In general, Bezier curves are described by systems of parametric equations that describe the path of the curve in the xy-plane over the interval $[0, 1]$.

The simplest type of Bezier curves is a **Bezier Line**, describe parametrically by joining the points $\mathbf{P}_0 = (x_0, y_0)$ and $\mathbf{P}_2 = (x_1, y_1)$ with a straight line. We can describe this construction parametrically by

$$\mathbf{P}(t) = \mathbf{P}_0(1 - t) + \mathbf{P}_1 t \tag{32.34}$$

In terms of the separate x and y components,

$$x(t) = x_0(1 - t) + x_1 t \tag{32.35}$$
$$y(t) = y_0(1 - t) + y_1 t \tag{32.36}$$

Quadratic Bezier curves are constructed as illustrated in figure 32.7. We draw a curve that connects points $\mathbf{P}_0$ and $\mathbf{P}_2$; the shape of this line is determined by the position of a third "guide point" or "handle" that we label $\mathbf{P}_1$. We then define parametrizations of the line segments $\overline{\mathbf{P}_0\mathbf{P}_1}$ and $\overline{\mathbf{P}_1\mathbf{P}_2}$ as

$$\mathbf{P}_{01}(t) = \mathbf{P}_0(1 - t) + \mathbf{P}_1 t \tag{32.37}$$
$$\mathbf{P}_{12}(t) = \mathbf{P}_1(1 - t) + \mathbf{P}_2 t \tag{32.38}$$

Finally, we parametrize the line segment from $\mathbf{P}_{01}$ to $\mathbf{P}_{12}$:

$$\mathbf{P}(t) = (1 - t)\mathbf{P}_{01}(t) + t\mathbf{P}_{12}(t) \tag{32.39}$$

The **Bezier Quadratic** is the curve traced out by $\mathbf{P}(t)$ as t goes from $t = 0$ to $t = 1$. Substituting the expressions for $\mathbf{P}_{01}$ and $\mathbf{P}_{12}$ gives

$$\mathbf{P}(t) = (1 - t)[(1 - t)\mathbf{P}_0 + t\mathbf{P}_1] + t[(1 - t)\mathbf{P}_1 + t\mathbf{P}_2] \tag{32.40}$$
$$= (1 - t)^2\mathbf{P}_0 + 2t(1 - t)\mathbf{P}_1 + t^2\mathbf{P}_2 \tag{32.41}$$

In terms of the x and y coordinates, the **quadratic Bezier interpolants** are:

$$x(t) = (1 - t)^2 x_0 + 2t(1 - t)x_1 + t^2 x_2 \tag{32.42}$$
$$y(t) = (1 - t)^2 y_0 + 2t(1 - t)y_1 + t^2 y_2 \tag{32.43}$$

Bezier quadratics are used, for example, to describe true-type fonts. The spline functions constructed in this way have slopes tangent to the line segment $\overline{\mathbf{P}_{01}\mathbf{P}_{12}}$.

The **Bezier Cubic** has a similar construction, except that there are two **control points** $\mathbf{P}_1$ and $\mathbf{P}_2$ instead of just one. As before we construct the line segments $\overline{\mathbf{P}_0\mathbf{P}_1}$, $\overline{\mathbf{P}_1\mathbf{P}_2}$ and $\overline{\mathbf{P}_2\mathbf{P}_3}$. At any time $t \in [0, 1]$, we define points on these three segments by

$$\mathbf{P}_{01}(t) = (1 - t)\mathbf{P}_0 + t\mathbf{P}_1 \tag{32.44}$$
$$\mathbf{P}_{12}(t) = (1 - t)\mathbf{P}_1 + t\mathbf{P}_2 \tag{32.45}$$

Figure 32.7: The Bezier quadratic is the parabola traced out by **P** as it moves at a constant velocity from $\mathbf{P}_{01}$ to $\mathbf{P}_{12}$, while $\mathbf{P}_{01}$ is moving from $\mathbf{P}_0$ to $\mathbf{P}_1$ and $\mathbf{P}_{12}$ is moving from $\mathbf{P}_1$ to $\mathbf{P}_2$.

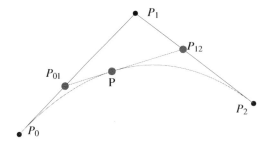

Figure 32.8: Construction of the Bezier Cubic spline.

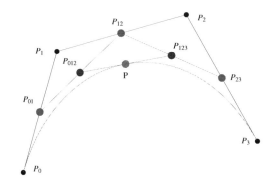

$$\mathbf{P}_{23}(t) = (1-t)\mathbf{P}_2 + t\mathbf{P}_3 \tag{32.46}$$

Next, construct line segments $\overline{\mathbf{P}_{01}\mathbf{P}_{12}}$ and $\overline{\mathbf{P}_{12}\mathbf{P}_{23}}$ and define their parametrization on $[0, 1]$ as follows:

$$\mathbf{P}_{012}(t) = (1-t)\mathbf{P}_{01}(t) + t\mathbf{P}_{12}(t) \tag{32.47}$$
$$\mathbf{P}_{123}(t) = (1-t)\mathbf{P}_{12}(t) + t\mathbf{P}_{23}(t) \tag{32.48}$$

Finally we construct the line segment $\overline{\mathbf{P}_{012}\mathbf{P}_{123}}$ with parametrization

$$\mathbf{P}(t) = (1-t)\mathbf{P}_{012}(t) + t\mathbf{P}_{123}(t) \tag{32.49}$$
$$= (1-t)[(1-t)\mathbf{P}_{01}(t) + t\mathbf{P}_{12}(t)] + t[(1-t)\mathbf{P}_{12}(t) + t\mathbf{P}_{23}(t)] \tag{32.50}$$
$$= (1-t)^2\mathbf{P}_{01}(t) + 2t(1-t)\mathbf{P}_{12}(t) + t^2\mathbf{P}_{23}(t) \tag{32.51}$$
$$= (1-t)^2[(1-t)\mathbf{P}_0 + t\mathbf{P}_1] + 2t(1-t)[(1-t)\mathbf{P}_1 + t\mathbf{P}_2] \tag{32.52}$$
$$+ t^2[(1-t)\mathbf{P}_2 + t\mathbf{P}_3]$$
$$= (1-t)^3\mathbf{P}_0 + 3t(1-t)^2\mathbf{P}_1 + 3t^2(1-t)\mathbf{P}_2 + t^3\mathbf{P}_3 \tag{32.53}$$

Figure 32.9: Alternate notation for Bezier cubic splines.

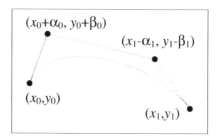

The Cartesian coordinates of the point $\mathbf{P}$ constructed in this ware are

$$x(t) = (1-t)^3 x_0 + 3t(1-t)^2 x_1 + 3t^2(1-t)x_2 + t^3 x_3 \tag{32.54}$$

$$y(t) = (1-t)^3 y_0 + 3t(1-t)^2 y_1 + 3t^2(1-t)y_2 + t^3 y_3 \tag{32.55}$$

Bezier cubics in this form are used to describe Postscript fonts.

Because we have a cubic parametrization there are a total of eight coefficients (four each for x and y), which we have described by the coordinates of the points $P_0, P_1 P_2, P_3$. By uniqueness, there can be only curve that matches our restriction, and so any derivation of the Bezier cubics must, of necessity give the same curve.

An alternate notation as illustrated in figure 32.9 is more apropos to the usage in many graphics applications. We join to the two points

$$\mathbf{P}_0 = (x_0, y_0) \tag{32.56}$$

$$\mathbf{P}_1 = (x_1, y_1) \tag{32.57}$$

in such a way that the slopes at $\mathbf{P}_0$ and $\mathbf{P}_1$ are the same as the vectors $\mathbf{Q}_0 - \mathbf{P}_0$ and $\mathbf{Q}_1 - \mathbf{P}_1$ where

$$\mathbf{Q}_0 = (x_0 + 3\alpha_0, \ y_0 + 3\beta_0) \tag{32.58}$$

$$\mathbf{Q}_1 = (x_1 - 3\alpha_1, \ y_1 - 3\beta_1) \tag{32.59}$$

for some constants α and β. The numbers 3 are used by convention though they are not present in all implementations.

As before we find a parametric representation of the curve $(x(t), \ y(t))$ on the interval $t \in [0, 1]$, subject to the conditions

$$\begin{array}{cccc} x(0) = x_0 & x(1) = x_1 & x'(0) = 3\alpha_0 & x'(1) = 3\alpha_1 \\ y(0) = y_0 & y(1) = y_1 & y'(0) = 3\beta_0 & y'(1) = 3\beta_1 \end{array} \tag{32.60}$$

The solution is

$$x(t) = x_0 + 3\alpha_0 t + [3(x_1 - x_0) - 3(2\alpha_0 + \alpha_1)]t^2 + \tag{32.61}$$
$$[2(x_0 - x_1) + 3(\alpha_0 + \alpha_1)]t^3$$

$$y(t) = y_0 + 3\beta_0 t + [3(y_1 - y_0) - 3(2\beta_0 + \beta_1)]t^2 + \tag{32.62}$$
$$[2(y_0 - y_1) + 3(\beta_0 + \beta_1)]t^3$$

The variation used for Postscript fonts is based on the positions of the two points (x_0, y_0) and (x_3, y_3) and their handles (x_1, y_1) and (x_2, y_2) rather than the derivatives, so it has a slightly different form,

$$x(t) = (1 - t)^3 x_0 + 3t(1 - t)^2 x_1 + 3t^2(1 - t)x_2 + t^3 x_3 \tag{32.63}$$
$$y(t) = (1 - t)^3 y_0 + 3t(1 - t)^2 y_1 + 3t^2(1 - t)y_2 + t^3 y_3 \tag{32.64}$$

Higher degree Bezier curves are defined using additional control points. The points give a sequence of line segments that "pull" the curve towards them, with the Bezier curve parallel to the first and last segment.

$$x(t) = \sum_{i=0}^{n} \binom{n}{i} x_i (1 - t)^{n-i} t^i \tag{32.65}$$

$$y(t) = \sum_{i=0}^{n} \binom{n}{i} y_i (1 - t)^{n-i} t^i \tag{32.66}$$

A generalization to higher dimensions is given by **Bezier Surfaces**.[6] The general form of a Bezier Surface is given in terms of $(m+1)(n+1)$ points $(x_{0,0}, y_{0,0}, z_{0,0}), \ldots, (x_{m,n}, y_{m,n}, z_{m,n})$ as

$$x(s,t) = \sum_{i=0}^{n} \sum_{j=0}^{m} \binom{n}{i} \binom{m}{j} s^i (1 - s)^{n-i} t^j (1 - t)^{n-j} x_{i,j} \tag{32.67}$$

$$y(s,t) = \sum_{i=0}^{n} \sum_{j=0}^{m} \binom{n}{i} \binom{m}{j} s^i (1 - s)^{n-i} t^j (1 - t)^{n-j} y_{i,j} \tag{32.68}$$

$$z(s,t) = \sum_{i=0}^{n} \sum_{j=0}^{m} \binom{n}{i} \binom{m}{j} s^i (1 - s)^{n-i} t^j (1 - t)^{n-j} z_{i,j} \tag{32.69}$$

where $s, t \in [0, 1]$.

Exercises

1. Let $y = e^x$. Construct Lagrange iterpolating polynomial on the interval $0, 1$ using $n = 2$, $n = 3$, $n = 4$ and $n = 5$ points.

2. Go to the Bureau of labor statistics data site (http://data.bls.gov/cgi-bin/surveymost?cw) and download the consumer price index for the Western Region,

   for the last ten years, as a spreadsheet. Save the data as a csv file and read it into Python. Then plot the data as a scatter plot. Fit a cubit spline.

3. Implement Lagrange interpolation. Then use it with a sliding window on the data set from the previous exercise.

---

[6] Also invented by Pierre Bezier in 1972

Chapter 33

Finding Zeros (Roots)

A **root** or a **zero** of a function is a number x where where $f(x)$ crosses the x axis, i.e., the solution of the equation $f(x) = 0$. Not all functions have roots, and some functions will have many roots.

> **Definition 33.1. Root**
>
> A number r is said to be a root of a function $f(x)$ if $f(r) = 0$.

Figure 33.1: The Intermediate Value Theorem tells us that any continuous function with end points on opposite sides of the x axis must cross the x axis at least once.

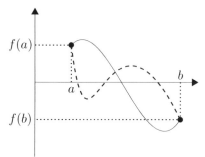

The existence of a root of a **continuous** function in the interval (a, b) is guaranteed by the **intermediate value theorem** if $f(a)f(b) < 0$. The condition $f(a)f(b) < 0$ ensures that $f(a)$ and $f(b)$ have different signs and therefore lie on opposite sides of the x axis. Since $y = 0$ is between $f(a)$ and $f(b)$, there is at least one point r between a and b such that $f(r) = 0$ (see figure 33.1 for two examples of such functions).

> **Theorem 33.1. Intermediate Value Theorem**
>
> Let $f(x)$ be continuous on $[a, b]$ and $f(a) \neq f(b)$. Then $\forall y \in$ ($\min(f(a), f(b))$, $\max(f(a), f(b))$), $\exists c \in (a, b)$ such that $y = f(c)$.

Bisection

The simplest algorithm for finding roots is called **bisection**. It assumes we already know two points a and b, one on either side of the root. As discussed above, the intermediate value theorem ensures that there is a root in (a, b) if $f(a)f(b) < 0$. By convention, we will choose the names such that $a < r < b$. (If the names are given to us in the other order, just switch them.)

The basic idea is to split the interval $[a, b]$ in half. We define c as the midpoint[1]

$$c = a + \frac{b - a}{2} \tag{33.1}$$

First, we check to see if $f(c) = 0$. If it is, we are done, because c is the root. If not, we check the sign of $f(a)f(c)$.

If $f(a)f(c) > 0$ then a and c are on the same side of the root, so $r \in (c, b)$. We relabel c as the new a, and repeat until the interval is sufficiently small.

If $f(a)f(c) < 0$ then a and c are on different sides of the root, so $r \in (a, c)$. We relabel c as the new b, and repeat until the interval is sufficiently small (figure 33.2).

We stop iterating when

$$\Delta = b - a < \epsilon \tag{33.2}$$

where ϵ is some desired tolerance (an input parameter). This method is summarized in algorithm 33.1. The algorithm includes two additional suggestions to improve performance.

1. It might take a long time to reach the desired ϵ, so it always a good idea to include a counter and terminate after some number N steps regardless of how close you've gotten (stop after, say, 10,000 steps). This is especially important when you are debugging the program.

2. As you get closer and closer to the root, the product $f(a)f(c)$ will get smaller and smaller, and could run into the level of machine accuracy. It is better to check the product $\text{Sign}(f(a))\text{Sign}(f(b))$ rather than the product $f(a)f(c)$.

Because the size of the interval is halved each time, the total number of iterations will be the smallest integer n such that

$$\left(\frac{1}{2}\right)^n |b - a| < \epsilon \tag{33.3}$$

Solving for n,

$$n \approx \log_2\left(\frac{|b - a|}{\epsilon}\right) \tag{33.4}$$

As $n \to \infty$, the iterates will approach the exact root. This leads to the following theorem.

---

[1]Refer to equation 7.7 to see why we calculate the midpoint this way and not as $(a + b)/2$.

Figure 33.2: The first three iterations of a bisection algorithm. The interval is halved in size after each iteration.

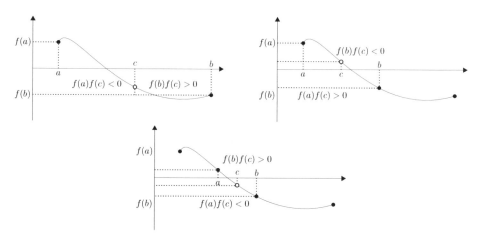

Theorem 33.2. The bisection algorithm converges.

Suppose $f(x)$ is continuous and has a root at $x = r$. Then $\forall \epsilon > 0$, $\exists N$ such that

$$|f(c_n) - f(r)| < \epsilon \qquad (33.5)$$

$\forall\, n > N$, where c_n is the midpoint after n steps of the bisection algorithm.

Fixed Point Iteration

Even though algorithm 33.1 eventually converges, it can be be very slow. Better methods depend on the concept of fixed point iteration, such as the Babylonian root finding algorithm (algorithm 3.1).

Definition 33.2. Fixed Point

A number p is called a **fixed point** of the function $f(x)$ if $p = f(p)$.

You may have played the following game when you were a kid: type a number into a calculator and press the same function button over and over again until nothing changes any more. Usually you will get an error; sometimes you will get a nonsense sequence; and sometimes it will converge to something. This is an example of fixed point iteration.

Example 33.1. Guess the fixed point of $y = \sqrt{x}$ using a calculator and the $\boxed{\sqrt{}}$ key starting with a first guess of $x_0 = 16$.

The following sequence was generated with a TI-36 (which has 10 digit accu-

---

Algorithm 33.1 Bisection algorithm

---

input: f, a, b,tolerance ϵ, maximum steps N

 1: **if** $f(a) = 0$ **then**
 2:    **return** a   There is a root at a.
 3: **else if** $f(b) = 0$ **then**
 4:    **return** b   There is a root at b.
 5: **end if**
 6: **if** $a > b$ **then**
 7:    $a, b \leftarrow b, a$ Force $a < b$
 8: **end if**
 9: $\Delta \leftarrow 0.5 * (b - a)$; $i \leftarrow 0$
10: **if** $f(a)f(b) > 0$ **then**
11:    Print error message and stop.
12: **end if**
13: **while** $\Delta > \epsilon$ **and** $i < N$ **do**
14:    $r \leftarrow a + \Delta$
15:    **if** $f(r) = 0$ **then**
16:       **return** r Root is at the midpoint.
17:    **end if**
18:    **if** $\text{sign}(f(a))\text{sign}(f(r)) < 0$ **then**
19:       $b \leftarrow r$ Root is on left half of interval.
20:    **else**
21:       $a \leftarrow r$ Root is on right half of interval.
22:    **end if**
23:    $\Delta \leftarrow 0.5 * (b - a)$ Find new midpoint.
24:    $i \leftarrow i + 1$ Increment step counter.
25: **end while**
26: **return** r

---

racy):

$$x_0 = 16 \tag{33.6a}$$

$$x_1 = \sqrt{x_0} = \sqrt{16} = 4 \tag{33.6b}$$

$$x_2 = \sqrt{x_1} = \sqrt{4} = 2 \tag{33.6c}$$

$$x_3 = \sqrt{x_2} = \sqrt{2} = 1.414213562 \tag{33.6d}$$

$$x_4 = \sqrt{x_3} = \sqrt{1.414213562} = 1.1892070115 \tag{33.6e}$$

$$x_5 = \sqrt{x_4} = \sqrt{1.1892070115} = 1.090507733 \tag{33.6f}$$

$$\vdots$$

Eventually, after around 30 iterations, the calculator displays something like

$$\boxed{1.0000000000} \tag{33.6g}$$

on all subsequent iterations, because

$$\sqrt{1.0000000000} = 1.0000000000 \qquad (33.7)$$

In fact, example 33.1 found the fixed point of the square root function

$$f(x) = \sqrt{x} \qquad (33.8)$$

to within the machine epsilon of the calculator (1 part in 10^{10}), namely, the point where

$$x = f(x) = \sqrt{x} \qquad (33.9)$$

Equation 33.9 has only two solutions: $x = 1$ and $x = 0$. The calculator converged on the first of these solutions. Had we started with any positive number, we still would have converged on the solution $x = 1$, regardless of which number we typed in for x_0. Had we started with $x = 0$ we would have converged on the other root, $x = 0$, and had we started with a negative number, we would have gotten an error message.

The fixed point we found in example 33.1 occurred at the intersection of $y = f(x) = \sqrt{x}$ and $y = x$. This will always be the case; this follows immediately from the definition of a fixed point, that $f(p) = p$. *A fixed point of $f(x)$ always occurs at an intersection of the two curves $y = f(x)$ and $y = x$.* If the $f(x)$ does not intersect the line $y = x$, then it does not have a fixed point.

> **Theorem 33.3. Existence of Fixed Points**
>
> A continuous function $f(x)$ will have a fixed point if and only if it crosses the line $y = x$.

> **Theorem 33.4.**
>
> Every continuous bounded function on the real numbers has a fixed point.

Proof. Since $f(x)$ is bounded then there is some positive number M such that

$$|f(x)| < M \qquad (33.10)$$

for all x. Choose $x = a$ such that $a < -M$. Let $g(x) = f(x) - x$. Then

$$g(a) = f(a) - a > -M - a > 0 \qquad (33.11)$$

Choose $x = b$ such that $b > M$. Then

$$g(b) = f(b) - b = M - b < 0 \qquad (33.12)$$

Since $g(a)$ and $g(b)$ have different signs, there is some number r, $a < r < b$, such that $g(r) = 0$. This follows from the intermediate value theorem (theorem 33.1). Hence at $x = r$, $f(r) = r$, i.e., r is a fixed point. Thus a fixed point exists. $\square$

During fixed point iteration we are computing a sequence of repeated function applications. For some function $g(x)$, and some starting value x_0, we compute the numbers

$x_1, x_2, \ldots,$ where

$$x_1 = g(x_0) \tag{33.13a}$$
$$x_2 = g(g(x_0)) = g^2(x_0) \tag{33.13b}$$
$$x_3 = g(g(g(x_0))) = g^3(x_0) \tag{33.13c}$$
$$\vdots$$
$$x_n = g^n(x_0) \tag{33.13d}$$

where we have used the notation $g^k(x)$ to denote the repeated application of the function $g(x)$ k times. This is summarized more succinctly in algorithm 33.2.

Algorithm 33.2 Fixed point iteration. This algorithm will find the fixed point of $f(x)$ using a starting value of x_0.

---

input: f, x_0,tolerance ϵ, maximum steps N
 1: $\Delta \leftarrow \infty$
 2: $x \leftarrow x_0$
 3: $i \leftarrow 0$
 4: **while** $\Delta > \epsilon$ **and** $i < N$ **do**
 5:     $x_{old} \leftarrow x$
 6:     $x \leftarrow f(x_{old})$
 7:     $\Delta \leftarrow |x - x_{old}|$
 8:     $i \leftarrow i + 1$ Increment step counter.
 9: **end while**
10: **return** x as **fixedpoint**(f, x_0, ϵ, N)

We can write a naive fixed point algorithm to find the root of any function using fixed point iteration as follows. If $x = r$ is a root of the function $f(x)$, then by definition of a root, $f(r) = 0$. If we define the function

$$g(x) = x - f(x) \tag{33.14}$$

then $g(r) = r - f(r) = r$, i.e., *the root of $f(x)$ is a fixed point of $g(x) = x - f(x)$.* The naive algorithm is illustrated in algorithm 33.3.

Unfortunately, algorithm 33.3 is not guaranteed to converge, and will sometimes diverge quite catastrophically.

Example 33.2. Write a Python program to find a root of $f(x)$ using fixed point iteration. Demonstrate that it converges to the correct answer for $f(x) = x^2 - 1/2$
using $x_0 = .5$ and diverges using $x_0 = 2$.

Theorem 33.5. Convergence of Fixed Point Iteration

Suppose that $f(x) \in C^1[a,b]$ such that[a]

$$f(x) : [a,b] \mapsto S \subset [a,b] \qquad (33.15)$$

Then $f(x)$ has a fixed point in $[a,b]$.

Furthermore, if there exists some positive constant K, where $0 < K < 1$, such that

$$|f'(x)| \leq K \qquad (33.16)$$

for all $x \in [a,b]$, then $f(x)$ has a unique fixed point $p \in [a,b]$, and algorithm 33.2 will converge to p for any starting $x_0 \in [a,b]$.

[a]By $C^1[a,b]$ we mean the set of all continuous differentiable functions with continuous derivatives on (a,b)

Algorithm 33.3 Naive root finding using fixed point iteration. This algorithm attempts to find the root of $f(x)$ using fixed point iteration on $g(x) = f(x) - x$.

input: f, x_0, tolerance ϵ, maximum steps N

1: $\Delta \leftarrow \infty$
2: $x \leftarrow x_0$
3: $i \leftarrow 0$
4: $g(x) \leftarrow x - f(x)$
5: **while** $\Delta > \epsilon$ and $i < N$ **do**
6:     $x_{old} \leftarrow x$
7:     $x \leftarrow g(x_{old})$
8:     $\Delta \leftarrow |x - x_{old}|$
9:     $i \leftarrow i + 1$
10: **end while**
11: **if** $i = N$ **then**
12:     **return** "Algorithm did not converge"
13: **end if**
14: **return** x

```
def naiveFPRoot(f, x0, epsilon, N, PRINT=True):
    g = (lambda x : x - f(x))
    r=x0;i=0;Delta = float("inf")
    while i<N and abs(Delta) > epsilon:
        i+=1;  rnew = g(r)
        Delta = abs(rnew -r)
        r = rnew
        if PRINT: print i, Delta, r
    return r
```

Defining the function $f(x) = x^{-.5}$ using **lambda x:x*x-.5**, and we iterate starting with $x_0 = .5$,

```
>>> naiveFPRoot(lambda x:x*x-.5, .5, .0001, 25)
1 0.25 0.75
2 0.0625 0.6875
3 0.02734375 0.71484375
4 0.0110015869141 0.703842163086
5 0.00460620946251 0.708448372548
6 0.00189909656654 0.706549275982
7 0.000788120609447 0.707337396591
8 0.00032619261663 0.707011203975
9 0.000135157454216 0.707146361429
10 5.59764821843e-05 0.707090384947
0.707090384947524
>>>
```

We appear to have converged rather smoothly to the correct root of ≈ 0.70709. However, if we start from further away, the iterates rapidly diverge beyond the range of storable numbers.

```
>>> naiveFPRoot(lambda x:x*x-.5, 2, 0.0001, 25)
1 3.5 -1.5
2 1.75 -3.25
3 10.0625 -13.3125
4 176.72265625 -190.03515625
5 36112.860611 -36302.8957672
6 1317900240.59 -1317936543.48
7 1.73695673264e+18 -1.73695673396e+18
8 3.01701869565e+36 -3.01701869565e+36
9 9.1024018099e+72 -9.1024018099e+72
10 8.28537187088e+145 -8.28537187088e+145
11 6.86473870388e+291 -6.86473870388e+291
12 inf -inf
13 nan -inf
-inf
```

If we try to find the square root of another number, such as $\sqrt{4}$, the algorithm will not converge even for starting values very close to the correct solution.

```
>>> naiveFPRoot(lambda x:x*x-4.0, 2.00001, .00001, 25)
1 4.00001000003e-05 1.9999699999
2 0.000119999499995 2.0000899994
3 0.000360005699871 1.9997299937
4 0.0010799522961 2.000809946
5 0.00324043999743 1.997569506
6 0.00971606870371 2.0072855747
7 0.0291953784088 1.97809019629
8 0.0871591753267 2.06524937162
9 0.265254966978 1.79999440464
10 0.760020143258 2.5600145479
11 2.55367448546 0.00634006244185
12 3.99995980361 4.00629986605
```

```
13 12.0504386167 -8.04413875066
14 60.7081682399 -68.7523069906
15 4722.87971653 -4791.63202352
16 22959733.4488 -22964525.0808
17 5.27369412188e+14 -5.27369435152e+14
18 2.78118521133e+29 -2.78118521133e+29
19 7.7349911797e+58 -7.7349911797e+58
20 5.98300885501e+117 -5.98300885501e+117
21 3.57963949591e+235 -3.57963949591e+235
22 inf -inf
23 nan -inf
-inf
```

The problem with this algorithm is that the sufficient conditions for convergence are very rarely met. Thus the algorithm is not guaranteed to converge.

Newton's Method

Newton's method, which you probably studied in elementary calculus, will (almost) always work. As we will see, Newton's method is a form of fixed point iteration, though it does not use the same iterating function discussed previously.

Designate the true root by p, and let p_0 be a first guess for p. We can project the tangent line of $f(x)$ from the point $(p_0, f(p_0))$ down to where it intersects with the x-axis at $(p_1, 0)$.

Since $f(x)$ is decreasing in the directing from p_0 towards the true root p, the intersection point p_1 on the x axis *should* be between p_0 and p (unless there is too much strange curvature in $f(x)$ between p_0 and p). See figure 33.3.

Figure 33.3: Derivation of Newton's method.

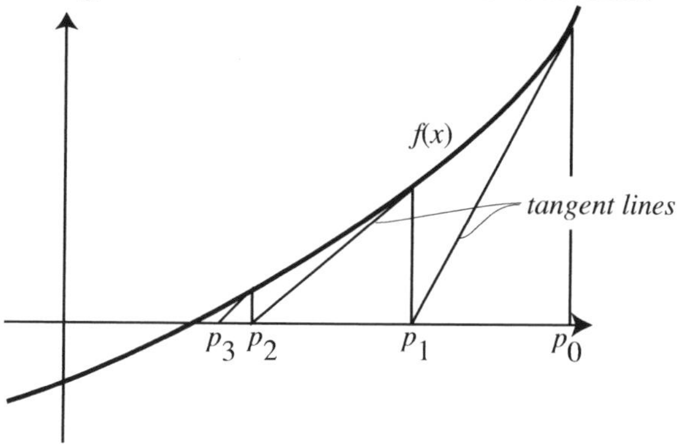

The slope of the straight line connecting the points $(p_0, f(p_0))$ and $(p_1, 0)$ is

$$f'(p_0) = \text{slope} = \frac{\text{rise}}{\text{run}} = \frac{f(p_0) - 0}{p_0 - p_1} = \frac{f(p_0)}{p_0 - p_1} \tag{33.17}$$

Solving for p_1,

$$p_1 = p_0 - \frac{f(p_0)}{f'(p_0)} \tag{33.18}$$

This gives us the well known formula for **Newon's Method**

$$p_{n+1} = p_n - \frac{f(p_n)}{f'(p_n)} \tag{33.19}$$

It is generally more convenient, however, to express 33.19 directly as a fixed point iterable function. Given $f(x)$, define

$$g(x) = x - f(x)/f'(x) \tag{33.20}$$

Then a root is at the fixed point of $g(x)$.

Algorithm 33.4 Newton's method to find a root of $f(x)$

---

input: f, f', x_0, tolerance ϵ, maximum steps N
1: $g(x) \leftarrow x - f(x)/f'(x)$
2: $r \leftarrow$ **fixed point**$(g(x), x_0, \epsilon, N)$ (from algorithm 33.2)
3: **return** r

Newton's method converges much more quickly than bisection. To see why this happens, we can expand $f(x)$ in a Taylor series about the true root p. Since $f(p) = 0$,

$$f(p + \epsilon) \approx f(p) + \epsilon f'(p) + \frac{1}{2}\epsilon^2 f''(p) + \cdots \tag{33.21}$$

$$\approx \epsilon f'(p) + \frac{1}{2}\epsilon^2 f''(p) + \cdots \tag{33.22}$$

where the second line follows because at a root $f(p) = 0$. Similarly,

$$f'(p + \epsilon) \approx f'(p) + \epsilon f''(p) + \cdots \tag{33.23}$$

Let ϵ_i be the error after the ith iteration. Then since

$$x_{i+1} = x_i - \frac{f(x_i)}{f'(x_i)} \tag{33.24}$$

we have

$$\epsilon_{i+1} - \epsilon_i = (x_{i+1} - p) - (x_i - p) = x_{i+1} - x_i \tag{33.25}$$

$$= -\frac{f(x_i)}{f'(x_i)} = -\frac{\epsilon_i f'(p) + \frac{1}{2}\epsilon_i^2 f''(p) + \cdots}{f'(p) + \epsilon_i f''(p) + \cdots} \tag{33.26}$$

Solving for ϵ_{i+1},

$$|\epsilon_{i+1}| \approx \left| \frac{\epsilon_i \left(f'(p) + \epsilon_i f''(p) + \cdots\right) - \left(\epsilon_i f'(p) + \frac{1}{2}\epsilon_i^2 f''(p)\right)}{f'(p) + \epsilon_i f''(p) + \cdots} \right| \approx \left| \frac{\epsilon_i^2 f''(p)|}{2f'(p)} \right| \tag{33.27}$$

The number $k = |f''(p)/2f'(p)|$ is a constant, so we end up with $|\epsilon_{i+1}| \approx k|\epsilon_i|^2$

By comparison, the bisection algorithm has $\epsilon_{i+1} = \frac{1}{2}|\epsilon_i|$

The quadratic factor results in Newton's method converging much more quickly than the bisection algorithm. Newton's method is said to **converge quadratically**, while bisection is said to **converge linearly**.

Theorem 33.6. Convergence of Newton's Method

Let $f(x) \in C^1[a, b]$ have a root $p \in [a, b]$ such that $f'(p) \neq 0$. Then $\exists \delta > 0$ such that $\forall x_0 \in I$, given by

$$I = [p - \delta, p + \delta] \qquad (33.28)$$

Newton's method with first guess x_0 and subsequent iterations given by

$$x_{n+1} = g(x_n) \qquad (33.29)$$

where

$$g(x) = x - \frac{f(x)}{f'(x)} \qquad (33.30)$$

will converge, i.e, $x_n \to p$ as $n \to \infty$.

Under certain conditions Newton's method will not converge, even if a root does exist. For example, by theorem 33.6 if the derivative is not continuous in the entire interval then it will fail. The function $f(x) = x/\sqrt{|x|}$ provides an example of this situation. The derivative is everywhere continuous except at the origin where it becomes infinite. The plot of $f(x)$ is also a mirror image of itself through the origin. In this case Newton's method can lead to cyclic iteration. A similar case can occur if the initial point is chosen on the edge of an open interval of convergence, as with $f(x) = x/(1 + x^2)$ at $x = 1/\sqrt{3}$. In both cases we have a situation where $x_{n+1} = -x_n$ and the function is a mirror image of itself. The same thing happens with $f(x) = x^2$ if $x = \sqrt{5/3}$.

Figure 33.4: When Newton's method fails. Left: $f(x) = x/|x|$ has an infinite derivative at the origin. Center: $f(x) = x/(1 + x^2)$ is a mirror image of itself. Newton's method converges on the interval $(-1/\sqrt{3}, 1/\sqrt{3})$, diverges outside this interval, and oscillates right on the endpoints. Right: $f(x) = x^2$ has a local minimum, but no root, at $x = 0$. Newton oscillation can become trapped if $x_0 = \sqrt{5/3}$.

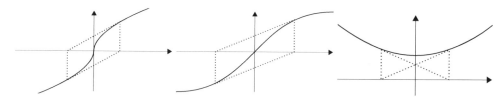

A variation on the Newton's method called the Damped Newton's Method can fix these situations by checking if successive iterations decrease in magnitude. If they do not, the interval is halved, until they do. The damped Newton method will always converge to either a root or to a local minimum (algorithm 33.5).

Algorithm 33.5 Damped Newton's method to find a root (or minimum value) of $f(x)$

---

input: f, f', x_0, tolerance ϵ, maximum steps N

1:   $\Delta \leftarrow f(x_0)/f'(x_0)$
2:   $x \leftarrow x_0$
3:   $f_{new} \leftarrow f(x_0)$
4: **while** $\Delta > \epsilon$ and $i < N$ **do**
5:     $f_{old} \leftarrow f_{new}$
6:     $x_{new} \leftarrow x - \Delta$
7:     $f_{new} = f(x_{new})$
8:     $j \leftarrow 0$
9:     **while** $|f_{new}| \geq |f_{old}|$ and $j < N$ **do**
10:       $\Delta \leftarrow \Delta/2$
11:       $x_{new} \leftarrow x - \Delta$
12:       $f_{new} \leftarrow f(x_{new})$
13:       $j \leftarrow j + 1$
14:     **end while**
15:     $x \leftarrow x_{new}$
16:     $\Delta \leftarrow f(x)/f'(x)$
17:     $i \leftarrow i + 1$
18: **end while**
19: **return** x

Exercises

1. Write a function that implements Newton's method using fixed point iteration. Use Newton's method to find all roots of $f(x) = x^2 - 4.6x + 5$.

2. Implement both Newton's method and Bisection to find the solution to solve $x = \cos x$. Measure the computation time using **time.time()** for each method. You may have to run your programs a large number of times to get a reasonably accurate number. Compare your results.

3. The **secant method** uses both x_{n-1} and x_{n-2} to determine x_n. The derivative at x_n is estimated using the divided difference

$$f'(x_n) \approx \frac{f(x_{n-1}) - f(x_{n-2})}{(x_{n-1} - x_{n-2})}$$

Replacing this expression in the formula for Newton's method gives

$$x_n = x_{n-1} - \frac{f(x_{n-1})(x_{n-1} - x_{n-2})}{f(x_{n-1}) - f(x_{n-2})}$$

Implement the secant method and compare it to Newton's method. Use it to find the roots of $y = -x^3 - \cos x$.

Chapter 34

Least Squares

Here we consider the following problem: Given some set of data points in the xy-plane

$$\{(x_i, y_i) : i = 1, 2, ..., n\} \tag{34.1}$$

what is the "best fit" curve $f(x)$ to data?

In this chapter we will define "best fit" to mean that that sum of the vertical distances between the observations y_i and the predictions $f(x_i)$ are minimized. This technique is called the **method of least squares** or **linear regression**. The fundamental assumption underlying regression analysis is that **there is no noise or measurement error in the x values**. For example, data may be collected at fixed, known discrete time intervals, so the value of each x_i is know precisely.

When there is noise or error in both the x and the y variables, regression analysis is sometimes still performed. However, care must be taken. If the error bars in one variable are significantly larger than the error bars in the other axis, the axis with the smaller error bars should be chosen as the independent (x) coordinate. If the error bars have comparable magnitude or the noise has a comparable distribution along both axes, **principal component analysis** (PCA; chapter 41) should be performed first to determine the underlying geometry of the data set. PCA is analogous to the physics problem of making a coordinate transformation into the reference frame of a spinning (American) football during a pass – the dynamics are much more easily understood if your main axis is oriented along the spin axis of the football.

Linear Regression

In linear regression, the target function is $f(x) = mx + b$ for some undetermined constants m and b. We can define an **objective function** $g(m, b)$ to be minimized by

Figure 34.1: The sum of all the vertical distances is minimized in linear regression.

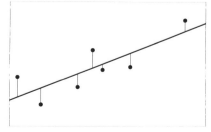

$$g(m,b) = \sum_{i=1}^{n} |f(x_i) - y_i|^2 = \sum_{i=1}^{n} (mx_i + b - y_i)^2 \tag{34.2}$$

To find m and b, we set the partial derivatives $\partial g/\partial m$ and $\partial g/\partial b$ equal to zero.

$$0 = \frac{\partial g}{\partial b} = \frac{\partial}{\partial b} \sum_{i=1}^{n} (mx_i + b - y_i)^2 = \sum_{i=1}^{n} 2(mx_i + b - y_i) \tag{34.3a}$$

$$= 2 \sum_{i=1}^{n} (mx_i + b - y_i) \tag{34.3b}$$

Dividing by 2 and separating the three sums

$$0 = \sum_{i=1}^{n} (mx_i + b - y_i) = \sum_{i=1}^{n} mx_i + \sum_{i=1}^{n} b - \sum_{i=1}^{n} y_i \tag{34.3c}$$

$$= m \sum_{i=1}^{n} x_i + nb - \sum_{i=1}^{n} y_i = mX + nb - Y \tag{34.3d}$$

where

$$X = \sum_{i=1}^{n} x_i \text{ and } Y = \sum_{i=1}^{n} y_i \tag{34.3e}$$

Similarly,

$$0 = \frac{\partial g}{\partial m} = \frac{\partial}{\partial m} \sum_{i=1}^{n} (mx_i + b - y_i)^2 = \sum_{i=1}^{n} 2x_i (mx_i + b - y_i) \tag{34.4a}$$

$$= 2 \sum_{i=1}^{n} x_i (mx_i + b - y_i) \tag{34.4b}$$

Dividing by 2 and separating the three sums as before

$$0 = \sum_{i=1}^{n} x_i (mx_i + b - y_i) = \sum_{i=1}^{n} mx_i^2 + b \sum_{i=1}^{n} x_i - \sum_{i=1}^{n} x_i y_i \tag{34.4c}$$

$$= m \sum_{i=1}^{n} x_i^2 + bX - \sum_{i=1}^{n} x_i y_i = mA + bX - C \tag{34.4d}$$

where

$$A = \sum_{i=1}^{n} x_i^2 \text{ and } C = \sum_{i=1}^{n} x_i y_i \tag{34.4e}$$

Equations 34.3d and 34.4d give us a a system of two linear equations in two variables m and b. Multiplying equation 34.3d by A and equation 34.4d by X gives

$$0 = A(mX + nb - Y) = AXm + Anb - AY \tag{34.5a}$$

$$0 = X(mA + bX - C) = AXm + X^2b - CX \tag{34.5b}$$

Subtracting,

$$0 = Anb - AY - X^2 b + CX = b(An - X^2) + CX - AY \qquad (34.6)$$

and therefore

$$b = \frac{AY - CX}{An - X^2} \qquad (34.7)$$

If we instead multiply equation 34.3d by X and equation 34.4d by n we obtain

$$0 = X\left(mX + nb - Y\right) = mX^2 + nXb - YX \qquad (34.8a)$$

$$0 = n\left(mA + bX - C\right) = nAm + nXb - nC \qquad (34.8b)$$

Subtracting,

$$0 = m\left(X^2 - nA\right) - (YX - nC) \qquad (34.9)$$

Solving for m and substituting the definitions of A, C, X and Y, gives

$$m = \frac{XY - nC}{X^2 - nA} \qquad (34.10)$$

Algorithm 34.1 Algorithm for linear regression.

---

input: $((x_1, y_1), \ldots, (x_n, y_n))$
1: $X \leftarrow \sum_{i=1}^{n} x_i$
2: $Y \leftarrow \sum_{i=1}^{n} y_i$
3: $A \leftarrow \sum_{i=1}^{n} x_i^2$ (or: $A \leftarrow \mathbf{x} \cdot \mathbf{x}$)
4: $C \leftarrow \sum_{i=1}^{n} x_i y_i$ (or: $C \leftarrow \mathbf{x} \cdot \mathbf{y}$)
5: $D \leftarrow X^2 - nA$
6: $m \leftarrow (XY - nC)/D$
7: $b \leftarrow (CX - AY)/D$
8: **return** m, b

Except for a multiplication by (-1), the denominator in 34.10 is the same as in 34.7. It is convenient to label this denominator as $D = X^2 - nA$. Then the regression equations become $b = (CX - AY)/D$ and $m = (XY - nC)/D$, as summarized in algorithm 34.1.

Matrix Form. As an aside, we note that instead of solving first for b and then for m, we could have rearranged equations (34.3d) and (34.4d) as

$$bn + m\sum_{i=1}^{n} x_i = \sum_{i=1}^{n} y_i \qquad (34.11a)$$

$$b\sum_{i=1}^{n} x_i + m\sum_{i=1}^{n} x_i^2 = \sum_{i=1}^{n} x_i y_i \qquad (34.11b)$$

In matrix form, this becomes

$$\begin{bmatrix} n & \sum x_i \\ \sum x_i & \sum x_i^2 \end{bmatrix} \begin{bmatrix} m & b \end{bmatrix} = \begin{bmatrix} \sum y_i \\ \sum x_i y_i \end{bmatrix} \qquad (34.11c)$$

Solving the matrix equation for $[m, b]^{\mathrm{T}}$ gives the same result.

Statistical Form. It is sometimes useful o express the quantities A, C, D, X, and Y in terms of known statistical quantities, in particular, the sample standard deviations s_x and s_y, where

$$s_x^2 = \frac{\sum_i (x_i - \bar{x})^2}{n-1}, \text{ and } s_y^2 = \frac{\sum_i (y_i - \bar{y})^2}{n-1}, \tag{34.12}$$

where the sample means are $\bar{x} = \frac{1}{n}\sum x_i = X/n$ and $\bar{y} = \frac{1}{n}\sum y_i = Y/n$; and the correlation

$$r = \frac{1}{n-1}\sum_i \left(\frac{x_i - \bar{x}}{s_x}\right)\left(\frac{y_i - \bar{y}}{s_y}\right). \tag{34.13}$$

Since s_x and s_y are constants in the sum (34.13),

$$(n-1)rs_x s_y = \sum_i (x_i - \bar{x})(y_i - \bar{y}) \tag{34.14a}$$

$$= \sum_i (x_i y_i - \bar{x} y_i - \bar{y} x_i + \overline{xy}) \tag{34.14b}$$

$$= \sum_i x_i y_i - n\overline{xy} = C - \frac{1}{n}XY \tag{34.14c}$$

Similarly, the observed sample variance s_x^2 satisfies

$$(n-1)s_x^2 = \sum_i (x_i - \bar{x})^2 \tag{34.15a}$$

$$= \sum (x_i^2 - 2x_i \bar{x} + \bar{x}^2) \tag{34.15b}$$

$$= \sum x_i^2 - n\bar{x}^2 = A - \frac{1}{n}X^2 \tag{34.15c}$$

Therefore from (34.10)

$$m = \frac{XY - nC}{X^2 - nA} = \frac{C - \frac{1}{n}XY}{A - \frac{1}{n}X^2} = \frac{(n-1)rs_x s_y}{(n-1)s_x^2} = r\frac{s_y}{s_x} \tag{34.16}$$

Similarly, from (34.7),

$$b = \frac{AY - CX}{An - X^2} = \frac{AY - CX}{n(n-1)s_x^2} \tag{34.17a}$$

$$= \frac{AY - X(\frac{1}{n}XY + (n-1)rs_x s_y)}{n(n-1)s_x^2} \tag{34.17b}$$

$$= \frac{AY - X(\frac{1}{n}XY)}{n(n-1)s_x^2} - \frac{X((n-1)rs_x s_y)}{n(n-1)s_x^2} \tag{34.17c}$$

$$= \frac{Y}{n} \times \frac{(A - X^2/n)}{(n-1)s_x^2} - \frac{X}{n} \times \frac{rs_y}{s_x} \tag{34.17d}$$

$$= \frac{1}{n}Y - \frac{1}{n}mX = \bar{y} - m\bar{x} \tag{34.17e}$$

Algorithm 34.2 Algorithm for linear regression (statistical).

---

input: $((x_1, y_1), \ldots, (x_n, y_n))$ as $\mathbf{x}$, $\mathbf{y}$

1: $\bar{x} \leftarrow \text{mean}(\mathbf{x})$
2: $\bar{y} \leftarrow \text{mean}(\mathbf{y})$
3: $s_x \leftarrow \text{StandardDeviation}(\mathbf{x})$
4: $s_y \leftarrow \text{StandardDeviation}(\mathbf{y})$
5: $r \leftarrow \text{correlation}(\mathbf{x}, \mathbf{y})$
6: $m \leftarrow r s_y / s_x$
7: $b \leftarrow \bar{y} - m\bar{x}$
8: **return** m, b

Polynomial Least Squares

We can generalize the least squares problem to a polynomial of any degree n. Suppose we replace the objective function used previously with a polynomial of degree $n - 1$

$$P(x) = c_1 + c_2 x + \cdots + c_n x^{n-1} \tag{34.18}$$

If there are n data points $(x_1, y_1), \ldots, (x_m, y_m)$, then a perfect fit would give

$$c_1 + c_2 x_1 + \cdots + c_n x_n^{n-1} = y_1 \tag{34.19}$$

$$\vdots \tag{34.20}$$

$$c_1 + c_2 x_m + \cdots + c_n x_m^{n-1} = y_m \tag{34.21}$$

However, in any practical problem $m > n$ and usually $m \gg n$, so the system is (extremely) overdetermined. Thus

$$\begin{bmatrix} 1 & x_1 & x_1^2 & \cdots & x_1^{n-1} \\ 1 & x_2 & x_2^2 & & x_2^{n-1} \\ \vdots & & & & \\ 1 & x_m & x_m^2 & \cdots & x_m^{n-1} \end{bmatrix} \begin{bmatrix} c_1 \\ c_2 \\ \vdots \\ c_m \end{bmatrix} = \begin{bmatrix} y_1 \\ y_2 \\ \vdots \\ y_m \end{bmatrix} + \mathbf{r} \tag{34.22}$$

where $\mathbf{r}$ is a vector of **residuals** to be minimized. Our goal is find the vector $\mathbf{c}$ that minimizes $\mathbf{r}$, where

$$\mathbf{Ac} = \mathbf{y} + \mathbf{r} \tag{34.23}$$

i.e., find $\mathbf{c}$ to minimize the distance

$$|\mathbf{r}| = |\mathbf{Ac} - \mathbf{y}| \tag{34.24}$$

If we denote the jth column of $\mathbf{A}$ by $\mathbf{a}_j$, where

$$\mathbf{a}_j = \begin{bmatrix} x_1^{j-1} \\ x_2^{j-1} \\ \vdots \\ x_m^{j-1} \end{bmatrix} \tag{34.25}$$

then

$$\mathbf{A} = \begin{bmatrix} \mathbf{a}_1 & | & \mathbf{a}_2 & | & \cdots & | & \mathbf{a}_{n-1} \end{bmatrix} \tag{34.26}$$

and

$$\mathbf{Ac} = c_1\mathbf{a}_1 + c_2\mathbf{a}_2 + \cdots + c_n\mathbf{a}_n = \sum c_j\mathbf{a}_j \tag{34.27}$$

We minimize the objective function

$$g(c_1, \ldots, c_n) = |\mathbf{r}|^2 = \mathbf{r}^{\mathrm{T}}\mathbf{r} = (\mathbf{Ac} - \mathbf{y})^{\mathrm{T}}(\mathbf{Ac} - \mathbf{y}) \tag{34.28}$$

by setting the derivatives $\partial g / \partial c_i = 0$:

$$0 = \frac{\partial}{\partial c_i}\left((\mathbf{Ac} - \mathbf{y})^{\mathrm{T}}(\mathbf{Ac} - \mathbf{y})\right) \tag{34.29}$$

$$= \left(\frac{\partial}{\partial c_i}(\mathbf{Ac} - \mathbf{y})^{\mathrm{T}}\right)(\mathbf{Ac} - \mathbf{y}) + (\mathbf{Ac} - \mathbf{y})^{\mathrm{T}}\frac{\partial}{\partial c_i}(\mathbf{Ac} - \mathbf{y}) \tag{34.30}$$

But from (34.27)

$$\frac{\partial}{\partial c_i}\mathbf{Ac} = \mathbf{a}_i \tag{34.31}$$

Thus

$$0 = (\mathbf{a}_i)^{\mathrm{T}}(\mathbf{Ac} - \mathbf{y}) + (\mathbf{Ac} - \mathbf{y})^{\mathrm{T}}\mathbf{a}_i \tag{34.32}$$

Distributing the transposes,

$$0 = \mathbf{a}_i^{\mathrm{T}}\mathbf{Ac} - \mathbf{a}_i^{\mathrm{T}}\mathbf{y} + \mathbf{c}^{\mathrm{T}}\mathbf{A}^{\mathrm{T}}\mathbf{a}_i - \mathbf{y}^{\mathrm{T}}\mathbf{a}_i \tag{34.33}$$

Rearranging,

$$\mathbf{a}_i^{\mathrm{T}}\mathbf{y} + (\mathbf{a}_i^{\mathrm{T}}\mathbf{y})^{\mathrm{T}} = \mathbf{a}_i^{\mathrm{T}}\mathbf{Ac} + (\mathbf{a}_i^{\mathrm{T}}\mathbf{Ac})^{\mathrm{T}} \tag{34.34}$$

Each of these terms is a number, so we can omit the transpose on the second term on each side of the equation,

$$2\mathbf{a}_i^{\mathrm{T}}\mathbf{y} = 2\mathbf{a}_i^{\mathrm{T}}\mathbf{Ac} \tag{34.35}$$

Dividing by 2 and taking into account that the equation is true for all $i = 1, 2, \ldots, n-1$,

$$\mathbf{A}^{\mathrm{T}}\mathbf{y} = \mathbf{A}^{\mathrm{T}}\mathbf{Ac} \tag{34.36}$$

Equations 34.36 are called the **Normal Equations** of the system. This can be simplified to

$$\mathbf{Mc} = \mathbf{b} \tag{34.37}$$

where $\mathbf{M} = \mathbf{A}^{\mathrm{T}}\mathbf{A}$ and $\mathbf{b} = \mathbf{A}^{\mathrm{T}}\mathbf{y}$. The elements of the matrix $\mathbf{M}$ and the vector $\mathbf{b}$

are completely determined by the input data. The only unknowns are the coefficients of the polynomial, which are listed from lowest order to highest order, in the vector $\mathbf{c}$. $\mathbf{c}$ can be found by solving the linear system, as discussed in chapter 30. This is most easily done with `c=np.linalg.solve(M,b)`, which returns a numpy array containing the coefficients.

The matrix $\mathbf{M} = \mathbf{A}^{\mathrm{T}}\mathbf{A}$ is an $n \times n$ symmetric matrix, known as the **normal matrix** given by

$$\mathbf{A}^{\mathrm{T}}\mathbf{A} = \begin{bmatrix} 1 & 1 & \cdots & 1 \\ x_1 & x_2 & \cdots & x_m \\ x_1^2 & x_2^2 & \cdots & x_m^2 \\ \vdots & & & \vdots \\ x_1^{n-1} & x_2^{n-1} & \cdots & x_m^{n-1} \end{bmatrix} \begin{bmatrix} 1 & x_1 & x_1^2 & \cdots & x_1^{n-1} \\ 1 & x_2 & x_2^2 & & x_2^{n-1} \\ \vdots & & & & \\ 1 & x_m & x_m^2 & \cdots & x_m^{n-1} \end{bmatrix} \tag{34.38}$$

$$= \begin{bmatrix} m & \sum x_i & \sum x_i^2 & \sum x_i^3 & \cdots & \sum x_i^{n-1} \\ \sum x_i & \sum x_i^2 & \sum x_i^3 & \cdots & & \vdots \\ \sum x_i^2 & \sum x_i^3 & & & & \\ \sum x_i^3 & & & & & \\ \vdots & & & & & \vdots \\ \sum x_i^{n-1} & \cdots & & & \cdots & \sum x_i^{2(n-1)} \end{bmatrix} \tag{34.39}$$

The right hand side of equation 34.37 is given by the column vector

$$\mathbf{b} = \mathbf{A}^{\mathrm{T}}\mathbf{y} = \begin{bmatrix} 1 & 1 & \cdots & 1 \\ x_1 & x_2 & \cdots & x_m \\ x_1^2 & x_2^2 & \cdots & x_m^2 \\ \vdots & & & \vdots \\ x_1^{n-1} & x_2^{n-1} & \cdots & x_m^{n-1} \end{bmatrix} \begin{bmatrix} y_1 \\ y_2 \\ \vdots \\ y_m \end{bmatrix} = \begin{bmatrix} \sum y_i \\ \sum x_i y_i \\ \sum x_i^2 y_i \\ \vdots \\ \sum x_i^{n-1} y_i \end{bmatrix} \tag{34.40}$$

Thus the normal equations in their full glory become

$$\begin{bmatrix} m & \sum x_i & \sum x_i^2 & \sum x_i^3 & \cdots & \sum x_i^{n-1} \\ \sum x_i & \sum x_i^2 & \sum x_i^3 & \cdots & & \vdots \\ \sum x_i^2 & \sum x_i^3 & & & & \\ \sum x_i^3 & & & & & \\ \vdots & & & & & \\ \sum x_i^{n-1} & \cdots & & & \cdots & \sum x_i^{2(n-1)} \end{bmatrix} \begin{bmatrix} c_1 \\ c_2 \\ \vdots \\ c_{n-1} \end{bmatrix} = \begin{bmatrix} \sum y_i \\ \sum x_i y_i \\ \sum x_i^2 y_i \\ \vdots \\ \sum x_i^{n-1} y_i \end{bmatrix} \tag{34.41}$$

For linear regression, the degree of the polynomial is $n - 1 = 1$ or $n = 2$ (n gives the dimension of the matrix, which is one larger than the degree of the fit). Thus

$$\begin{bmatrix} m & \sum x_i \\ \sum x_i & \sum x_i^2 \end{bmatrix} \begin{bmatrix} c_0 \\ c_1 \end{bmatrix} = \begin{bmatrix} \sum y_i \\ \sum x_i y_i \end{bmatrix} \tag{34.42}$$

Algorithm 34.3 Algorithm for polynomial least squares.

input: points $((x_1, y_1), \ldots, (x_m, y_m))$, degree n

1: **for** $j \in 1, \ldots, m$ **do**
2:     $\mathbf{a}_j \leftarrow [1, x_j, x_j^2, \ldots, x_j^{n-1}]$ $\mathbf{a}_j$ is row j of $\mathbf{A}$
3: **end for**
4: $\mathbf{M} \leftarrow \mathbf{A}^{\mathrm{T}} \mathbf{A}$
5: $\mathbf{b} \leftarrow \mathbf{A}^{\mathrm{T}} \mathbf{y}$ $\mathbf{y}$ is column vector in input y_i
6: $\mathbf{c} \leftarrow \mathrm{LinearSolve}(\mathbf{M}, \mathbf{b})$
7: **return** $\mathbf{c}$ $\mathbf{c}$ is a vector of coefficients of the Least Squares polynomial

---

The variables A and X defined in algorithm 34.1, along with the number of points m, comprise the normal matrix, and the variables Y and C form the vector $\mathbf{b}$ on the right hand side. The variable D in the algorithm is the determinant of the matrix, and thus the earlier algorithm is actually inverting the matrix to solve for the slope and y-intercept.

How good is good enough?

The inherent danger in polynomial least squares is over-fitting: attempting to fit a polynomial of too high of a degree to a data set. In figure 34.2 we show the result of fitting the US population data from chapter 32. That data set had 10 points, and can be precisely fit by the degree 9 polynomial illustrated in the figure. The precise fit matches every single grid point. However, it also displays features that are not reflected in the actual population, like the hump between 1900 and 1910.

Figure 34.3 shows a plot of the function $f(x) = 10 + (x-1)(x-2.1)(x-2.9)(x-4.1)(x-5.3)$ along with a collection of noisy data based on this function. The noisy data was produced by adding $\pm.5$ alternately to the y values. No noise was added along the x axis.

```
def f(x):
    return 10+(x-1.)*(x-2.1)*(x-2.9)*(x-4.1)*(x-5.3)
fv = np.vectorize(f)
xvals=np.arange(1,5.5,.3)
n=len(xvals)
yvals=np.array([0.5*(-1)**j for j in range(n)])+fv(xvals)
```

Python has a built in polynomial fitting function **np.polyfit()**, which will generate the coefficients for any degree **n** and return them as a Numpy array. Thus

```
coefs=np.polyfit(xn, yn, n)
```

will return a list of $n+1$ coefficients $c_0, c_1, \ldots, c_n$ to $P(x) = \sum_{k=0}^{n} c_k x^k$. To determine the y-values you need to evaluated this polynomial; you can do this with the function **polyval** for either a point **x0**, as

```
y0 = np.polyval(coef,x0}
```

Figure 34.2: Overfitting of the US population data from chapter 32.

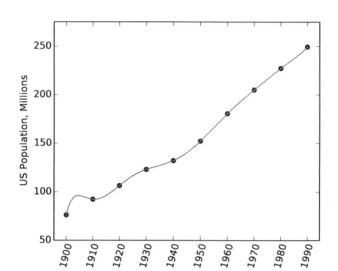

Figure 34.3: A noisy data set.

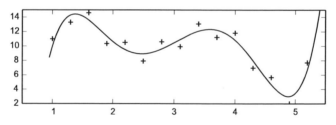

will return a single y value; or for an array **x**, as

```
y=np.polyval(coef,x)
```

will return an array **y** whenever **x** is an array. Figure 34.4 shows the results of fitting the randomized data set in figure 34.3 for several different degree polynomials.

If we don't know anything about the underlying function $f(x)$, how can we ever say one of these functions is better than the others? If our data points are (x_i, y_i) and our degree-j fit is given by $P_j(x)$, one thing we can do is calculate a root mean square error of the observed minus the predicted values:

$$\epsilon_j = \sqrt{\frac{1}{n} \sum_i (y_i - P_j(x_i))^2} \qquad (34.43)$$

However, as we increase the degree of the fit, the total root mean square residual error

Figure 34.4: Result of fitting the noisy data set shown in figure 34.3 with polynomials of several different degrees.

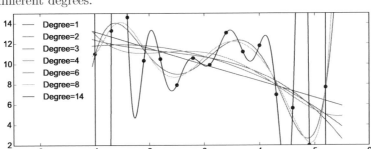

will *always* continue to decrease! When the degree of the fit reaches $m - 1$, where m is the number of data points, then we are able to find a polynomial that fits every point exactly and has an RMS error of zero. We know this from the Lagrange Interpolation Theorem (theorem 32.1), which expressly constructs a formula for the polynomial.

This occurs in the plot at the bottom figure 34.4. This does not mean we are doing any better. All we are doing is fitting a polynomial to the noise, which is not what we want. We want to find a polynomial that fits the underlying data, and not the noise.

One thing we can do is to split our data set up into two smaller data sets, which we can call S_1 and S_2. We put aside a smaller portion of the data, say around 25% (chosen randomly), into set S_2, which we call the **test set**. We leave the remaining data in set S_1, which call the **training set**. We can randomly re-arrange the dataset in place using the numpy function **np.random.shuffle**; then we only have to pick off our data.

```
np.random.shuffle(dataet)
k=int(.75*float(len(dataset))) # pick approximately 75%
train=dataset[:k]
test=dataset[k:]
```

We do all of our polynomial fits on the training set, but we calculate our errors on the test set. *Thus none of the data that we measure the error on is used to compute the fit* (figure 34.6).

Figure 34.5 shows the results of the following experiment. For each degree d from 1 through 12, data set S was split up into two data sets, S_1 and S_2. S_1 contained 75% of the data and S_2 the other 25%. The selections were made randomly. A polynomial of degree d was fit to the data in set S_1, and then tested with set S_2. Errors were calculated at each data point in S_2. A **predicted** y value, the value predicted by the fit, and an **observed** data value, the y value in S_2, were recorded. The root mean square error was calculated and then the original data was reshuffled and the process repeated for a total of 100 runs (at each degree). The results are shown in figure 34.5.

In figure 34.5 we see a significant increase in the RMS errors for $n > 6$ (note the logarithmic scale on the y axis). Increasing the degree beyond $n = 6$ clearly does not help. Both $n = 5$ and $n = 6$ are about the same, and are not easily distinguishable here as either being better than the other. Referring back to figure 34.4, both of these fits are essentially indistinguishable (visually). But figure 34.5 tells us something that

Figure 34.5: Root mean square fit errors on test set, using fits determined by training set. Each + corresponds to a different shuffling and splitting of the original data into a test and training set pair. The circles show the mean of the RMS errors.

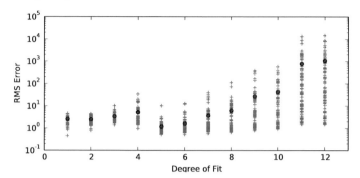

figure 34.4 does not, namely, that increasing the fit beyond 6 does not help, and, in fact, is likely to make things worse.

Variance-Bias Trade-off. What is really happening can be described with probability theory. Let $y = f(x)$ be the actual function that we are sampling at some number of points, so that the true values of the function are $y_1, y_2, \ldots, y_n$ at $x_1, x_2, \ldots, x_n$. Since this function is deterministic, its expectation is $E[y_i] = y_i$. However, there is some irreducible noise in the data which we will described by its variance $\text{var}[y] = \sigma^2$. Let $\hat{y}$ be some numerical approximation (estimate) of y that we have determined from a noisy sampling of the data. What is expected difference between our estimate and the actual true function?

$$E[(y_i - \hat{y})_i^2] = E[y_i^2 + \hat{y}_i^2 - 2y_i\hat{y}_i] = E[y_i^2] + E[\hat{y}_i^2] - 2y_i E[\hat{y}_i] \qquad (34.44)$$

Next, we appeal to the following result from probability theory: for any variable x, $\text{var}[x] = E[x^2] - E[x]^2$. Rearranging gives $E[x^2] = \text{var}[x] + E[x]^2$. Applying this to each of the first two terms in eq. 34.44 gives

$$E[(y_i - \hat{y})_i^2] = \text{var}[y_i] + E[y_i]^2 + \text{var}[\hat{y}_i] + E[\hat{y}_i]^2 - 2y_i E[\hat{y}_i] \qquad (34.45a)$$

$$= \sigma^2 + \text{var}[\hat{y}_i] + (y_i^2 - 2y_i E[\hat{y}_i] + E[\hat{y}_i]^2) \qquad (34.45b)$$

$$= \sigma^2 + \text{var}[\hat{y}_i] + (y_i - E[\hat{y}_i])^2 \qquad (34.45c)$$

$$= \sigma^2 + \text{var}[\hat{y}_i] + E[y_i - \hat{y}_i]^2 \qquad (34.45d)$$

The first terms is the irreducible error, due to noise. In general, you cannot do anything to avoid this and it provides a lower limit on your fit. The second term is the variance in the model, and it describes fluctuations in your description of the data, or what you think you know about the data. As you increase the number of parameters in a model, the variance increases. The variance gives the variation in the predicted values of your model for different realizations of your model, e.g, for different training sets. The third term gives the bias. It gives the actual difference between the model and the true value you are trying to predict. The bias decreases as you add more parameters to the model, because you are improving the model. The bias varies for any given value of y_i when

Figure 34.6: The data splitting process.

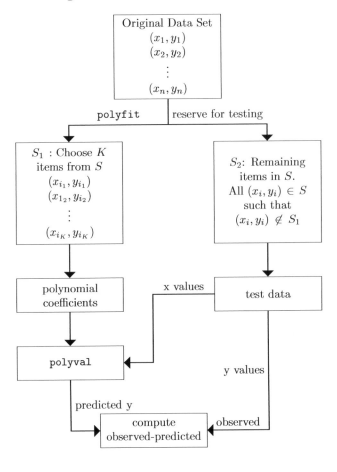

you change the training set and calculate a new set of parameters, so we calculate the expected value in the its definition, based on building the model a large number of times.

Multiple Linear Regression

Suppose we have p observations of an n-dimensional data set that we write as row vectors

$$y_1 = [x_1, x_2, \ldots, x_n]_1 \tag{34.46a}$$

$$y_2 = [x_1, x_2, \ldots, x_n]_2 \tag{34.46b}$$

$$\vdots$$

$$y_p = [x_1, x_2, \ldots, x_n]_p \tag{34.46c}$$

We want to approximate these observations by the best fit plane

$$y = c_0 + c_1 x_1 + c_2 x_2 + \cdots + c_n x_n \tag{34.47}$$

using the method of least squares. The observations tell us that a perfect fit would give

$$c_0 + c_1 x_{11} + c_2 x_{21} + \cdots + c_n x_{n1} = y_1 \tag{34.48a}$$
$$c_0 + c_1 x_{12} + c_2 x_{22} + \cdots + c_n x_{n2} = y_2 \tag{34.48b}$$

$$\vdots$$

$$c_0 + c_1 x_{1p} + c_2 x_2 2p + \cdots c_n x_{np} = y_p \tag{34.48c}$$

where the first index refers to the vector component and the second index to the observation number. This can be rewritten as the matrix equation

$$\begin{bmatrix} 1 & x_{11} & x_{21} & \cdots & x_{n1} \\ 1 & x_{12} & x_{22} & \cdots & x_{n2} \\ \vdots & & & & \vdots \\ 1 & x_{1p} & x_{2p} & \cdots & x_{np} \end{bmatrix} \begin{bmatrix} c_0 \\ c_1 \\ \vdots \\ c_n \end{bmatrix} = \begin{bmatrix} y_0 \\ y_1 \\ \vdots \\ y_n \end{bmatrix} \tag{34.49}$$

Defining the matrix on the left as $\mathbf{A}$ and the two column vectors as $\mathbf{c}$ and $\mathbf{y}$, any real solution will have some residual error $\mathbf{r}$, where

$$\mathbf{Ac} = \mathbf{y} + \mathbf{r} \tag{34.50}$$

The goal is to find the values of the vector $\mathbf{c}$ that minimize the residual distance

$$|\mathbf{r}| = |\mathbf{AC} - \mathbf{y}| \tag{34.51}$$

We have already solved this problem (with a different matrix $\mathbf{A}$) for polynomial least squares (see equations 34.22 through 34.36). The solution is

$$\mathbf{A}^T \mathbf{y} = \mathbf{A}^T \mathbf{Ac} \tag{34.52}$$

The matrix $= \mathbf{A}^T \mathbf{A}$ is symmetric and hence invertible, and therefore

$$\mathbf{c} = (\mathbf{A}^T \mathbf{A})^{-1} \mathbf{Ay} \tag{34.53}$$

If we define the column vectors $\mathbf{u}_j^T = [1, x_{1j}, x_{2j}, x_{3j}, \ldots, x_{nj}], j = 1, 2, \ldots, p$, then

$$\mathbf{A}^T \mathbf{A} = \begin{bmatrix} \mathbf{u}_1 | \cdots | \mathbf{u}_p \end{bmatrix} \begin{bmatrix} \mathbf{u}_1^T \\ \mathbf{u}_2^T \\ \vdots \\ \mathbf{u}_p^T \end{bmatrix} = \begin{bmatrix} p & \sum x_{1i} & \sum x_{2i} & \cdots & \sum x_{ni} \\ \sum x_{1i} & \sum x_{1i}^2 & \sum x_{1i}x_{2i} & \cdots & \sum x_{1i}x_{ni} \\ \sum x_{2i} & \sum x_{2i}x_{1i} & \sum x_{2i}^2 & \cdots & \vdots \\ \vdots & & & & \vdots \\ \sum x_{ni} & \cdots & & & \sum x_{ni}^2 \end{bmatrix} \tag{34.54}$$

If the observations have three variables $[x_i, y_i, z_i]$, then

$$\mathbf{A}^T\mathbf{A} = \begin{bmatrix} p & \sum x_i & \sum y_i & \sum z_i \\ \sum x_i & \sum x_i^2 & \sum x_i y_i & \sum x_i z_i \\ \sum y_i & \sum y_i x_i & \sum y_i^2 & \sum y_i z_i \\ \sum z_i & \sum z_i x_i & \sum z_i y_i & \sum z_i^2 \end{bmatrix} \tag{34.55}$$

Algorithm 34.4 Algorithm for multivariate linear regression.

---

input: Observations $\mathbf{x}_1, \mathbf{x}_2, \ldots, \mathbf{x}_p$ and values $y_1, y_2, \ldots, y_p$

1: **for** $j \in 1, \ldots, p$ **do**
2:     $\mathbf{a}_j \leftarrow [1, x_{j1}, x_{j2}, \ldots, x_{jn}]$ $\mathbf{a}_j$ is row j of $\mathbf{A}$
3: **end for**
4: $\mathbf{M} \leftarrow \mathbf{A}^T\mathbf{A}$
5: $\mathbf{b} \leftarrow \mathbf{A}^T\mathbf{y}$ $\mathbf{y}$ is column vector in input y_i
6: $\mathbf{c} \leftarrow \textbf{LinearSolve}(\mathbf{M}, \mathbf{b})$
7: **return** $\mathbf{c}$ The solution is $y = c_1 + c_2 x_1 + c_3 x_3 + \cdots + c_n x_n$

Example 34.1. Solve the normal equations to perform multiple linear regression on the following data set, where the first column contains y values, and the remainder of each row contains the corresponding $\mathbf{x}$ vector.

```
 1  0.416,-1.036,3.001,-0.623,-2.539,1.302
 2  0.442,-3.754,-0.579,4.960,4.462,1.974
 3  -10.295,-4.614,-4.067,3.732,-2.544,3.746
 4  -0.110,0.135,-2.498,4.190,1.874,-1.508
 5  2.318,-4.469,1.744,-2.650,0.854,-2.534
 6  12.276,1.192,4.857,-4.827,0.266,4.090
 7  -6.168,-1.357,2.808,3.715,-4.272,4.074
 8  -9.573,-2.641,-3.141,1.445,-4.279,1.472
 9  -4.872,-4.081,3.682,-1.139,-4.745,2.281
10  11.060,3.031,1.263,-0.312,2.711,3.191
11  -9.790,-3.436,-2.767,4.326,-1.949,1.015
12  2.791,-4.771,-1.336,1.780,4.821,3.061
13  14.337,3.723,4.469,-4.640,1.673,-3.314
14  1.718,4.718,3.021,1.069,-3.327,-2.503
15  -0.015,3.316,1.049,0.157,-4.442,0.125
16  -7.816,0.684,-3.803,3.080,-3.944,1.185
17  16.812,2.101,3.394,-4.657,4.598,-2.363
18  -6.650,-3.228,2.172,2.440,-2.582,-2.150
19  13.530,1.812,-3.681,-4.531,3.778,4.017
20  2.846,-4.386,-3.825,-0.877,3.498,0.359
```

Brute-force Python code for doing the calculation is

```python
1  import numpy as np
2  with open("data.txt","r") as f:   # read the data
3      data=f.readlines()
4  A=[]; y=[]                 # generate matrix A and vector y
5  for line in data:
6      values = line.strip().split(",")
```

```
 7      values = map(float, map(lambda x:x.strip(), values))
 8      y.append(values[0])
 9      values=[1.0]+values[1:]   # prepend x with 1
10      A.append(values)
11   A=np.array(A); y = np.array(y)
12   AT=A.T; ATA = AT.dot(A)
13   b = AT.dot(y)
14   c=np.linalg.solve(ATA, b)   # solve linear system
15   for ci in c: print "%.3f" %(ci),   # print to three digits
```

The output is

```
2.392 0.970 0.502 -1.014 1.466 0.270
```

which implies that the fit is

$$y = 2.392 + 0.970x_1 + 0.502x_2 - 1.014x_3 + 1.466x_4 + 0.270x_5.$$

Multiple Regression with statsmodel. The easiest way to do multiple regression in Python in to use **statsmodels**. Using the package **statsmodels** instead, the equivalent code (starting on line 12; we still have to form the **A** and **y** matrices properly)

```
import statsmodels.api as sm
model=sm.OLS(y, A)
res=model.fit()
for ci in res.params: print "%.3f" %(ci),
```

The output (not shown here) is identical. Even more information can be produced with the **statsmodel summary()** function. The output of **print res.summary()** for this example is shown below.

```
                          OLS Regression Results
==============================================================================
Dep. Variable:                      y   R-squared:                       0.999
Model:                            OLS   Adj. R-squared:                  0.998
Method:                 Least Squares   F-statistic:                      2022.
Date:                Tue, 17 Feb 2015   Prob (F-statistic):           1.72e-19
Time:                        15:52:38   Log-Likelihood:                 -5.0440
No. Observations:                  20   AIC:                             22.09
Df Residuals:                      14   BIC:                             28.06
Df Model:                           5
==============================================================================
                 coef    std err          t      P>|t|      [95.0% Conf. Int.]
------------------------------------------------------------------------------
const          2.3922      0.093     25.728      0.000      2.193      2.592
x1             0.9701      0.030     31.995      0.000      0.905      1.035
x2             0.5021      0.034     14.902      0.000      0.430      0.574
x3            -1.0140      0.034    -29.720      0.000     -1.087     -0.941
x4             1.4660      0.027     53.730      0.000      1.407      1.524
x5             0.2697      0.036      7.486      0.000      0.192      0.347
==============================================================================
Omnibus:                        1.143   Durbin-Watson:                   1.659
Prob(Omnibus):                  0.565   Jarque-Bera (JB):                0.866
Skew:                           0.196   Prob(JB):                        0.648
Kurtosis:                       2.058   Cond. No.                        5.05
==============================================================================
```

Exercises

1. Using the data from chapter 23 exercise 1, do a linear regression. Calculate the values of the slope and intercept yourself, e.g., by using eqs. (34.7) and (34.10) or (34.16) and (34.17e).

2. Repeat exercise 1, but this time do it by first forming the matrix (34.42), and then solving for the unknown coefficients using **np.linalg.solve**.

3. Repeat exercise 1, but this time do it by using **np.polyfit** with a degree 1 fit.

4. Write a python function **normal_matrix(x,n)** that forms the normal matrix $M=A^T A$ and column vector **b** (see equation (34.42)) for a degree n polynomial fit, and return them as a tuple **(M,b)**.

5. Using the function you wrote in exercise 4, for the systems **Mc=b** for degree $p=2$, 3, 4, 6, 9, 12, and 15 fits. Solve the system using **np.linalg.solve**.

6. Repeat the previous exercise using **np.polyfit**.

7. Plot the solutions you found in exercise 6 in a single column of plots, one degree per plot, using **subplot**. Make a scatter plot of the original data in each subplot. Verify that the polynomial fits are smooth lines, and not connected lines joining the data points.

8. Go to the Bureau of labor statistics data site (http://data.bls.gov/cgi-bin/surveymost?cw) and download the consumer price index for the Western Region, for the last ten years, as a spreadsheet. Save the data as a csv file and read it into Python. Then plot the data as a scatter plot. Find the optimal polynomial fit by splitting the data into test and training sets and repeating the process at least 100 times.

Chapter 35

Nonlinear Regression

Linear vs Nonlinear Regression

In linear regression, a function is described by a linear combination of model parameters. The coefficients of the model parameters themselves need not be linear in the function variables. For example

$$\hat{y}(x) = ax^2 + bx + c \qquad (35.1)$$

is linear in the model parameters a, b, and c. Finding $\hat{y}$ given a set of values $\{(x_i, y_i), ...\}$ by minimizing the RSS difference is an example of linear regression, and the values of the coefficients can be found by solving the normal equations. Similarly, it is possible to find an appropriate set of normal equations for any model

$$\hat{y}(x) = a_1 f_1(x) + b_1 f_2(x) + a_3 f_3(x) + \cdots + a_n f_n(x) \qquad (35.2)$$

for any combination of linear and/or nonlinear functions $f_1, \ldots, f_n$.

Sometimes a model of a data set cannot be expressed as a linear combination of its parameters, such as

$$\hat{y} = a\left[1 + \frac{b}{\sqrt{c + dx^2}}\right] \qquad (35.3)$$

In this case, $\hat{y}$ depends nonlinearly on the coefficients a, b, c, and d, and so it is not possible to explicitly find a system of normal equations. It may be possible to find a transformation that makes the equations linear, but the resulting minimization process will not necessarily carry over – an example of this will be given with the simple exponential fit given below.

Since there is no closed form solution we will need to iterate. Rather than describing the optimization process here, we will illustrate the procedure by example below.

Fitting an Exponential

Suppose we have a collection of data points that we believe can be correctly modeled by an exponential function plus some noise.

$$f(x) = Ce^{mx} + n(x) = e^{mx+b} + n(x) \qquad (35.4)$$

Here $C = e^b$ is a positive constant and $n(x)$ is noise, e.g., due to measurement error. This is one of the most common equations found in mathematical models of natural phenomena. It describes things as varied as radioactive decay, population growth under certain conditions, heating and cooling, the accrual of interest on a bank deposit, and capacitative charging.

Consider the following data, which gives the population of the United States at 10 year intervals in thousands of people.

1790	3929	1850	23191	1910	92228	1970	203302
1800	5308	1860	31433	1920	106021	1980	226542
1810	7239	1870	38558	1930	123202	1990	248709
1820	9638	1880	50189	1940	132164		
1830	12866	1890	62979	1950	151325		
1840	17069	1900	76212	1960	179323		

Figure 35.1: US population in thousands.

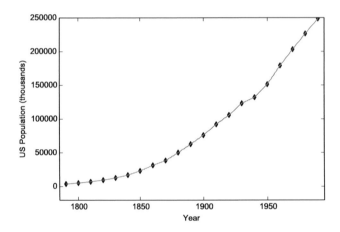

This data is plotted in figure 35.1; it certainly *looks like* an exponential curve. The question becomes, *can we accurately fit* an exponential curve to this data?

More specifically, can we find numbers m and b such that

$$P(t) = e^{mt+b} \tag{35.5}$$

gives a "good fit" to the data, in some sense? (The parameters m and b are intentionally chosen here to resemble the parameters m and b in the equation for a line $y = mx + b$.)

In linear least squares, we found that the best fit is the one that minimizes the sum of the square distances of the errors. If the data points are at (x_i, y_i) for $i = 1, 2, .., n$, and we are fitting the curve $y = f(x)$, then we minimized the sum

$$S = \sum_{i=1}^{n} (f(x_i) - y_i)^2 \tag{35.6}$$

For linear and polynomial functions f, we can minimize this sum exactly by setting the partial derivatives (with respect to each of the parameters) equal to zero, because we get a systems of linear equations in the unknown parameters. Unfortunately, if we try to do this with the exponential,

$$S = \sum_{i=1}^{n}(e^{ax_i+b_i} - y_i)^2 \tag{35.7}$$

the partial derivatives with respect to the model parameters a and b are nonlinear in a and b. So instead of plowing through the hopelessly nonlinear equations trying to find the impossible solution, lets try a more naive approach. This method is actually incorrect, though it is described quite widely on the internet.[1]

The idea is simple: if we expect $y = e^{ax+b}$, let $u = \ln y$. Then

$$u = \ln y = ax + b \tag{35.8}$$

is linear in x. Mathematically we perform the map

$$(x_i, y_i) \mapsto (x_i, u_i) \text{ where } u_i = \ln y_i, i = 1, 2, \ldots, n \tag{35.9}$$

To produce a *new data set* $\{(x_1, u_1), \ldots, (x_n, u_n)\}$ that replaces the original data set $\{(x_1, y_1), \ldots, (x_n, y_n)\}$. Looking at (35.8), an linear regression of u on x will gives us the values of m and b in the *model*

$$u(x) = mx + b \tag{35.10}$$

Inverting the transformation (35.9), $u_i = \ln y_i$, gives $y_i = e^{u_i}$. Extrapolating this to the *model* (35.10) (this step is not really mathematically justified) gives

$$y = e^u = e^{mx+b} \tag{35.11}$$

which is exactly the model we are looking for.

We can do exactly this in Python. First, define the data points.

```
USPOP=[3929, 5308,7239,9638,12866,17069,23191,31433,
   38558,50189,62979,76212,92228,106021,123202,
   132164, 151325,179323,203302,226542,248709]
USYR =[1790,1800,1810,1820,1830,1840,1850,1860,1870,1880,
   1890,1900,1910,1920,1930,1940,1950,1960,1970,1980,1990]
```

Next, do a linear fit of $\ln(p)$ *vs.* time. To reduce the chances of numerical roundoff error we will measure time $t = 0$ from the first data point (1790), although this is not really necessary.

```
import numpy as np
xvals=[X-1790 for X in USYR]
logpop=np.log(USPOP)
m,b=np.polyfit(xvals,logpop,1)
```

The returned values are

```
0.0207689449969 8.67175820593
```

---

[1] I was taught to solve the problem this way in undergraduate labs.

We plot the results of the fit figure 35.2. To do this we defined a function to return the value of the predicted fit as a function of x.

```
def predicted(x):
    return np.exp(m*x+b)
```

Then we can use **pyplot** to plot the exponential over an array of points.

```
import matplotlib.pyplot as plt
plt.scatter(xvals, USPOP, label="Actual_Population")
pdata=[predicted(x) for x in xvals]
plt.plot(xvals,pdata, c="red", label="Least_Squares_Log")
plt.xlabel("Year")
plt.ylabel("US_Population_(thousands)")
plt.xticks(range(10,201,50), range(1800,1991,50))
plt.xlim(-5,205)
plt.ylim(-20000,400000)
plt.legend(loc="best")
```

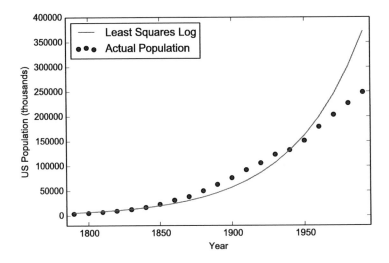

Figure 35.2: U. S. population exponential fit with $m = 0.0207$ and $b = 8.671$.

Improving the Fit: Brute Force

For some reason the prediction (given by the least squares fit) in figure 35.2 does not look very good. The nature question to ask is: "why not?" The answer to this question is that the least squares fit we have found this way – somewhat naively – does not actually minimize the sum (35.7); instead, we are minimizing

$$S = \sum_i \left(mx_i + b_i - \ln y_i \right)^2. \tag{35.12}$$

To verify that that the minimums are different, we will do a brute-force (exhaustive) calculation over (m, b) space and see if there are other combinations of m and b that will give a better result. In general, not a good way to proceed for extremely large data sets (e.g., in the thousands or millions of data points). But for our data set, it is quite reasonable to do a brute-force scan of (m, b) space.[2] At each point we will calculate the root[3] mean sum

$$R = \left[\sum_{i=1}^{n} (e^{mx_i + b_i} - y_i)^2 \right]^{1/2} \tag{35.13}$$

as a function of m and b. With the time values still in **xvals** and the popuation values still in **USPOP**, we can do this with

```
def rmspop(m, b):
    def pred(x,m,b):
        return np.exp(m*x+b)
    preds=[pred(x,m,b) for x in xvals]
    rss = sum([(y1-y2)**2 for y1,y2 in zip(preds, USPOP)])
    return np.sqrt(rss)
```

We can plot out this distance using a contour plot in (m, b) space. The minimum should be at the bottom of a valley (figure 35.3). We can plot the landscape, then blow it up and estimate the value of the minimum manually to get a good value of the minimum without doing an exhaustive search. To plot the landscape,

```
A=[[rmspop(M,B) for M in np.linspace(0.0,.04,25)]
    for B in np.linspace(1,15,200)]
cp=contourf(A)
colorbar(cp)
```

To add the original point, it must be scaled to the 25×200 array **A**.

```
xpoint=25*(.0207-.0)/(.04-0)
ypoint=200*(8.617-1)/(15-1)
scatter([xpoint],[ypoint],
    label="Logarithmic_Least_Squares",
    s=75, facecolor="pink")
```

After we find the minimum, we can also add it to the plot. We use the same scaling. Of course since we found the point manually by blowing up the plot, the value is approximate.

```
PLUSXpoint=25*(.015-.0)/(.04-0)
PLUSYpoint=200*(9.5-1)/(15-1)
scatter([PLUSXpoint],[PLUSYpoint],marker="D", s=75,
        facecolor="white", label="Landscape_Minimum")
```

It can be verified that the RMS value is smaller at $(0.015, 9.5)$ than the original value of $(0.0217, 8.617)$ by substitution into **rmspop**:

---

[2] Suppose we perform the calculation at each of 200 values for both m and b, or a total of 40,000 (m, b) pairs. At each point we compute a sum over 21 data points. This is a perfectly reasonable number of calculations to perform (with a computer).

[3] We are taking the root so that the numbers don't get too big.

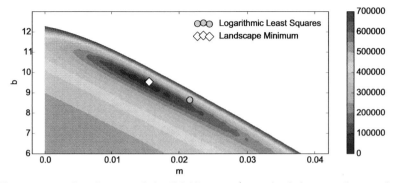

Figure 35.3: Landscape of the RMS error (35.13) of the population data.

```
rmspop(.0207, 8.617), rmspop(0.015, 9.5)
```

```
(128915.98119364001, 44022.051609003756)
```

As we see from figure 35.4, the values at the landscape minimum do appear to give a much better approximation to the original data.

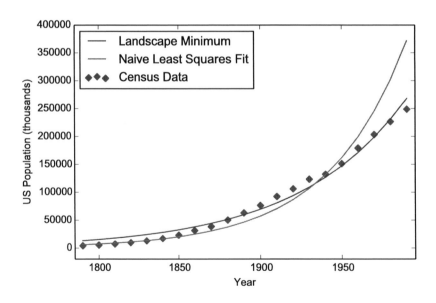

Figure 35.4: U. S. population with naive least squares fit, and optimal least squares fit.

An easier way to do this is to use the function **scipy.optimize.leastsq**. The function **leastsq** will minimize (35.6) for any function.

To use **leastsq** to solve the present problem, we must first define a function **F**. (We don't have to call it **F**; we could call it anything we want.) The function **F** includes information about f and computes a list of the differences between the actual and predicted values of the model at each point in the data. For example, if f depends on some parameters p, q, ...; **f** is a formula for f in terms of **x**, **p**, **q**, ...; and we have observations **yobs** and data points **xdata**,

```
def F((p,q,...), xdata, yobs):
        ypred = [f(p,q,x) for x in xdata]
        return [obs-pred for obs,pred in zip(yobs,ypred)]
```

We define **f** as a function within **F**, e.g., for the exponential fit,

```
def F((m, b), times, pops):
    def f(t,m,b):
        return np.exp(m*t+b)
    preds=[f(t,m,b) for t in times]
    return [actual-pred(t,m,b) for actual,t in zip(pops,times)]
```

Then the optimization would be performed with **leastsq**.

```
from scipy.optimize import leastsq as L
opt=L(func, (msave,bsave),args=(xvals,USPOP))
mopt,bopt=opt[0]
print "m_=",mopt,"b_=", bopt, "rms_=",rmspop(mopt, bopt)
```

```
m = 0.0147084845973 b = 9.54763631546 rms = 43691.116890814432
```

The solution we found manually is very close to this minimum solution.

Logistic Regression

Logistic regression is typically used when the dependent variable consists of discrete, rather than continuous values. In statistics such variables are called categorical variables. Examples are gender, eye color, or which courses a student is taking this semester. The independent variable is still continuous. An alternative perspective is to treat this as a classification problem: which subsets of the domain get mapped to which discrete elements of the range? In machine learning the discrete elements are typically referred to as *classes* or *class labels*, but we will avoid that nomenclature to avoid any confusion with python classes.

Theory

In the simplest case there are two categories C_1 and C_0. We want to find a probability function $P(C_i|x)$ that will make this assignment. Let

$$y = P(C_1|x) \tag{35.14}$$

Then since there are only two categories,

$$1 - y = P(C_0|x) \tag{35.15}$$

The log of the odds ratio for C_1 is

$$z = \ln \frac{y}{1-y} = \text{logit}(y) \tag{35.16}$$

Solving for y gives

$$y = \frac{1}{1 + e^{-z}} \tag{35.17}$$

It can be shown that for normally distributed variables, z depends linearly on x.[4] Thus we have the logistic function

$$y = \frac{1}{1 + e^{-(ax+b)}} \tag{35.18}$$

where a and b are undetermined parameters.

Implementation

Logistic Regression is typically implemented using an iterative maximum likelihood estimator. A maximum likelihood estimator (MLE) finds the maximum value of the likelihood or log-likelihood function (e.g., (35.18)), or the most probable outcome. Under certain conditions, such as those discussed in this chapter, a MLE will produce the same result as least squares minimization. Typical iteration methods include variations on gradient descent algorithms, which attempt to follow the shortest path to an energy minimum (e.g., the minimum RSS error) by iterating on a formula similar to Newton's method.[5] We will refer only to the version of logistic regression implemented in scikit-learn in the remainder of this chapter.

Example 35.1. Generate a simulated data set of 1500 age 12 children, consisting of 800 boys (mean height 149.0488164 cm; standard deviation 3.7468166 cm) and 700 girls (mean height 151.1913253 cm; standard deviation 3.674342. Assume a normal distribution.

We can generate the data using **np.random.normal**.

```
boys=np.random.normal(149.0488164,3.7468166,800)
girls=np.random.normal(151.1913253,3.7468166,700)
```

Histograms are plotted with **matplotlib.pyplot.hist** (fig. 35.5).

The same data is plotted according to category "boy" or "girl" in figure 35.6. The following will convert **boys** and **girls** to arrays for plotting.

```
b=[[x,0] for x in boys]
g=[[x,1] for x in girls]
```

```
bg = np.array(b+g)    # concatenate lists, convert to array
heights=bg[:,0]       # first column of array
zerosones=bg[:,1]     # second column
```

It is difficult to really understand figure 35.6 because many of the points lie on top of one-another. Although the figure clearly shows the different categories, it is not clear where

---

[4]See E. Alpaydin, *Introduction to Machine Learning*, 2nd. ed., Chapter 10.5.
[5]See chapter 3.3.2 of Y. Abu-Mostafa et. al., *Learning from Data* for a detailed discussion of the gradient descent algorithm for logistic regression.

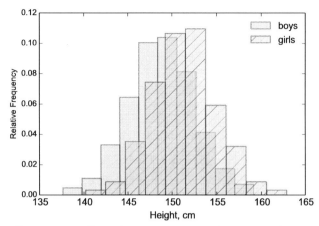

Figure 35.5: Distributions generated in example 35.1.

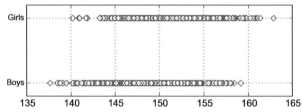

Figure 35.6: Simulated data generated in example 35.1. The plot is produced with
`plt.scatter(heights,zerosones)`.

the points may be bunched up, or if the data is distributed in any sort of meaningful
way. Another way to illustrate the data is to replace the discrete categorization of ones
and zeros with a proportion. On the y axis we can plot the proportion, out of the total,
of data points in category 1 out of the total, as a function of x. Since each data point
represents the same proportion, we have to break the data up into equally spaced bins
along the x-axis, as we do with an histogram.

```
def bindata(xdata, zerosones, m, M, nbins):
    Delta=float(M-m); N = nbins+1
    binmins=np.linspace(m,M,N)
    zeros, ones = N*[0], N*[0]
    binvals=[int(nbins*(x-m)/Delta) for x in xdata]
    for flag,b in zip(zerosones,binvals):
        if flag>0:
            ones[b]+=1   # histogram of ones
        else:
            zeros[b]+=1 # histogram of zeros
    sizes = [x+y for x,y in zip(ones, zeros)] # total histogram
    proportions=[float(x)/float(y) if y>0 else 0 for x,y \
                in zip(ones, sizes) ]
    return (binmins, proportions, sizes)
```

Typically some ten to twenty bins are good. Then we can count the number of actual values in each category. The y axis is the proportion of girls out of the total, $G/(B+G)$. To get the data for fig. 35.7 a call such as this would work:[6]

```
xv, yv, sv = bindata(heights, zerosones, m, M, 15 )
plt.scatter(xv, yv, s=sv, c="white", edgecolor="magenta")
```

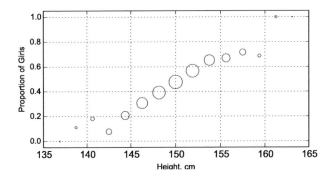

Figure 35.7: Distributions generated in example 35.1 illustrated as proportion of girls in bins of width 2 cm. in height. The markers are proportional in size to the total number of students in each bin.

We will perform logistic regression on the data set using the function

```
sklearn.linear_model.LogisticRegression()
```

The package **sklearn** is part of a package called scikit-learn.[7] The python name of the package is **sklearn**. The logistic regression function in **sklearn** is very general, and a complete discussion is way beyond the scope of this text. To set up your data for logistic regression,

- The x values can either

  ▶ Represent continuous floating point values (such as our height values) as an $n \times 1$ array (assuming there are n data points):

    ```
    X=np.array([[value],[value],..,[value]])
    ```

  ▶ Represent vectors of continuous floating point values as arrays,

    ```
    X=np.array([[value, value, ..., value],
                [value, value, ..., value],..,
                [value, value, ..., value]])
    ```

- The y values should be an array (of the same length as the x array) of ones and zeros[8] indicating which of the two classes each corresponding x value belongs to.

---

[6]The code actually plots the symbols at the *left* edge of each bin, which will be corrected in exercise 5.
[7]See http://scikit-learn.org/stable/documentation.html.
[8]Multi-class logistic regression is also possible; see the scikit-learn documentation if you are interested.

Finally, **sklearn** has a convenient function **train_test_split** that will separate your data randomly into a test set (say around a quarter of the data) and a training set (the rest of the data). We can save the test set for later to see how well the prediction works.

Each time we perform a logistic regression we have to instantiate a new python class object called **LogisticRegression()**. We instantiate this object by typing in

```
LR=LogisticRegression()
```

This means that **LR** (or whatever we choose to name it) is a new logistic regression object. We access this class object using its methods. To actually perform the logistic regression, we have to pass data to **LR** and ask it to do something with this data. The real work is done by the **fit** method. If we have put our training data in **XTRAIN** and **YRAIN** then we can perform the fit with

```
LR.fit(XTRAIN,YTRAIN)
```

The output of the fit is stored inside the class object. To access this information we have to use additional methods. We are interested in three particular parameters. The first one of these is R^2 (the coefficient of determination). If the x and y test data are in the arrays **XTEST** and **YTEST** then we can get R^2 by inquiring

```
LR.score(XTEST,YTEST)
```

The coefficient of determination gives the fraction of the variance that is explained by the model. For linear models $R^2 = r^2$ where r is the Pearson correlation coefficient. In general,

$$R^2 = 1 - \frac{\text{RSS}}{\text{TSS}} \tag{35.19}$$

Here RSS is the **residual sum square error** after computing the fit,

$$\text{RSS} = \sum (y_i - f(x_i))^2 \tag{35.20}$$

and TSS is the **total sum square error**

$$\text{TSS} = \sum (y_i - \bar{y})^2 \tag{35.21}$$

In general, values of R^2 closer to 1 are better. However, a high value of R^2 is not sufficient to tell you whether or not the correct model was used to describe your data.[9]

The other two parameters we are interested in are the values of a and b in the logistic equation 35.18. Those are given by the methods **coef_** and **intercept_**, each of which returns an array. There is only one intercept, so the intercept is an array of length one, and you can just pull off the zeroth element.

```
b=LR.intercept_[0]
```

The coefficient will be an array containing an array of coefficients of length equal to the dimension of the x data. If your x data was a single variable then **LR.coef_** $\rightarrow$ **[[value]]**, and you can extract it as

---

[9]See James et. al., *An Introduction to Statistical Learning*, Chapter 3; or https://en.wikipedia.org/wiki/Coefficient_of_determination.

```
a=LR.coef_[0][0]
```

If the x data is an a array of vectors, then the coefficient format is `[[value, value, ...,value]]`, and eq. 35.18 generalizes to

$$y = \frac{1}{1 + e^{-\left(\sum a_i x_i + b\right)}} \tag{35.22}$$

Example 35.2. Use `sklearn` to perform logistic regression on the boy/girl data set from example 35.1. First we set up the data arrays. In this case, since the numbers are in the range 135 to 165, we will shift the x-axis values to avoid the potential for numerical errors.

```
from sklearn.linear_model import LogisticRegression
from sklearn.cross_validation import train_test_split
m=min(heights)
y=np.array(zerosones)
X=np.array([[x-m] for x in heights])
```

Next we will divide the data up into a test set and a training set. We will use 75% of the data for training.

```
x_train,x_test,y_train,y_test = train_test_split(X, y,test_size=0.25)
```

Finally we can perform the logistic regression in the training set.

```
LR=LogisticRegression()
LR.fit(x_train, y_train)
```

The logistic regression has been performed. To get the results, we can inquire the object `LR` for the values computed. We are interested in three values in particular: R^2 (the coefficient of determination), and the values of a and b in the logistic equation 35.18,

```
R2=LR.score(x_test,y_test)
a=LR.coef_[0][0]
b=LR.intercept_[0]
print "R^2=",R2,"a=",a,"b=",b
```

```
R^2= 0.645333333333 a= 0.176737238599 b= -2.81985553203
```

The a and b values can be used to define a function for plotting. Any **x** offset value **m** that was used previously must also be taken into account (fig. 35.8).

```
from math import e
def f(x):
    return 1.0/(1.0+e**(-a*x-b))
xvals = np.linspace(135,165,100)
yvals = [f(x-m) for x in xvals]
plt.plot(xvals,yvals, c="red")
```

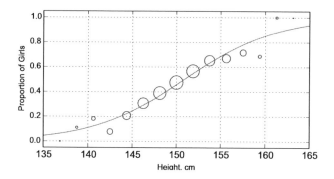

Figure 35.8: Logistic regression fit plotted with data from fig. 35.7.

It is also sometimes informative to print the logistic regression fit with the ones and zeros prediction (fig. 35.9).

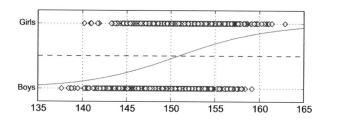

Figure 35.9: Logistic regression fit plotted with data from fig. 35.6.

sklearn also has some built in metrics that can be used to evaluate the fit using the test data. These include a calculation of the confusion matrix, the precision, the recall and the f1 score.

We define a **positive** as a y value that corresponds to class C_1 and a **negative** as y value that corresponds to class C_0. A correctly predicted value is called **true** and and incorrectly predicted value is called **false**:

		Actual Class	
		C_0	C_1
Predicted	C_0	TN (True Negative)	FN (False Negative)
Class	C_1	FP (False Positive)	TP (True Positive)

The **precision** gives the ratio of true positives to total positives. It gives the proportion of values, among all those *predicted* to be in category C_1, which were predicted correctly. For the example above, it would be the ratio of the number of girls correctly predicted to be girls (numerator) to the total number of children predicted to be girls.

$$P = \frac{TP}{TP + FP} \tag{35.23}$$

The **recall** has the same numerator but the denominator is the sum of the true positives and the false negatives, that is, a count of the number of x values to be in category C_1. It gives the proportion of values, among those that are *actually* in category C_1, that are predicted correctly:

$$R = \frac{TP}{TP + FN} \tag{35.24}$$

In the best of all worlds we would like a predictor with both high precision and high recall (i.e., near 1).

The F_1 score[10] is the harmonic mean of precision and recall;

$$F_1 = \frac{2PR}{P + R} \tag{35.25}$$

The reason for using a harmonic mean rather than a true average is illustrated by the following example:[11] Suppose the recall is high ($R \approx 1$) and the precision is low ($P \ll 1$). Then the arithmetic mean is around 0.5 while the harmonic mean is $\approx 2P$.

Example 35.3. Use **sklearn** to print the metrics and confusion matrix.

```
from sklearn import metrics
predictions=LR.predict(x_test)
print metrics.classification_report(y_test,predictions)
```

	precision	recall	f1-score	support
0.0	0.57	0.67	0.61	200
1.0	0.52	0.42	0.47	175
avg / total	0.55	0.55	0.55	375

The two lines labeled **0.0** and **1.0** give the values using first the class with $y = 0$ and then the class with $y = 1$ as C_1. The support is the total number of items in each class in the test set.

```
confusion_matrix = metrics.confusion_matrix(y_test,predictions)
print confusion_matrix
```

```
[[133  67]
 [101  74]]
```

A color plot is a useful visualization of the confusion matrix.

```
plt.matshow(confusion_matrix)
plt.title("Test_Data_Set_Confusion_Matrix")
plt.colorbar(); plt.ylabel("True_Label"); plt.xlabel("Predicted_Label")
```

---

[10]see K. Murphy, *Machine Learning*, section 5.7.2.3; https://en.wikipedia.org/wiki/F1_score
[11]Murphy op.cit.

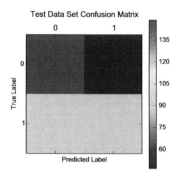

Logistic Regression in `statsmodels`

As an alternative to using scikit-learn, it is even easier to use the logistic regression function in **statsmodels**. The main difference is the rest of the library. **statsmodels** is devoted primarily to statistics, while **sklearn** is devoted to machine learning. The main difference is that the **fit** method does not automatically provide an intercept; to force one, we need to add a column of ones to the x data. The y data remains as before. Starting with the lists **zerosones** and **heights** that we used in example 35.2. We will add the offset **m** as we did previously for easy comparison.

```
YVALS=np.array([u for u in zerosones])
XVALS=np.array([[1,u-m] for u in heights])
```

Then we can do logistic regression as follows.

```
import statsmodels.api as sm
model=sm.Logit(YVALS,XVALS)
results=model.fit(method="bfgs")
print results.summary()
```

Logit Regression Results

Dep. Variable:			y	No. Observations:		1500
Model:			Logit	Df Residuals:		1498
Method:			MLE	Df Model:		1
Date:		Sat, 02 Jan 2016		Pseudo R-squ.:		0.08468
Time:			17:52:33	Log-Likelihood:		-948.63
converged:			True	LL-Null:		-1036.4
				LLR p-value:		4.624e-40

	coef	std err	z	P>|z|	[95.0% Conf. Int.]	
const	-3.0657	0.248	-12.352	0.000	-3.552	-2.579
x1	0.1947	0.016	12.174	0.000	0.163	0.226

Note that the coefficients are very similar to the values used previously.[12]

---

[12] For more details see http://statsmodels.sourceforge.net/devel/examples/generated/ example_discrete.html#logit-model.

Exercises

1. The Hill function $y = \dfrac{Ax^n}{B^n + x^n}$ is often a good fit for predicted the concentration of proteins in complex biochemical reactions, where x is the concentration of a stimulation protein (input) and y is the concentration of the measured output protein. Using the following input data,

```
x=[1,  5, 10, 15, 20, 25, 30, 35, 40]
y=[1,  4,  7, 25, 66, 83, 90, 95, 98]
```

   use the brute-force approach (exhaustive search) to fit a Hill function to the data. Assume that $A = 100$ and find B and n.

2. Implement exercise 1 using **leastsq** from **scipy.optimize** instead of exhaustive search.

3. Can you do exercise1 using a logistic function? What function should you use? Implement the solution.

4. Show that the log odds ratio (eq. 35.16) is linear in x for one dimensional normally distributed data, $\text{logit}(y) = ax + b$ for some numbers a and b.

5. Fix the function to group the data in bins and plot the binned proportion data where the symbols are proportional to size of the data in the plot, as illustrated in figure 35.7, so that the points are plotted in the center of the bins and not the left edges. Verify your results by reproducing the simulation in the text of two overlapping normally distributed populations.

6. In the boy/girl student example, we assumed that all the students could be described by a single normal distribution. This is a faulty assumption because at the age of 12 children are still growing. According to the Center for Disease Control, the average heights in cm. for children based on their age in months is

Age	Boys	Girls
132	144.37	143.98
144	149.05	151.19
156	156.09	157.16

Generate a random sample of 15 children composed of 800 boys and 700 girls. Assume that the children's ages are uniformly distributed between 12 and 13 years old (144 and 156 months old). A uniform sample of **n** numbers between zero and one can be generated with **np.random.random(n)**; to get a uniform sample between 12 and 13, add 12 to the array. Based on this age, use the least squares fit to the data in the table produce a mean height μ for students of that age. Then use **np.random.normal(mu,sigma)** to generate a random height for that student. Assume that the standard deviation is 3.5 cm. Finally, repeat the logistic regression example performed in the text. Plot the probability curve and the proportion of girls as a function of height.

7. In a simple random sample (SRS) of college freshman, a student's performance was measured as whether or not he or she graduated within six years of matriculation as a function of their grade point average (GPA) at the end of the first semester in college. Here are the GPA's of the students who graduated:

```
GPAS_GRADS=[2.2,2.27,2.4,2.45,2.46,2.5,
2.63,2.65,2.65,2.72,2.72,2.74,2.86,2.9,
2.93,3.0,3.0,3.04,3.05,3.05,3.18,3.24,
3.26,3.27,3.33,3.33,3.42,3.43,3.43,
3.46,3.5,3.5,3.52,3.52,3.52,3.56,3.57,
3.6,3.6,3.6,3.68,3.77,3.93]
```

Here are the GPA's of the students who did not graduate;

```
GPAS_NONGRADS=[0.0,0.0,0.0,0.0,0.43,
1.4,1.5,1.7,1.75,1.85,1.9,2.0,2.0,2.0,
2.08,2.14,2.18,2.23,2.35,2.35,2.4,2.65,
2.66,2.79,2.85,2.99,3.05,3.36,3.5,3.52,
3.65,4.0]
```

Using logistic regression, determine the probability that a student will graduate within six years at this university as a function of their first semester GPA.

Chapter 36

Differential Equations

When we talk about solving differential equations, what we really mean is that we are finding a numerical solution of an initial value problem.

Definition 36.1. Initial Value Problem

An initial value problem is composed of a differential equation and an initial condition:

$$\mathbf{y}' = \mathbf{f}(t, \mathbf{y}) \tag{36.1a}$$

$$\mathbf{y}(t_0) = \mathbf{y}_0 \tag{36.1b}$$

If there is only a single variable, equations 36.1 become

$$\frac{dy}{dt} = f(t, y) \tag{36.2a}$$

$$y(t_0) = y_0 \tag{36.2b}$$

where t_0 and y_0 are known, fixed constants. If there are multiple variables, then we collect them together in the vectors $\mathbf{y}$.

Example 36.1. Accrued interest. If you invest an amount P (dollars) at time $t = 0$, and accumulate wealth at an interest rate r, then the total investment A will grow at a rate proportional to the amount present.

$$\frac{dA}{dt} = rA \tag{36.3a}$$

$$A(0) = P \tag{36.3b}$$

The exact solution to this initial value problem is the well known "Pert" equation $A = Pe^{rt}$. This can be verified by direct substitution.

Example 36.2. The **Lorenz Equations** are a system of three inter-related differential equations that describe atmospheric convection.

$$x' = \sigma(y - x) \tag{36.4a}$$

$$y' = \rho x - xz - y \tag{36.4b}$$

$$z' = xy - \beta z \tag{36.4c}$$

where $\beta = 8/3$, $\sigma = 10$, and $\rho = 28$ are fixed constants. In the notation of (36.1), this can be written as $\mathbf{y}' = \mathbf{f}(t, \mathbf{y})$, where

$$\mathbf{y} = \begin{bmatrix} x & y & z \end{bmatrix}^{\mathrm{T}} \tag{36.5}$$

and

$$\mathbf{f}(t, \mathbf{y}) = \begin{bmatrix} \sigma(y - x) \\ \rho x - xz - y \\ xy - \beta z \end{bmatrix} \tag{36.6}$$

Even though t is not explicitly part of the function $\mathbf{f}(t, \mathbf{y})$ it is still present implicitly through the dependence of each of the variables on t.

A typical initial condition for the Lorenz system would be

$$\mathbf{y}_0 = \begin{bmatrix} 0 & 1 & 0 \end{bmatrix}^{\mathrm{T}} \tag{36.7}$$

The solution of the Lorenz equations in three dimensions has chaotic properties and displays a characteristic "butterfly" shape (figure 36.1).

Figure 36.1: The solution of the the Lorenz system is a locus of points in three dimensions whose path is described by the chaotic butterfly shape.

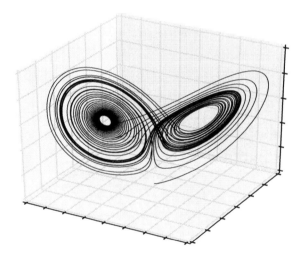

Numerical Solutions of Differential Equations

A solution to (36.2) is a function $\phi(t)$ (possibly a vector function if there are multiple variables) that satisfies both the differential equation and initial condition, i.e.,

$$\phi'(t) = f(t, \phi(t)) \tag{36.8a}$$
$$\phi(t_0) = y_0 \tag{36.8b}$$

Comparing (36.8) to (36.2) we see that for $\phi(t)$ to be a solution means we can replace y everywhere in the original equation by its explicit formula $\phi(t)$ and the equation is correct. Thus we say that $y = \phi(t)$ is a solution.

Solving (36.2) means finding a function $\phi(t)$ that satisfies the original equation.

Solution

The **solution** of an initial value problem is a **function**.

Numerically, this means our solution will be a list of points on the plot of the solution:

$$(t_0, y_0), (t_1, y_1), (t_2, y_2), \ldots, (t_n, y_n) \tag{36.9}$$

Numerical Solution

The **numerical solution** of an initial value problem is a **list of points**.

For the remainder of this chapter, we will assume that the points are evenly spaced along in the t direction, i.e., we define a **grid** so that

$$t_i = t_0 + kh, \ \ k = 0, 1, 2, \ldots \tag{36.10}$$

where h is some small fixed number. In fact, this fixed spacing is not necessary, but it is easier to understand the techniques if we make this restriction. Variable grid spacings are discussed in advanced textbooks on numerical analysis.

Thus our solution will be a list or sequence of points. If we need to know the value of the solution in between two of the grid points, we can interpolate.

Euler's Method

Using our fixed grid, we can approximate the slope between two points (t_n, y_n) and (t_{n+1}, y_{n+1}) as approximately

$$\frac{y_{n+1} - y_n}{t_{n+1} - t_n} = \frac{y_{n+1} - y_n}{h} \qquad (36.11)$$

We use this ratio to approximate the slope at t_n, which is given by $y'_n(t_n)$. Since

$$y' = f(t, y) \qquad (36.12)$$

we also can approximate

$$y'(t_n) \approx f(t_n, y_n) \qquad (36.13)$$

to give us

$$\frac{y_{n+1} - y_n}{h} \approx f(t_n, y_n) \qquad (36.14)$$

Solving for y_{n+1} gives us an iteration formula,

$$y_{n+1} = y_n + h f(t_n, y_n) \qquad (36.15)$$

Equation 36.15 is call **Euler's Method**.

Algorithm 36.1 Euler's method to solve the initial value problem $y' = f(t, y)$, $y(t_0) = y_0$.

---

input: $f(t, y)$, t_0, y_0, h, t_{max}
1: $t = t_0$
2: $y = y_0$
3: $k = 0$
4: **while** $t < t_{max}$ **do**
5:     $y_{k+1} \leftarrow y_k + h f(t_k, y_k)$
6:     $t_{k+1} \leftarrow t_k + h$
7:     $k \leftarrow k + 1$
8: **end while**
9: **return** $((t_0, y_0), (t_1, y_1), (t_1, y_2), \ldots, (t_n, y_n))$

The only change in algorithm 36.1 for a system is in line 5, where we would have one line for each component of the update.

Example 36.3. Write a Python program to solve the initial value problem $y' = y + t$, $y(0) = 1$, on the interval $[0, 1]$, with a step size of $h = .1$ using Euler's method. First, we write a program for $f(t, y) = y + t$.

```
def f(t,y):
    return y+t
```

Next, we write a function **euler** to calculate the solution. We don't have to count the indices because we can just use Python's **append** function to append the values to the end of a growing list.

```
def euler(t0,y0,h,tmax):
    t, y = t0, y0
    td, yd = [t0], [y0]
    while t<tmax:
        y = y + h*f(t,y)
        yd.append(y)
        t=t+h
        td.append(t)
    return(td,yd)
```

Then to call the program and print out a list of the points, one pair per line,

```
>>> (tvals, yvals)=euler(0,1,.1,1)
>>> for x, y in zip(tvals, yvals):
...    print "%7.2f_%7.2f" %(x,y)
...
  (some values omitted)
    0.90      2.82
    1.00      3.19
    1.10      3.61
>>>
```

To plot the solution,

```
>>> imort matplotlib.pyplot as plt
>>> plt.plot(tvals,yvals)
>>> show()
```

In an ipython notebook with **%matplotlib inline** enabled, the **show()** is not required. The **plot** output is shown in figure 36.2.

Figure 36.2: Output of 36.3.

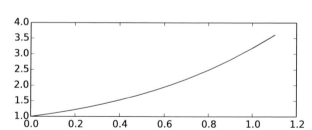

In general, the smaller the step size (h), the better the accuracy of the solution. As a result a lot of iterations can be required to get an good solution. For Euler's method, if the step size is large, individual updates can go wildly astray (figure 36.3).

Many other methods have been developed that improve on Euler's method. The most commonly used ones are collections of methods known as Runge-Kutta methods (RK), Adam-Bashforth methods (AB, good for non-stiff systems), and Backward Differentiation methods (BDF Methods, good for stiff systems). Most of these methods are much

Figure 36.3: Example of a solving a **stiff** initial value problem with Euler's method: $y' = -5ty^2 + 5/t - 1/t^2$, $y(1) = 1$, for different step sizes.

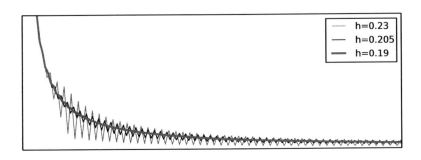

more efficient that Euler's method, but each one has its own limitations. Fortunately there are many programming libraries that include highly efficient implementations and will automatically choose a method for you, or allow you to select a method. For more details on the advantages and disadvantages of the different methods, see any textbook on the numerical solution of differential equations.

Using odeint to Solve IVPs

In Python, we can use **scipy.integrate.odeint** to solve initial value problems. Odeint uses one of the most efficient libraries ever developed for numerical integration, called LSODA. LSODA[1] is part of a larger FORTRAN library called ODEPACK, and automatically switches between stiff (BDF) and non-stiff (Adams) solvers depending on the nature of the problem. The different solvers in ODEPACK are among the best debugged and most popular solvers in use for solving differential equations.

For a one-variable differential equation, the basic call to **odeint** is

```
y = odeint(f, y0, times)
```

where **times** is a (numpy) array of values for the t-axis at which you want to know the output. The initial value of **times** corresponds to the first value, **times[0]**. The return value **y** is an array of values of the solution at the requested times.

---

[1]The acronym stands for Livermore Solver for Ordinary Differential equations with Automatic switching. Other modules in ODEPACK include LSODE,the basic solver; LSODES, a stiff solver; LSODAR, that also solves algebraic equations (roots), LSODPK, a Krylov-method solver; LSODKR, Krylov with root finding; LSODI, LSOIBT and LSODIS, for implicit systems. See Hindmarsh, "ODEPACK, a Systematized Collection of ODE Solvers," in *Scientific Computing*, ed. R. Stepleman (1983), Elsevier, for more details.

Example 36.4. Repeat example 36.3 using **odeint** instead of implementing Euler's method.

```
from scipy.integrate import odeint
from numpy import linspace
import matplotlib.pyplot as plt

def f(y,t):                       # define the RHS of the ODE
    return(y+t)

tvals = linspace(0,1.0,11)        # define the time points
y0 = 1.0                          # initial conditions
yvals = odeint(f, y0, tvals)      # solve the IVP
for t, y in zip(tvals, yvals):    # print the solution
    print "%7.2f_%7.2f" %(tv)
plt.plot(tvals, yvals)            # plot the solution
```

For a system of equations, the calling sequence is the same, but both **f** and **y0** will be arrays of the same length. The return value is an array of pairs of (x, y) values, one pair at each time point. To separate the array of x values from the array of y values, we can use the array transpose operation.

Example 36.5. Write a Python program to solve the Van der Pol system

$$x' = 10y \tag{36.16a}$$

$$y' = 10(1 - x^2)y - x \tag{36.16b}$$

with initial conditions $x(0) = y(0) = 1$. Plot graphs on the interval $[0, 10]$ of both variables, and also plot the solution in the xy plane.

```
import numpy as np
from scipy.integrate import odeint
import matplotlib.pyplot as plt

def f(v,t):
    xdot = 10.0*v[1]
    ydot = 10.0*(1-v[0]**2)*v[1]-v[0]
    return np.array([xdot,ydot])

times = np.linspace(0,10.0,1001)
v0=np.array([1.0,1.0])
solution=odeint(f,v0,times) # define solution times

(xvals,yvals)=solution.T    # separate (x,y) pairs

fig, (ax1,ax2) = plt.subplots(nrows=1,ncols=2)
ax1.plot(xvals,yvals)
ax2.plot(times,xvals, linestyle="--")
ax2.plot(times,yvals)
```

The resulting plot is shown in figure 36.4.

Table 36.1. `scipy.integrate.odeint` Parameters and Keywords

`odeint(func, y0, t, **kwargs)` integrates a differential equation or a system of differential equations. It returns an array **y** containing the values of the solution with the initial value as the first entry (first row if multivariate). If **full_output=True** it will return a tuple **y,infodict**, where **infodict** is a dictionary of additional information.[a]

Parameter	Description
`func`	Function to be integrated.
`y0`	Initial condition (may be array).
`t`	Time points at which output is to be returned. The initial condition must correspond to the first time point.

Keyword	Description
`args`	Additional arguments to pass to **func**.
`atol`	Absolute error tolerance' total=**rtol*abs(y)+atol**.
`col_deriv`	If **TrueDfun** defines derivatives by column rather than row. Columns are faster.
`Dfun`	Callable function that gives the gradient (Jacobian) of **func**.
`full_output`	If **True** a dictionary of of additional outputs is returned.
`h0`	Optional initial step size.
`ixpr`	Set to **True** to print a message when method changes.
`hmax`	Optional maximum allowed step size.
`hmin`	Optional minimum allowed step size.
`ml,mu`	Jacobian band width.
`mxhnil`	Optional maximum allowed number of messages to print.
`mxordn`	Optional maximum allowed order for the non stiff Adams solver.
`mxords`	Optional maximum allowed order for the stiff BDF solver.
`mxstep`	Optional maximum allowed numbers of steps.
`printmessg`	If **True** a convergence message is printed.
`rtol`	Relative error tolerance; total =**rtol*abs(y)+atol**.
`tcrit`	Optional array of know critical points.

[a]For more details see `http://docs.scipy.org/doc/scipy-0.14.0/reference/generated/scipy.integrate.odeint.html#scipy-integrate-odeint`

Generic integration with `ode`

The **ode** method provides a generic wrapper for the numerical integration of initial value problems using the available solvers. It gives you more control over individual options than **odeint** should you need it. A summary of the methods used by **ode** are summarized in tables 36.2 and 36.3.

Example 36.6. Use **vode** with a BDF solver to solve the IVP

$$y' = \frac{0.009y + \cos(5t + 2y)}{5 - \cos t + 3y}, y(1) = 1$$

Figure 36.4: Solution of Van der Pol eqn. Left: in xy plane; Right: $x(t), y(t)$.

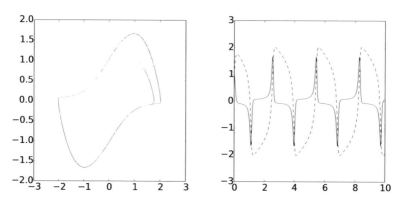

on the interval $[1,15]$, stopping at intervals of $\Delta t = 0.01$ to manually accrue to the output. Plot the accrued results.

```
1  import matplotlib.pyplot as plt
2  from scipy.integrate import ode
3  def f(t, y):
4      return  .009*y+np.cos(5*t+2*y)/(5-np.cos(t+3*y))
5
6  solver=ode(f).set_integrator("vode", method="bdf")
7  solver.set_initial_value(1,1)
8
9  t=[1]; y=[1]
10 while solver.successful() and solver.t<15:
11     solver.integrate(solver.t+.01)
12     t.append(solver.t)
13     y.append(solver.y[0])
14
15 plt.plot(t,y,color="k")
16 plt.set_xlim(1,15)
17 plt.title(r"$y'=.009y+\frac{\cos(5t+2y)}{5-\cos(t+3y)}$")
```

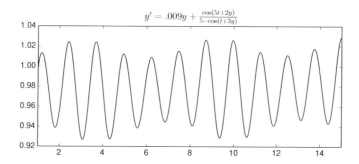

> **Table 36.2.** `scipy.integrate.ode` methods
>
> `ode(f,jac=None)` is a generic interface for for numerical integrators that solve differential equations of the form $y'(t) = f(t, y)$ with optional jacobian (keyword `jac`) that gives df/dy.
>
> | Method | Description |
> | --- | --- |
> | `integrate(t,step=0)` | Solve the differential equation $y' = f(t, y)$ for $y = y(t)$. |
> | `set_f_params(*args)` | Set extra parameters for the user defined function being integrated. |
> | `set_initial_value(y, [t])` | Sets the initial condition $y(t) = y_0$ |
> | `set_integrator` | Integrator, table 36.3. |
> | `set_jac_params(*args)` | Sets extra parameters for any user supplied jacobian. |
> | `set_solout(solout)` | `solout(t,y)` is a user supplied callable function that is called at each integrator step. |
> | `successful()` | Boolean to determine if integration was successful. |

Stream Plots and the Phase Plane

In a stream plot of a two dimensional system, small arrows are used to indicate the direction of the tangent line to the solution of the differential equation at every point in the xy plane. You do not have to solve an initial value problem to actually produce a stream plot, because the slopes are given directly in the equation itself. For example, consider the van der Pol oscillator

$$x' = 10x \qquad (36.17a)$$
$$y' = 10(1 - x^2)y - x \qquad (36.17b)$$

At any point (x, y), the slope of the tangent line is given by the ratio of the right hand sides, because

$$\frac{dy}{dx} = \frac{y'}{x'} = \frac{10(1 - x^2)y - x}{10x} \qquad (36.18)$$

To avoid problems that may arise due to vertical tangent lines, we will instead calculate the angle θ that the tangent line makes with the horizontal. This can be computed with the `atan2` function. When for $x' \neq 0$,

$$\tan \theta = \frac{y'}{x'} \qquad (36.19)$$

The `atan2(x,y)` function examines the quadrant of the point `(x,y)` to determine whether the angle should be in the interval $[0, \pi]$ or $[\pi, 2\pi]$. If $x = 0$, then it need only look at the sign of y to determine whether the angle is $\pi/2$ (and arrow pointing vertically upwards) or $3\pi/2$ (for an arrow pointing downwards).

Table 36.3. `scipy.integrate.ode.set_integrator`

`ode.set_integrator(name, **kwargs)` selects the integrator used by **ODE**.

name	Description and keywords to `set_integrator`
`"lsoda"`	Real valued solver, with automatic method switching between a non-stiff Adams method and a stiff BDF method.
`"vode"`	Real valued variable ordinary differential equation solver. Uses an implicit Adams for non-stiff problems and BDF for stiff problems.[a]
`"zvode"`	Complex valued solver.

keyword	description
`atol`	Abs. tolerance
`rtol`	Rel. tolerance
`lband`	Jacobian band width
`rband`	Jacobian band width
`with_jacobian`	Flag to turn on Jacobian
`nsteps`	Max. steps allowed
`first_step`	First stepsize
`min_step`	Min step size
`max_step`	Max step size
`max_order_ns`	Max Adams order (12)
`max_order_s`	Max BDF order (5)
`max_hnil`	Max num messages
`ixpr`	Extra message flag

See http://www.netlib.org for details on this solver.

`"dopri5"`	Explicit 4(5) Runga-Kutta method.
`"dop853"`	Explicit 8(5,3) Runga-Kutta method.

keyword	description
`atol`	Abs. tolerance
`rtol`	Rel. tolerance
`nsteps`	Max. steps allowed
`first_step`	First stepsize
`max_step`	Max step size
`safety`	Safety factor for step selection
`ifactor`	Max. step increase
`dfactor`	Max. step decrease
`beta`	β for step size control
`verbosity`	Negative integer to turn off messages.

Suppose we were to define the function **f(v,t)** to solve the van der Plot oscillator, e.g., with **odeint**.

```
def f(v,t):
    xdot = 10.0*v[1]
    ydot = 10.0*(1-v[0]**2)*v[1]-v[0]
    return np.array([xdot,ydot]))
```

The we could calculate the angle θ at any point (x, y) with the function **angle(x,y)** defined here. Observe that our definition of **angle** will work with **any** function (for a two-dimensional system) that is compatible with **odeint**, not just the van der Pol function, so long as it does not depend explicitly on time.

```
from math import atan2
def angle(x, y):
    xdot,ydot=f([x,y],[])
    theta=atan2(ydot,xdot)
    return theta
Angle = np.vectorize(angle)
```

The **np.vectorize(angle)** defines a new function **Angle**, and allows us to use **angle** on entire numpy vectors in a single command, without having to loop through the vectors one point at a time.

Next, to get the stream plot we need to generate (a) the positions of the arrows; and (b) the graphical display of the arrows themselves. Once we have the first, the second is easy: we can use the **plt.quiver** function:

```
plt.quiver{X,Y,U,V}
```

where **X** and **Y** are arrays containing the x and y coordinates of the tails of the arrows, and **U** and **V** are arrays containing the heads of the arrows, measured with respect to the tail. So **X**, **Y**, **U** and **V** should all be the same length. But consider the arrow at point (x, y). If it corresponds to a tangent line with direction θ, an arrow with length ℓ with have coordinates $(\cos\theta, \sin\theta)$, measured in local coordinates with respect to the tail of the arrow. If we create an array **theta** that contains the angles of all the slopes, so that **theta[i,j]** has the slope angle of arrow at point (**X[i]**, **Y[i]**), then the plot of **all** the arrows (assuming we want arrows of length 1) will be generated by

```
plt.quiver(X,Y,np.cos(theta),np.sin(theta))
```

The easiest way to get the position of the arrows is using **np.meshgrid**, which is a two-dimensional extension of **np.linspace**. To understand **meshgrid**, consider the following example.

```
>>>x=np.linspace(1,5,5)
>>>y=np.linspace(10,40,3)
>>>X,Y=np.meshgrid(x,y)
>>> X
array([[ 1.,   2.,   3.,   4.,   5.],
       [ 1.,   2.,   3.,   4.,   5.],
       [ 1.,   2.,   3.,   4.,   5.]])
>>> Y
array([[ 10.,   10.,   10.,   10.,   10.],
       [ 25.,   25.,   25.,   25.,   25.],
       [ 40.,   40.,   40.,   40.,   40.]])
```

Reading **across** the array for **X**, each row is copy of **x**. Reading **down** the array for **Y**, each column is a copy of **y**. Thus we can get the row and column index (in the matrix sense) of an $n_x \times n_y$ array, where n_x and n_y are the lengths of **x** and **y** respectively:

```
for i in range(len(x)):
    for j in range(len(y)):
        print (X[j,i],Y[j,i]),
    print
```

will produce the following output:

```
(1.0, 10.0) (1.0, 25.0) (1.0, 40.0)
(2.0, 10.0) (2.0, 25.0) (2.0, 40.0)
(3.0, 10.0) (3.0, 25.0) (3.0, 40.0)
(4.0, 10.0) (4.0, 25.0) (4.0, 40.0)
(5.0, 10.0) (5.0, 25.0) (5.0, 40.0)
```

It is often useful to plot one or more actual solutions on the plot. In the xy plane, these are sometime called *trajectories*, and the plots of the trajectories (or solutions) in the xy plane are sometimes called phase plots (or phase portraits). To get the trajectory plot we must actually solve the differential equation. For example, we would add a block of code such as the following, after plotting our quiver.

```
1  times = np.linspace(0,10.0,1001)
2  v0=np.array([0.1,0.1])
3  solution=odeint(f,v0,times)
4  xvals, yvals=solution.T
5  plt.plot(xvals,yvals)
```

We would typically repeat lines 2 through 5 several times, with different initial conditions, to illustrate a number of different trajectories.

Example 36.7. Make a stream plot with **plt.quiver** for the van der plot equations

Collecting together our code, we don't have to loop through the indices, since **quiver** is vectorized, and expects a **meshgrid**-based input. In fact, the following is sufficient, once both **Angle** and **f** have been defined (see figure 36.5).

```
import numpy as np
import matplotlib.pyplot as plt
from math import atan2

def f(v,t):        # define the RHS of the ODE
    xdot = 10.0*v[1]
    ydot = 10.0*(1-v[0]**2)*v[1]-v[0]
    return np.array([xdot,ydot]))

def angle(x, y):  # define the Angle function
    xdot,ydot=f([x,y],[])
    theta=atan2(ydot,xdot)
    return theta
Angle = np.vectorize(angle)
x=np.linspace(-3,3,25)
y=np.linspace(-3,3,25)
X,Y=np.meshgrid(x,y)
theta=Angle(X,Y)
q=plt.quiver(X,Y,np.cos(theta), np.sin(theta))
```

Figure 36.5: Left: Stream plot for the van der Pol equations. Right: Stream plot with with several trajectories.

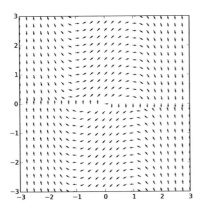
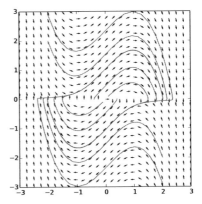

Exercises

1. Implement Euler's method manually (do not use **odeint**). Use it to solve each of the following initial value problems on the intervals shown, for step sizes of h=1, 0.5, 0.1, and 0.01. Use pyplot to plot the solutions for the different step sizes in different colors.

   (a) $y' = 3y - x$, $y(0) = 1$, on (0,10).

   (b) $y' = 1 - x + 2y$, $y(0) = 1$, on (0,5).

   (c) $y' = x^2 + y^2$, $y(0) = 1$, on (1,3).

   (d) $y' = \sqrt{x + y}$, $y(1) = 4$, on (1,3).

2. The four-term Runge-Kutta method method is defined by the iteration formulas

$$k_1 = f(x_n, y_n)$$

$$k_2 = f\left(x_n + \frac{1}{2}h, y_n + \frac{1}{2}hk_1\right)$$

$$k_3 = f\left(x_n + \frac{1}{2}h, y_n + \frac{1}{2}hk_2\right)$$

$$k_4 = f(x_n + h, y_n + hk_3)$$

$$y_{n+1} = y_n + \frac{h}{6}(k_1 + 2k_2 + 2k_3 + k_4)$$

Implement a Runge-Kutta solver and use it to solve $y' = 3x + 4y$, $y(0) = 1$ on the interval (0,1) with $k = .1$. Compare your results with Euler's method and the exact solution.

3. Write a function **ODESYS(a,b,c,d,times)** to solve a system of linear differential equations

$$x'(t) = ax + by$$
$$y'(t) = cx + dy$$

where a, b, c and d are any real constants. Use **odeint**. Here **times** is the same as the corresponding list of times input to **odeint**, and the output is the same as the output of **odeint**. Let **A** be the matrix of coefficients

$$\mathbf{A} = \begin{bmatrix} a & b \\ c & d \end{bmatrix}$$

In each of the following cases, solve the system and plot (a) plot both x and y as a function of time; (b) plot y as a function of x.

   (a) Using a matrix **A** with two positive eigenvalues.

   (b) Using a matrix **A** with one positive and one negative eigenvalue.

   (c) Using a matrix **A** with two purely imaginary (conjugate) eigenvalues.

   (d) Using a matrix **A** with two complex conjugate eigenvalues with negative real parts.

4. Use **odeint** to solve the predator-prey Lotka Volterra model

$$n'(t) = n(t)(a - bp(t))$$
$$p'(t) = p(t)(cn(t) - d)$$

where $n(t)$ is the predator and $p(t)$ is the prey population in thousands and a, b, c, and d are positive constants. Use initial conditions $(n, p) = (4, 2)$ and $a = 1$, $b = 2$, $c = 1$, $d = 2$. Try solving for a duration of time (0,50). Plot your solutions in two ways: (a) Both $n(t)$ and $p(t)$ in different colors as a function of time on the same figure. (b) $n(t)$ as a function of $p(t)$. Interpret your plots.

5. The following data set from a trapping company is based on the number of fur pelts harvested for **hares** and **lynx**, in 1000s per year, in Northwest Canada, for the years from 1900 to 1920. It can be used to estimate the populations of each species, assuming that the number of pelts harvested is proportional to the population of each species.

```
hares=[30,47.2,70.2,77.4,36.3,
      20.6,18.1,21.4,22,25.4,
      27.1, 40.3,57,76.6,52.3,
      19.5,11.2,7.6,14.6,
      16.2,24.7]
lynx=[4,6.1,9.8,35.2,59.4,41.7,
     19,13,8.3,9.1,7.4,8,12.3,
     19.5,45.7,51.1,29.7,15.8,
     9.7,10.1,8.6]
```

In this exercise you will fit this data to the Lotka Volterra system

$$n'(t) = n(t)(a - bp(t))$$
$$p'(t) = p(t)(cn(t) - d)$$

where $n(t)$ is the predator and $p(t)$ is the prey population, and a, b, c, and d are positive constants.

(a) Letting $n(t)$ denote the predator (lynx) population and $p(t)$ the prey (hare) population as a function of time, use a numerical approximation

$$y'(t) \approx \frac{y(t_{i+1}) - y(t_i)}{t_{i+1} - t_i}$$

to get a numerical estimate of $n'(t)$ and $p'(t)$ at the first 20 time points, i.e., lists $\{n_0', n_1', n_2', \dots\}$ and $\{p_0', p_1', p_2', \dots\}$.

(b) Define two new variables $x(t) = n'(t)/n(t)$ and $y(t) = p'(t)/p(t)$. Find numerical estimates of the functions $x(t)$, $y(t)$ as lists $\{x_0, x_1, x_2, \dots\}$ and $\{y_0, y_1, y_2, \dots\}$

(c) Rearranging the Lotka Volterra equations gives

$$x(t) = \frac{n'(t)}{n(t)} = a - bp(t)$$

$$y(t) = \frac{p'(t)}{p(t)} = cn(t) - d$$

Thus x is a linear function of p, and y is a linear function of p. Using the data sets you calculated in the previous two steps, do a linear regression of x on p to determine the best fit coefficients a and b, and a linear regression of y on n to get the coefficients c and d.

(d) Using the values of a, b, c, and d you just found, solve the Lotka Volterra equations numerically for 21 years using **odeint**. Use the first data values as the first data points from the trapping data. Plot your numerical solution as a pair of smooth curves (that are a function of times) and do a scatter plot of the data points on the same figure. Interpret your results.

6. Make phase portraits with arrows representing the stream of the following systems of differential equations. Choose enough sets of initial conditions to convince yourself that you have found representative solutions.

(a) $x' = y$, $y' = -4 \sin x$

(b) $x' = 1$, $y' = \cos(xy)$

(c) $x' = y^2 - x^2$, $y' = x^2 + y^2 - 2$

(d) $x' = y$, $y' = x - x^3 - y$

Chapter 37

Discrete Systems

In a **discrete time dynamical systems**, changes occur only in **discrete steps** which we call times $k = 0, 1, 2, \ldots$. The state n_{i+1} of the system at time $i + 1$ then depends on the states of the system at all previous times $k = 0, 1, 2, \ldots, i$:

$$n_{i+1} = f(n_0, n_1, n_2, \ldots, n_i) \tag{37.1}$$

In a **single step process**, we have

$$n_{i+1} = f(n_i) \tag{37.2}$$

This is really fixed point iteration. For example, if a patient is given one dose of some medication every day, when each new dose is given there is still some medication left in the body from the previous day, since not all of it has been used up. If a fraction $\alpha < 1$ is left at the end of each day

$$n_{i+1} = \alpha n_i + 1 \tag{37.3}$$

We can predict what will happen by calculating the solution by brute force. Suppose that $\alpha = 0.8$. Fixed point iteration is done on line 7 here:

```
1   from matplotlib.pyplot import *
2   def f(n):
3       return 0.8*n+1
4   n=0;  y=[n]
5   x=range(0,15)
6   for i in x[1:]:
7       n = f(n)
8       y.append(n)
9   scatter(x,y)
10  plot(x,y)
11  show()              # see figure 37.1
```

From figure 37.1 it looks as if the points are approaching a **steady state value** of $n_i \approx 5$ as $i \to \infty$. This steady state value is the same as the fixed point of $f(x)$, which occurs when $x = f(x)$ (def. 33.2). This occurs when

$$n = f(n) = \alpha n + 1 \tag{37.4}$$

Solving for n gives

$$n = \frac{1}{1 - \alpha} \tag{37.5}$$

When $\alpha = .8$ (as we used in figure 37.1), $n = 5$. To see what is happening at each iteration, we can draw a **cobweb plot**. Starting with a guess at n_0 (on the x-axis), we

Figure 37.1: Solution of eq. 37.3. The lines that connect the points are added for display purposes only; the solution is only defined at the discrete points defined by the dots.

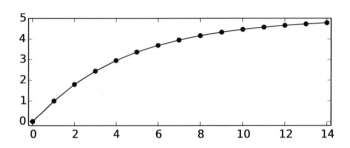

project to the line $y = x$ (see figure 37.2); the line $y = x$ is the dashed line). From the line $y = x$ we project to the curve of $f(n)$. This gives the first iteration, n_1. Then for each successive iteration, we (a) first project horizontally to the line $y = x$, then (b) vertically to the function $f(n)$. This gives the next iteration (the black dots). Following the arrows on this cobweb, we see that they approach the fixed point where the curves of $y = x$ and $y = f(x)$ intersect (the ring in figure 37.2).

Algorithm 37.1 Algorithm for a cobweb plot.

input: f, x_0 (starting point), N (maximum iterations)

1: $p_1 \leftarrow \mathbf{Plot}(y = x)$	Make a plot of $y = x$
2: $p_3 \leftarrow \mathbf{Plot}(y = f(x))$	Make a plot of $y = f(x)$
3: $x \leftarrow x_0$	Initialize
4: **for** $j \in 0, 2, 4, 6, \ldots, n$ **do**	
5: $\quad x' \leftarrow f(x)$	Next fixed point iteration
6: $\quad (x_j, y_j) \leftarrow (x, x')$	Vertical segment
7: $\quad (x_{j+1}, y_{j+1}) \leftarrow (y_j, y_j)$	Horizontal segment
8: $\quad x \leftarrow x'$	
9: **end for**	
10: $p_3 \leftarrow \mathbf{Plot}((x_0, y_0), \ldots, (x_1, y_n))$	Plot all segments
11: **return** (p_1, p_2, p_3)	Overlay all three plots

Sometimes interesting things can happen when fixed point iteration does not converge. For example, consider the function

$$n_{i+1} = n_i - n_i^2 + 2 \tag{37.6}$$

This function has fixed points at $n \pm \sqrt{2}$:

$$n = f(n) = n - n^2 + 2 \implies n = \sqrt{2} \tag{37.7}$$

However, fixed point iteration is not guaranteed to converge in *any* interval that includes $\sqrt{2}$ (see theorem 33.5). To guarantee convergence, we require (among other things) that

Figure 37.2: Cobweb plot for $n_{i+1} = .8n_i + 1$.

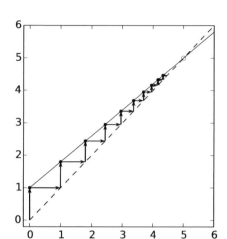

there exist a positive constant $K < 1$ such that $|f'(n)| < K$. But

$$|f'(n)| = |1 - 2n| \tag{37.8}$$

and therefore

$$\left|f'\left(\sqrt{2}\right)\right| = \left|1 - 2\sqrt{2}\right| \approx 1.8 > 1 \tag{37.9}$$

Since f is continuous near $\sqrt{2}$, there is no interval containing $\sqrt{2}$ for which $|f'(n)| < K < 1$. What does happen if we try to use this function to compute the square root? Here is a simple calculation:

```
>>> z=1.4
>>> for i in range(10):
...     z=z-z*z+2.0
...     print z
1.44
1.3664
1.49935104
1.25129749885
1.68555206822
0.844466293538
2.13134297262
-0.411279894303
1.41956895424
1.4043929384
>>>
```

Even though we started very close to the correct answer, it looks like things are bouncing around all over the place! But if we continue the iteration (say for 100 steps) something

Figure 37.3: Cobweb of first 500 interations on $f(n) = n - n^2 + 2$, starting from $n_0 = 1.44$. The fixed point is shown with a diamond and the line segments connect each of last 300 iterations. Round markers show the period 3 cycle at approximately (0.55, 2.25, -.80) to which iteration is converging.

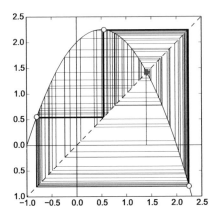

very interesting starts to happen. Here are the last 10 of the next 100 iterations.

```
-0.804360116051
0.548644687655
2.24763369436
-0.804223529673
0.549000984648
2.2475989035
-0.804101927527
0.549318162621
2.24756771884
-0.803992931916
```

While the system is not converging to a fixed point, it does seem to be **converging to a pattern**. That pattern is very close to the sequence of three numbers (0.55, 2.25, -0.80) (to two decimal points precision; see figure 37.3). This is called a **period 3 cycle.**

Period 3 cycles are important indicators of something even more important in dynamical systems, namely chaos. Whenever a system has a period-3 cycle, it also has a cycle of period n for every integer n. This was proven by Sarkovskii in 1964.[1]

Since Sarkovskii's original result was not disseminated outside of Russia at the time, a special case of it was re-discoverd by Li and Yorke a decade later.[2]

---

[1] [Ukraunskyi matematychnyi zhurnal] "Coexistence of cycles of a continuous map of a line into itself." (in Russian) **16**:61-71 (1964). Accessible proofs of Sarkovskii's theorem are given in R. Devaney, *An Introduction to Chaotic Dynamical Systems*, Addison Wesley (1989); and also in X-C Huang, "From Intermediate Value Theorem to Chaos." *Mathematics Magazine*, **65**(2):91-103.

[2] Tsien-Yien Li and James Yorke "Period Three Implies Chaos." *Am. Math. Monthly*, **82**(10):985-992 (1975).

Theorem 37.1. Sarkovskii (1964)

Order the natural numbers as follows:

$$3 \prec 5 \prec 7 \prec 9 \prec \cdots$$
$$2 \cdot 3 \prec 2 \cdot 5 \prec 2 \cdot 7 \prec 2 \cdot 9 \cdots \prec$$
$$2^2 \cdot 3 \prec 2^2 \cdot 5 \prec 2^2 \cdot 7 \prec 2^2 \cdot 9 \prec \cdots$$
$$2^3 \cdot 3 \prec 2^3 \cdot 5 \prec 2^3 \cdot 7 \prec 2^3 \cdot 9 \prec \cdots \qquad (37.10)$$
$$\vdots \prec \cdots$$
$$\cdots \prec 2^5 \prec 2^4 \prec 2^3 \prec 2^2 \prec 2 \prec 1$$

Suppose that f has a least one period p point x_p. Then for every q such that $p \prec q$ in this ordering, f also has a point x_q with least period q.

Theorem 37.2. Period 3 Implies Chaos (Li & Yorke, 1975)

Let $f : J \mapsto J \subset \mathbb{R}$ be continuous. If there is a point $a \in J$ such that $b = f(a)$, $c = f(b)$, and $a = f(c)$ (see figure 37.4) then for every integer $k = 1, 2, \ldots$ there is a point $x_k \in J$ having least period k, i.e., such that $f^k(x_k) = x_k$ and $f^j(x_k) \neq x_k$ for all $j = 1, 2, \ldots, k - 1$.

Figure 37.4: Mapping of a period 3 cycle on a closed interval.

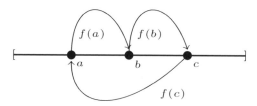

Some insight into the onset of chaos can be obtained by examining the **logistic map**.

$$x_{n+1} = ax_n(1 - x_n) \qquad (37.11)$$

where $a > 0$ is a (known) fixed constant. This is a type of normalized population model where the first term represents the birth rate and the second term represents intra-species competition for resources. A fixed point exists when

$$x = f(x) = ax(1 - x) = ax - ax^2 \qquad (37.12)$$

Rearranging,

$$x(ax + (1 - a)) = 0 \qquad (37.13)$$

Thus fixed points exist at $x = 0$ and $x^* = (a-1)/a$ (see figure 37.5).

Figure 37.5: The logistic map $x_{n+1} = ax_n(1-x_n)$ and the fixed point at $x^* = (a-1)/a$.

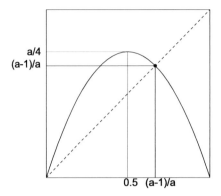

To see when fixed point iteration is guaranteed to converge,

$$|f'(x)| = |a - 2ax| = a|(1 - 2x)| \tag{37.14}$$

because we define the logistic map assuming that $a > 0$. Then if we pick any starting point in the interval $(0, 1)$,

$$0 < x < 1 \tag{37.15}$$

Multiplying by -2 and adding 1,

$$1 > 1 - 2x > -1 \tag{37.16}$$

Equivalently, $|1 - 2x| < 1$, and therefore

$$|f'(x)| = a|1 - 2x| < a \tag{37.17}$$

Normally we restrict $a > 1$ because this equation originates in problems in population biology. The fixed point theorem will guarantee convergence if $a < 1$. But this is not terribly interesting. If $0 < a < 1$ and $0 < x_0 < 1$ then

$$x_1 = ax_0(1 - x_0) < ax_0 \tag{37.18a}$$
$$x_2 = ax_1(1 - x_1) < ax_1 < a^2 x_0 \tag{37.18b}$$
$$x_n < a^n x_0 \to 0 \text{ as } n \to \infty \tag{37.18c}$$

If $a < 1$ and $x_0 > 1$ then $x_1 = ax_0(1 - x_0) < 0$ because $1 - x_0 < 0$. Since negative values in a population model are not physically realizable, and zero populations are terminal, we must restrict $a > 1$.

Focusing solely on the fixed point (rather than the whole interval), iteration is only guaranteed to converge in some interval about x^* if

$$|f'(x^*)| = |a - 2ax^*| = \left| a - 2a\left(\frac{a-1}{a}\right)\right| = |2 - a| \le K < 1 \tag{37.19}$$

for some positive constant K. This is only possible if $|2 - a| < 1$, or $1 < a < 3$.

Two more fixed points seem to magically appear as you increase a past 3. This is called a **bifurcation**. As a gets even larger, even more fixed points appear. To understand what is happening, it is easier to consider $f^2(x)$:

$$f^2(x) = f(f(x)) = f(ax(1-x)) \tag{37.20a}$$

$$= a[ax(1-x)][1 - ax(1-x)] \tag{37.20b}$$

$$= a^2 x(1-x)(1 - ax + ax^2) \tag{37.20c}$$

When $a = 3$,

$$f^2(x) = 9x(1-x)(1 - 3x + 3x^2) \tag{37.21}$$

This has fixed points when $f^2(x) = x$, i.e., when,

$$x = 9x(1-x)(1 - 3x + 3x^2) \tag{37.22}$$

Besides the fixed point at $x = 0$, the remaining fixed points occur at

$$1 = 9(1-x)(1 - 3x + 3x^2) \tag{37.23}$$

Figure 37.6: Left: Bifurcation of the logistic map at $a = 3$. Observe that the single fixed point separates into a pair that slowly moves apart from one other as a increases beyond 3.0. Right: Bifurcation of the logistic map at $a = 1 + \sqrt{6} \approx 3.4495$. Each fixed point is replaced by a triple, consisting of the original plus two new points. In each case $f^4(x)' > 0$ through the middle point of the triple, and $f^4(x)' < 0$ through the other two points. This indicates that the outer points are stable and the inner point is unstable.

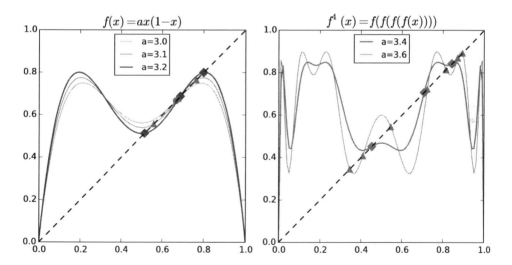

Rearranging equation 37.23

$$0 = 27x^3 - 54x^2 + 36x - 8 \tag{37.24a}$$

$$= (3x)^3 - 3(3x)^2(2) + 3(3x)(2^2) - 2^3 \tag{37.24b}$$

$$= (3x - 2)^3 \tag{37.24c}$$

Hence a single fixed point exists at $x^* = 2/3$ when $a = 3$. This is the same location as the original fixed point. For a infinitesimally larger, this fixed point splits up into two different fixed points (figure 37.6). The fixed point of $f(x)$ also changes slightly as a increases, but not as much as the new fixed points. Examining figure 37.5, we see that the downward valley in the middle of the plot of $f^2(x)$ just passes through the curve of $y = x$ as a passes through 3. For $a > 3$, the curve of $f^2(x)$ intersects $y = x$ three times; for $a < 3$, they only intersect once.

When $a = 1 + \sqrt{6} \approx 3.4495$, each of the of the diamonds in figure 37.6 (left) bifurcates into two new fixed points (figure 37.6, right). This is because at this point, the function $f^4(x)$ has developed additional "valleys" that push through the line $y = x$, causing new fixed points, just as $f^2(x)$ did at $a = 3$.

The bifurcation process can be illustrated by plotting the value of the fixed point as a function of the bifurcation parameter a. For the logistic map, when $a < 3$, the **bifurcation diagram** has only a single curve. At $a = 3$, this single curve divides into two curves, and at $a = 1 + \sqrt{6}$, each of these curves divide into two more curves (figure 37.7). The bifurcation diagram in figure 37.7 is plotted using a brute-force numerical

Figure 37.7: Bifurcation diagram of the logistic map. The bifurcation parameter a is shown on the x-axis, and the value of the stable fixed points are shown on the y-axis.

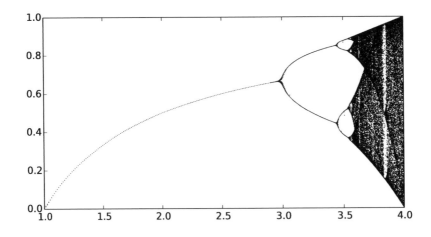

approach. Because of the algorithm used to generate this plots, none of the curves for the unstable fixed points are shown. In the brute-force algorithm, the x axis was first discretized into 1000 points, each one representing a different value of a. For each point a along the a axis, $N = 500$ random starting points $x_0, \ldots, X_{N-1}$ were chosen in the interval $(0, 1)$. Fixed point iteration was used on each of the N points for $n = 500$ iterations. Each of the final values $(a, f^n(x_j))$, for $j = 0, \ldots, N - 1$, was then plotted.

Exercises

1. The **tent map** is defined on the interval [0,1] as the function

$$f(x) = a \begin{cases} x, & x < 1/2 \\ 1 - x, & x \geq 1/2 \end{cases}$$

where $a > 0$ is any real, positive constant. When $a > 1$, the tent map has two fixed points. Determine the locations of the two fixed points as a function of a.

2. Draw a bifurcation plot of the tent map as described below in exercise 4.

3. Determine when the logistic map bifurcates into 2,3, 4, 5, 6, and 8 stable fixed points. You may want to solve the equations numerically.

4. One way to generate a bifurcation diagram of the logistic map is via a Monte Carlo simulation. You discretize the x axis into the desired pixel accuracy, say in increments of 0 in the interval $1 \leq x \leq 4$. Then for each value of x, you pick a large number of random starting values m in the interval $(0, 1)$, say with **np.random.rand()**. Using the value of x as your a value, run the logistic map a large number N (say 500) of times with each starting value. This will generate a large number of ending values. If N is sufficiently large enough then the ending values will each be within one pixel of the corresponding y values of the bifurcation diagram. Generate a bifurcation diagram in this manner.

5. Write a python function **cobweb(f, x0, n, xmin, xmax, ymin, ymax)** to draw a cobweb plot of fixed point iteration, where

f is the name of function to plot; **x0** is the starting point value of x; **n** is the number of fixed point iterations to perform; **xmin** and **xmax** are the minimum and maximum values of the x axis on the plot and **ymin** and **ymax** are the minimum and maximum values of the y axis on the plot.

Demonstrate that your cobweb plot works with the function call

```
cobweb(cos, 1.0, 200,0, 1.5, 0,
                    1)
```

6. Draw cobweb plots for the tent map at intervals of 0.1 on the interval[0.5,2.5]. Pick any starting point. To visualize what is happening, you may want to make a movie. The easiest way to do this is not with python. Save each cobweb plot as a **.png** file with the same x- and y-axis limits and size (use **fig.set_size_inches()**), for example. Then use a command line utilite such as **avconv** (available at https://libav.org/download.html) to convert the **.png** files to a movie. If you save the **.png** files sequentially in a folder such as **cobweb001.png, cobweb002.png,**... then the command line for **avconv** is

```
avconv "cobweb%03d.png"
            tentmapmovie.avi
```

To convert to a **.mov** file replace **.avi** with **.mov**. You will probably want to change your stepping interval to a smaller number, such as 0.01, so that you generate a large number of frames.

Chapter 38

Fractals

Fractal's are geometric figures that display recursive **self-similarity** upon magnification. At every level of magnification, one can find copies of the entire original figure. However, the images are not space-filling and therefore, even when imagined drawn to completion, would not have a topological dimension of 2 like the plane. Because of the recursive self-similarity these fractals are considered to have have a fractional dimensions - somewhat larger than 1 and smaller than 2. The term "fractal" was first used by Benoît Mandelbrot (b. 1924), to refer to a an object whose **Hausdorff dimension** exceeds its **topological dimension**. We will use a simplification of the Hausdorff dimension here, called the **Fractal dimension.**

Definition 38.1. Fractal

A **fractal** in $\mathbb{R}^n$ is a subset of $\mathbb{R}^n$ that (a) is self-similar, and (b) has fractal dimension exceeding its topological dimension.

Before we elaborate on these concepts lets consider some early examples of fractals.

The Weierstrass Function

The first published example of a fractal is given by the Weierstrass Function in 1872 (figure 38.1),

$$f(x) = \sum_{k=0}^{\infty} a^k \cos(b^k \pi x) \tag{38.1}$$

where $0 < a < 1$ and b is any positive odd integer such that $ab > 1 + 3\pi/2$. Weierstrass's function is commonly quoted in analysis textbooks as an example of a function that is everywhere continuous but nowhere differentiable. The first n terms of the Weirstrass's function can be calculated

```
from numpy import pi, cos, linspace
def f(x,n):
    return(sum(
       map(lambda n: a**n*cos(x*pi*b**n),
       linspace(0,n,n))))
```

Figure 38.1: Weierstrass's function at three different spatial resolutions. The boxes in each of the top two images show the plot below it. The sum was truncated after 250 terms.

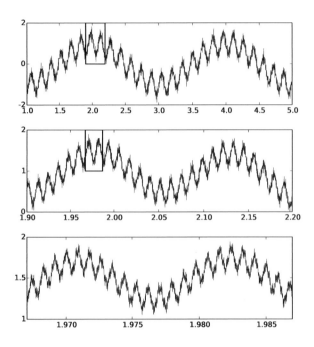

Koch Curve

The Koch curve[1] is another early fractal that is constructed as follows (see figure 38.2):

1. Divide a line segment into 3 equal parts.
2. Construct an equilateral triangle on the middle segment.
3. Remove the middle segment.
4. Repeat the process on each segment.
5. Repeat ad-infinitum

We can infer a recursive implementation to construct the Koch curve from figure 38.3. Define the vector $\mathbf{v} = \mathbf{Q} - \mathbf{P}$. Then regardless of the orientation of the line segment $\overline{\mathbf{PQ}}$,

$$\mathbf{A} = \mathbf{P} + \frac{1}{3}\mathbf{v} \tag{38.2}$$

$$\mathbf{C} = \mathbf{P} + \frac{2}{3}\mathbf{v} \tag{38.3}$$

---

[1]First described by Niels Fabian Helge von Koch (1870-1924)

Figure 38.2: First five iterations of the Koch curve. The shape in (b) is shrunk by a factor of 3 and mapped to each sub-segment of itself to produced the shape (c). Then (b) is shrunk b an additional factor of 3 and mapped to (c) to produced (d), and so forth.

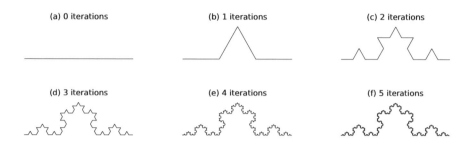

A normal vector to **v** (with the same magnitude) is obtained by a 90 degree rotation (equivalent to flipping the coordinates and changing the sign of one of them).

$$\mathbf{n} = \begin{bmatrix} 0 & -1 \\ 1 & 0 \end{bmatrix} \mathbf{v} \tag{38.4}$$

Each segment has one third the length of $|\mathbf{v}|$, and point **B** is projected out a distance $\sqrt{3}/2$ orthogonally to segment $\overline{\mathbf{PQ}}$. Hence

$$\mathbf{B} = \frac{1}{2}(\mathbf{P} + \mathbf{Q}) + \frac{\sqrt{3}}{6}\mathbf{n} \tag{38.5}$$

Thus at each iteration, points **A**,**B**, and **C** are calculated according to equations 38.2 through 38.5. One Python implementation follows.

Figure 38.3: Geometry of the Koch curve.

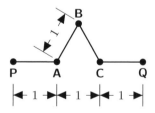

```
1  def koch(start, finish,n):
2      if n<=0:
3          return(zip(start, finish))
4      P=array(start); Q=array(finish)
5      V=Q-P
```

```
6     # Normal vector
7     M=np.array([[0,-(np.sqrt(3.0)/6.0)],
8                 [(np.sqrt(3.0)/6.0),0]])
9     N=M.dot(V)
10    # Three intermediate points
11    A=P+(1.0/3.0)*V
12    B=0.5*(Q+P)+N
13    C=P+(2.0/3.0)*V
14
15    # calculate x and y for edge
16    if n<=1:
17        xvals,yvals = zip(*map(list,[P,A,B,C,Q]))
18        return(xvals, yvals)
19    # make recursive call
20
21    starts=[P,A,B,C]
22    stops=[A,B,C,Q]
23    results = map(lambda x, y : koch(x,y,n-1), starts, stops)
24
25    # unpack and flatten
26    xvals, yvals = zip(*results)
27    xvals= [x for subl in map(list, xvals) for x in subl]
28    yvals= [y for subl in map(list, yvals) for y in subl]
29    return(xvals, yvals)
```

The function **koch(P,Q,n)** is called with the coordinates **P** and **Q** of the left and right end points and the number of iterations. It returns a lists of x values and a list of y values that can be plotted.

If the number of iterations is fewer than or equal to zero, then it returns the endpoints of the original line, converted to x and y lists.

Lines 4 through 12 calculate the points **A**, **B** and **C** as described. The input lists are converted to Numpy Arrays to make the vector additions easier.

If $n \leq 1$, the program only requires a single iterations, and the list of points **[P,A,B,C,Q]** is converted to lists of x values and y values and returned in lines 14 through 16.

Otherwise, more than one iteration was required. On lines 20 through 22, the **koch** is called recursively and separately on each of the intervals **[P,A]**, **[A,B]**, **[B,C]**, **[C,Q]**. On lines 25 through 27 the results are combined into a single list and, converted to x and y values, and returned.

A single Koch curve with 5 iterations can be generated with

```
from matplotlib.pyplot import *
x,y=koch([0,0],[3,0],5)
plot(x,y)
show()
```

The collection of Koch curves shown as a single figure 38.2 was generated as follows.

```
fig, axx=subplots(nrows=2,ncols=3)
n=0
labels=[" (a) "," (b) "," (c) "," (d) "," (e) "," (f) "]
for row in 0,1:
    for column in 0,1,2:
        ax=axx[row,column]
        x,y=koch([0,0],[3,0],n)
        ax.plot(x,y,lw=.5,c="k")
        mytitle=labels[n]+str(n) + " iterations"
        print mytitle
        ax.set_title(mytitle, fontsize=7)
        ax.set_aspect("equal")
        ax.axis("off")
        ax.set_ylim(-.1,.9)
        n+=1
show()
```

Figure 38.4: First five iterations of the Koch snowflake.

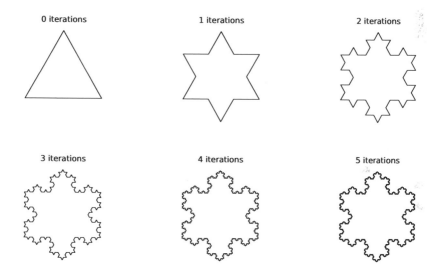

A similar object, the Koch snowflake (figure 38.4), is generated by repeating this process on each side of an equilateral triangle. Since **Koch** does not care about the orientation of the initial line, the snowflake is produced by three calls to **Koch**.

```
1  def snowflake(n):
2      xb,yb=koch([1,0],[0,0],n)
3      xl,yl=koch([0,0], [.5,.5*np.sqrt(3)], n)
4      xr,yr=koch([.5,  .5*np.sqrt(3)], [1,0], n)
5      xsides=[xl, xr, xb]
```

```
6     ysides=[yl, yr, yb]
7     xvals=[x for side in xsides for x in side]
8     yvals=[y for side in ysides for y in side]
9     return(xvals, yvals)
```

The Koch Snowflake has an interesting property: it has a bounded area but an infinite perimeter. To see this, Let N_k be the number of sides of the snowflake after step k.

$$N_0 = 3 \tag{38.6a}$$

$$N_1 = 4 \times 3 = 12 \tag{38.6b}$$

$$N_2 = 4 \times 12 = 4^2 \times 3 \tag{38.6c}$$

$$N_3 = 4^3 \times 3 \tag{38.6d}$$

$$\vdots$$

$$N_k = 4N_{k-1} = 4^k \times 3 \tag{38.6e}$$

Let L_k be the the length of each line segment after the kth step. Assume the original triangle has edges of length 1. Since the length is divided by 3 each time,

$$L_k = \frac{1}{3^k} \tag{38.7}$$

Let P_k be the perimeter after step k:

$$P_k = N_k L_k = 4^k \times 3 \times \frac{1}{3^k} = 3\left(\frac{4}{3}\right)^k \tag{38.8}$$

Hence $P_k \to \infty$ as $k \to \infty$.

Perimeter of Koch Snowflake

The Koch snowflake has infinite perimeter but finite area!

Serpiński Triangle

The Serpiński triangle[2] (figure 38.5) is obtained by recursively removing pieces of a triangle and has a similar algorithm.

1. Construct any triangle T with a base parallel to the $x-$axis.
2. Construct a new triangle T' by shrinking T to half its height and half its width.
3. Make three copies of T', positioning one on each corner of T.
4. Repeat with the smaller triangles.

It can be drawn in Python by the following recursive function.

---

[2] 1915, Waclaw Sierpiński, 1881-1969.

Figure 38.5: Sierpinski Triangle after 8 iterations.

```
from matplotlib.pyplot import *
import numpy as np
def sierpinski(points, n):
    if n<=0:
        return
    if n<=1:
        xvals,yvals=map(list,zip(*points))

        xvals.append(xvals[0])
        yvals.append(yvals[0])
        plot(xvals,yvals,c="k",linewidth=.5)
        return
    A,B,C=map(np.array, points)
    AB=(A+B)/2.0
    BC=(B+C)/2.0
    CA=(C+A)/2.0
    sierpinski([A,AB,CA],n-1)
    sierpinski([AB,B,BC],n-1)
    sierpinski([CA,BC,C],n-1)
```

Figure 38.5 was then produced by the following code.

```
sierpinski([[0,0],[1,0],[.5,1]],8)
axis("equal")
axis("off")
show()
```

Fractal Dimension

> **Definition 38.2. Topological Dimension**
>
> A set S has **topological dimension** 0 if every point has arbitrarily small neighborhoods whose boundaries do not intersect the set.
>
> A set has **topological dimension** k if each point in S has arbitrarily small neighborhoods whose boundaries meet S in a set of dimension $k-1$ and k is the least non-negative integer for which this holds.

Example 38.1. A line has topological dimension 1. Every neighborhood of P intersects the line in a pair of points of dimension 0.

Figure 38.6: Topological dimension of a line.

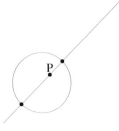

Example 38.2. A planar region has topological dimension 2.

Example 38.3. The Sierpinski Triangle has topological dimension of 1.

> **Definition 38.3. Self-Similar**
>
> A set S is called **self-similar** if S can be subdivided into k congruent subsets, each of which can be magnified by a constant factor M to yield the whole set S.

An example is given by the square in figure 38.7

Figure 38.7: Every small square in the grid is congruent, and can be magnified by 17 in each dimensions to obtain the larger 17×17 square.

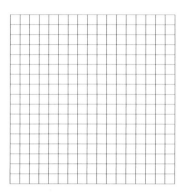

Definition 38.4. Fractal Dimension

Suppose that S can be subdivided into k congruent pieces, each of which may be magnified by a factor of M to yield S. Then the **fractal dimension** D of S is

$$D = \frac{\log k}{\log M} = \frac{\log\,(\text{number of pieces})}{\log\,(\text{magnification factor})} \tag{38.9}$$

Example 38.4. A line segment can be decomposed into n self-similar objects which, when magnified by n, reproduce the line. This gives us an object of fractal dimension 1.

Example 38.5. A square of size $n \times n$ can be decomposed into n^2 self-similar objects which, when magnified by n, reproduce the square. This gives us an object of fractal dimension 2. To see this, we have a number of duplicates $k = n^2$ and magnification $M = n$, hence

$$D = \frac{\log n^2}{\log n} = 2 \tag{38.10}$$

Example 38.6. A cube can be decomposed into n^3 self-similar objects which, when magnified by n, reproduce the cube. This gives us an object of fractal dimension 3, because there are n^3 objects, but each sub-object can be magnified by n to give the original:

$$D = \frac{\log n^3}{\log n} = 3 \tag{38.11}$$

Example 38.7. Sierpinski Triangle. The whole triangle can be decomposed into $k = 3$ three congruent triangles. Each triangle can be magnified by a factor of

$M = 2$ to retrieve the original. Thus the fractal dimension is

$$D = \frac{\log 3}{\log 2} \approx 1.584 \tag{38.12}$$

It can also be subdivided into 9 triangles that are $1/4$ the size of the original, or 27 triangles that are $1/8$ the size of the original, etc., all of which give the same fractal dimension.

Example 38.8. The Koch Curve. Each side is decomposed into $k = 4$ pieces, each of which can be magnified by $M = 3$ to obtain the original shape. Therefore the fractal dimension is

$$D = \frac{\log 4}{\log 3} \approx 1.261 \tag{38.13}$$

Similarly, it can be decomposed into 16 pieces, each of which is $1/9$ the size of the original, or into 4^k pieces which are each $1/3^k$ as big as the original. The dimension is still $\log 4/\log 3$.

Example 38.9. The Cantor Set. A Cantor set is obtained by starting with a straight line segment, and removing the middle third iteratively, as illustrated in figure 38.8. After one iteration, we have two sub-intervals, each of which is $1/3$ the

Figure 38.8: Iteration towards the Cantor Set

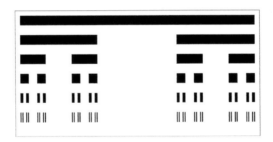

length of the original. After two iterations we have 4 sub-intervals, each of which is $1/9$ the length of the original. After the kth step, we have 2^k sub-intervals, each of which is $1/3^k$ the length of the original.

Hence the fractal dimension is given by

$$D = \frac{\log 2^k}{\log 3^k} = \frac{\log 2}{\log 3} \approx 0.6309 \tag{38.14}$$

which is more than a point but less than a line.

Here we reiterate the definition of a fractal.

> **Definition 38.5. Fractal**
>
> A **fractal** is a subset of $\mathbb{R}^n$ which is self-similar and whose fractal dimension exceeds its topological dimension.

Attractors and the Julia Set

> **Definition 38.6. Iterated Function System**
>
> Let $0 < \beta < 1$ and let $\mathbf{P}_1, \ldots, \mathbf{P}_n$ be a sequence of points in the plane. An **iterated function system** is the collection of functions $\mathcal{A} = \{A_1, A_2, \ldots, A_n\}$, where
> $$A_i(\mathbf{P}) = \beta(\mathbf{P} - \mathbf{P}_i) + \mathbf{P}_i$$
> for each $i = 1, 2, \ldots, n$.

> **Definition 38.7. Attractor**
>
> Let $\mathcal{A}$ be an iterated function system. The set of points to which an arbitrary set in the plane converges is called the **attractor** of the system.

Example 38.10. The Cantor set is the attractor of the following iterated function system. Let $\mathbf{P}$ be represented by the column matrix $\begin{bmatrix} x \\ y \end{bmatrix}$, and define

$$A_0 \begin{bmatrix} x \\ y \end{bmatrix} = \frac{1}{3} \begin{bmatrix} x \\ y \end{bmatrix} \tag{38.15}$$

$$A_1 \begin{bmatrix} x \\ y \end{bmatrix} = \frac{1}{3} \begin{bmatrix} x - 1 \\ y \end{bmatrix} + \begin{bmatrix} 1 \\ 0 \end{bmatrix} \tag{38.16}$$

Then $\mathcal{A} = \{A_0, A_1\}$ is an iterated function system. If you generate the sequence $\mathbf{P}_1, \mathbf{P}_2, \ldots$, by randomly selecting a choice $s_i = 0$ or $s_i = 1$ for each i, so that

$$\mathbf{P}_{i+1} = \begin{cases} A_0(\mathbf{P}_i), & \text{if } s_i = 0 \\ A_1(\mathbf{P}_i), & \text{if } s_i = 1 \end{cases} \tag{38.17}$$

then the attractor of $\mathcal{A}$ is the Cantor set (figure 38.9). The following code will generate a picture of the attractor.

```
import random
from matplotlib.pyplot import *
A0= lambda P: ((P[0]/3., P[1]/3.))
A1= lambda P: ((1+(P[0]-1)/3., P[1]/3.))
```

```
5   def iterate(n,p):
6       x=p
7       for i in range(n):
8           x = A0(x) if random.randint(0,1)==0 else A1(x)
9       return(x)
```

```
10  def Cantor(npts):
11      startingPoint = (random.random(), random.random())
12      return zip(*[iterate(25,startingPoint)
13          for i in range(npts)])
14
15  x,y = Cantor(500)
16  scatter(x,y,c="k",marker=",", s=0.01)
17  show()
```

Figure 38.9: The attractor generated by equation 38.10.

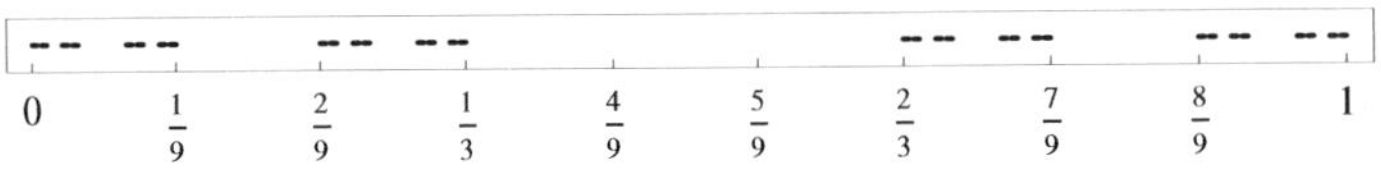

Example 38.11. Appolonian Gasket. The following is an iterated function system on the Complex plane $\mathbb{C}$. Let

$$f(z) = \frac{3}{1 + \sqrt{3} - z} - \frac{1 + \sqrt{3}}{2 + \sqrt{3}} \qquad (38.18)$$

Iterate by choosing one of the following randomly at each step:

$$z_{n+1} = \text{randomly select one of} \begin{cases} f(z_n) \\ \frac{1}{2}(-1 + i\sqrt{3})f(z_n) \\ \frac{1}{2}(-1 + i\sqrt{3})f(z_n) \end{cases} \qquad (38.19)$$

The attractor is called an Apollonian gasket.[3]

The critical result from analysis that we require is the Boundary mapping theorem, which states that interior points of sets map to interior points (figure 38.11).

---

[3] Named for Apollonius of Perga (262-190 BC). Apollonius considered what happens if you constructed three identical circles that are each tangent to on another, and all tangent to a single larger circle. He then proposed constructing additional internal circles that are tangent to subsets of three of these circles. One of these is shown in the circle at the center of the figure. Additional circles can be inscribed between this center circle and the three medium sized circles. We can also place circles inside the three sectors between the medium circles, and iterate ad-infinitum. The result is the Apollonian fractal that consists of a collection of gaskets.

Figure 38.10: Left:Apollonian Gasket. Middle: Apollonian Circles. Right: Apollonian Fractal generated with **apollon.py** by Ludger Sandig which can be found at `https://github.com/lsandig/apollon`.

Figure 38.11: Illustration of the Boundary Mapping Theorem

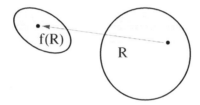

Theorem 38.1. Boundary Mapping Theorem

Let $f(z)$ be a complex function; let R be a closed set of the complex plane; and let $z^* \in R$ be any interior point of R (not on its boundary). Then $f(z^*)$ is an interior point of $f(R)$.

When we apply the Boundary Mapping theorem to an iterated function system in complex space we obtain Julia sets.[4] A Julia Set is obtained as follows. Let

$$R(z) = \frac{P(z)}{Q(z)} \qquad (38.20)$$

be any rational complex function where P and Q have no common divisors. When fixed point iteration is applied to $R(z)$, a sequence of points will be generated that either approaches infinity or does not approach infinity. The boundary between the points that approach infinity and those that do not is called the **Julia Set**.

---

[4]The Julia Set (Gaston Julia[5], 1893-1978) was described as early as 1918 but did not become widely known until colorful images were generated in the 1960s by Mandelbrot and others.

Definition 38.8. Orbit

Let $f(z)$ be a function on the complex plain. The **orbit of $f(z)$ starting at z_0** is the sequence of points $z_0, z_1, z_2, \ldots$ in the complex plane generated by using fixed point iteration

$$z_{k+1} = f(z_k) \tag{38.21}$$

For example, nearly every quadratic map

$$z_{k+1} = z_k^2 + c \tag{38.22}$$

has a fractal Julia set. This particular set has been extensively studied. Images of the Julia Set can be plotted on a rectangle by dividing the rectangle into a $p \times q$ (p, q integers) grid of points. Choose some "large" real number R (e.g., $R \sim 100$). Pick any point on the grid as z_0 and count the number of iterations until $|z_k| > R$ (this is called the **escape time**). If the escape radius R is never reached, the value of R is returned. This process is then repeated using every *other* point in the grid as z_0. This results in a $p \times q$ matrix whose values are between 1 and M. Treating this matrix as an image (e.g., assigning colors to the interval $[1, M]$) generates the well known pictures of Julia Sets (figure 38.12).

Algorithm 38.1 Algorithm to find the Julia Set of $f(z)$.

---
input: f,$R_{\max}$ (escape radius); $N_{\max}$ (escape count); p, q (image dimensions in pixels); $x_0, y_0, x_{\max}, y_{max}$ (domain boundaries)

1: $\Delta x \leftarrow (x_{max} - x_0)/p$
2: $\Delta y \leftarrow (y_{max} - y_0)/q$
3: **for** $k \leftarrow 0, \ldots, p$ **do**
4:     $x \leftarrow x_0 + k\Delta x$
5:     **for** $j \leftarrow 0, \ldots, q$ **do**
6:         $y \leftarrow y_0 + j\Delta y$
7:         $z \leftarrow z + iy$
8:         $n \leftarrow 1$
9:         **while** $|z| < R_{\max} \wedge n < N_{\text{nmax}}$ **do**
10:            $z \leftarrow f(z)$
11:            $n \leftarrow n + 1$
12:        **end while**
13:        **if** $|z| > R$ **then**
14:            $A_{kj} \leftarrow 0$ Escaped
15:        **else**
16:            $A_{ij} \leftarrow 1$ Converged
17:        **end if**
18:    **end for**
19: **end for**

Definition 38.9. Bounded Orbit

The orbit of z under $f(z)$ is **bounded** if there exists a K such that $|f^n(z)| < K$ for all n, and is called **unbounded** if no such K exists.

Definition 38.10. Julia Set

The **filled Julia Set** of $f(z)$ is the set of all points whose orbits are bounded. The **Julia Set** of $f(z)$ is the boundary of the filled Julia set.

Figure 38.12: Self-similarity of the quadratic Julia Set for $c = -0.8 - .15i$ and $N_{max} = 100$. On the bottom is a magnification of the area shown in the box on the top. The image is colored with a diverging **PuOr** colormap that counts the number of iterations until escape.

Under fixed fixed point iteration in $\mathbb{R}^2$, some functions will also converge to a collection of points which when taken together form a fractal. These limit sets are also known as **chaotic** (or **strange**) **attractors**.

Example 38.12. The Hénon Map[6]

$$(x_{n+1}, y_{n+1}) = (1 - ax_n^2 + y_n, bx_n) \tag{38.23}$$

has a chaotic attractor for certain values of the constants a and b (figure 38.13).

We can visualize the chaotic attractor by picking any initial point and performing a large number of fixed point iterations using equation 38.23. The result shown in figure 38.13 (left) used 100,000 points.

By doing fixed point iteration starting from each point in a gridded region of $\mathbb{R}^2$ (like we did to find the colorized Julia sets in $\mathbb{C}$), we can count the number of iterations it takes to diverge to some specific distance from the origin. For $a = .2$ and $b = 1.01$ the colored escape figure for the Henon map, we end up with a shape that resembles a turbulent vortex, as shown in figure 38.13 (right).

Figure 38.13: Left: Hénon attractor for $a = 1.4$ and $b = 0.3$, an example of a strange attractor in the real plane. Right:Iterations to escape to 100 for $a = 0.2$ and $b = 1.01$ in the Hénon Map.

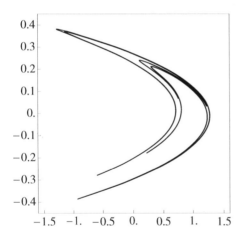 

---

[6]M. Hénon. A two-dimensional mapping with a strange attractor. Comm. Math. Physics. 50:69-77 (1976)

Exercises

1. The Hénon Map is found by obtaining the sequence of iterations

$$(x_0, y_0), (x_1, y_1), (x_2, y_x), \ldots$$

where

$$(x_{i+1}, y_{i+1}) = (a - \alpha x_i^2 + by_i, \gamma x_i)$$

Starting from $(x_0, y_0) = (0, 0)$. Write a function **HenonMap(x, y, a, b, alpha, beta)** that performs a single step in this iteration, i.e., it returns (x_{i+1}, y_{i+1}) given (x_i, y_i)

2. Read problem 1. Write a function **HenonIterate(n)** that returns a list of the first n iterations of the Hénon Map using $a = 1.4$, $b = 0.3$, $\alpha = 1$, $\gamma = 1$.

3. Plot at least 10,000 points in the Hénon attractor. This is the attractor of the Hénon map. Hint: see exercises 1 and 2.

4. Plot the Hénon Whirlwhind (fig. 38.13, right). With a slight modification of the parameters the Hénon Whirlwind becomes the Hénon Sting Ray (shown below). See if you can find such a set of parameter modifications.

5. Write a program to plot the Julia set for $f(x) = z^2 + C$ where $C = 0.360284 + 0.100376j$.

6. Plot the Mandelbrot Set. The Mandelbrot Set is the set of all complex numbers c such that fixed point iteration on $f(z) = z^2 + c$, starting from $z_0 = 0$, converges. The Mandelbrot Set is itself a fractal.

7. Look up the Mandelbrot Set on Wikipedia. Modify your program from the previous problem to plot (in color) each of the following:

(a) Seahorse   (c) Island

(b) Seahorse tail   (d) Satellite

8. The Koch curve is a special case of a **de Rham curve**. A de Rham curve is found by performing fixed point iteration in the complex plane. One type of Koch curve is call a **Koch-Peano** curve, which is found by starting at some point z_0 and picking the next points by flipping a coin. If it comes up heads,

$$z_1 = a\bar{z}$$

and if it comes up tails,

$$z_1 = a + (1 - a)\bar{z}$$

where $\bar{z}$ is the complex conjugate and a is a constant. The process is repeated, flipping a coin each time.

(a) For $a = \frac{1}{2} + i\frac{\sqrt{3}}{6}$ you should get the Koch curve. You can simulate the coin flipping by using **np.random.rand()**, which returns a random number between 0 and 1. If it is less than 0.5, pick heads; if it is greater than 0.5, pick tails. Perform at least 10000 iterations and then do a scatter plot in the complex plane. To get this scatter plot, extract the real parts of the results (**x=z.real**) as the x values and the imaginary parts (**y=z.imag**) as the y values.

(b) Repeat the process to plot a **Koch-Peano** curve, which uses $a = 0.6 + 0.37i$, and for $a = 0.6 + 0.45i$

9. A **Cesàro** Curve is calculated the same way as a Koch Peano curve (see previous exercise), except the iteration formulas are

$$z_1 = az$$

and

$$z_1 = a + (1 - a)z$$

Plot Cesàro curves for $a = 0.3 + 0.3i$ and $a = 0.5 + 0.5i$.

Chapter 39

Estimating pi

Algorithms for estimating π are almost as old as civilization itself, and the estimate $22/7$ is one of the oldest. For example, the Great Pyramid at Giza[1] has perimeter/height ratio of $44/7$ which is very nearly 2π, with only 0.04% error. The Rhind Papyrus[2] gives $\pi \approx 256/81 \approx 3.16049$. Yajnavalkya[3] gave a value of $256/81$, and Archimedes[4] estimated that $223/71 < \pi < 22/7$.

Method of Inscribed Polygons

In this technique π is estimated by calculating the perimeter of a sequence of polygons with 2^n of edges inscribed in a unit circle. As the $n \to \infty$, the perimeters of the polygons approaches the circumference of the circle. Let π_n be the ratio of the perimeter of the nth polygon to the diameter of the circle. Then we expect $\pi_n \to \frac{1}{2}\pi$ as $n \to \infty$ (since the diameter is 2). The perimeter P_n of the nth polygon is

$$P_n = 2^n H_n \tag{39.1}$$

where H_n is the length of the outer edge. Therefore

$$\pi_n = \frac{1}{2}P_n = 2^{n-1} H_n \tag{39.2}$$

To get a formula for H_n, we look at the H_2 and H_3. At $n = 2$, we are inscribing a square in a circle of radius 1, and divide the square into four right triangles, each with hypotenuse $H_2 = \sqrt{2}$ (see fig. 39.1, left). Then

$$\pi_2 = 2^{2-1} H_2 = 2\sqrt{2} \approx 2.82843 \tag{39.3}$$

When $n = 3$ we divide each central angle in half. Define the points **A**, **B**, and **C**, and the distance a as shown in figure figure 39.1 (right). Triangle $\triangle$**ABC** can be decomposed into two right triangles. Using the Pythagorean theorem on the inner triangle,

$$(1 - a)^2 + \left(\frac{H_2}{2}\right)^2 = 1 \tag{39.4}$$

---

[1] Built sometime around 2500 BC.

[2] Written in Egypt around 1650 BC; it was discovered during illegal excavations in the mid 19th century. It was purchased first by Henry Rhind and later the British Museum.

[3] A vedic (Indian) sage, who lived c. 900 BC.

[4] A Greek mathematician who lived in Syracuse, 287 - 212 BC, and died during the Roman invasion.

Figure 39.1: Left: A square inscribed in a unit circle. Right: One segment of an octagon inscribed in a unit circle is obtained by spliting each of the triangles on the left in half.

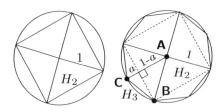

Solving for a,

$$a = 1 - \sqrt{1 - \left(\frac{H_2}{2}\right)^2} \tag{39.5}$$

Using the Pythagorean theorem on the outer triangle

$$H_3^2 = a^2 + \left(\frac{H_2}{2}\right)^2 \tag{39.6}$$

Substituting the expression for a (eq. 39.5) int (39.6) gives

$$H_3^2 = \left[1 - \sqrt{1 - \left(\frac{H_2}{2}\right)^2}\right]^2 + \left(\frac{H_2}{2}\right)^2 = 2 - 2\sqrt{1 - \left(\frac{H_2}{2}\right)^2} \tag{39.7}$$

Therefore (since $H_2 = \sqrt{2}$),

$$H_3^2 = 2 - 2\sqrt{1 - \left(\frac{\sqrt{2}}{2}\right)^2} = 2 - \sqrt{2} \tag{39.8}$$

$$\pi_3 = 2^2 H_3 = 4\sqrt{2 - \sqrt{2}} \approx 3.06147 \tag{39.9}$$

By a similar argument

$$H_4^2 = 2 - 2\sqrt{1 - \left(\frac{H_3}{2}\right)^2} \tag{39.10}$$

and in general

$$H_n^2 = 2 - 2\sqrt{1 - \left(\frac{H_{n-1}}{2}\right)^2} \tag{39.11}$$

so our n^{th} estimate of π is $\pi_n = 2^{n-1} H_n$. Algorithm 39.1 gives $\pi \approx 3.1415914$ after ten iterations, correct to the fifth decimal place.

Scientific Computation: Python Hacking for Math Junkies

Algorithm 39.1 Calculation of π using the method of polygons

input: n

1: $H \leftarrow \sqrt{2}$, $p \leftarrow 2$

2: **for** $i \leftarrow 3, \ldots, n$ **do**

3:     $H \leftarrow \sqrt{2 - 2\sqrt{1 - (H/2)^2}}$

4:     $p \leftarrow 2p$

5:     $\pi_i \leftarrow pH$

6: **end for**

7: **return** π_n

Method of Archimedes

Archimedes found both an upper and lower bounds on π. In addition to inscribing polygons, he also circumscribed polygons. Let I_n and C_n be the perimeters of any n-gons that are inscribed and circumscribed about a circle of radius $1/2$. Since the circle has (by definition) circumference π, then

$$I_n < \pi < C_n \tag{39.12}$$

for all n. He derived the following recurrence relationships:

$$C_{2n} = \frac{2C_n I_n}{C_n + I_n} \text{(circumscribed polygon)} \tag{39.13a}$$

$$I_{2n} = \sqrt{C_{2n} I_n} \text{(inscribed polygon)} \tag{39.13b}$$

Archimedes used $n = 6 \cdot 2^k$ for $k = 0, 1, .., 4$ (i.e., hexagon, 12-gon, 24-gon, 48-gon, 96-gon) to obtain

$$3.1408 \approx \frac{223}{71} < \pi < \frac{22}{7} \approx 3.1429 \tag{39.14}$$

Archimedes did not explain how he computed the square roots, and expressed each result as a rational number.

Taylor Series Method

More accurate methods are based on infinite series expansions. Setting $\pi/4$ in the Taylor series expansion for the arctangent,

$$\tan^{-1} x = x - \frac{1}{3}x^3 + \frac{1}{5}x^5 - \frac{1}{7}x^7 + \ldots \tag{39.15}$$

gives

$$\frac{\pi}{4} = 1 - \frac{1}{3} + \frac{1}{5} - \frac{1}{7} + \ldots \tag{39.16}$$

Unfortunately this converges very slowly. Even after a million iterations it is no better than the method of polygons after 10 iterations.

n	π_n
10	3.2323158
100	3.1514934
1,000	3.1425917
10,000	3.1416926
100,000	3.1416027
1,000,000	3.1415937

John Machin (1680-1752) showed that the series

$$\frac{\pi}{4} = 4\tan^{-1}\frac{1}{5} - \tan^{-1}\frac{1}{239} \tag{39.17}$$

converges much more quickly. Machin's formula (39.17) can be derived using the trigono-metric identity for the sum of arc-tangents,

$$\tan^{-1} A \pm \tan^{-1} B = \tan^{-1}\frac{A \pm B}{1 \mp AB} \tag{39.18}$$

Therefore

$$2\tan^{-1}\frac{1}{5} = \tan^{-1}\frac{1}{5} + \tan^{-1}\frac{1}{5} = \tan^{-1}\left[\frac{\frac{1}{5}+\frac{1}{5}}{1-\frac{1}{5}\cdot\frac{1}{5}}\right] = \tan^{-1}\frac{5}{12} \tag{39.19}$$

$$4\tan^{-1}\frac{1}{5} = \tan^{-1}\frac{5}{12} + \tan^{-1}\frac{5}{12} = \tan^{-1}\left[\frac{\frac{5}{12}+\frac{5}{12}}{1-\frac{5}{12}\cdot\frac{5}{12}}\right] = \tan^{-1}\frac{120}{119} \tag{39.20}$$

Combining these together gives

$$4\tan^{-1}\frac{1}{5} - \tan^{-1}\frac{1}{239} = \tan^{-1}\frac{120}{119} - \tan^{-1}\frac{1}{239} \tag{39.21}$$

$$= \tan^{-1}\left[\frac{\frac{120}{119}-\frac{1}{239}}{1+\frac{120}{119}\cdot\frac{1}{239}}\right] \tag{39.22}$$

$$= \tan^{-1}\frac{28561/28441}{28561/28441} \tag{39.23}$$

$$= \tan^{-1} 1 = \frac{\pi}{4} \tag{39.24}$$

If we define the series

$$f(x,n) = \sum_{k=0}^{n}\frac{x^{2k+1}(-1)^k}{2k+1} \tag{39.25}$$

then

$$\pi = \lim_{n\to\infty} 4\left(4f\left(\frac{1}{5},n\right) - f\left(\frac{1}{239},n\right)\right) \tag{39.26}$$

We can implement this recursively in Python.

```
def f(x,n):
    if n>=1:
        mult = -1.0 if n%2==1 else 1.0
        last = (mult)*(x**(2.0*n+1))/(2.0*n+1.0)
        return f(x,n-1)+ last
    else:
        return x

def F(n):
    return 4*(4*f(.2,n)-f(1.0/239.0,n))

for n in range(10):
    print n, F(n)
```

This converges much more quickly:

```
0 3.18326359833
1 3.14059702933
2 3.14162102933
3 3.14159177218
4 3.1415926824
5 3.14159265262
6 3.14159265362
7 3.14159265359
8 3.14159265359
9 3.14159265359
```

Machin-like formulas have been used to calculate over a trillion digits of π. Yasumasa Kanada[5] and his colleagues used formulas like[6]

$$\pi = 176 \tan^{-1} \frac{1}{57} + 28 \tan^{-1} \frac{1}{239} - 48 \tan^{-1} \frac{1}{682} + 96 \tan^{-1} \frac{1}{12943} \qquad (39.27)$$

$$\frac{\pi}{4} = 12 \tan^{-1} \frac{1}{49} + 32 \tan^{-1} \frac{1}{57} - 5 \tan^{-1} \frac{1}{239} + 12 \tan^{-1} \frac{1}{110443} \qquad (39.28)$$

$$\frac{\pi}{4} = 44 \tan^{-1} \frac{1}{57} + 7 \tan^{-1} \frac{1}{239} - 12 \tan^{-1} \frac{1}{682} + 24 \tan^{-1} 112943 \qquad (39.29)$$

Files containing their results are posted on the lab website FTP server.

Brent-Salamin Algorithm

An iteration based on results of Gauss and Legendre was developed by Richard Brent and Eugene Salamin[7]. and forms the basis of the popular **superpi** program that runs

---

[5]see http://pi2.cc.u-tokyo.ac.jp/
[6]The first of these was discovered by Carl Størmer (1857-1957).
[7]E. Salamin (1975) Computation of π Using Arithmetic-Geometric Mean. *Mathematics of Computation.* **30**(135):565-570; R.P. Brent (1975). Multiple Precision Zero-Finding methods and the Complexity of Elementary Function Evaluation. In *Analytic Computational Complexity* (ed. J.F. Traub). New York: Academic Press.

under Windows. The Salamin-Brent Algorithm sets initial values $a_0 = 1$, $b_0 = 1/\sqrt{2}$, $t_0 = 1/4$, and $p_0 = 1$, then repeats the following calculation until the desired accuracy is reached:

$$a_{n+1} = \frac{a_n + b_n}{2} \tag{39.30}$$

$$b_{n+1} = \sqrt{a_n b_n} \tag{39.31}$$

$$t_{n+1} = t_n - p_n(a_n - a_{n+1})^2 \tag{39.32}$$

$$p_{n+1} = 2p_n \tag{39.33}$$

$$\pi_{n+1} = \frac{(a_n + b_n)^2}{4t_n} \tag{39.34}$$

This algorithm converges very quickly, with the number of correct digits approximately doubling with every iteration.

BBP Formulas

The BBP formula allows the computation of the nth digit of π without knowing any of the first $n - 1$ digits.[8] The formula is:

$$\pi = \sum_{n=0}^{\infty} \left(\frac{4}{8n + 1} - \frac{2}{8n + 4} - \frac{1}{8n + 5} - \frac{1}{8n + 6} \right) \left(\frac{1}{16} \right)^n \tag{39.35}$$

The algorithm is implemented as follows. Let

$$S_n = \sum_{k=0}^{\infty} \frac{1}{16^k(8k + j)} \tag{39.36}$$

Then

$$\pi = 4S_1 - 2S_4 - S_5 - S_6 \tag{39.37}$$

Define the notation $\{x\} = x \mod 1$, the fractional part of x. Then

$$\{16^n S_p\} = \left\{ \sum_{k=0}^{n} \frac{16^{n-k}}{8k + p} + \sum_{k=n+1}^{\infty} \frac{16^{n-k}}{8k + p} \right\} \tag{39.38}$$

$$= \left\{ \sum_{k=0}^{n} \frac{\{16^{n-k} \mod (8k + p)\}}{8k + p} + \sum_{k=n+1}^{\infty} \frac{16^{n-k}}{8k + p} \right\} \tag{39.39}$$

Define

$$s_p(n) = \sum_{k=0}^{n} \frac{\{16^{n-k} \mod (8k + p)\}}{8k + p} \tag{39.40}$$

---

[8]Bailey, D. H.; Borwein, P. B.; and Plouffe, S. "On the Rapid Computation of Various Polylogarithmic Constants." Math. Comput. 66, 903-913, 1997, which is available at http://crd.lbl.gov/~dhbailey/dhbpapers/digits.pdf. For details on the numerical implementation on computing π, see http://crd.lbl.gov/~dhbailey/dhbpapers/bbp-alg.pdf

Then the nth hex-digit of π is given by

$$d_n = \lfloor 16 \{4\{s_1(n)\}2\{s_4(n)\} - \{s_5(n)\} - \{s_6(n)\}\}\rfloor \qquad (39.41)$$

where $\lfloor x \rfloor$ denotes the greatest integer less than or equal to x.

Spigot Algorithms

The BBP algorithm is a type of **spigot** algorithm. These are algorithms that can pour out digits one at a time, independent of earlier digits in the sequence. BBP gives a spigot for the base 16 digits of π – you just turn on the spigot and the digits pour on out. You don't have to worry about using up the machine precision once you get to 16 digits. Or you can just start at digit 1-trillion and go from there. Unfortunately no equivalent **series**-based spigot method has been found for π. However a repeated product does exist. Rabinowitz and Wagon[9] showed that the series

$$\pi = \sum_{k=0}^{\infty} \frac{(k!)^2 2^{k+1}}{(2k+1)!} \qquad (39.42)$$

expands to the form

$$\frac{\pi}{2} = 1 + \frac{1}{3}\left[1 + \frac{2}{5}\left[1 + \frac{3}{7}\left[1 + \frac{4}{9}\left[1 + \cdots\right]\right]\right]\right] \qquad (39.43)$$

Comparing this to the expansion

$$\pi \approx 3.14159\cdots = 3 + \frac{1}{10}\left[1 + \frac{1}{10}\left[4 + \frac{1}{10}\left[1 + \frac{1}{10}\left[5 + \frac{1}{10}\left[9 + \cdots\right]\right]\right]\right]\right] \qquad (39.44)$$

they observed that (39.43) is like a mixed-radix expansion in the mixed-based $\left(\frac{1}{3}, \frac{2}{5}, \frac{3}{7}, \frac{4}{9}, \cdots\right)$, in which $\pi = 2.222\ldots$. Gibbons[10] figured out how to convert each digit from base m to base n by observing that the successive multiplications in (39.43) can be written as linear fractional transformations.

$$\pi = \left[2 + \frac{1}{3} \times\right]\left[2 + \frac{2}{5} \times\right]\left[2 + \frac{3}{7} \times\right] \cdots \left[2 + \frac{k}{2k+1} \times\right] \cdots \qquad (39.45)$$

Each of the transforms can be represented by a 2×2 matrix, and the spigot represented by a Python generator. Gibbons' original algorithm was published in Haskell but the translation can be made almost literally word for word. To print out, e.g., the first 1000 digits of π,

```
p=spigot()
for i in range(1000):
    print next(p),
```

---

[9]S. Rabinowitz and S. Waggon (1995) "A Spigot Algorithm for the Digits of Pi." *Am. Math. Month.* **102**:195-203.

[10]J. Gibbons (1975) "Unbounded spigot algorithm for the digits of Pi." *Am. Math. Monthly.* **113**:318-328.

Here is a Python translation of Gibbons' `spigot` code.

```python
def spigot():
    q,r,t,k,n,l = 1,0,1,1,3,3
    while True:
        if 4*q+r-t < n*t:
            yield n
            q,r,t,k,n,l = (10*q,10*(r-n*t),t,k,
                           (10*(3*q+r))/t-10*n,l)
        else:
            q,r,t,k,n,l = (q*k,(2*q+r)*l,t*l,k+1,
                (q*(7*k+2)+r*l)/(t*l),l+2)
```

Buffon's Needle

This method calculates π experimentally via a Monte-Carlo simulation.[11]   Buffon's method is a version of the acceptance-rejection method for producing sequences of random numbers. Generate n pairs of uniform random numbers (x, y) in the unit box $[-1, 1] \times [-1, 1]$. The area of of this box is 4. The we count the number of points m that fall within the unit circle; these points satisfy $x^2 + y^2 <= 1$. We expect the ratio m/n to equal the ratio of the area of the circle to the area of the square. Since the circle has radius $r = 1$, its area is π. Hence

$$\frac{m}{n} \approx \frac{\pi}{4} \tag{39.46}$$

so our numerical estimate is $\pi \approx 4m/n$ (figure 39.2).

Figure 39.2: Left: Acceptance-Rejection method for estimation of π. Right: Definition of parameters in and Buffon's Needle method.

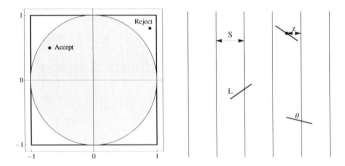

Buffon did not actually use a circle; instead his idea was to drop an object of length L (e.g., a needle) on a surface that contains parallel lines a distance S units apart, where $S > L$. If the object is dropped n times and x of those times it falls on one of the parallel lines, then

$$\pi \approx \frac{2nL}{xS} \tag{39.47}$$

---

[11] It was invented in 1777 by G.L. Leclerc de Buffon (1707-1788)

To see this suppose the center of the needle falls a distance z from a line. Then the uniform probability density function (PDF) of z between 0 and $S/2$ is $f(z) = 2/S$. Let the acute angle between the needle and the line be θ. The uniform PDF of θ on $[0, \pi/2]$ is $g(\theta) = 2/\pi$. The joint PDF is the product

$$f(z, \theta) = \frac{4}{S\pi} \tag{39.48}$$

A needle crosses the line if

$$z \leq \frac{L}{2} \sin \theta \tag{39.49}$$

so the probability that a needle will cross the line is

$$P = \int_{\theta=0}^{\pi/2} \int_{z=0}^{(L/2)\sin\theta} \frac{4}{s\pi} dz d\theta = \frac{4}{s\pi} \int_0^{\pi/2} \frac{L}{2} \sin\theta d\theta = \frac{2L}{S\pi} \tag{39.50}$$

If we drop n needles and x of them touch the line then we expect

$$\frac{x}{n} \approx P = \frac{2L}{s\pi} \tag{39.51}$$

Solving for π gives equation 39.47. A modern twist on Buffon's method is given in the WikiHow article "How to Calculate Pi by Throwing Frozen Hot Dogs."[12]

Exercises

1. Determine the initial conditions (the values of I_3 and C_3) for the method of Archimedes (see equations 39.13).

2. Write a program using the method of Archimedes (equations 39.13) that will calculate the value of π to machine accuracy using the method of Archimedes, and print out (a) the number of iterations required, and (b) the number of sides of the polygon. Start the method with I_3 and C_3 (triangles), which have perimeters that you can determine by hand (or using Python). You may not use any assumed or built in value for π to determine when the iteration has converged.

3. Write a function that calculates the arctangent of x using the first n terms of the Taylor series (39.15) as $f(x, n)$ using (39.25),

$$\tan^{-1} x = x - \frac{1}{3}x^3 + \frac{1}{5}x^5 - \frac{1}{7}x^7 + \dots$$
$$= \sum_{k=0}^{\infty} \frac{x^{2k+1}(-1)^k}{2k + 1}$$

4. Use Machin's formula for π, (39.17),

$$\pi = 4 \left(4 \tan^{-1} \frac{1}{5} - \tan^{-1} \frac{1}{239} \right)$$

to calculate π to machine accuracy iteratively. How many iterations are required?

5. Do ex. 4 using Størmer's formula (39.27).

6. Do ex. 4 using Kanada's formula (39.28).

7. Do ex. 4 using Kanada's formula (39.29).

8. Implement Gibbon's spigot algorithm (see the code on page 378) and use it to print a table of the first 100,000 digits of π (to the right of the decimal point), pretty-printed so that there are: 100 digits per line; a space after each group of 10 digits; a blank line after each 10'th line; and with the first column annotated, as in 100, 200, 300, ...

9. Implement a Buffon's needle-like method using the acceptance/rejection method. Imagine we have a circular dartboard that has a radius of 1 that is circumscribed by a square. When we throw darts at the board, they either fall inside the circle, or outside the circle but inside the square. The area

---
[12]See http://www.wikihow.com/Calculate-Pi-by-Throwing-Frozen-Hot-Dogs.

of the circle is π. The area of the square is 4. So the probability of a dart landing inside the circle is $\pi/4$. The same argument applies if our dartboard only consists of the portion in the first quadrant. The function **numpy.random.random_sample()** will return a random number with a uniform probability of being in the interval $[0,1)$. Write a program to estimate π by throwing one million darts.

10. Implement a simulation of Buffon's need method using a board marked with parallel lines separated by a distance S. Throw needles of length L at the board; each needle will land with a random location that is some distance z from a line and has an angle θ. Assume that z falls with a uniform probably density on $[0, S/2]$ and θ falls with a uniform probability on $[0, \pi/2]$. Run your program for $n=100$, 1000, 10,000 100,000 and one million throws, assuming $S > L$. What happens if you vary the length L?

Chapter 40

Singular Value Decomposition

The **Singular Value Decomposition** is a factoring of a matrix $\mathbf{X}$ into three parts, written as

$$\mathbf{X} = \mathbf{U}\Sigma\mathbf{V}^{\mathrm{T}} \tag{40.1}$$

While all matrices have a singular value decomposition (SVD), when $\mathbf{X}$ is square, there is an intuitive description of the process: a rotation, followed by a scaling, followed by another rotation. In any decomposition, the first and third matrix are orthogonal, that is, they are composed of mutually perpendicular unit vectors; and the middle matrix is a diagonal matrix whose entries are called the **singular values** of $\mathbf{X}$. This SVD is widely used in statistical and data analysis applications.

Theorem 40.1. Singular Value Decomposition

Any $n \times m$ matrix $\mathbf{X}$ can be uniquely decomposed as a product

$$\mathbf{X} = \mathbf{U}\Sigma\mathbf{V}^{\mathrm{T}} \tag{40.2}$$

where $\mathbf{U}$ is an $n \times k$ orthogonal matrix, Σ is a $k \times k$ diagonal matrix, and $\mathbf{V}$ is an $m \times k$ orthogonal matrix.

The SVD has a geometric interpretation when $\mathbf{X}$ is a real, square 2×2 matrix. Think of the matrix $\mathbf{X}$ as an operator that transforms a vector $\mathbf{v}$, as in $\mathbf{v} \mapsto \mathbf{X}\mathbf{v}$. Then the SVD writes this transformation as

$$\mathbf{v} \mapsto \mathbf{X}\mathbf{v} = \mathbf{R}_2\mathbf{S}\mathbf{R}_1\mathbf{v} \tag{40.3}$$

where $\mathbf{R}_1$ and $\mathbf{R}_2$ are orthogonal matrices, and $\mathbf{S}$ is diagonal. Since $\mathbf{R}_1$ is orthogonal, it first rotates $\mathbf{v} \mapsto \mathbf{v}' = \mathbf{R}_1\mathbf{v}$ in a new coordinate system. Then the diagonal matrix expands (if $s_i > 1$) or compresses (if $s_i < 1$) the components of $\mathbf{v}'$ along the x' and y' axis. Finally, $\mathbf{R}_2$ is like an "unwinding" rotation, that brings the the expanded vector back, without changing its length.

Definition 40.1. Singular Values

Let $\mathbf{X} = \mathbf{U}\Sigma\mathbf{V}^{\mathrm{T}}$ be the Singular Value Decomposition of $\mathbf{X}$. Then the values on the diagonal of Σ are the **singular values** of $\mathbf{X}$.

> **Theorem 40.2. Singular Value Decomposition Algorithm**
>
> Let $\mathbf{X}$ be any matrix over $\mathbb{R}$. Then $\exists$ orthogonal matrices $\mathbf{V}$ and $\mathbf{U}$ such that
>
> $$\mathbf{X} = \mathbf{U}\Sigma\mathbf{V}^{\mathrm{T}} \tag{40.4}$$
>
> where Σ is a diagonal matrix of singular values of $\mathbf{X}$, and in particular, for any orthonormal bases, $(\mathbf{v}_1, \ldots, \mathbf{v}_n)$ and $(\mathbf{u}_1, \ldots, \mathbf{u}_n)$, the matrices given by
>
> $$\mathbf{U} = \left[\ \mathbf{u}_1\ \middle|\ \ldots\ \middle|\ \mathbf{u}_n\ \right] \tag{40.5}$$
> $$\mathbf{V} = \left[\ \mathbf{v}_1\ \middle|\ \ldots\ \middle|\ \mathbf{v}_n\ \right] \tag{40.6}$$
>
> form a singular value decomposition given by equation 40.4, where the $\mathbf{v}_j$ are normalized eigenvectors of $\mathbf{S} = \sqrt{\mathbf{X}^{\mathrm{T}}\mathbf{X}}$ and $\mathbf{u}_j = \Sigma\mathbf{v}_j$, where
>
> $$\mathbf{X} = \Sigma\mathbf{S} = \Sigma\sqrt{\mathbf{X}^{\mathrm{T}}\mathbf{X}} \tag{40.7}$$
>
> and the elements of Σ are the square roots of the eigenvalues of $\mathbf{S}$.

Algorithm 40.1 Algorithm for the singular value decomposition.

---

input: $\mathbf{M}$

1: $\mathbf{v}_1, \mathbf{v}_2, \ldots \leftarrow$ **Eigenvectors** $(\mathbf{M}^{\mathrm{T}}\mathbf{M})$
2: $\mathbf{u}_1, \mathbf{u}_2, \ldots \leftarrow$ **Eigenvectors** $(\mathbf{M}\mathbf{M}^{\mathrm{T}})$
3: $\mathbf{S} \leftarrow$ **Diagonal**(**Eigenvalues** $(\mathbf{M}^{\mathrm{T}}\mathbf{M}))$
4: $\mathbf{V} \leftarrow \left[\ \mathbf{v}_1^{\mathrm{T}}\ \middle|\ \mathbf{v}_2^{\mathrm{T}}\ \middle|\ \cdots\ \right]$
5: $\mathbf{U} \leftarrow \left[\ \mathbf{u}_1^{\mathrm{T}}\ \middle|\ \mathbf{u}_2^{\mathrm{T}}\ \middle|\ \cdots\ \right]$
6: **repeat**
7:     **if** $\mathbf{U}\mathbf{S}\mathbf{V}^{\mathrm{T}} = \mathbf{M}$ **then**
8:         **return** $(\mathbf{U}, \mathbf{S}, \mathbf{V})$
9:     **end if**
       Flip the direction of one of the column vectors of $\mathbf{U}$ or $\mathbf{V}$
10: **until** all permutations have been checked.

One practical application of the SVD is data compression, which we will illustrate here with an example from image analysis. We can expand the SVD of $\mathbf{X}$ by the singular matrix Σ. Suppose the singular values are $s_1, s_2, \ldots$, in decreasing order. These singular values are arranged along the diagonal of Σ, so

$$\mathbf{X} = \mathbf{U}\Sigma\mathbf{V}^{\mathrm{T}} = s_1\mathbf{u}_1\mathbf{v}_1^{\mathrm{T}} + s_2\mathbf{u}_2\mathbf{v}_2^{\mathrm{T}} + \cdots + s_n\mathbf{u}_n\mathbf{v}_n^{\mathrm{T}} \tag{40.8}$$

The 600×800 image shown on the bottom right of figure 40.1 has 600 singular values. Storing the entire image as an array of integer pixels requires $600 \times 800 = 480,000$ bytes of memory. Each component in equation 40.8 requires $600 + 800 + 1 = 1301$ bytes of storage. Using only the first 320 components reduces the required storage to $320 \times 1301 = 390,300$ bytes. If only the first 160 components are used, then only 208,160 bytes are required.

Figure 40.1: Image compression using the singular value decomposition when it is truncated using only the n largest singular components, indicated by the numbers above each figure. The original figure, which has 600 singular values, is shown on the bottom right.

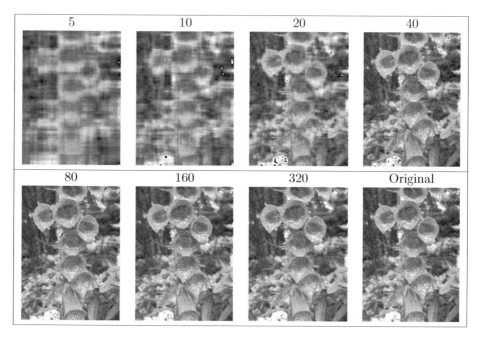

To see why this works, we refer to figure 40.2. The sum in equation 40.8 is strongly dominated by the largest singular values, which are orders of magnitude larger than the smallest singular values. The terms with small s_i do not make a significant contribution to the total matrix, and thus many of them can be ignored.

The SVD can be calculated in Numpy using **numpy.linalg.svd** (see table 30.1). Using the python imaging package **image** to read the image, we can do the calculation of the first **n** components as follows:

```python
import Image
import numpy as np
g=Image.open("flower.jpg")
A=np.asarray(g) # convert to an array
U, Sigma, V = np.linalg.svd(A)
UT=U.T            # transpose
M = np.zeros_like(A)
for j in range(n):  # Compute matrix product
    B=np.outer(UT[j], V[j]) * Sigma[j]
    M=M+B
i=Image.fromarray(np.unit8(M)) # convert to image
i.save("modified-flower-file.jpg") # to save the file
i.show() # to show the picture on screen
```

Figure 40.2: The singular values of the image shown in figure 40.1 are dominated by a few of the largest values. This plot shows the singular values, arranged in order, on a logarithmic scale.

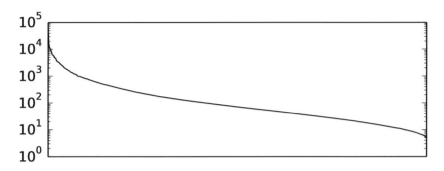

Exercises

1. Find the SVD of each of the following matrices, and then verify that the SVD decomposition works using numpy.

   (a) $\begin{bmatrix} 1 & 3 \\ 0 & -1 \end{bmatrix}$

   (b) $\begin{bmatrix} 5 & 0 & 3 \\ -.5 & 6 & 2 \end{bmatrix}$

   (c) $\begin{bmatrix} 7 & -3 & 2.5 \\ 0 & 1 & 0 \\ .2 & 0 & .3 \end{bmatrix}$

2. Let A be a 2×2 matrix . Let x and y represent unit vectors along the x and y axis, $x' = Ax$, $y' = Ay$. Write a program whose input is A (representing A as a numpy array) and which does the following:

   (a) FInd the SVD of A using `numpy.linalg.svd`

   (b) Plot each of the following pairs of vectors in a different square subplot as arrows: $\{V^T x, V^T y\}$ (in black); $\{\Sigma V^T x, \Sigma V^T y\}$ (in red); $\{UV^T x, UV^T y\}$ (in blue).

3. The square root of a matrix is A is a matrix M such that $M^2 = A$. We write $M = \sqrt{A}$. Write a python program to find the square root of A, a square 2×2 numpy array.

Hints:

   (a) If A is diagonalizable, i.e., if there exists a matrix U such that $D = U^{-1}AU$, where D is diagonal, then $\sqrt{A} = U\sqrt{D}U^{-1}$

   (b) The columns of U are the eigenvectors of A.

   (c) What is the square root of a diagonal matrix? When is A diagonalizable?

4. The polar decomposition of a real, square matrix A is written as $A = M\sqrt{A^T A}$, where M is an isometry (a length-preserving transformation matrix). Write a program to find the polar decomposition of a matrix A.

5. Find or take a photograph of a high-contrast object like a can of cola. Convert it to a gray scale image using a graphics program, or via the techniques of chapter 43. Convert the gray scale image to a numpy array and compute the SVD of the image. Compute the truncated SVD using equation 40.8 for n=5, 10, 20, 40, 60, 80,... up to the maximum number of singular values in the full image. Display each of the truncated images. Interpret your results.

Chapter 41

Principal Component Analysis

Suppose we have a collection of data points $(x_1, y_1), \ldots, (x_m, y_m)$. In higher dimensions we represent each data point by a vector $\mathbf{x}$ that we call the **feature vector**. The individual components of each feature vector are called its features. When we are dealing with xy data, the features are the x and y coordinates of each data point.

In linear regression we find a line $y = f(x)$ that minimizes the sum of the vertical distances between the points and the line. This is sometimes called the regression of y on x. This is only meaningful if all of the noise (error) is in the y-direction. If the noise is only in the x direction, we can switch coordinates and find what statisticians call the regression of x on y rather than the regression of y on x. But if there is noise along both axes what we really want is to find the line that minimizes the *perpendicular* distances to the points.

Figure 41.1: The Principal Components of a data set. Left: Minimizing the distance to a line. Right: the Principal axes.

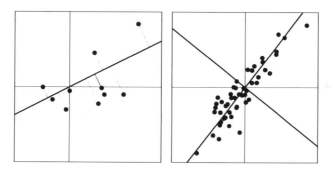

It is useful to collect together all of the data points into a single **feature matrix**. Each row of the feature matrix contains a single data point. Thus if our data consists of a collection of points in the xy plane, the feature matrix will look like

$$\mathbf{X} = \begin{bmatrix} x_1 & y_1 \\ x_2 & y_2 \\ \vdots & \vdots \\ x_m & y_m \end{bmatrix} \tag{41.1}$$

Definition 41.1. Feature Matrix

Suppose we have a k-dimensional data set with m vectors $\mathbf{x}_1, \ldots, \mathbf{x}_m$, that we write as row vectors

$$\mathbf{x}_j = [x_{j1}, x_{j2}, \ldots, x_{jk}], \, j = 1, \ldots, m \tag{41.2}$$

Then we define the **feature matrix** $\mathbf{X}$ as a matrix whose rows are composed of the data points:

$$\mathbf{X} = \begin{bmatrix} \mathbf{x}_1 \\ \vdots \\ \mathbf{x}_m \end{bmatrix} \tag{41.3}$$

Usually we will want to have the data **zero-centered**, that is, transformed to a new coordinate system so that the average values in each axis are at the origin. If

$$\mu_x = \frac{1}{m} \sum_{j=1}^{m} x_j \text{ and } \mu_y = \frac{1}{m} \sum_{j=1}^{m} y_m \tag{41.4}$$

then the zero centered matrix (for a data set in the plane) will look like

$$\mathbf{X} = \begin{bmatrix} x_1 - \mu_x & y_1 - \mu_y \\ x_2 - \mu_x & y_2 - \mu_y \\ \vdots & \vdots \\ x_m - \mu_x & y_m - \mu_y \end{bmatrix} \tag{41.5}$$

The **scatter matrix** $\mathbf{X}^{\mathrm{T}}\mathbf{X}$ occurs frequently in statistical analysis. For two dimensional data, it is computed as

$$\mathbf{X}^{\mathrm{T}}\mathbf{X} = \begin{bmatrix} x_1 - \mu_x & y_1 - \mu_y \\ x_2 - \mu_x & y_2 - \mu_y \\ \vdots & \vdots \\ x_m - \mu_x & y_m - \mu_y \end{bmatrix}^{\mathrm{T}} \begin{bmatrix} x_1 - \mu_x & y_1 - \mu_y \\ x_2 - \mu_x & y_2 - \mu_y \\ \vdots & \vdots \\ x_m - \mu_x & y_m - \mu_y \end{bmatrix} \tag{41.6}$$

$$= \begin{bmatrix} x_1 - \mu_x & \cdots & x_m - \mu_x \\ y_1 - \mu_y & \cdots & y_m - \mu_y \end{bmatrix} \begin{bmatrix} x_1 - \mu_x & y_1 - \mu_y \\ x_2 - \mu_x & y_2 - \mu_y \\ \vdots & \vdots \\ x_m - \mu_x & y_m - \mu_y \end{bmatrix} \tag{41.7}$$

$$= \begin{bmatrix} \sum(x_j - \mu_x)^2 & \sum(x_j - \mu_x)(y_j - \mu_y) \\ \sum(x_j - \mu_x)(y_j - \mu_y) & \sum(y_j - \mu_y)^2 \end{bmatrix} \tag{41.8}$$

$$= (m - 1)\mathrm{cov}(\mathbf{X}) \tag{41.9}$$

where $\mathrm{cov}(\mathbf{X})$ is the covariance matrix of the data set that is represented by $\mathbf{X}$. Note that this proportionality only works if the data set is centered.

> ### Definition 41.2. Scatter Matrix
>
> Let $\mathbf{X}$ be a centered feature matrix. Then the **scatter matrix** $\mathbf{S}$ (also called the **covariance matrix**, $\mathbf{cov}(\mathbf{X})$), is
>
> $$\mathbf{S} = \mathbf{X}^{\mathrm{T}}\mathbf{X} = \mathrm{cov}(\mathbf{X}) \tag{41.10}$$

> ### Definition 41.3. Principal Direction
>
> The **principal directions** of the centered data set 41.5 are the eigenvectors of the covariance matrix $\mathbf{S}$.

> ### Definition 41.4. Principal Components
>
> The **principal components** of a data set $\mathbf{X}$ are the projections of the data set onto its principal directions.

In particular, once you know the principal directions $\mathbf{v}_i$ of a centered data set $\mathbf{X}$, then the principal components of that data set are the projections $\mathbf{X}\mathbf{v}_i$. If the $\mathbf{v}_i$ are the column vectors of a matrix $\mathbf{V}$, then we compute $\mathbf{X}\mathbf{V}$. This is sometimes used for data set **dimensionality reduction**. It is not unusual for a data set to be oriented in such a way that many of its principal components are dominant. We can choose the projection of the data set into the subspace represented by the dominant components to get a lower dimensional representation that contains nearly all of the information that is contained in the original data set.

> ### Theorem 41.1. Principal Component Calculation Theorem
>
> Let $\mathbf{X}$ represent a zero centered data set with singular value decomposition $\mathbf{X} = \mathbf{U}\Sigma\mathbf{V}^{\mathrm{T}}$. Then the principal directions of $\mathbf{X}$ are the column vectors of $\mathbf{V}$.

Proof. We expand the matrix $\mathbf{S} = \mathbf{X}^{\mathrm{T}}\mathbf{X}$ using its singular value decomposition,

$$\mathbf{S} = \mathbf{X}^{\mathrm{T}}\mathbf{X} = (\mathbf{U}\Sigma\mathbf{V}^{\mathrm{T}})^{\mathrm{T}}(\mathbf{U}\Sigma\mathbf{V}^{\mathrm{T}}) \tag{41.11}$$

Since the transpose of a product is the product of the transposes in the reverse order,

$$\mathbf{S} = \mathbf{V}\Sigma\mathbf{U}^{\mathrm{T}}\mathbf{U}\Sigma\mathbf{V}^{\mathrm{T}} \tag{41.12}$$

Since $\mathbf{U}$ is is orthogonal, then $\mathbf{U}^{\mathrm{T}}\mathbf{U} = \mathbf{I}$ (the identity matrix), and thus

$$\mathbf{S} = \mathbf{V}\Sigma^2\mathbf{V}^{\mathrm{T}} \tag{41.13}$$

Right multiplying by $\mathbf{V}$,

$$\mathbf{S}\mathbf{V} = \mathbf{V}\Sigma^2\mathbf{V}^{\mathrm{T}}\mathbf{V} = \mathbf{V}\Sigma^2\mathbf{I} = \mathbf{V}\Sigma^2 \tag{41.14}$$

because **V** is orthogonal. Since Σ is diagonal, so is Σ^2. If s_i, $i = 1, 2, \ldots, k$ are the numbers on the diagonal of Σ, then $s_1^2, s_2^2, \ldots, s_k^2$ are on the diagonal of Σ^2.

Let $\mathbf{v}_1, \mathbf{v}_2, \ldots, \mathbf{v}_k$ be the column vectors of **V**. Then $\mathbf{SV} = \mathbf{V}\Sigma^2$ becomes

$$\mathbf{S}\left[\,\mathbf{v}_1\,\middle|\,\mathbf{v}_2\,\middle|\,\cdots\,\middle|\,\mathbf{v}_k\,\right] = \left[\,\mathbf{v}_1\,\middle|\,\mathbf{v}_2\,\middle|\,\cdots\,\middle|\,\mathbf{v}_k\,\right]\begin{bmatrix} s_1^2 & 0 & \cdots & 0 \\ 0 & s_2^2 & & \vdots \\ \vdots & 0 & \ddots & 0 \\ 0 & \cdots & 0 & s_k^2 \end{bmatrix} \tag{41.15}$$

$$= \left[\,s_1^2\mathbf{v}_1\,\middle|\,s_2^2\mathbf{v}_2\,\middle|\,\cdots\,\middle|\,s_k^2\mathbf{v}_k\,\right] \tag{41.16}$$

Equating the columns,
$$\mathbf{Sv}_j = s_j^2\mathbf{v}_j, \, j = 1, 2, \ldots, k \tag{41.17}$$

Thus the s_j^2 are the eigenvalues of **S** and the $\mathbf{v}_j$ are the corresponding eigenvectors. It is customary to order these so that $s_1^2 \geq s_2^2 \geq \cdots \geq s_k^2$.

Algorithm 41.1 Principal Components of a Data Set.

---
input: Data set represented by zero-centered matrix **X**
1: $\mathbf{U}, \Sigma, \mathbf{V}^{\mathrm{T}} \leftarrow \mathbf{SVD(X)}$
2: **return** $\left[\,\mathbf{v}_1\,\middle|\,\mathbf{v}_2\,\middle|\,\cdots\,\middle|\,\mathbf{v}_k\,\right]$ (column vectors of **V**)

All of the matrix operations required to perform principal component analysis can be found in the numpy package **numpy.linalg**. To illustrate this, we can extract the cost of gasoline per gallon and the cost of electricity per kilowatt hour from the US Bureau of Labor Statistics (http://data.bls.gov/cgi-bin/surveymost?ap). We have extracted this data at monthly intervals into two lists **g** and **e** for the ten year period 2004 through 2014. We can create a data array **x** with

```
>>> X=np.array([g,e]).T
>>> print X
[[ 1.592  0.091]
 [ 1.672  0.091]
 ...
 [ 2.56   0.135]]
```

To center the data, we need to subtract the mean of the x values from each x values, and the mean of the y values from each y values. The numpy function **np.mean** returns an array of mean values calculated along each axis. We use this to define a centering function for any matrix of centered values.

```
def centerArray(M):
    mu = np.mean(M, 0)
    return M-mu
```

When we center the data, each value is measured from its mean.

```
1  >>> X=centerArray(X)
2  >>> print X
```

```
3    [[ -1.32008333e+00  -2.99166667e-02]
4     [ -1.24008333e+00  -2.99166667e-02]
5     ...
6     [ -2.50833333e-02   1.30833333e-02]
7     [ -3.52083333e-01   1.40833333e-02]]
```

We can obtain the direction vectors of the principal components using the singular value decomposition.

```
>>> U, S, V=np.linalg.svd(X)
>>> print "The first PC is ", V[0]
>>> print "The second PC is ", V[1]
The first PC is  [ 0.99988131  0.01540671]
The second PC is  [-0.01540671  0.99988131]
```

To visualize the principal component, we want to construct a line through the center point (μ_x, μ_y) (the same point that was used to center the data) and in the direction of the principal value. We can use the parameterization of a line to do this. If **C** is the center point then the line is the locus of all points **C**+t**P**, where **P** is the vector **v**[0] computed above. We pick points t that will take our line off-scale to the left and right to get two end points, and then use the **plot** function.

```
PC=v[0]
mug = np.average(g)
mue = np.average(e)
center=np.array([mug,mue])
P=center - 3*PC[0]
Q=center + 3*PC[0]
plot([P[0],Q[0]], [P[1],Q[1]], color="k",linewidth=3)
```

After adding scales and labels, the plot looks like this.

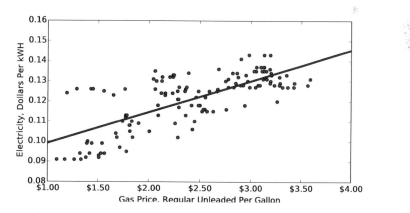

To see how PCA can be used for dimensionality reduction consider the 3D data set:

```
rawdata=np.array([[8.3, -41.0, 28.7],[ 6.5, -38.5, 29.5],
                  [0.5, -39.2, 28.6],[ 1.6, -41.8, 28.0],
                  [5.0, -37.6, 30.0],[-0.1, -40.3, 28.1],
                  [6.1, -42.2, 28.2]])
```

Centering the data gives

```
>>> X=centerArray(rawdata); np.round(X,2)
array([[ 4.31, -0.91, -0.03],
       [ 2.51,  1.59,  0.77],
       [-3.49,  0.89, -0.13],
       [-2.39, -1.71, -0.73],
       [ 1.01,  2.49,  1.27],
       [-4.09, -0.21, -0.63],
       [ 2.11, -2.11, -0.53]])
```

To reduce the dimensionality, we compute the SVD and project the data onto each component.

```
>>> U, S, V = np.linalg.svd(X)
>>> np.round(np.dot(X, V.T),2)
array([[-4.27, -1.09, -0.12],
       [-2.61,  1.62, -0.09],
       [ 3.47,  0.97, -0.1 ],
       [ 2.48, -1.73,  0.17],
       [-1.18,  2.72,  0.19],
       [ 4.13, -0.21, -0.11],
       [-2.01, -2.27,  0.06]])
```

We drop the 3rd column to get the projection onto the first two components. We can also do this with **sklearn**.

```
>>> from sklearn.decomposition import PCA
>>> pca = PCA(n_components=2)
>>> np.round(pca.fit_transform(X),2)
array([[-4.27, -1.09],
       [-2.61,  1.62],
       [ 3.47,  0.97],
       [ 2.48, -1.73],
       [-1.18,  2.72],
       [ 4.13, -0.21],
       [-2.01, -2.27]])
```

Setting **components=2** in **sklearn.decomposition.PCA** we perform the SVD and extract the first two components, the same as computed previously. If we had included all of the components we would still get the same answer for the first two:

```
>>> from sklearn.decomposition import PCA
>>> pca = PCA(n_components=3)
>>> np.round(pca.fit_transform(X),2)
array([[-4.27, -1.09, -0.12],
       [-2.61,  1.62, -0.09],
       [ 3.47,  0.97, -0.1 ],
       [ 2.48, -1.73,  0.17],
       [-1.18,  2.72,  0.19],
       [ 4.13, -0.21, -0.11],
       [-2.01, -2.27,  0.06]])
```

In addition, **sklearn** will tell us how much of the variance in the data is accounted for by each principal component:

```
>>> pca.explained_variance_ratio_
array([ 0.76254115,  0.23613593,  0.00132292])
```

Thus 76% of the variation occurs in the first component and 24% in the second component. Only about 0.13% of the variation is accounted for by the third principal component, which illustrates how it is reasonable to ignore the third dimension in this data set (fig. 41.2).

Figure 41.2: Left: nearly planar data set, plotted in three dimensions. Right: projection to plane of first two principal components.

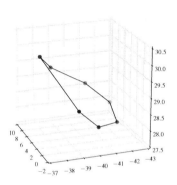 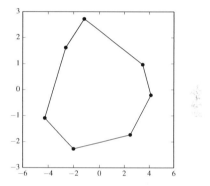

Exercises

1. Write a function that will generate a n points randomly scattered in $\mathbb{R}$ with a Gaussian probability density, centered at the origin and with standard deviations σ_x and σ_y.

2. Modify the function you wrote in exercise 1 to have a center at (h, k) and with the axes rotated by an angle θ.

3. Generate a Gaussian cloud centered at $(3, 5)$ with standard deviations $(2, 1)$, rotated by 30 degrees. Find the principal axes

of the cloud using PCA.

4. Generate Gaussian clouds centered at $(1, 2)$, $(0, 0)$, $(3, 0)$ and $(4, -2)$ with standard deviations $(2,1)$, $(1.5, 1)$, $(1,1)$, $(1,1)$ and sizes 150, 400, 300, 250 points, respectively. Make a scatter plot. Use **scipy.cluser.vg.kmeans2** to cluster the data using $k =2,3,4,5$, and 6 clusters. For each value of k, generate a plot with the points in each cluster plotted in a different color.

Chapter 42

Clustering

Given a set of points $S = \{\mathbf{p}_1, \mathbf{p}_2, \dots\}$, can we identify a non-overlapping, partition of $S = S_1 \cup S_2 \cup \cdots$ such that each of the S_i represents a physically meaningful piece of information about the data? Each object that we identify in a data set is called a **cluster**, and the problem of correctly identifying all the clusters in a set is called **clustering**. The 2D images in figure 42.1 are simple examples consisting of easily partitionable sets of points. We can easily pick out the blobs, facial features and sinusoidial waves by eye. Automatic clustering is another story altogether, and many different algorithms for clustering have been devised to solved these, and other, sorts of problems.[1]

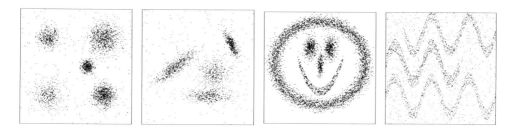

Figure 42.1: Examples of two dimensional data sets to be clustered.

In general the problem is of more practical interest in high dimensional data sets. For example, clustering can identify the products that customers buy at the say time. A retailer could use this information to offer other products for purchase, either via store signs, coupons on the back of receipts, or pop-up browser ads. Rather than give a comprehensive view of clustering, we will discuss three of the most popular methods: **k-means**, **DBSCAN**, and **hierarchical** clustering.

Centroid-Based Clustering: k-means

In the **k-means** centroid based clustering algorithm we identify a single characteristic point for each cluster that is **responsible** for each point in the cluster. These points represent cluster centroids. The input to the algorithm is the number of clusters N. Since we have no idea where the centroids should be, we place N points $\mathbf{C}_1, \dots, \mathbf{C}_N$, at random locations in the space spanned by the data set. Next, we calculate the distance between each point $\mathbf{p}_i$, $i = 1, \dots, n$ and each responsible point $\mathbf{C}_j$, $j = 1, \dots, N$. We assign point $\mathbf{p}_i$ to cluster k if $\mathbf{p}_i$ is closer to $\mathbf{C}_k$ than it is to any of the other $\mathbf{C}_j$ for

---

[1] For a textbook level review of clustering see M. Zaki and W. Meira (2014) *Data Mining and Analysis: Fundamental Concepts and Algorithms*, chapters 13-17, pp. 333-466.

$j \neq k$. In other words, point $\mathbf{p}_i$ is assigned to the center k that *minimizes* the distance $\|\mathbf{C}_k - \mathbf{p}_i\|$ over all values of k. We say that

$$\kappa_i = \operatorname*{argmin}_k \|\mathbf{C}_k - \mathbf{p}_i\| \tag{42.1}$$

where κ_i is the new cluster assignment for point i. The argmin function means return the argument (e.g., input value) that minimizes the given function, rather than returning the value of the function itself. Thus $\operatorname{argmin}(f(x))$ means the value of x that minimizes $f(X)$. Next, we adjust the cluster centers to be the centroids of the new assignments.

$$\mathbf{C}_k = \frac{\sum_{j=1}^n I_{kj}\mathbf{p}_j}{\sum_{j=1}^n I_{kj}} \tag{42.2}$$

Here I_{ij} is an **indicator function**, so that $I_{kj} = 1$ if $\mathbf{p}_j$ is in cluster k, and zero otherwise. We then repeat the process until centers have converged numerically.

The k-means centroids will converge to Voronoi centers (chapter 31) of their identified clusters. Unfortunately, there may be more than one solution, so k-means should be run multiple times with different starting points to verify that an optimal solution is reached. As illustrated in figure 42.2, while it works well with well-separated Gaussian clouds, guessing the correct number of clusters is crucial. Using a value of k that is too small or too big will result in grouped or artificially split clusters, and if the clusters are too close, they may not be well separated.

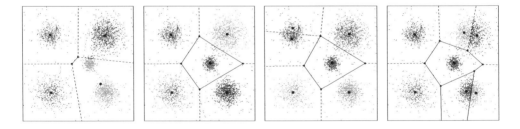

Figure 42.2: Clustering of Gaussian clouds with k-means (each cluster shown in a different color), for $k = 4, 5, 6, 7$, and the corresponding Voronoi diagrams of the cluster centers. The frame on the far left has too few clusters, and the two frames on the right artificially splits clusters. Furthermore, for $k = 5$, part of the cluster in the upper right is included in the center cluster.

The k-means algorithm is implemented in **scipy.cluster.vq**. The data should be defined as an array of vectors, e.g.,

```
X=np.array([[x1,y1,..],
            [x2,y2,..],..,
            [xn,yn,..]])
```

In two dimensions, if your x and y values are in the data arrays **x** and **y** respectively, then **X=np.array(zip(x,y)** will be sufficient. Then the clustering function is **kmeans2**

```
C,flags=kmeans2(X,k)
```

where **k** is the desired number of clusters. *The algorithm will always find **k** clusters.*[2]

kmeans2 returns two objects:

- **C**, a $k \times p$ (p = the data dimension) array of cluster centroids
- **flags**, where **flags[j]** is the cluster number of data point **X[j]**. To get a list of unique cluster labels, use **list(set(flags))**.

To extract the data for plotting:

```
from matplotlib import colors as clrs
colors=list(clrs.cnames)
for i in range(k):
    xdata = [p for p,q,f in zip(x,y,flags) if f==i]
    ydata = [q for p,q,f in zip(x,y,flags) if f==i]
    c=colors[i]
    plt.scatter(xdata,ydata,edgecolor=c,s=1)
```

Alternatively, you can assign a list of color names to the variable **colors**.

The k-means algorithm works best when the data can be separated into non-overlapping Gaussian blobs. When this is not the case, other methods may work better (fig. 42.3).

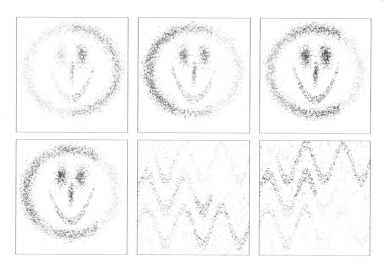

Figure 42.3: The k-means algorithm fails when the clusters are contorted. The smiley face uses $k = 2, 3, 4,$ and 5; and the sine waves use $k = 3$ and 4.

It turns out that k-means is actually a special case of the **Expectation-Maximization (EM)** clustering algorithm.[3] In the EM algorithm, rather than making a "hard" assignment of each point to a cluster, the clusters are assumed to be described by probability distributions. The two iterative steps in k-means of (1) minimizing the distances; and (2) calculating the cluster centers are replaced by expectation (E) and maximization (M) steps. In the E step, each point is assigned to the *most likely cluster*. In the M step,

---

[2]Full details are given at http://docs.scipy.org/doc/scipy-0.14.0/reference/generated/scipy.cluster.vq.kmeans2.html#scipy.cluster.vq.kmeans2

[3]For a proof see C.M.Bishop (2006) *Pattern Recognition and Machine Learning*, chapter 9.

the new probabilities are calculated based on the new assignments. The EM algorithm is implemented in the Python package **sklearn.mixture.GMM**.[4]

Topological Based Clustering - DBSCAN

The **DBSCAN** Algorithm[5] is follows the overall shapes of clusters by looking at points in very small neighborhoods of each other. There are two input parameters: ϵ, N. We use these to define the concept of an ϵ-**neighborhood** $N_\epsilon(\mathbf{p})$ of a point,

$$N_\epsilon(\mathbf{p}) = \{\mathbf{q}|\|\mathbf{p} - \mathbf{q}\| \leq \epsilon\} \tag{42.3}$$

There are three types of points in the algorithm: **core points** (those that fall inside a cluster); **border points** (on the edge of cluster; and **noise** (points that do not fall into any cluster.

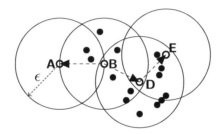

Figure 42.4: **B** and **D** are core points; **A** and **E** are border points. **A** is directly directly density reachable from **B** but not vice-versa (using $N = 5$). **E** is density reachable from **B** but not from **A**. **A** and **E** are density connected to each other by **B**

The following concepts behind DBSCAN are illustrated in figure 42.4.

- **p** is a core point if $|N_\epsilon(\mathbf{p})| \geq N$
- **p** is **directly density reachable from q** if (a) $\mathbf{p} \in N_\epsilon(q)$ and (b) $|N_\epsilon(\mathbf{q})| \geq N$.[6]
- **p** is **density reachable** from **q** if there is a sequence of points $\mathbf{q} = \mathbf{p}_1, \mathbf{p}_2, \ldots, \mathbf{p}_n = \mathbf{q}$ such that each $\mathbf{p}_{i+1}$ is directly density reachable form $\mathbf{p}_i$.
- **p** is **density connected** to **q** if there is a point **x** such that both **p** and **q** are density reachable from **x**.
- If S is a set of points, the C is a **cluster of points** in S if $\forall \mathbf{p}, \mathbf{q} \in C$, (a) if $\mathbf{p} \in C$ and **q** is density reachable from **p**, then $\mathbf{q} \in C$; and **p** is density connected to **q**.

The DBSCAN algorithm then proceeds through all the points **p** in set S. Let $C = \{\mathbf{p}\}$. Then C is expanded into the maximally density connected set containing **p**, by first examining each point in $N_\epsilon(\mathbf{p})$, and then recursively considering the ϵ neighborhood of the added points. This process is continued until all points have been clustered.

---

[4]http://scikit-learn.org/stable/modules/mixture.html
[5]Ester et. al (1996) *A density-based algorithm for discovering clusters in large spatial databases with noise*, KDD96, https://www.aaai.org/Papers/KDD/1996/KDD96-037.pdf The paper is easily readable by students.
[6]The absolute value on the set denotes the number of points in the set.

DBSCAN is implemented in `sklearn.cluster`.[7] In this case, **DBSCAN** is a class object that must be *created* by assigning data, and then queried to get results. The **DBSCAN** class has two parameters: `eps`, the parameter ϵ, the radius of the ϵ-neighborhood; and `min_samples`, corresponding to N, the minimum number of points required in the definition of the neighborhood. The class function `fit` takes one parameter `X`, an array of feature vectors. To cluster with $\epsilon = .1$ and $N = 5$,

```
from sklearn.cluster import DBSCAN
X=np.array([[x1,y1],[x2,y2],...,[xn,yn]])
db=DBSCAN(eps=.1, min_samples=5).fit(X)
```

We extract the clustering results from **DBSCAN.labels_**, which has a value once `fit` has been called. It contains an array of integers giving the class assignments. Points that are classified as noise are assigned a value of -1. If you want to make a color plot, you can determine a unique set of labels by converting to a **set** object.

```
labels=db.labels_
unique_labels = set(labels)
```

In this case you would have to assign `len(unique_labels)` color names for the clusters. This can be done the same way we plotted the results for k-means. The results of applying DBSCAN to the smiley face and sine waves from fig. 42.1 are shown in fig. 42.5

Figure 42.5: Clustering with DBSCAN of the smileyface with $\epsilon = .09$ and $N = 10$ and the sinusoids with $\epsilon = .05$ and $N = 5$.

Hierarchical Clustering

The idea behind **hierarchical clustering** (HC) is that similar objects should be in the same cluster. Similarity is measured by a distance metric. HC algorithms are then used to build tree-like structures where each instance (point) is a single node of the tree. Methods are either "bottom-up" or "top-down." In an bottom-up HC algorithm, each point is considered as a separate node. Similar points are then joined together to form clusters; this process is repeated until all of the clusters have been joined together (**agglomerative clustering**). Alternatively, in the top-down approach all of the points

---

[7]http://scikit-learn.org/stable/modules/generated/sklearn.cluster.DBSCAN.html#sklearn.cluster.DBSCAN

can be considered to form one super-cluster, and then the clusters divided recursively (**divisive clustering**).

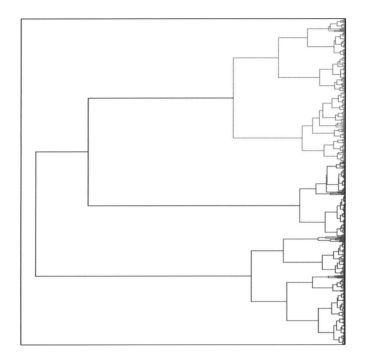

Figure 42.6: Dendrogram for the clouds from frame 2 in fig. 42.1.

Hierarchical clustering was one of the first[8] clustering algorithms developed, and hence there are many different implementations in both **scipy**[9] and **sklearn**.[10] In **scipy**, we first build a **linkage matrix** and then can identify the clusters from a **dendrogram**. The dendrogram is the tree-plot that shows how the clusters are built.

```
import scipy.cluster.hierarchy as HC
X=np.array([[x1,y1],[x2,y2],..,[xn,yn]])]
L=HC.linkage(X) # Build Linkage matrix
```

You can use the linkage matrix to plot a dendrogram. For the elliptical cloud data (frame 2 of fig. 42.1), the dendrogram shown in fig. 42.6 would suggest somewhere around three to ten clusters is appropriate. A more sophisticate analysis than just "eyeballing" the tree is required to determine an appropriate number mathematically.

```
p=HC.dendrogram(L, truncate_mode="none", orientation="right",
    no_labels=True)
```

---

[8]For example, J. Ward (1963) "Hierarchical Grouping to Optimize an Objective Function," *J. Am. Stat. Assn.* **58**(301):236-244 proposed a least-squares distance metric for agglomerative clustering.
[9]http://docs.scipy.org/doc/scipy/reference/cluster.hierarchy.html#module-scipy.cluster.hierarchy
[10]http://scikit-learn.org/stable/modules/generated/sklearn.cluster.AgglomerativeClustering.html#sklearn.cluster.AgglomerativeClustering

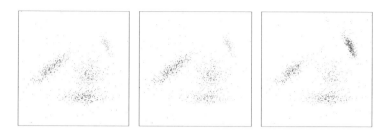

Figure 42.7: Hierarchical clustering of cloud data for 3, 4 or 5 clusters.

If we let **n** be the number of clusters we want, then we can extract the cluster labels as a array of integers with **fcluster**.

```
labels=HC.fcluster(L, n, 'maxclust')
```

fcluster returns an array that has the same length as the number of points in the original data **x**. We can plot the clusters as we did with the other clustering algorithms. The results for the clouds with $n = 3, 4, 5$ are shown in fig. 42.7.

Cluster Validation

When you look a picture like the smiley face or the cloud plots shown in this chapter you can tell immediately whether or not the algorithm worked and how many clusters you need to find. In general, however, this is not the case. Large databases may have millions of records, where each record has hundreds to thousands of components. It is difficult enough to visualize in three dimensions, much less a thousand-dimensional database. So we need some algorithm to tell us when we have found a suitable number of clusters. A complete discussion of this topic is beyond our scope;[11] we will mention two measures, but only briefly.

The most commonly used measure is the **silhouette coefficient**, which compares the points in each cluster with those in other clusters.[12] If $\mathbf{p}_i$ is in cluster C, let

$$\mu_i(\mathbf{p}_i) = \text{mean distance from } \mathbf{p}_i \text{ to points } \mathbf{q}_j \neq \mathbf{p}_i, \forall \mathbf{q}_j \in C$$
$$\mu_i'(\mathbf{p}_i) = \text{mean distance from } \mathbf{p}_i \text{ to points } \mathbf{q}_j, \forall \mathbf{q}_j \notin C$$
$$M_i(\mathbf{p}_i) = \max_j(\mu_i, \mu_i')$$

The the following silhouette score should be close to one:

$$S = \frac{1}{n} \sum_{i=1}^{n} \frac{\mu_i'(\mathbf{p}_i) - \mu_i(\mathbf{p}_i)}{M_i(\mathbf{p}_i)} \tag{42.4}$$

Terms in the sum that are more negative come from points that are closer to other

---

[11] For a good review see Zaki and Meira, op.cit., chapter 17.

[12] P.J.Rousseeuw(1987) "Silhouettes: A graphical aid to the interpretation and validation of cluster analysis." *J. Comp. Appl. Math.* **20**:53-65.

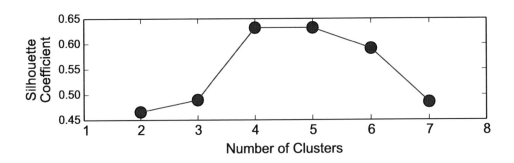

Figure 42.8: Silhouette score for k-means clustering of the Gaussian clouds from figure 42.2. The maximum value is at $k = 5$ clusters, but there is very little difference between 4 and 5. A visual inspection of the original data, however, tells us that there are clearly 5 clusters.

clusters; thus clusterings with an average closer to positive one are better-defined (figure 42.8). The silhouette score can be calculated via

```
\from sklearn.metrics import sillhouette_score
s=silhouette_score(X, labels)
```

Another common measure the **Calinski-Harabasz Index (CI Index)**, defined as[13]

$$I(k) = \left[\frac{n-k}{k-1} \right] \frac{\text{tr}\mathbf{S}'}{\text{tr}\mathbf{S}} \qquad (42.5)$$

where $\mathbf{S}$ and $\mathbf{S}'$ are the in-cluster and between-cluster scatter matrices (def. 41.2.) The idea here is to plot $I(k)$ as a function of the number of clusters k and look foe the "elbow," the point beyond which there is no significant change.

---

[13]T. Calinski, J. Harabasz, (1974) "A dendrite method for cluster analysis." *Commun. Statist.* **3**(1):127.

Chapter 43

Image Analysis

Image Representation

A digital image[1] can be represented by a two-dimensional array of numbers, where each number represents a single pixel. We will therefore find it convenient to represent an image by a function $f(r, c)$ that gives the intensity or color the pixel at row r and column c. Most of image processing is based on transforming this function. We will examine many of these transformations on the images shown in figure 43.2.

In **monochrome images** (black and white, figure 43.1) the number is either a zero or a 1. In **gray-scale images** (or **gray-level images**) the number represents an intensity value, usually between 0 and 255 (for 8-bit gray-scale); sometimes we normalize this to a real number between 0 and 1.

Figure 43.1: A 25×25 pixel monochrome representation of the Northridge N as a matrix of ones and zeros (left) and the image (right).

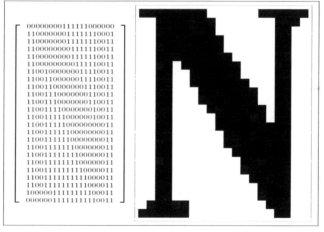

Colors are represented by tuples of three or four integers; there are several standard systems. The values are typically either 8-bit or 16-bit integers. In **RGB images**, three numbers represent Red, Green and Blue intensity levels (again, either in the range [0,1] or [0,255], depending on the implementation). With 8-bit values, there are $3 \times 8 = 24$ total bits, which allows the system to represent up to $2^{24} = 16,777,216$ different colors. With 16-bit values, up to $2^{48} = 281,474,976,710,656$ different colors

---

[1]An excellent reference on image analysis is R.C. Gonzalez and R.E.Woods, Digital Image Processing, 3rd Edition, Prentice Hall (2008).

Figure 43.2: Images used in this chapter. The pictures of the Hollywood sign[a] and of David Hilbert[b] are from Wikimedia.

[a]See `http://commons.wikimedia.org/wiki/File:Aerial_Hollywood_Sign.jpg` (released to public domain by photographer).
[b]See `http://commons.wikimedia.org/wiki/File:Hilbert.jpg` (public domain).

can be represented. Web pages also use the RGB system, with the three 8-bit numbers combined into a single six hexit representation.

In **CMY images** the numbers refer to Cyan, Magenta, and Yellow. The reason for the two systems is that most printers deposit pigments in each of the three CMY colors, but the light measured by most imaging systems is composed of RGB components. In fact, the two systems are equivalent, because when illuminated by white light, cyan pigment will not reflect any red; magenta pigment will not reflect any green light; and yellow pigment will not reflect any blue light. The conversion between the two systems is given by $C = 1 - R, M = 1 - G, Y = 1 - B$. Most printers also add a fourth pigment, black, which is the predominant color in printing; otherwise, equal amounts of each of the three other CMY pigments would have to be combined to produce black. The resulting system is called **CMYK**.

Physiological perception is described by a fourth representation, called **HSI** (for Hue, Saturation, Intensity). This system is sometimes useful in describing things in terms of observed colors like brown, which is easier to visualize than "a color that reflects 60% red, 40% green and 20% blue light." The conversion, where R, G, and B are normalized to [0,1], is given by the equations

$$\left.\begin{array}{l} H = \theta, \text{ if } B \leq G, \text{ and } 360 - \theta \text{ otherwise, where} \\[2mm] \theta = \cos^{-1} \dfrac{[(R - G) + (R - B)]/2}{\sqrt{(R - G)^2 + (R - B)(G - B)}} \\[4mm] S = 1 - \dfrac{3}{R + G + B} \times \min(R, G, B) \\[3mm] I = \dfrac{R + G + B}{3} \end{array}\right\} \qquad (43.1)$$

In Python's Pyplot library, the functions **imread**, **imshow**, and **imsave** can be used to read an image file into a matrix, display an image stored as a matrix on the screen, and save the image as a file.

However, there is a much more powerful package for image processing available called the **Python Imaging Library** or `pil` or `image`. To read in and display the file `hollywood.jpg` with `image`, its as easy as this:

```
import Image
picture=Image.open("hollywood.jpg")
picture.show()
```

To get some basic information about the figure, once its been imported, we can look at the pictures property values.

```
>>> print picture.format
JPEG
>>> print picture.size
(1666, 761)
>>> print picture.mode
RGB
```

If we are only interested in working with a particular part of the picture, we can crop it. The function `crop(box=(left,upper,right,lower)` will return a cropped version of the picture. The various values are measured in pixels, where (0,0) is at the upper left hand corner of the image (this is standard in image processing). So to crop around the letter H in the Hollywood sign,

```
H = picture.crop(box=(200,300,400,600))
H.show()
H.save("H.jpg")
```

This gives a little picture that looks like this:

Unlike Pyplot, the `show()` command does not tie up your console – it spawns a separate process (using a program called ImageMagick) in a different window to display the file.

Intensity Transformation

Intensity transformations convert one set of pixel values to another set of pixel values,

$$g(x,y) = \mathbf{T}[f(x,y)] \tag{43.2}$$

for some transformation operator $\mathbf{T}$. Presumably this transformation will provide some kind of information about or enhancement of the image.

The most important transformations that we will perform on images are: (1) contrast enhancement; (2) Noise reduction; and (3) Feature identification. In this subsection we we will discuss contrast enhancement. Noise reduction and feature identification are often performed with the transformations and filtering techniques discussed in the subsequent subsections.

Table 43.1. The Python Imaging Package - Module Image

Functions	Returns
`new(mode,size, color)`	A new image. **color** optional.
`open(file, mode)`	Inputs image from a file.
`blend(im1,im2,alpha)`	Image with pixels $x_1(1-\alpha_1)+x_2\alpha$
`composite(im1,im2,mask)`	Interpolates between the **im1**, **im2**. **mask** is an image of α's.
`eval(image,f)`	Evaluates function **f** pixelwise on **f**.
`fromstring(mode,size,data)`	Reads a new image from a string.
`merge(mode,bands)`	Merges images from different bands.

Method	Returns
`im.convert(mode)`	Converts image to another mode. Typical modes are **"L"** (short for luminance, but really means grayscale; **"RGB"**; **"CMYK"**
`im.copy()`	Returns a copy of the image.
`im.crop(box)`	Crops the image. **box** is a 4-tuple with the pixel locations of the left, top, right, and bottom coordinates, where (0,0) is the top left hand corner.
`im.filter(filter)`	Filters an image. See table 43.3.
`im.fromstring(data)`	Like the **fromstring()** function, but loads the data into the image **im**.
`im.getbands()`	Tuple with names of the bands, e.g, (**"R","G","B"**) for an RGB image.
`im.getbbox()`	A tight auto-crop of the image.
`im.getcolors()`	A list of the colors in the image.
`im.getdata()`	A flattened list with the pixel values.
`im.getextrema()`	The maximum and minimum pixel values.
`im.getpixel(x,y)`	The value of the pixel at (x,y).
`im.histogram()`	Histogram of **im** (as list of pixel counts).
`im.paste(image, box)`	Paste **image** into **im** at **box**.
`im.point(F)`	Maps table/function **F** to **im**.
`im.putpixel(xy,color)`	Sets the pixel value at the given location.
`im.resize(size,filter)`	Resizes **im**.
`im.rotate(angle)`	Rotates **im**.
`im.save(file)`	Saves to a file.
`im.show(file)`	Shows **im** on the screen.
`im.thumbnail(size)`	Creates a thumbnail image.
`im.transform()`	Transforms the image. Table 43.4
`im.transpose()`	Image transpose.

[a]For more details see http://effbot.org/imagingbook/image.htm# tag-Image.Image.transform.

Table 43.2. Python Image Library `image` attributes

Attribute	Returns
`format`	File format, or **None**.
`mode`	The image mode, as a string:
	`"1"` (1 Bit, B&W)
	`"L"` (8 Bit, grayscale)
	`"LA"` (like `"L"` with alpha)
	`"P"` (8 bit, mapped to a palette)
	`"RGB"` (3×8 bit, color)
	`"RGBA"` (4×8 bit color with transparency mask)
	`"RGBa"` (RGB with alpha)
	`"RGBX"` (RGB with padding)
	`"CMYK"` (4×8 bit color
	`"YCbCr"` (3×8 bit color video format)
	`"I"` (signed 32 bit integers)
	`"F"` (32 bit floating point pixels.
`size`	Image size as (width, height)
`palette`	Color palette table.
`info`	Information dictionary of image metadata.

Suppose we have a low contrast image, such as the upper left-hand corner of the picture of the Hollywood sign, behind the trees (the box in the top image of figure 43.3). The original image was in color; it was converted to a gray scale image in the figure. Cropping to the 75×350 pixel corner area and gray scale conversion was done with

```
corner=picture.crop(box=(0,0,350,75))
graycorner=corner.convert("L")
```

Figure 43.3: Top: Hollywood sign after grey conversion. Bottom Left: Top left hand corner, expanded. Bottom Right: Top left hand corder after contrast stretching.

The cropped corner is expanded and shown by itself on the bottom left of figure 43.3; we see that it is very light and low in contrast. This is because nearly all of the pixels are very close to 1, as all of the intensities are very high.

To get an idea of the distribution of intensities across an image we would calculate an image histogram using the function **histogram**. This function actually returns a list of pixel values for each color level in the figure, not an actual plot of the histogram. The histogram of the intensities of the cropped corners is shown on the left of figure 43.4. To plot this type of histogram, we would use the **bar** function from **pyplot**.

```
h=graycorner.histogram()
from matplotlib.pyplot import *
for i,j in zip(range(len(h)), h):
    bar(i,j,color="white")
xlim(0,255)
show()
```

The original figure (the Hollywood sign) had 256 gray levels. Thus the histogram data has 256 values. If we were to plot the entire histogram directly without collecting the data into larger bins, it would be a very busy plot. For example, the histograms in fig. 43.4 combine 16 adjacent bins together for plotting.

```
fullHistogram=corner.histogram()
binnedHistogram = [sum(fullHistogram[i*16:(i+1)*16])
    for i in range(16)]
```

Figure 43.4: Histograms of the images in fig. 43.3 before (left) and after (right) contrast stretching.

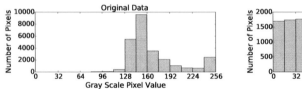 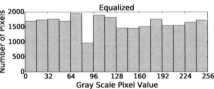

The idea of contrast stretching is to expand the range of intensity values in the image so that all usable values are utilized. Returning to the histogram of the cropped corner from figure 43.3 that is shown on the left of figure 43.4, we observe that there is some minimum intensity i_{min} and some maximum intensity i_{max} that we want to stretch to the entire range [0,1]. Typically this is done with a linear stretch, such as

$$g(x,y) = \frac{f(x,y) - i_{min}}{i_{max} - i_{min}} \tag{43.3}$$

If we apply this sort of stretching function to the cropped corner, we end up with the image shown on the bottom right of figure 43.3. The histogram of the modified image is shown on the right hand side of figure 43.4.

One way to do contrast stretching is to map the image through a lookup table and the **point** function. If we define a table **T** with the new starting values for each of the 256 bins and pass this to **picture.point(T)**, then **point** will remap **picture** so that each new bin starts with the assigned values. This is done in the following code.

```
def equalize(picture):
    grayscale=picture.convert("L")
    Histogram = grayscale.histogram()
    LookUpTable = []
    levels=len(Histogram)
    average = sum(Histogram)/256
    n = 0
    for i in range(256):
        LookUpTable.append(n / average)
        n = n + Histogram[i]
    return picture.point(LookUpTable)
```

In lines 8 through 11, **LookUpTable** is assigned the following values:

$$0, \frac{H_0}{\mu}, \frac{H_0 + H_1}{\mu}, \frac{H_0 + H_1 + H_2}{\mu}, \dots \tag{43.4}$$

Where the histogram is $\{H_0, H_1, H_2, \dots\}$, and $\mu = \frac{1}{256} \sum_i H_i$. These are the number of aggregate pixels that are required in each bin to most nearly linearize the distribution. Thus **equalize(picture)** performs a linear contrast equalization.

Another common contrast enhancement technique is called Gamma correction. A gamma correction uses the non-linear transformation

$$g(x,y) = c[f(x,y)]^\gamma \tag{43.5}$$

for some real positive constants c and γ (see figure 43.5).

Figure 43.5: Left: Gamma correction function for $c = 1$ and different values of γ. Right: Gamma transformations of the image in 43.3 using $\gamma = 1/2, 1, 2, 4$ (top to bottom) and $c = 1$

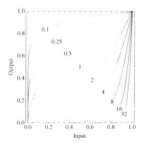

Spatial Filtering

Intensity transforms may be either linear or non-linear. The most common transformation we will use is a **linear spatial filter**. Spatial filters consider all the pixels in some neighborhood of (x, y) and generate the transformed value at that location based on a fixed formula. For example, we may use a 3×3 linear spatial filter, which considers the pixels to the left, right, above, below, and diagonally adjacent. The transformed image is then given by

$$g(x, y) = \sum_{p=-1}^{1} \sum_{q=-1}^{1} k(p, q) f(x + p, y + q) \qquad (43.6)$$

This is an example of a **neighborhood** filter because it only uses information in the neighborhood of pixel (x, y). For example, a filter that averages each pixel with its 8 near neighbors is

$$g(x, y) = \frac{1}{9} \sum_{p=-1}^{1} \sum_{q=-1}^{1} f(x + p, y + q) \qquad (43.7)$$

We will be primarily interested in linear filters of the form

$$K(x, y) \otimes f(x, y) = \sum_{p=-X}^{X} \sum_{q=-Y}^{Y} K(p, q) f(x + p, y + q) \qquad (43.8)$$

where $K(p, q)$ is called the **filter** and the operation $\otimes$ is known as **convolution**, defined by the right hand side of equation 43.8. Conceptually we think of sliding a square box of dimensions $(2X + 1) \times (2Y + 1)$ pixels over parts of the image, and replacing the pixel in the center of the box with a weighted average that is described by the filter K. In general we we want our transformation to be normalized, so that

$$g(x, y) = \frac{K(x, y) \otimes f(x, y)}{\sum_{p=-X}^{X} \sum_{q=-Y}^{Y} K(p, q)} \qquad (43.9)$$

Typically the filter or **kernels** can be represented by grids such as

$$K_1 = \frac{1}{9} \times \begin{array}{|c|c|c|} \hline 1 & 1 & 1 \\ \hline 1 & 1 & 1 \\ \hline 1 & 1 & 1 \\ \hline \end{array}, \qquad K_2 = \frac{1}{16} \times \begin{array}{|c|c|c|} \hline 1 & 2 & 1 \\ \hline 2 & 4 & 2 \\ \hline 1 & 2 & 1 \\ \hline \end{array} \qquad (43.10)$$

These are examples of **smoothing** filters. All of the weights in the kernel are positive and give a numerical approximation to $\iint K(p, q) f(x + p, y + q) dp dq$. The first example ($K_1$) replaces each pixel by the average of it's intensity and the intensity of its adjacent pixels (figure 43.6); the second example (K_2) replaces the pixel with a weighted average. The idea of these filters is to remove random noise, which is usually characterized by sharp, spiky transitions. Unfortunately, edges are also characterized by these sharp transitions so smoothing tends to make the image appear blurry; this is especially pronounced for larger filters.

One of the purposes of smooth filtering is to remove unnecessary data that might cause confusion in feature identification. This is illustrated by the process of **thresholding**:

Figure 43.6: Smoothing using the fixed average (K_1 in eq. 43.10) for filters of size 3, 7, 9, 15, 25, and 50. Compare with the original image in figure 43.2.

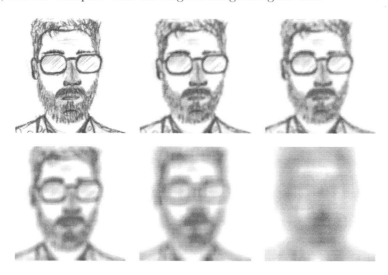

transform every value in the image to either a zero or a 1, depending on whether it is above or below a given threshold. As shown in figure 43.7 this can remove details but still allow the identification of gross features.

Table 43.3. Image Filtering in Python Image Library

Method	Description
`im.filter(filter)`	Filters an image, typically using a filter provided by `ImageFilter`. Existing filters include: `ImageFilter.BLUR` `ImageFilter.CONTOUR` `ImageFilter.EDGE_ENHANCE` `ImageFilter.EDGE_ENHANCE_MORE` `ImageFilter.EMBOSS` `ImageFilter.FIND_EDGES` `ImageFilter.SMOOTH` `ImageFilter.SMOOTH_MORE` `ImageFilter.SHARPEN`
ImageFilter Methods	
`RankFilter(size,rank)`	Creates a rank filter
`MinFilter(size=3)`	Minimum pixel value filter
`MedianFilter(size=3)`	Medium pixel value filter
`MaxFilter(size=3)`	Maximum pixel value filter
`ModeFilter(size=3)`	Mode of pixel values filter

Figure 43.7: Result of thresholding at .7 after smoothing with filters of size 1, 3, 5, 7, 9, 11, 13, 15, 25, and 50. The image at the top left (using the identity 1×1 filter) shows the result of thresholding the original image.

Edge Detection

Sharpening filters are the opposite of smoothing filters: their purpose is to highlight transitions in intensity, rather than hide them, primarily for the purpose of identifying edges between features in objects. Sharpening is generally obtained by differentiating the image in some way, just as smoothing is obtained by integration. Consider the definition of a derivative from calculus:

$$\frac{\partial f(x,y)}{\partial x} = \lim_{h \to 0} \frac{f(x+h,y) - f(x,y)}{h} \tag{43.11}$$

If we measure distance in terms of pixels, then the smallest non-zero distance is a single pixel; approximating $h \approx 1$ pixel will give us a numerical estimate of the derivative:

$$f_x(x,y) \approx f(x+1,y) - f(x,y) \tag{43.12}$$

This is called a **forward** approximation for the derivative at (x,y) because it uses the interval $(x, x+1)$ to approximate $f'(x,y)$. The corresponding **backward** approximation is

$$f_x(x,y) \approx f(x,y) - f(x-1,y) \tag{43.13}$$

because it uses the interval $(x-1, x)$. The backward approximation at x is also equal to the forward approximation at $x - 1$. Taking their difference gives an approximation for the second derivative:

$$\begin{aligned} f_{xx}(x,y) &\approx f_x(x,y) - f_x(x-1,y) \\ &\approx f(x+1,y) - 2f(x,y) + f(x-1,y) \end{aligned} \tag{43.14}$$

Sharp spikes occur at the transitions in the first derivative, while pairs of spikes, one

Figure 43.8: Numerical derivatives of a gray-scale image. The Northridge N on the left is illustrated in gray levels, with white $= 1$ and black $= 0$. The edges taper through intermediate levels in various shades of gray. On the right is $f(x)$ along the horizontal line; $f'(x)$ (middle) and $f''(x)$ (bottom).

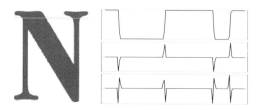

up/one-down, occur in the second derivatives. The second derivative is more useful for edge detection because the passage through zero between the spikes helps to more precisely pin down its location.

Since equation 43.14 only calculates a derivative in the $x-$direction, only changes in intensity as we move parallel to the $x-$axis will be detected. Thus it will react most strongly to edges that are mainly parallel to the $y-$ axis (vertical edges). To get horizontal edges, we want to calculation f_{yy} instead of f_{xx}

$$f_{yy} \approx f(x, y+1) - 2f(x, y) + f(x, y-1) \tag{43.15}$$

and to get edges in all directions, we need to calculate the Laplacian:

$$\nabla^2 f(x, y) = f_{xx}(x, y) + f_{yy}(x, y) \tag{43.16}$$

Hence we get the following **Laplacian Filter** (see figure 43.9):

$$\nabla^2 f \approx f(x+1, y) + f(x-1, y) + f(x, y+1) + f(x, y-1) - 4f(x, y) \tag{43.17}$$

Figure 43.9: Second derivative filters. Left to right: derivatives in the x-axis; the y-axis; along both diagonals simultaneously; along both x- and y- axes simultaneously; and Laplacian.

1	−2	1		1	1	1		1	0	1		0	1	0		1	1	1
1	−2	1		−2	−2	−2		0	−4	0		1	−4	1		1	−8	1
1	−2	1		1	1	1		1	0	1		0	1	0		1	1	1

A variation on this is given by the Sobel Operators.[2] If we define

$$H(x, y) = S_x(x, y) \otimes f(x, y)$$
$$V(x, y) = S_y(x, y) \otimes f(x, y) \tag{43.18}$$

---

[2]I.E.Sobel. Camera Models and Machine Perception. Ph.D. Dissertation, Stanford University (1970).

Figure 43.10: Comparison of Filters. The original image is shown on the left, followed by second derivative filters for Vertical, Horizontal, Diagonal, Vertical plus Horizontal lines, and Laplacian. The filtered images have been color-reversed for clarity.

the transformation is

$$g(x,y) = \sqrt{H(x,y)^2 + V(x,y)^2}$$ (43.19)

where

$$S_x = \begin{array}{|c|c|c|} \hline -1 & 2 & -1 \\ \hline 0 & 0 & 0 \\ \hline -1 & 2 & -1 \\ \hline \end{array} \qquad S_y = \begin{array}{|c|c|c|} \hline -1 & 0 & -1 \\ \hline 2 & 0 & 2 \\ \hline -1 & 0 & -1 \\ \hline \end{array}$$ (43.20)

An even better algorithm is given by the **Canny edge detection** model. Canny[3] observed that noise is described by a Gaussian distribution and found that the optimal Kernel for noise removal is given by

$$G(x,y) = e^{-(x^2+y^2)/(2\sigma^2)}$$ (43.21)

To use this Kernel, we first smooth the image:

$$F(x,y) = G(x,y) \otimes f(x,y)$$ (43.22)

and then apply the Sobel technique using F instead of f. The different methods are compared in figure 43.11.

The Python function **scipy.misc.imfilter** provides several types of image filtering. See http://docs.scipy.org/doc/scipy-0.14.0/reference/generated/scipy. misc.imfilter.html#scipy.misc.imfilter for more details.

---

[3]J. Canny. A Computational Approach for Edge Detection. IEEE Transactions on Pattern Analysis Machine Intelligence. 8(6):679-698 (1986).

Figure 43.11: Comparison of Laplace, Sobel, and Canny algorithms (left to right).

Morphology

So far the image analysis techniques we have examined transform images from one format to another; given one array of pixels, we convert it to another set of pixels. We generally do this to make the picture look better. But we don't just look at pictures, we get information from them. Given an image, we want to extract attributes of that image; usually this involves identifying certain higher level shapes like blobs, lines and spots. To us these things have meaning: the blobs may be peoples' faces; the spots their eyes; and the lines their eyeglasses. Only by some way recognizing these intermediate level features can we hope to eventually perform higher level recognition and analysis of pictorial data.

The first step, of course, is to often to make the picture look better: remove noise, smooth or sharpen the edges, somehow increase its useful information content. The subject of image **morphology** deals with describing the geometric structure of the image such as convex hulls, boundaries and skeletons of the image. The field is heavily based on the discipline of mathematical morphology. Morphological operations on images include the following:

Erosion and Dilation. **Erosion** removes components of an image by contracting boundary elements such as lines; it is useful for removing connections between elements that we think should not be there. **Dilation** increases the visibility of small features by expanding boundary elements; it is useful for bridging gaps between elements that we think really should not be there. Mathematically we define the Erosion of binary image A by B as

$$\text{Erosion}(A, B) = A \ominus B = \{z | B_z \subseteq A\} \tag{43.23}$$

Figure 43.12: Top: Original image (left), dilation (center), and erosion (right). Bottom row: Opening (left) and Closing (right). The borders are not part of the images.

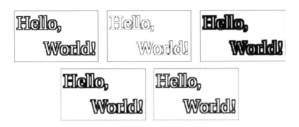

where B_z is the translation of image B by z; and the dilation of A by B is

$$\text{Dilation}(A, B) = A \oplus B = \bigcup_{b \in B} A_b \qquad (43.24)$$

For gray scale images, the definitions are given point-wise (at point $a \in A$), by

$$(A \ominus B)(a) = \inf_{a \in B}[A(z) - B(z - a)]$$
$$(A \oplus B)(a) = \sup_{b \in B}[A(z) - B(z - a)] \qquad (43.25)$$

Opening and Closing. These are global generalizations of erosion and dilation. Opening smooths the contours of an image by removing protrusions and narrow connections:

$$A \circ B = (A \ominus B) \oplus B \qquad (43.26)$$

Closing fuses narrow breaks and eliminates small holes,

$$A \bullet B = (A \oplus B) \ominus B \qquad (43.27)$$

Boundary Extraction. This is similar to edge detection, in that it finds the boundaries of regions in an image. The operations

$$T(A) = (A - (A \ominus B))^c$$
$$S(A) = (A - (A \oplus B)) \qquad (43.28)$$

can both do this. Here I^C is the complement of image I,

$$I(x, y)^c = 1 - I(x, y) \qquad (43.29)$$

and image subtraction is defined point-wise by subtracting pixels:

$$(A - B)(x, y) = A(x, y) - B(x, y) \qquad (43.30)$$

Figure 43.13: Boundary subtraction.

Hello,   Hello,   Hello,
     World!   World!   World!

Hole Filling. A **hole** is defined as a background region surrounded by a connected border of foreground pixels. Hole filling is sometimes called image completion. Hole filling is defined as the following transformation: given an **indicator** point inside a hole, fill the entire hole, e.g., set all the pixels to 1. Let I be the image and $P_0(x, y)$ be an array that only has 1's at the indicator points, and zeros elsewhere. Then define the sequence

$$P_k = (P_{k-1} \oplus B) \bigcap I^c, \text{ where } B = \begin{pmatrix} 0 & 1 & 0 \\ 1 & 1 & 1 \\ 0 & 1 & 0 \end{pmatrix} \tag{43.31}$$

Holes are filled when the fixed point is reached, i.e., $P_k = P_{k-1}$.

Connected Components. In a binary image, two adjacent pixels are said to be **connected** if they are both 1. A pixel is said to be **connected** to the pixel next to it if the two pixels are connected. **Adjacency** can be defined in several ways. The most common are: (a) they are **4-adjacent** if they are above, below, left, or right of one another; and (b) they are **8-adjacent** if they 4-adjacent or diagonally touching. Given any two pixels, they are considered connected if there is some path between them consisting of adjacent connected pixels. Given any pixel, its **connected component** is the set of all pixels that are connected to it. The extraction of connected components is similar to the process of hole filling. Here we define an array of indicator pixels $S_0(x, y)$ where there is one pixel turned on in each connected component. Then we do fixed point iteration on

$$S_k = (S_{k-1} \oplus B) \bigcap I \tag{43.32}$$

Here B is a matrix that defines adjacency: for 4-connectedness it is like the matrix in equation 43.31; for 8-connectedness it would be a matrix of all-ones.

Segmentation

The next step is to divide the picture into subregions that are somehow distinct from one another. This process of separating out the different regions is known as image **segmentation**. Usually we do some sort of edge detection before we do segmentation, e.g., with a Laplacian, Sobel, or Canny Filter. If the image is noisy we may actually want to blur it first

The simplest segmentation method is **thresholding**. Every pixel in the image is converted into either 1's or 0's depending on whether or not it is above a given threshold. This works well if the items we are attempting to identify are in high contrast with the

Figure 43.14: Left: Cross-section of the shoot apical meristem of Arabidopsis Thaliana obtained via confocal microscopy. Center: Segmentation after blurring and extraction of the morphological boundary by thresholding at $T = 0.84$. Right: Segmentation of fig 43.2a by blurring and thresholding at $T = 0.65$.

background environment. Each connected component then defines a particular segment of the image.

One very popular segmentation technique is the **Watershed Transform**. The concept is based on treating the array of pixels as a topological map. Bright pixels are at the tops of mountains and dark pixels are at the bottoms of valleys (or vice-versa). If we drop water on any given pixel it will either (a) stay where it is, if it is at the bottom of a valley; (b) roll down the hill in a unique direction (given by the direction of steepest decrease); or (c) may move in one of two directions, if it is on a ridge line. We define a **watershed** as the set of all points that will fall to a particular minimum (there may be several adjacent pixels at the bottom of the basis that satisfy this minimum). The lines at the crests of the hills are called **watershed lines**. The idea is to punch holes at the bottom of each basin and slowly pump water in from the bottom, flooding the image. As the water rises, each basin slowly fills, and will eventually overflow from one watershed into another watershed. When this happens we construct an infinitely high dam to prevent water from flowing between the regions. We continue to pump water in, extending the lengths of our dams as necessary. At the end of the process, the collection of dams gives the watershed lines of the image. The problem with watershed is that the domains need to be seeded – somebody or some algorithm needs to determine where to "punch the holes" that are used to start filling in the individual domains.

scipy-ndimage

Scipy includes a large number of convolution, filtering, and morphological image processing functions such as multidimensional correlation; Gaussian and Laplacian filtering; shifts, splines, and geometric transforms; histograms and data extraction; dilation, erosion, opening, closing, and morphological transformation; and Fourier analysis. You should definitely check into this package before you attempt to reinvent any image processing software on your own.[4]

scikit-image

The Python imaging library is not the only external source for image analysis software. Scikit-image[5] is another large package of open source image processing software. Scikit-image is an extension of Scipy-image that provides a large number of morphology, filtering, and segmentation packages that are already built and ready to use.

opencv

Opencv[6] is a collection of open source software packages for computer vision written in C/C++ with wrappers for a number languages that include Python. They have a collection of tutorials[7] you can follow to learn how to use opencv for image processing; feature detection and description; tracking; image reconstruction; machine learning; denoising; and object detection.

---

[4]See `http://docs.scipy.org/doc/scipy-0.14.0/reference/ndimage.html`, or the tutorial at `http://scipy-lectures.github.io/advanced/image_processing/` for more information.

[5]For more detail see `http://scikit-image.org/docs/0.10.x/`

[6]See `http://opencv.org/`

[7]See `http://docs.opencv.org/trunk/doc/py_tutorials/py_tutorials.html`

Table 43.4. `Image.transform` Methods

`im.transform(size,method,data)`
`im.transform(size,method,data,filter)`

Parameter	Description
`method`	**"EXTENT"** - a rectangular region. **data** is a 4-tuple (x_0, y_0, x_1, y_1) that specifies where the data should be sampled in the original image.
	"AFFINE" - affine transformation. **data** is an 6-tuple (a, b, c, d, e, f). The transformation is $(x, y) \mapsto (ax + by + c, dx + ey + f)$.
	"QUAD" - quadrilateral mapping. **data** is an 8-tuple $(x_0, y_0, x_1, y_1, x_2, y_2, x_3, y_3)$ which contains the upper left, lower left, lower right, and upper right corners, in that order.
	"MESH" - map a mesh. **data** contains a list of rectangles in the same format as **"QUAD"**.
	"PERSPECTIVE". **data** is an 8-tuple (a, b, c, d, e, f, g). The transformation is $(x, y) \mapsto \left(\dfrac{ax + by + c}{gh + hy + 1}, \dfrac{dx + ey + f}{gx + hy + 1} \right)$
`filter`	**"NEAREST"** - nearest neighbor.
	"BILINEAR" - 2×2 linear interpolation.
	"BICUBIC" - 4×4 splines.

Exercises

1. Write a function to convert RGB, as a tuple of three real numbers each in the range (0,1), to a tuple (H, S, I).

2. Find a picture on the internet that you like working with. It should be something that is not to detailed and has a reasonable amount of contrast, like a picture of a cola can. If you prefer, you can take a photo with a camera or cell phone. Read it in using PIL. Display the picture. Determine its size and mode.

3. Convert your picture to at least two other file formats and save them.

4. Generate and save a monochrome (grays scale) image from your picture and save it.

5. Crop a region in the bottom right corner of your original color picture into a new variable and save it.

6. Compute and plot a histogram of you gray scale image.

7. Equalize the gray scale image and compare the before and after histograms.

8. Apply smoothing filters of at sizes 3, 5, 9 and 15 to your image. What do you observe? What happens if you threshold after each filter is applied on the original image?

9. Compare the contour, emboss, and sharpen filters in PIL.

10. Write a function to do Laplacian filtering and apply it to your image.

11. Write functions that do Horizontal and Vertical Sobel edge detection.

12. Write a Canny edge detector.

Chapter 44

Satellite orbits

In this chapter we will consider the problem of building up larger programs from smaller ones. The idea is this: if you have one very big problem to solve, it is easier to break it down into smaller pieces and then put all of the pieces together rather than trying to solve everything all at once. This is a formed of **systems analysis** called **top-down development**.

We will apply this to the study of a particular application, namely, that of predicting the trajectory of a satellite in orbit around the earth. We will first study the physics, then look at the basic algorithm, breaking it down into pieces.

However, don't expect to learn any software engineering here. We are going to hack out the solution by implementing the physics as directly and quickly as we can.

Overview of the Problem

We want to be able to predict the **sub-satellite position** (or **ground track**), on the surface of the earth, of a near-earth orbiting satellite (such as the International Space Station) as a function of time. We will accomplish this goal using slightly-perturbed Keplerian motion, and by taking into account the rotation of the Earth. Here is a summary of the basic facts from physics.

- According to **Kepler's theory** (which we will later derive from Newton's theory using a point-mass approximation for the earth) the satellite's orbit is **an ellipse with one focus of the ellipse at the center of the Earth**.

- **The ellipse is constrained to lie in a plane** that is tilted at some angle with Earth's equatorial plane.

- The Earth is actually slightly blimpy, and is not a point mass. This causes a torque to be exerted on the satellite. **As a result, the orbit plane rotates about the Earth's polar axis**. This rotation causes the orbit vector to be perturbed.

- Because **the Earth rotates** under the plane of the orbit, **the ground track drifts west**. To see this, consider the plane of the orbit. A typical orbital period is about 100 minutes. Consider where the orbit plane crosses the surface of the Earth; without rotation, it will return to the same spot 100 minutes later. But because the Earth is rotating, the orbit will appear to drift westward.

So how would we put these pieces together to predict the location at some time $t = 1$, given the location at some time $t = 0$? Here is our "Basic Algorithm:"

Algorithm 44.1 Orbital algorithm, pass 1

---

input: Initial state vector (position, velocity of satellite)
1: **for** each time step Δt **do**
2:     1) Determine satellite movement in the 2D orbital plane using Kepler.
3:     2) Figure out how much the orbit plane has rotated.
4:     3) Convert the 2D position in the orbit to a 3D Earth-centered xyz.
5:     4) Convert the Earth-centered xyz to latitude/longitude, accounting for Earth
    rotation.
6: **end for**
7: **return**

Orbits are Elliptical

Elliptical orbits[1] are predicted by Newton's law of gravity. Let r_S and r_E be the position of the satellite and the position of the earth in some inertial coordinate frame, and denote their respective masses by m and M. Then Newton's law of gravity, in combination with Newton's second law of motion says that the force on the satellite by the Earth is given by

$$m\mathbf{r}_S'' = -GmM\frac{\mathbf{r}_S - \mathbf{r}_E}{|\mathbf{r}_E - \mathbf{r}_S|^3} \tag{44.1}$$

while the equal and opposite force on the Earth, by the satellite, is given by

$$M\mathbf{r}_E'' = -GmM\frac{\mathbf{r}_E - \mathbf{r}_S}{|\mathbf{r}_E - \mathbf{r}_S|^3} \tag{44.2}$$

where the derivative is taken with respect to time. Divide the first equation by m, the second by M, and subtract, to get

$$\mathbf{r}'' = -G(M + m)\frac{\mathbf{r}}{|\mathbf{r}|^3} \tag{44.3}$$

where

$$\mathbf{r} = \mathbf{r}_S - \mathbf{r}_E \tag{44.4}$$

Define the **reduced mass of the system** as

$$\mu = G(M + m) \approx GM \approx 3.986 \times 10^{14} \text{ m}^3/\text{sec}^2 \tag{44.5}$$

The approximation is valid because $M \approx 5 \times 10^{24}$ kg and the heaviest satellites sent into orbit are 10,000 kg, so that $m \ll M$ is reasonable.

The **fundamental equation of motion** is then, from equations 44.3 and 44.4,

$$\mathbf{r}'' = \frac{d^2\mathbf{r}}{dt^2} = -\frac{\mu\hat{\mathbf{r}}}{r^2} \tag{44.6}$$

where $\hat{\mathbf{r}}$ is a unit vector in the same direction as $\mathbf{r}$. Taking the cross product of (44.6)

---

[1]Technically, orbits are conic sections, which include parabolas and hyperbolas, but we will ignore that distinction for now and only focus on near-earth circular orbits.

with **r** gives

$$\mathbf{r} \times \mathbf{r}'' = -\mathbf{r} \times \left(\frac{\mu \hat{\mathbf{r}}}{r^2} \right) = \mathbf{0} \tag{44.7}$$

because the cross product of any vector with itself is zero:

$$\mathbf{r} \times \mathbf{r} = \mathbf{0} \tag{44.8}$$

Next, we consider the following derivative, which we can calculate with the product rule:

$$\frac{d}{dt}(\mathbf{r} \times \mathbf{r}') = \mathbf{r} \times \mathbf{r}'' + \mathbf{r}' \times \mathbf{r}' \tag{44.9}$$

The first term is zero by (44.7), and the second term is zero because it is a cross product of a vector with itself. This gives

$$\frac{d}{dt}(\mathbf{r} \times \mathbf{r}') = \mathbf{0} \tag{44.10}$$

Define the **angular momentum density vector** as

$$\mathbf{h} = \mathbf{r} \times \mathbf{r}' \tag{44.11}$$

Thus

$$\frac{d\mathbf{h}}{dt} = \mathbf{0} \tag{44.12}$$

This gives us conservation of angular momentum.

Law of Conservation of Angular Momentum

$$\mathbf{h} = \mathbf{c}(\text{constant}) \tag{44.13}$$

Take the cross product of the fundamental equation of motion (44.6) with the angular momentum vector,

$$\mathbf{r}'' \times \mathbf{h} = -\left(\frac{\mu \hat{\mathbf{r}}}{r^2} \right) \times (\mathbf{r} \times \mathbf{r}') \tag{44.14}$$

To evaluate the vector triple product $\hat{\mathbf{r}} \times (\mathbf{r} \times \mathbf{r}')$ we will use the "BAC-CAB" identity

$$\mathbf{a} \times (\mathbf{b} \times \mathbf{c}) = \mathbf{b}(\mathbf{a} \cdot \mathbf{c}) - \mathbf{c}(\mathbf{a} \cdot \mathbf{b}) \tag{44.15}$$

hence

$$\hat{\mathbf{r}} \times (\mathbf{r} \times \mathbf{r}') = \mathbf{r}(\hat{\mathbf{r}} \cdot \mathbf{r}') - \mathbf{r}'(\hat{\mathbf{r}} \cdot \mathbf{r}) \tag{44.16}$$

Since $\mathbf{r} = r\hat{\mathbf{r}}$,

$$\hat{\mathbf{r}} \times (\mathbf{r} \times \mathbf{r}') = \frac{1}{r}(\mathbf{r}(\mathbf{r} \cdot \mathbf{r}') - r^2\mathbf{r}') \tag{44.17}$$

Hence from equation (44.14)

$$\mathbf{r}'' \times \mathbf{h} = -\left(\frac{\mu}{r^3} \right)(\mathbf{r}(\mathbf{r} \cdot \mathbf{r}') - r^2\mathbf{r}') \tag{44.18}$$

Since r is the magnitude of **r**, then r' is the rate of change of **r** in a direction parallel to

r. Hence

$$r' = \frac{dr}{dt} = \hat{\mathbf{r}} \cdot \mathbf{r}' = \frac{1}{r}\mathbf{r} \cdot \mathbf{r}' \tag{44.19}$$

Substituting this into (44.18) gives

$$\mathbf{r}'' \times \mathbf{h} = -\left(\frac{\mu}{r^3}\right)(\mathbf{r}rr' - r^2\mathbf{r}') = -\left(\frac{\mu}{r^2}\right)(\mathbf{r}r' - r\mathbf{r}') \tag{44.20}$$

But by the quotient rule

$$\frac{d}{dt}\left(\frac{\mathbf{r}}{r}\right) = \frac{r\mathbf{r}' - \mathbf{r}r'}{r^2} \tag{44.21}$$

Hence

$$\mathbf{r}'' \times \mathbf{h} = \mu\frac{d}{dt}\left(\frac{\mathbf{r}}{r}\right) \tag{44.22}$$

We can rewrite this as

$$\mathbf{v}' \times \mathbf{h} = \mu\frac{d}{dt}\left(\frac{\mathbf{r}}{r}\right) \tag{44.23}$$

where $\mathbf{v} = \mathbf{r}'$. Reversing the order of the cross product,

$$\mathbf{h} \times \mathbf{v}' = -\mu\frac{d}{dt}\left(\frac{\mathbf{r}}{r}\right) \tag{44.24}$$

Multiply both sides of the equation by dt, and integrate

$$\int \mathbf{h} \times \mathbf{v}'\, dt = -\mu \int \frac{d}{dt}\left(\frac{\mathbf{r}}{r}\right) dt \tag{44.25}$$

Since **h** is a constant we can pull it out of the integral on the left. Further, we can write $\mathbf{v}' = d\mathbf{v}/dt$ so that

$$\mathbf{h} \times \int \frac{d\mathbf{v}}{dt}\, dt = -\mu \int \frac{d}{dt}\left(\frac{\mathbf{r}}{r}\right) dt \tag{44.26}$$

By the fundamental theorem of calculus,

$$-\mathbf{h} \times \mathbf{v} = \mu\frac{\mathbf{r}}{r} + \mathbf{C} \tag{44.27}$$

where **C** is a (vector) constant of integration. The standard notation is define an **eccentricity vector** $\mathbf{e} = \mathbf{C}/\mu$, so that

$$\mathbf{v} \times \mathbf{h} = \mu\left(\frac{\mathbf{r}}{r} + \mathbf{e}\right) \tag{44.28}$$

The reason for the name eccentricity will become apparent later. Taking the dot product of (44.28) with **r** gives

$$(\mathbf{v} \times \mathbf{h}) \cdot \mathbf{r} = \mu\left(\frac{\mathbf{r}}{r} + \mathbf{e}\right) \cdot \mathbf{r} = \mu(r + \mathbf{r} \cdot \mathbf{e}) \tag{44.29}$$

Using the vector identity $(\mathbf{a} \times \mathbf{b}) \cdot \mathbf{c} = (\mathbf{c} \times \mathbf{a}) \cdot \mathbf{b}$, and then substituting the definition of angular momentum ($\mathbf{h} = \mathbf{r} \times \mathbf{v}$, from equation (44.11)),

$$(\mathbf{v} \times \mathbf{h}) \cdot \mathbf{r} = (\mathbf{r} \times \mathbf{v}) \cdot \mathbf{h} = \mathbf{h} \cdot \mathbf{h} = h^2 \tag{44.30}$$

where h is the constant magnitude of the angular momentum per unit mass. Substituting (44.30) into (44.29) gives us

$$h^2 = \mu(r + \mathbf{r} \cdot \mathbf{e})$$ (44.31)

Define θ as the angle between $\mathbf{r}$ and the constant vector $\mathbf{e}$. Then

$$h^2 = \mu(r + re \cos \theta) = \mu r(1 + e \cos \theta)$$ (44.32)

Solving for r

$$r = \frac{h^2/\mu}{1 + e \cos \theta}$$ (44.33)

This is the equation from analytic geometry for an ellipse with **semi-parameter** $p = h^2/\mu$ and eccentricity e, in polar coordinates. The semi-parameter is more commonly written in terms of the semi-major axis and eccentricity as

$$p = a(1 - e^2)$$ (44.34)

Thus we get the following result.

Orbit Position in Polar Coordinates

The distance r from the center of the earth is

$$r = \frac{a(1 - e^2)}{1 + e \cos \theta}$$ (44.35)

Here a is semi-major axis, e is eccentricity, θ is central angle measured from the point of closest approach, and $h^2 = \mu a(1 - e^2)$.

The Vis-Viva Equation

The potential energy for a satellite of mass m in the earth's gravity is

$$E_{potential} = -\frac{\mu m}{r}$$ (44.36)

where $\mu = GM$, as defined previously, and the kinetic energy is

$$E_{kinetic} = \frac{1}{2}mv^2$$ (44.37)

where v is the velocity, as defined in the previous section. By the **law of energy conservation** the total energy $\mathcal{E}$ is a constant

$$\mathcal{E} = E_{kinetic} + E_{potential} = \frac{1}{2}mv^2 - \frac{\mu m}{r}$$ (44.38)

Let r_1, v_1 and r_2, v_2 be the position and velocity of a satellite at two different points in its orbit. Then by energy conservation,

$$\frac{1}{2}mv_1^2 - \frac{\mu m}{r_1} = \frac{1}{2}mv_2^2 - \frac{\mu m}{r_2} \tag{44.39}$$

Canceling out the common factor of m,

$$\frac{v_1^2}{2} - \frac{\mu}{r_1} = \frac{v_2^2}{2} - \frac{\mu}{r_2} \tag{44.40}$$

From equation 44.35, at $\theta = 0$, $r(0) = a(1 - e)$. This distance is called **perigee**, because it is the closest point to the origin.[2] Furthermore, at perigee the velocity and the radius are perpendicular to one another, so the magnitude of the angular momentum is $h = r_{perigee}v_{perigee}$. From the equation in the discussion following (44.35)

$$h^2 = \mu a(1 - e^2) = r_{perigee}^2 v_{perigee}^2 \tag{44.41}$$

Hence, since $r_{perigee} = a(1 - e)$,

$$v_{perigee}^2 = \frac{\mu a(1 - e^2)}{a^2(1 - e)^2} = \frac{\mu}{a}\frac{1 + e}{1 - e} \tag{44.42}$$

If we let r_1 be any point on the orbit, and r_2 be perigee, then equation (44.40) gives us

$$\frac{v^2}{2} - \frac{\mu}{r} = \frac{\mu}{2a}\frac{1 + e}{1 - e} - \frac{\mu}{a(1 - e)} = \frac{\mu}{2a}\left[\frac{1 + e}{1 - e} - \frac{2}{1 - e}\right] = -\frac{\mu}{2a} \tag{44.43}$$

Solving for v^2 gives the **Vis-Viva Equation**

Vis-Viva Equation

$$v^2 = \mu\left(\frac{2}{r} - \frac{1}{a}\right) \tag{44.44}$$

where v is the satellite velocity, r its distance from the center of the Earth, a the orbital semi-major axis, $\mu = GM$, G is Newton's universal constant of gravitation, and M is the mass of the earth.

Keplerian Orbits

We have shown that in the absence of any outside forces, when a satellite orbiting about the Earth is treated like a point mass we end up with elliptical orbits. This is the essence of Keplerian orbital dynamics. Kepler's orbital description provides a reasonable first order description of planetary motion and, in fact, only slight adjustments are necessary to get extremely accurate predictions of satellite orbits. Our description of elliptical motion in a plane is given by figure 44.1. We know from equation 44.35 that if we place the focus of the ellipse at the origin and the perigee (nearest point on the orbit to the

---

[2]It is only called perigee when the central body is Earth. If the central body is, eg., the sun, moon or Jupiter, we use the terms *perihelion*, *perilune*, or *perijove*. The general term is *periapsis*.

Figure 44.1: Description of an elliptical orbit. The origin is off-centered from the center of the ellipse by a distance ae along the x-axis.

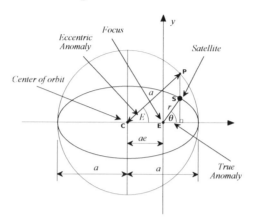

focus) on the positive x axis, then

$$r = \frac{a(1 - e^2)}{1 + e \cos \theta} \tag{44.45}$$

where θ, called the **true anomaly**, is the ordinary polar angular coordinate. The center of the ellipse in displaced from the origin by a distance ae to the left in this figure.

Suppose the satellite has polar coordinates (r, θ). Then in Cartesian coordinates,

$$(x, y) = (r \cos \theta, \ r \sin \theta) \tag{44.46}$$

Form the following construction, as illustrated in figure 44.1

1. Construct a circle of radius a circumscribing the ellipse.
2. Drop a perpendicular line ℓ from the satellite's location **S** to the x axis.
3. Denote by **P** the intersection of ℓ and the circle.
4. Draw a line segment from **P** to the center **C** of the circle.
5. The angle $E = \angle$**PCE** (**E** is the focus) is called the **eccentric anomaly**.

In terms of the eccentric anomaly,

$$a \cos E = ae + x \tag{44.47}$$

hence

$$x = a(\cos E - e) \tag{44.48}$$

Using (44.46) in (44.45)

$$r = \frac{a(1 - e^2)}{1 + ex/r} \tag{44.49}$$

Cross-multiplying and solving for r,

$$r = a(1 - e^2) - ex = a(1 - e^2) - ea(\cos E - e) \qquad (44.50)$$

$$= a - ae^2 - ea \cos E + ae^2 = a(1 - e \cos E) \qquad (44.51)$$

By the Pythagorean theorem,

$$y^2 = r^2 - x^2 = a^2(1 - e \cos E)^2 - a^2(\cos E - e)^2 \qquad (44.52)$$

$$= a^2(1 - 2e \cos E + e^2 \cos^2 E - \cos^2 E + 2e \cos E - e^2) \qquad (44.53)$$

$$= a^2(1 + e^2 \cos^2 E - \cos^2 E - e^2) \qquad (44.54)$$

$$= a^2(1 - e^2)(1 - \cos^2 E) \qquad (44.55)$$

so that

$$y = a\sqrt{1 - e^2} \sin E \qquad (44.56)$$

We don't have to worry about getting the correct sign of y because the the sign of $\sin E$ will always give us the correct quadrant.

Differentiating (using (44.48) and (44.56))

$$\frac{dx}{dt} = -a \sin E \frac{dE}{dt} \qquad (44.57)$$

$$\frac{dy}{dt} = a\sqrt{1 - e^2} \cos E \frac{dE}{dt} \qquad (44.58)$$

From the definition of angular momentum, $\mathbf{h} = \mathbf{r} \times \mathbf{v}$. In the coordinate frame shown, with the z axis out of the plane of the paper,

$$\mathbf{h} = \begin{vmatrix} \mathbf{i} & \mathbf{j} & \mathbf{k} \\ x & y & 0 \\ x' & y' & 0 \end{vmatrix} = \mathbf{k}(xy' - yx') \qquad (44.59)$$

Hence

$$h = a(\cos E - e)\left(a\sqrt{1 - e^2} \cos E\right) E' + (a\sqrt{1 - e^2} \sin E)(a \sin E)E' \qquad (44.60)$$

$$= a^2 \sqrt{1 - e^2} \left[(\cos E - e) \cos E + \sin^2 E\right] E' \qquad (44.61)$$

$$= a^2 \sqrt{1 - e^2}(1 - e \cos E)E' \qquad (44.62)$$

From equation 44.35, $h^2 = \mu a(1 - e^2)$, hence

$$\mu a(1 - e^2) = a^4(1 - e^2)(1 - e \cos E)^2 (E')^2 \qquad (44.63)$$

After some cancellation,

$$\mu = a^3(1 - e \cos E)^2 (E')^2 \qquad (44.64)$$

Dividing by a^3 and taking the square root,

$$\sqrt{\frac{\mu}{a^3}} = (1 - e \cos E)E' \qquad (44.65)$$

Let t_P be the time at which the satellite passes through perigee. Multiply equation (44.65) by dt and integrate from t_P:

$$\int_{t_P}^{t} \sqrt{\frac{\mu}{a^3}}\, dt = \int_{E(t_p)}^{E(t)} (1 - e \cos E) E'\, dt \qquad (44.66)$$

Pulling out the constant on the left hand side and integrating it, and writing $E'dt = dE$

$$\sqrt{\frac{\mu}{a^3}}(t - t_P) = \int_{E(t_p)}^{E(t)} (1 - e \cos E)\, dE = (E - e \sin E)\Big|_{0}^{E(t)} = E - e \sin E \qquad (44.67)$$

where the last step follows because $E(t_p) = 0$.

Mean Motion

The **mean motion** is

$$n = \sqrt{\frac{\mu}{a^3}} \qquad (44.68)$$

where $\mu = GM$ and a is the semi-major axis, gives an equivalent velocity as if the satellite were moving in a circular orbit at a fixed velocity with the same period.

In terms of the mean motion, the angular position of the satellite can be found at any later time from equation (44.67) by solving **Kepler's Equation**.

Kepler's Equation

$$E - e \sin E = n(t - t_P) = M \qquad (44.69)$$

Where E is the eccentric anomaly, e is the orbital eccentricity, M is mean anomaly, t_P is the time of periapsis passage, and n is the mean motion.

The number M, defined by the last equal sign of (44.69) is called the **Mean Anomaly**. The Mean Anomaly is an equivalent angle that changes linearly in time.

Mean Anomaly

The **mean anomaly** is an equivalent angle that changes linearly in time.

If we let τ be the period of the satellite, then the eccentric anomaly will be 2π. This gives

$$2\pi = n\tau = \tau\sqrt{\frac{\mu}{a^3}} \qquad (44.70)$$

Squaring both sides of the equation and rearranging gives Kepler's third law.

Kepler's Third Law of Planetary Motion

$$\frac{4\pi^2}{\mu}a^3 = \tau^2 \qquad\qquad (44.71)$$

This shows that Kepler's famous result, that the square of the period is proportional to the cube of the semi-major axis, follows from Newton's laws of motion.

Now we are able to produce an algorithm that predicts the position of a satellite in its orbital plane. Given the orbital elements a, e, and time of perigee passage t_p, we calculate the position of the satellite in the plane of the ellipse using algorithm 44.2.

Algorithm 44.2 Algorithm **OrbitPosition** for motion in a Keplerian orbit.

input: Orbital elements **v** that include: a (semi-major axis); e (orbital eccentricity); t_p (time of perigee passage); t (current time); ϵ (a very small number, tolerance, say 10^{-10}

1: $n \leftarrow \sqrt{mu/a^3}$
2: $M \leftarrow n(t - t_p)$
3: $E \leftarrow M$
4: **while** $|E - M| > \epsilon$ **do**
5: $\quad E \leftarrow M + e\sin E$ Fixed point iteration for E
6: **end while**
7: $x \leftarrow a(\cos E - e)$
8: $y \leftarrow a\sqrt{1 - e^2}\sin E$
9: **return** (x, y) as **OrbitPosition**(**v**, t)

We want to define a function **OrbitPosition**(**v**, t) that will take as its input a Keplerian input vector $\mathbf{v} = (a, e, i, \Omega, \omega, M)$ at some time $t = 0$, and determine the position and (x, y), as measured in the plane of the orbit, a time t later.

Note that the x coordinate here is the coordinate parallel to the **p** axis (the axis through the center of the orbit to perigee), and the y coordinate is the coordinate parallel to the **q** axis (in the plane of the axis, through the focus, normal to **p**), so it might be better to call these numbers (p, q) rather than (x, y).

We can now revise algorithm 44.1. For input, NASA provides orbital elements in two forms, either with the mean anomaly M or the time of periapsis passage t_p. If t_p is given, the mean anomaly can be recovered from equations 44.68 and 44.69.

Out of the Plane: Kepler's Elements

We have shown that in the absence of external perturbations the orbit is an ellipse. We also now know how to calculate the trajectory in that ellipse. The next step to to orient that ellipse in three dimensions.

Because the problem is three dimensional, every vector has three components. Because Newton's law is a second order differential equation, there are two initial conditions because two integrations are performed. So two constants are required in each coordinate

---

Algorithm 44.3 Orbital algorithm, pass 2

---

input: Orbital element vector $\mathbf{v} = (a, e, i, \Omega, \omega, M)$
1: **for** Each time point t **do**
2:   1) $(p, q) \leftarrow$ **OrbitPosition**$(\mathbf{v}, t)$
3:   2) Figure out how much the orbit plane has rotated.
4:   3) Convert the 2D position in the orbit to a 3D Earth-centered xyz.
5:   4) Convert the Earth-centered xyz to latitude/longitude, accounting for Earth rotation.
6: **end for**
7: **return**

Figure 44.2: Definition of the Keplerian elements used to orient an orbital plane in space.

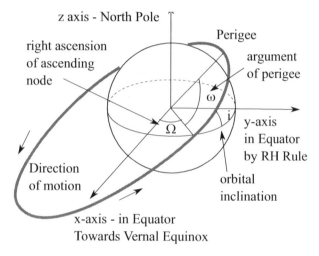

for a total of six constants. In Cartesian coordinates we could start with the coordinates (x, y, z) and the velocity (x', y', z') for our six numbers.

Instead of using position and velocity for his six coordinates, Kepler defined a set of six parameters based on the geometry of the problems. Three of these parameters, a, e, and t_p, describe the position of the satellite within the ellipse.

The other three parameters tell the orientation of the ellipse in space (see figure 44.2). In this coordinate system, the origin is at the center of the Earth, but:

1. The **x** axis points to the intersection of the Earth's equatorial plane and its orbital plane, called the first point in Aries or the **vernal equinox**.
2. The **z** axis points through the north pole.
3. The **y** axis is 90 degrees lies in the plane of the Earth's equator in such a way that the three axes make a right-handed coordinate system.

In this frame, we now define three additional parameters.

Table 44.1. Typical Orbital Elements for the International Space Station

Cartesian Elements (J2K)		Kepler Elements (M50)	
Element	Value	Element	Value
x, meters	-5107606.49	a, meters	6780663.07
y, meters	-1741563.23	e, dimensionless	.0011495
z, meters	-4118273.08	i, degrees	51.52894
x', m/sec	4677.962842	ω, degrees	38.42846
y', m/sec	4677.962842	Ω, degrees	341.20455
z', m/sec	-3800.652800	M, degrees	191.97036

Epoch: 2015:044:12:00:00.000 UTC. Cartesian elements are in an inertial mean of year 2000 frame of reference, and the Kepler elements are the mean (averaged) elements in an inertial mean of year 1950 frame of reference.

Source: http://spaceflight.nasa.gov/realdata/elements/

1. i, the **orbital inclination**, or angle between the plane of the orbit an the earth's equitorial plane;
2. Ω, the **right ascension of ascending node**, the angle measured along the equator from the x-axis to the point where the orbital plane intersects the equatorial plane, going from south to north; and
3. ω, the **argument of perigee**, the angle measured in the plane of the orbit from the equatorial plane to the line from the center of the earth to perigee.

The vector $\mathbf{v} = (a, e, t_P, i, \Omega, \omega)$ gives us the initial conditions of the orbit. We can replace t_P by M and (mathematically) get the equivalent information from $\mathbf{v}_1 = (a, e, i, M, \Omega, \omega)$. The parameter t_p is physically measurable, while M must be calculated using Kepler's equation, so the first form is typically considered more reliable. NASA provides the elements in both forms and the conversion can be made using equations 44.68 and 44.69.

We already know how to calculate the position within the plane of the orbit. We need to know how to calculate the transformation matrix between the coordinates in the $(\mathbf{p}, \mathbf{q})$ plane and the **xyz** frame we have just defined. We will do this by first extending the $(\mathbf{p}, \mathbf{q})$ plane into a 3D coordinate frame.

1. **p** axis points from the center of the Earth towards perigee.
2. **q** axis points from the center of the Earth, in the plane of orbit, to a point on the path of the orbit that is 90 degrees advanced from the satellite's motion.
3. **w** axis points from the center of the Earth and is orthogonal to the orbit plane so as to make **pqw** a right-handed coordinate frame.

We will designate unit vectors along each of the axes in the **pqw** frame as **p**, **q**, and **w**, and unit vectors in the **xyz** frame by **i**, **j**, **k**. The following sequence of rotations will transform the **xyz** frame to the **pqw** frame:

1. Rotate by Ω (right ascension of ascending node) about the z axis. Call the new x axis x'.

2. Rotate by i (inclination) about the x'-axis. Call the new z axis z''.
3. Rotate by ω (argument of perigee) about the z'' axis.

This will transform the axes as follows:

$$\mathbf{i} \to \mathbf{p}, \quad \mathbf{j} \to \mathbf{q}, \quad \mathbf{k} \to \mathbf{w} \tag{44.72}$$

Let $\mathbf{R_v}(\theta)$ be the standard rotation matrix about the axis $\mathbf{v}$. These can be found in any standard textbook on linear algebra. Then

$$\begin{bmatrix} \mathbf{p} \\ \mathbf{q} \\ \mathbf{w} \end{bmatrix} = \mathbf{R_z}(\omega)\mathbf{R_x}(i)\mathbf{R_z}(\Omega) \begin{bmatrix} \mathbf{i} \\ \mathbf{j} \\ \mathbf{k} \end{bmatrix} \tag{44.73}$$

$$= \begin{bmatrix} \cos\omega & \sin\omega & 0 \\ -\sin\omega & \cos\omega & 0 \\ 0 & 0 & 1 \end{bmatrix} \begin{bmatrix} 1 & 0 & 0 \\ 0 & \cos i & \sin i \\ 0 & -\sin i & \cos i \end{bmatrix} \begin{bmatrix} \cos\Omega & \sin\Omega & 0 \\ -\sin\Omega & \cos\Omega & 0 \\ 0 & 0 & 1 \end{bmatrix} \begin{bmatrix} \mathbf{i} \\ \mathbf{j} \\ \mathbf{k} \end{bmatrix} \tag{44.74}$$

$$= \begin{bmatrix} \cos\omega & \sin\omega & 0 \\ -\sin\omega & \cos\omega & 0 \\ 0 & 0 & 1 \end{bmatrix} \begin{bmatrix} \cos\Omega & \sin\Omega & 0 \\ -\cos i\sin\Omega & \cos i\cos\Omega & \sin i \\ \sin i\sin\Omega & -\sin i\cos\Omega & \cos i \end{bmatrix} \begin{bmatrix} \mathbf{i} \\ \mathbf{j} \\ \mathbf{k} \end{bmatrix} \tag{44.75}$$

$$= \begin{bmatrix} \cos\omega\cos\Omega - \sin\omega\cos i\sin\Omega & \cos\omega\sin\Omega + \sin\omega\cos i\cos\Omega & \sin\omega\sin i \\ -\sin\omega\cos\Omega - \cos\omega\cos i\sin\Omega & -\sin\omega\sin\Omega + \cos\omega\cos i\cos\Omega & \sin i\cos\omega \\ \sin i\sin\Omega & -\sin i\cos\Omega & \cos i \end{bmatrix} \begin{bmatrix} \mathbf{i} \\ \mathbf{j} \\ \mathbf{k} \end{bmatrix} \tag{44.76}$$

Once we have the satellite's position (p, q) from **OrbitPosition**$(\mathbf{v}, t)$, then the orbital position in Earth centered coordinates is

$$\mathbf{r} = p\mathbf{p} + q\mathbf{q} \tag{44.77}$$

$$= p(p_x\mathbf{i} + p_y\mathbf{j} + p_z\mathbf{k}) + q(q_x\mathbf{i} + q_y\mathbf{j} + q_z\mathbf{k}) \tag{44.78}$$

$$= (pp_x + qq_x)\mathbf{i} + (pp_y + qq_y)\mathbf{j} + (pp_z + qq_z)\mathbf{k} \tag{44.79}$$

This is summarized in algorithm 44.4

Algorithm 44.4 Algorithm **PQ2XYZ** to convert from orbital position to earth centered coordinates.

input: (p, q), coordinates in (p, q) (from **OrbitPosition**)

1: $p_x \leftarrow \cos\omega\cos\Omega - \sin\omega\cos i\sin\Omega$
2: $p_y \leftarrow \cos\omega\sin\Omega + \sin\omega\cos i\cos\Omega$
3: $p_z \leftarrow \sin\omega\sin i$
4: $q_x \leftarrow -\sin\omega\cos\Omega - \cos\omega\cos i\sin\Omega$
5: $q_y \leftarrow -\sin\omega\sin\Omega + \cos\omega\cos i\cos\Omega$
6: $q_z \leftarrow \sin i\cos\omega$
7: $w_x \leftarrow \sin i\sin\Omega$
8: $w_y \leftarrow -\sin i\cos\Omega$
9: $w_z \leftarrow \cos i$
10: $\mathbf{r} \leftarrow (pp_x + qq_x)\mathbf{i} + (pp_y + qq_y)\mathbf{j} + (pp_z + qq_z)\mathbf{k}$
11: **return** $\mathbf{r}$

We are ready for a third pass at the orbit algorithm now.

Algorithm 44.5 Orbital algorithm, pass 3

---

input: Orbital element vector $\mathbf{v} = (a, e, i, \Omega, \omega, M)$

1: **for** At each time t **do**
2:     1) $(p, q) \leftarrow \mathbf{OrbitPosition}(\mathbf{v}, t)$
3:     2) Figure out how much the orbit plane has rotated.
4:     3) $(x, y, z) \leftarrow \mathbf{PQ2XYZ}(p, q)$
5:     4) Convert the Earth-centered xyz to latitude/longitude, accounting for Earth
        rotation.
6: **end for**
7: **return**

Perturbed Keplerian Orbits

In low earth orbits the main perturbing force that causes deviations from Keplerian
motion is due to the Earth's oblateness. To be really accurate – and for some purposes
this is required – there are hundreds of additional terms that need to be added to Newton's law of gravity. [3] It may also be necessary to include lunar and solar gravitational
effects. The general idea is to expand the gravity field as a sum of spherical harmonics:

$$V = \frac{\mu}{r} \left[1 + \sum_{n=2}^{\infty} \left(\frac{a}{r} \right)^n \sum_{m=0}^{n} P_{nm}(\sin\phi)(c_{nm}\cos m\lambda + s_{nm}\sin m\lambda) \right] \qquad (44.80)$$

The gravitational force then becomes

$$\mathbf{F} = -\nabla V = -\mathbf{r}\frac{\partial V}{\partial r} + \frac{\boldsymbol{\phi}}{r}\frac{\partial V}{\partial \phi} + \frac{\boldsymbol{\theta}}{r\sin\phi}\frac{\partial V}{\partial \theta} \qquad (44.81)$$

where P_{nm} are the associated Legendre Polynomials, and ϕ and λ are the geocentric
latitude and longitude. In practice, of course, the series cannot be taken to infinity as
not all terms have been measured. In the EGM2008 Gravity model the coefficients are
known to spherical harmonic degree 2159.[4] In the Newtonian approximation only the
first terms remains in the gravitational field,

$$V = \frac{\mu}{r} \text{ and } \mathbf{F} = -\mathbf{r}\frac{\partial V}{\partial r} = -\frac{\mu\mathbf{r}}{r^3} \qquad (44.82)$$

A simpler expansion that assumes the potential is an oblate spheroid and ignores other
variations is given by[5]

$$V = \frac{\mu}{r} \left[1 - \sum_{n=2}^{\infty} J_n P_n(\sin\phi) \right] \qquad (44.83)$$

---

[3]If you are interested I've written a paper with one way of describing these deviations. See Shapiro
  and Bhat, GTARG, the TOPEX/Poseidon Ground Track Maintenance Maneuver Targeting Program,
  AIAA Aerospace Design Conference, Irvine, Feb 16-19, 1993, AIAA Paper 93-1129.
[4]see http://earth-info.nga.mil/GandG/wgs84/gravitymod/egm2008/index.html
[5]Y Kozai, Second Order Solution of Artificial Satellite Theory Without Air Drag, Astronomical Journal,
  67:446 (1962).

The negative sign in the sum is a convention, and like the earlier approximation, the sum is rarely taken to very high degree. The principal perturbation is due to the J_2 effect, and we will ignore all higher order perturbations, as they are much smaller. The effect on the orbital elements is a constant rate of change, called a **secular** perturbation. The result (which we will not derive here) is

$$\frac{da}{dt} = \frac{de}{dt} = \frac{di}{dt} = 0 \tag{44.84}$$

$$\frac{d\Omega}{dt} = -\left(\frac{r_e}{a}\right)^2 \frac{3J_2 n \cos i}{2(1-e^2)^2} \tag{44.85}$$

$$\frac{d\omega}{dt} = -\left(\frac{r_e}{a}\right)^2 \frac{3J_2 n(5\cos^2 i - 1)}{4(1-e^2)^2} \tag{44.86}$$

$$\frac{dM}{dt} = n\left(1 - \left(\frac{r_e}{a}\right)^2 \frac{3J_2(1 - 3\sin^2 i \sin^2 \omega)}{2(1-e)^3}\right) \tag{44.87}$$

A good value for $J_2 \approx 0.000108263$. Here $r_e \approx 6378.140$ km is the approximate equatorial radius of the earth.

The next most important perturbation on low earth orbits is drag, which mainly affects the semi-major axis according to

$$\frac{da}{dt} = -\frac{\rho A C_D \mu a}{m}\left[1 - \frac{\omega_E}{n}\cos i\right]^2 \tag{44.88}$$

and has very little affect on the other elements. Here ρ is the atmospheric density at the altitude of the satellite; $C_D \approx 2.2$ the drag coefficient; A the satellite cross-sectional area normal to its direction of motion; and $\omega_E \approx 2\pi/86400$ radians/second the earth rotation rate.

Recalling Euler's method for solving an initial value problem, the numerical solution of

$$\frac{dy}{dt} = f(t, y) \quad y(t_i) = y_i \tag{44.89}$$

is given approximately by

$$y(t_{i+1}) = y(t_i) + \left.\frac{dy}{dt}\right|_{t=t_i}(t_{i+1} - t_i) = y(t_i) + \left.\frac{dy}{dt}\right|_{t=t_i}\Delta t \tag{44.90}$$

Based on this, a single-step in Euler's method for propagating the Kepler elements is given by **PropStep(v**, Δt) in algorithm 44.6.

This gives us the next iteration of our basic algorithm (pass 4).

Satellite Ground Track

To convert a satellite position to local sub-satellite ground track in latitude and longitude you must take into account the Earth's rotation. That is because the x axis, in which

---

Algorithm 44.6 Euler's method algorithm for **PropStep**.

input: Orbital element vector $\mathbf{v} = (a, e, i, \Omega, \omega, M)$; time step Δt.

1: $n \leftarrow \sqrt{\mu/a^3}$

2: $\Delta a \leftarrow -\dfrac{\rho A C_D \mu a}{m} \left[1 - \dfrac{\omega_E}{n} \cos i \right]^2 \Delta t$

3: $\Delta \Omega \leftarrow - \left(\dfrac{r_e}{a} \right)^2 \dfrac{3 J_2 n \cos i}{2(1 - e^2)^2} \Delta t$

4: $\Delta \omega \leftarrow - \left(\dfrac{r_e}{a} \right)^2 \dfrac{3 J_2 n (5 \cos^2 i - 1)}{4(1 - e^2)^2} \Delta t$

5: $\Delta M \leftarrow n \left(1 - \left(\dfrac{r_e}{a} \right)^2 \dfrac{3 \mu J_2 (1 - 3 \sin^2 i \sin^2 \omega)}{2(1 - e)^3} \right) \Delta t$

6: $\Delta \mathbf{v} \leftarrow (\Delta a, 0, 0, \Delta \Omega, \Delta \omega, \Delta M)$

7: $\mathbf{v} \leftarrow \mathbf{v} + \Delta \mathbf{v}$

8: **return** $\mathbf{v}$ as **PropStep**($\mathbf{v}$, Δt)

Algorithm 44.7 Orbital algorithm, pass 4

input: Orbital element vector $\mathbf{v} = (a, e, i, \Omega, \omega, M)$

1: **for** At each time t **do**

2:     1) $(p, q) \leftarrow$ **OrbitPosition**($\mathbf{v}, t$)

3:     2) $\mathbf{v} \leftarrow$ **PropStep**($\mathbf{v}, \Delta t$)

4:     3) $(x, y, z) \leftarrow$ **PQ2XYZ**(p, q)

5:     4) Convert the Earth-centered xyz to latitude/longitude, accounting for Earth rotation.

6: **end for**

7: **return**

---

the satellite coordinates are calculated, is fixed,[6] whereas the x axis for the longitude has a 24-hour period.

This relationship is given approximately by the formula[7]

$$\theta = 100.460618375 + 36000.770053608336t + 0.0003879333t^2$$
$$+ 15h + \frac{m}{4} + \frac{s}{240} \textbf{ mod } 360.0 \tag{44.91}$$

where t is the time since Jan. 1, 2000 in centuries, and h:m:s is the current time in hours, minutes, and seconds. The result of this formula is an angle in degrees. Then the longitude is

$$\text{longitude} = \tan^{-1} \frac{y}{x} - \theta \tag{44.92}$$

in degrees, where x and y are the satellite coordinates.

Now we have a bit of a complication, because we have to include an actual time, rather than just a relative time from the start of the calculation.

Let us create (exercise 44.9) a function **xyz2latlog** which takes as input a vector (x, y, z)

---

[6]Well, not really, it has a 26,000 year period, but is essentially fixed over the duration of your calculation.
[7]See P. K. Seidelmann, Explanatory Supplement to the Astronomical Almanac, US Naval Observatory, 1961.

at some absolute time (use whatever coordinates you want, such as Nov 17, 2010 at 9:43 AM), and converts it to the correct latitude and longitude. Times are typically much easier to work with if we convert them into a continuous real valued number of days from some arbitrary origin, such as Jan 1. 2000 at 12:00 AM. One way to do this is with the Python **DateTime** package.

```
>>> import datetime
>>> t=datetime(2015,1,7,10,07,14)
>>> tz=datetime.datetime(2000,1,1,0,0,0)
>>> t-tz
datetime.timedelta(5485, 36434)
>>> (t-tz).days
5485
>>> (t-tz).seconds
36434
```

Including **xyz2latlong**, our fifth iteration is given by algorithm 44.8.

Putting it all together, we can now write an Euler's method algorithm (algorithm 44.9) to predict the satellite orbit and ground track with the function **prop**.

Algorithm 44.8 Orbital algorithm, pass 5

---

input: Orbital element vector $\mathbf{v} = (a, e, i, \Omega, \omega, M)$
1: **for** At each time t **do**
2:     1) $(p, q) \leftarrow$ **OrbitPosition**$(\mathbf{v}, t)$
3:     2) $\mathbf{v} \leftarrow$ **PropStep**$(\mathbf{v}, \Delta t)$
4:     3) $(x, y, z) \leftarrow$ **PQ2XYZ**(p, q)
5:     4) $(\lambda, \theta) \leftarrow$ **xyz2latlong**$(x, y, z; t)$
6: **end for**
7: **return**

Algorithm 44.9 Orbit Propagation

---

input: Orbital element vector $\mathbf{v} = (a, e, i, \Omega, \omega, M)$; t_{start}, t_{tend}, Δt.
1: $t \leftarrow t_{\text{start}}$
2: **while** $t < t\_\text{end}$ **do**
3:     $(p, q) \leftarrow$ **OrbitPosition**$(\mathbf{v}, \Delta t)$
4:     $\mathbf{v} \leftarrow$ **PropStep**$(\mathbf{v}, \Delta t)$
5:     $(x, y, z) \leftarrow$ **PQ2XYZ**$((p, q), \mathbf{v})$
6:     $(\lambda, \theta) \leftarrow$ **xyz2latlong**$(x, y, z; t)$
7:     $t \leftarrow t + \Delta t$
8:     Print coordinates or plot on a map.
9: **end while**

After you produce a list of latitude and longitude coordinates describing the orbit, you can plot them on a map of the world. You just have to choose a map projection and add the list of map coordinates to the map as a line plot. You can do this with the Basemap package as described in chapter 45.

Exercises

1. The mean anomaly M and eccentric anomaly E are two different angles used to measure the position of an object within the plane of its orbit. They are related by Kepler's equation $M = E - e \sin E$, where e is the orbital eccentricity. Suppose that you are given the value of e, where $0 \leq e < 1$, and that you know the value of M. Write a program to solve for E using fixed point iteration.

2. Write a program that takes as input a satellite's Keplerian elements at a given time and converts them to Earth centered elements (xyz) at the same time.

3. Write a program that takes as input a satellite's Keplerian elements at a given time, and calculates the sub-satellite latitude and longitude at the same time.

4. Write a program that takes as input a set of Keplerian orbit elements at some time t, and predicts the orbital elements at some later time t', assuming that there are no perturbations on the orbit.

5. Modify the program in the previous exercise to also calculate the latitude and longitude at a fixed interval between t and t' and print out a table of values.

6. Modify the program in exercise 4 to include J_2 perturbations.

7. Modify the program in exercise 5 to include J_2 perturbations.

8. Look up the orbital elements of the international space station. Write a computer program to figure out when it will pass nearly overhead at night during the next 3 weeks. Check your predictions online at http://spotthestation.nasa.gov/.

9. Write the algorithm for **xyz2latlong**. Hint: see the discussion starting around eq. 44.91.

Chapter 45

Maps with Basemap

Once you have a history of the orbit as developed in chapter 44 it would be nice to be able to plot the ground track over time. Matplotlib has a toolkit called Basemap that is designed for plotting maps. It is called a toolkit because it is not part of the standard Matplotlib installation; all that means is that you have to install it separately after you install Matplotlib. Plotting satellite orbits is only one of many things you can do with Basemap.

The Basemap Toolkit will plot data on maps using Pyplot. It defines data structures that can be used by Matplotlib for plotting. It includes shoreline, river, lake, and political boundary data for all the continents, countries, and North American states and provinces. The data can be plotted in thirty different map projections, and you can mark data, graphics, and contours on the plot. You can also read shapefiles, the standard files used in geographic information systems (GIS) software.

The first thing you have to do is define the type of map projection you want, using the class **Basemap**. The keywords for this are summarized in table 45.1.

Basemap returns the map data structure **m** including the coastline in map projection coordinates. You can call the instance **m(lat, long)** to convert latitude and longitude in degrees to (x, y) projection coordinates in meters. The inverse transformation can be performed using the keyword **inverse**.

For the rectangular maps, the map boundaries can generally be specified by either the corners or by the height, width and center coordinates. The corners (**llcrnrlon**, **llcrnrlat**, **urcrnrlon**, **urcrnrlat**) and the center coordinates (**lon_0**, **lat_0**) are given in degrees of latitude and longitude; height and width (**height**, **width**) are given in degrees.

As a simple demonstration, the following code plots great-circle routes from Los Angles to London, Tokyo, Santiago, Johannesburg, Manilla and Sidney on different map projections. Great circles are formed by the intersections of a sphere with a plane that passes through the center of the sphere, and form the paths of shortest distance between two points.

```
1  from mpl_toolkits.basemap import Basemap
2  import numpy as np
3  from matplotlib.pyplot import *
4  m = Basemap(projection="vandg", lat_0=40,lon_0=-118)
5  # Longitude, Latitudes
6  Manilla=(120.9667,14.5833); Johannesburg=(28.0456, -26.2044)
7  LA=(-118.25, 34.05);        London=(0.08, 51.53)
8  Sydney=(151.2094, -33.86);  Tokyo=(139.6917, 35.6895)
9  Santiago=(-70.6667, -33.45)
```

```
10  m.drawgreatcircle(LA[0], LA[1], London[0], London[1])
11  m.drawgreatcircle(LA[0], LA[1],Manilla[0],Manilla[1])
12  m.drawgreatcircle(Sydney[0], Sydney[1], LA[0], LA[1])
13  m.drawgreatcircle(LA[0], LA[1], Tokyo[0], Tokyo[1])
14  m.drawgreatcircle(LA[0], LA[1],Johannesburg[0],
15     Johannesburg[1])
16  m.drawgreatcircle(LA[0], LA[1], Santiago[0], Santiago[1])
17  m.drawcoastlines()
18  m.fillcontinents()
19  m.drawparallels(np.arange(-90,90,10))
20  m.drawmeridians(np.arange(-180,180,30))
21  title('van_der_Grinten_Projection')
22  show()
```

This code will produce the plot on the left below.All other things being equal, transportation routes such as shipping and air travel would follow great circle routes. However, because of high-altitude wind speeds and ocean currents, these are not always the optimal routes. By changing the projection value to **"eck4"** in line 4 you get the figure on the right.

van der Grinten Projection

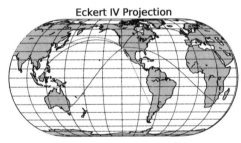

Eckert IV Projection

You have control over font sizes, background color, boundaries, line thickness, etc., on all geographic data. For example, the following will plot the great circle from Los Angeles to New York using a Polyconic projection, showing the state boundaries, rivers, and lakes.

```
m = Basemap(llcrnrlon=-120.,llcrnrlat=20.,\
            urcrnrlon=-45.,urcrnrlat=60.,\
            resolution='l',projection='poly',\
            lat_0=40.,lon_0=-75. )
LA=(-118.25, 34.05);    NY=(-74.0059,40.7129)
m.drawgreatcircle(LA[0],LA[1] NY[0],NY[1],lw=2,color="red")
m.drawcoastlines()
m.drawmapboundary(fill_color="lightblue")
m.fillcontinents(color="white", lake_color="lightblue")
m.drawcountries();  m.drawstates()
m.drawrivers(color="blue")
m.drawparallels(np.arange(20,60,5), linewidth=.25)
m.drawmeridians(np.arange(-120,-45,5), linewidth=.25)
title('Polyconic_Projection', fontsize="9")
show()
```

Polyconic Projection

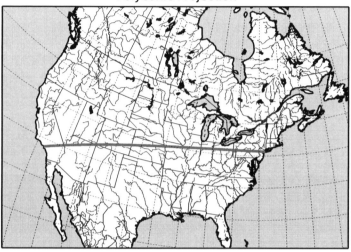

Table 45.1. Class `Basemap` Keywords[a]

`m=Basemap(**kwargs)`

Keyword	Description
area_thresh	Minimum size feature to plot, in square km. Defaults are 10000, 1000, 100, 10, 1 for c, l, i, h, f
ax	Axis instance for Pyplot.
elps	Geoid to use, e.g., "GRS80" or "WGS84". Overrides rsphere.
height	Height in meters of map.
lat_0	Center of map, latitude, degrees.
llcrnrlat	Latitude, lower left hand corner.
llcrnrlon	Longitude, lower left hand corner.
lon_0	Center of map, longitude, degrees.
projection	Map projection. Default is equidistant cylindrical coordinates. See table 45.2.
resolution	c: crude (default); l: low; i: intermediate; h: high; f: full.
rsphere	Radius of earth, or a pair of numbers giving the major and minor axes in meters.
urcrnrlat	Latitude, upper right hand corner.
urcrnrlon	Longitude, upper right hand corner.
width	Width in meters of map.

[a]For a complete list of all keywords and full descriptions on how to use them see http://matplotlib.org/basemap/api/basemap_api.html?highlight=basemap#module-mpl_toolkits.basemap

Table 45.2. Projections in Basemap (1 of 3)

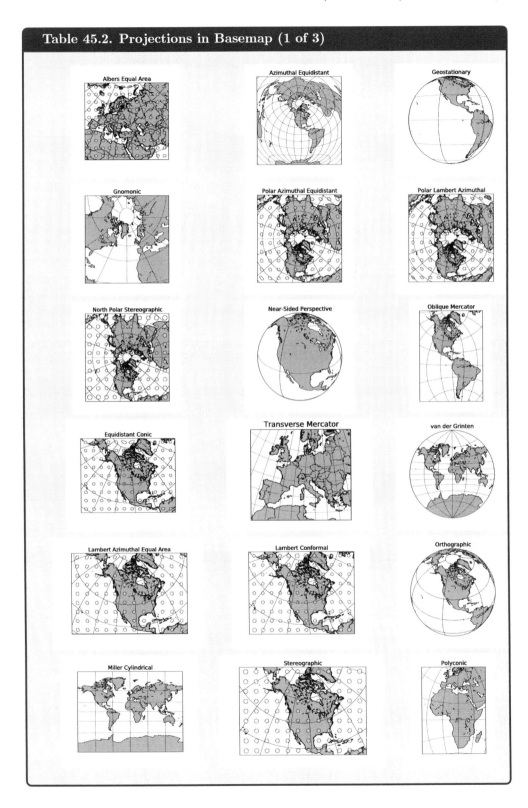

Table 45.2. Projections in Basemap (2 of 3)

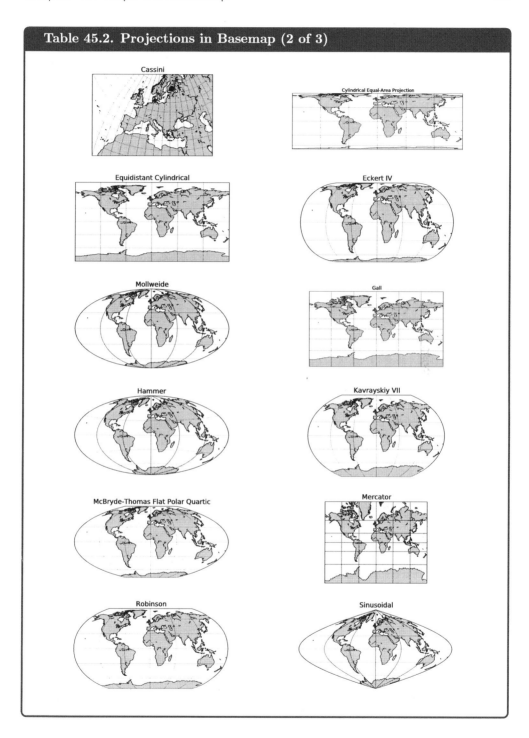

Table 45.2. Projections in Basemap (3 of 3)

Value of keyword **projection** in **Basemap**.

projection	Name		Projection	Name
"aeqd"	Azim. Equidistant		"omerc"	Oblique Mercator
"gnom"	Gnomonic		"tmerc"	Transverse Mercator
"ortho"	Orthographic		"poly"	Polyconic
"geos"	Geostationary		"mill"	Miller Cylindrical
"nsper"	Near-Sided Perspec.		"gall"	Gall Stereographic
"moll"	Mollweide		"cea"	Cylind. Equal-Area
"hammer"	Hammer		"lcc"	Lambert Conformal
"robin"	Robinson		"laea"	Lambert Azim. Eq.
"eck4"	Eckert IV			Ar.
"kav7"	Kavrayskiy VII		"stere"	Stereographic
"mbtfpq"	McBryde-Thomas		"eqdc"	Equidistant Conic
	Flat Polar Quartic		"aea"	Albers Equal Area
"sinu"	Sinusoidal		"npstere"	N. Polar Stereographic
"cyl"	Equidist. Cylindrical		"nplaea"	N. P. Lambert Azim.
"cass"	Cassini		"npaeqd"	N. Pol. Azim. Equid.
"merc"	Mercator		"vandg"	van der Grinten

Table 45.3. **Basemap** methods

Method[a,b]	Description
drawcoastlines	Draws all coastlines.
drawcountries	Draws all country boundaries.
drawgreatcircle	Draws a great circle. Example given in text.
drawmeridians(r)	Draws the meridians; **r** is a **range**.
drawparallels(r)	Draws the parallels; **r** is a **range**.
drawrivers	Draws all rivers.
drawmapboundary	Draws a boundary around the image. If a fillcolor is set, it can be used to fill the color of the oceans.
drawmapscale	Draws the map scale
drawstates	US, Mexico, and Canada state boundaries.
fillcontinents	Sets fill continent color.

[a]For a complete list, see http://matplotlib.org/basemap/api/basemap_api.html#matplotlib-basemap-toolkit

[b]Where appropriate, the following standard plotting keywords apply: **color**, **facecolor**, **fontsize**, **fontcolor**, **linewidth**, **linestyle**, and **zorder**.

Exercises

1. Write a program to draw a map centered on the city or town where you live plus/minus ten degrees latitude and longitude using a polyconic projection. If you live in North America, include state and province boundaries. Include rivers and national boundaries. Fill the land and water areas with different colors.

2. You are planning a trip from Los Angeles to Cape Town, South Africa. Unfortunately there are only 3 non-stops per week available, and none on the days that you would like the flow. You have choices between changing planes in New York, with an eight hour layover, and London with a three hour layover. Plot all three routes (Non-stop; via New York; and via London) on a single Eckert IV projection in different colors. Compute the total time it will take for each route assuming that the earth is round with a radius and 6378 km and that the plane travels with an average speed of 500 km/hour. How long does each route take? Which of the two one-stop routes are shorter in miles?

3. Suppose you are a planner for a delivery company that is based in Chicago and orders inventory from Delhi (India). You are considering two competing air carriers. One carrier flies direct from Delhi to Tokyo, then from Tokyo to Chicago, but has an 21 hour transfer time in Tokyo. The other carrier flies to London, then to Cincinnati, Ohio, and then to Chicago, with an eight hour transfer time each in London and Cincinnati. (a) Plot each flight path on a Robinson projection. Note that you will not be able to plot each path on the same figure. (b) Determine which which carrier will transport your shipment more quickly. Assume that the earth is round with a radius and 6378 km and that the plane travels with an average speed of 500 km/hour.

4. Write a program to plot the sub-satellite ground track of an orbit over a user-specified time period on a Mercator projection. Look up the orbital elements of the international space station and plot its ground track for the next 12 hours.

Appendix A

Complex Numbers

There is a one-to-one relationship between the elements of the complex plane (C) and the real plane $\mathbb{R}^2$. The complex plane is a particular treatment of $\mathbb{R}^2$ in which two operations, addition and multiplication, of points are defined in a special way.

Definition A.1. Complex Plane

The **Complex Plane** $\mathbb{C}$ is the set of all ordered pairs

$$z = (x, y), x, y, \in \mathbb{R}, \tag{A.1}$$

such that for any two complex numbers $w = (a, b) \in \mathbb{C}$, $z = (c, d) \in \mathbb{C}$, complex addition and multiplication are defined as follows

$$z + w = (a + c, b + d) \qquad \textbf{Complex Addition} \tag{A.2}$$
$$z \times w = (ac - bd, ad + bc) \qquad \textbf{Complex Multiplication} \tag{A.3}$$

An element of $\mathbb{C}$ is called a **Complex Number**.

Any complex number z can be divided up into two parts called the **real part**, $\mathrm{Re}\,(z)$, and the **imaginary part**, $\mathrm{Im}\,(z)$, so that z can be written as

$$z = (\mathrm{Re}\,(z), \mathrm{Im}\,(z)) \tag{A.4}$$

Definition A.2. Real Part

The **Real Part** of of a complex number $z = (x, y)$ is defined by

$$\mathrm{Re}\,z = \mathrm{Re}\,(x, y) = x \tag{A.5}$$

Definition A.3. Imaginary Part

The **Imaginary Part** of a complex number $z = (x, y)$ is defined by

$$\mathrm{Im}\,z = \mathrm{Im}\,(x, y) = y \tag{A.6}$$

Normal arithmetic occurs on the x-axis, so we call this the real axis.

Definition A.4. Real Axis

The **Real Axis** is defined as the subset of $\mathbb{C}$

$$\{z = (x,0) | x \in \mathbb{R}\} \tag{A.7}$$

Thus if $x \in \mathbb{R}$ then $(x,0) \in \mathbb{C}$, one will sometimes see things like

$$x = (x,0) \tag{A.8}$$

although the expression on the left is a real number and the expression on the right is a complex number. This works because the imaginary part of the right hand side is zero; hence we can use x and $(x,0)$ interchangeably. This is because the operations of addition and multiplication act as one would expect on two real numbers.

Definition A.5. Imaginary Axis

The **imaginary axis** is the set of complex numbers

$$\{z = (0,y) | y \in \mathbb{R}\} \tag{A.9}$$

Multiplication of a complex number by a real number is called **scalar multiplication**. Suppose

$$X = (x,0) \tag{A.10}$$

is any point on the real axis and $z = (a,b)$. Then

$$Xz = (x,0) \times (a,b) = (x \cdot a - b \cdot 0, x \cdot b + a \cdot 0) = (xa, xb) = x(a,b) = xz \tag{A.11}$$

This is the same as multiplying each component by the real number x, so we are justified in factoring out the real number.

Definition A.6. i

We use the symbol i to denote the complex number

$$i = (0,1) \tag{A.12}$$

Since $i = (0,1)$ by (A.12), then by A.3,

$$i^2 = (0,1) \times (0,1) = (0 \cdot 0 - 1 \cdot 1, 0 \cdot 1 + 1 \cdot 0) = (-1,0) = -1 \tag{A.13}$$

This is more commonly written as

$$i = \sqrt{-1} \tag{A.14}$$

More Common Notation. Since $i = (0,1)$ we can write any complex number $z = (a,b)$ as

$$z = (a,b) \tag{A.15}$$
$$= (a,0) + (b,0) \tag{A.16}$$
$$= a(1,0) + b(0,1) \tag{A.17}$$
$$= a + bi \tag{A.18}$$

where we have used the notation (A.8) to write $1 = (1,0)$ and (A.12) to write $i = (0,1)$.

Definition A.7. Normal Notation for Complex Numbers

If $z = (x, y) \in \mathbb{C}$ then we write

$$z = x + yi \tag{A.19}$$

Theorem A.1. Multiplication of Complex Numbers

Let $u = a + bi$ and $v = c + di$, where $a, b, c, d \in \mathbb{R}$. Then the complex number uv can be computed using the normal rules of multiplication over $\mathbb{R}$ supplemented by the equation $i^2 = 1$.

Proof. By equation (A.3)

$$uv = (a, b) \times (c, d) = (ac - bd, ad + bc) \tag{A.20}$$
$$= (ac - bd) + (ad + bc)i \tag{A.21}$$

But by the "normal" rules of multiplication,

$$uv = (a + bi)(c + di) = ac + adi + bci + bdi^2 \tag{A.22}$$
$$= (ac - bd) + (ad + bc)i \tag{A.23}$$

Theorem A.2. Properties of Complex Numbers

1. **Closure.** The set $\mathbb{C}$ is closed under addition and multiplication, i.e., whenever $w, z \in \mathbb{C}$ it follows that $w + z \in \mathbb{C}$ and $wz \in \mathbb{C}$.

2. **Commutative Property.**
$$\left. \begin{array}{c} w + z = z + w \\ wz = zw \end{array} \right\} \ \forall w, z \in \mathbb{C} \tag{A.24}$$

3. **Associative Property:**
$$\left. \begin{array}{c} (u + v) + w = u + (v + w) \\ (uv)w = u(vw) \end{array} \right\} \ \forall u, v, w \in \mathbb{C} \tag{A.25}$$

4. **Additive and Multiplicative Identities.** $\exists 0, 1 \in \mathbb{C}$ such that
$$\left. \begin{array}{c} z + 0 = 0 + z = z \\ z1 = 1z = z \end{array} \right\} \ \forall z \in \mathbb{C} \tag{A.26}$$

5. **Additive Inverse.** $\forall z \in \mathbb{C}$, $\exists$ unique $w \in \mathbb{C}$ such that $z + w = 0$, where $w = -z = (-1)(z)$.
$$z + (-z) = (-z) + z = 0 \tag{A.27}$$

6. **Multiplicative Inverse.** $\forall z \in \mathbb{C} (z \neq 0)$, $\exists$ unique $w \in \mathbb{C}$ such that $zw = wz = 1$, and we write $w = z^{-1} = 1/z$ so that
$$z(z^{-1}) = (z^{-1})z = 1 \text{ or} \tag{A.28}$$
$$z(1/z) = (1/z)z = 1 \tag{A.29}$$

7. **Distributive Property.**
$$u(w + z) = uw + uz, \ \forall u, w, z \in \mathbb{C} \tag{A.30}$$

Definition A.8. Complex Conjugate

Let $z = a + bi \in \mathbb{C}$. Then the **complex conjugate** of z is defined as

$$z^* = \overline{z} = a - bi \tag{A.31}$$

Using the complex conjugate gives us a way to extend the way we factor the difference of two squares. Recall from algebra that if $a, b \in \mathbb{R}$ then

$$a^2 - b^2 = (a - b)(a + b) \tag{A.32}$$

We now observe that if $z = a + bi$ then

$$zz^* = (a + bi)(a - bi) = a^2 + b^2 \tag{A.33}$$

Figure A.1: Geometry of a point in the complex plane.

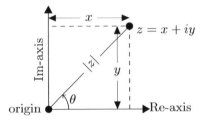

Definition A.9. Absolute Value

Let $z = a + bi \in \mathbb{C}$ where $a, b \in \mathbb{R}$. Then the **Absolute Value of** of z is defined as the positive square root,

$$|z| = \sqrt{zz^*} = \sqrt{a^2 + b^2} \tag{A.34}$$

Theorem A.3. Properties of the Complex Conjugate

$$z + z^* = 2\mathrm{Re}\,z, \ \forall z \in \mathbb{C} \tag{A.35}$$

$$z - z^* = 2i\mathrm{Im}\,z, \ \forall z \in \mathbb{C} \tag{A.36}$$

$$\overline{z + w} = z^* + w^*, \ \forall z, w \in \mathbb{C} \tag{A.37}$$

$$\overline{zw} = (z^*)(w^*), \ \forall z, w \in \mathbb{C} \tag{A.38}$$

$$(z^*)^* = z, \ \forall z \in \mathbb{C} \tag{A.39}$$

$$|wz| = |w||z|, \ \forall w, z \in \mathbb{C} \tag{A.40}$$

Appendix B

Vectors and Matrices

Vectors

Definition B.1. Vector

A **vector v** is an object with a **magnitude** and **direction**.

A vector, of and by itself, is not fixed to any particular location in space. There is a common visualization (that we will use) in which vectors are represented by arrows in $\mathbb{R}^n$. If we place the tail of the arrow at the origin then its point will be at some point $\mathbf{P}$. We can represent the point by its coordinates. In 3 dimensions,

$$\mathbf{P} = (x, y, z) \tag{B.1}$$

Vectors are typically represented by the coordinates of the point we have just described. In this case we will usually write the vector in its **column** form

$$\mathbf{v} = \begin{bmatrix} x \\ y \\ z \end{bmatrix} \tag{B.2}$$

We will sometimes write the vector in its row form as

$$\mathbf{v} = \begin{bmatrix} x & y & z \end{bmatrix} \tag{B.3}$$

Because there is a one-to-one relationship between the set of all vectors in $\mathbb{R}^n$ and the points in $\mathbb{R}^n$, the representations (B.1) are (B.3) are often used interchangeably, although they represent different objects. One will have to determine from the context which one is intended. In higher dimensions we will replace the symbols $x, y, z, \ldots$ with $x_1, x_2, \ldots, x_n$, and write (B.3) as

$$\mathbf{v} = \begin{bmatrix} v_1 & v_2 & \cdots & v_n \end{bmatrix} \tag{B.4}$$

To save space, we will sometimes write the column form by $\mathbf{v} = \begin{bmatrix} v_1 & v_2 & \cdots & v_n \end{bmatrix}^{\mathrm{T}}$ where the T is read as **transpose**.

The magnitude of $\mathbf{v}$ is defined as the Euclidean length of the line segment from the origin to the point at its tip.

Definition B.2. Vector Magnitude

The **magnitude** or **absolute value** or **length** of a vector $\mathbf{v}$ is given by the positive square root

$$v = |\mathbf{v}| = \sqrt{v_1^2 + v_2^2 + \cdots + v_n^2} \tag{B.5}$$

We can visualize the angle between two vectors by placing their tails at the same point in space. Since the two arrows will fall in a single plane (or $n - 1$ dimensional subspace), we define the angle between the vectors as the angle between the arrows in that plane.

Definition B.3. Angle Between Vectors

If we place $\mathbf{v}$ and $\mathbf{w}$ at the origin so that their tips are at points $\mathbf{P}$ and $\mathbf{Q}$, respectively, then the angle between $\mathbf{v}$ and $\mathbf{w}$ is defined to be the angle between the line segments $\overline{OP}$ and $\overline{OQ}$.

We will define angles in higher dimensions in terms of the dot product.

Definition B.4. Dot Product

Let $\mathbf{v}$ and $\mathbf{w}$ be vectors. Their **dot product** is given by

$$\mathbf{v} \cdot \mathbf{w} = v_1 w_1 + v_2 w_2 + v_3 w_3 + \cdots + v_n w_n \tag{B.6}$$

The angle θ between two vectors is defined in terms of the normal trigonometric cosine function.

$$\mathbf{v} \cdot \mathbf{w} = |\mathbf{v}||\mathbf{w}| \cos \theta \tag{B.7}$$

The sum of two vectors $\mathbf{v}$ and $\mathbf{w}$ is a vector $\mathbf{x}$ given by

$$\mathbf{x} = \left[\begin{array}{cccc} v_1 + w_1 & v_2 + w_2 & \cdots & v_n + w_n \end{array} \right]^{\mathrm{T}} \tag{B.8}$$

If $k \in \mathbb{R}$, then the **scalar product** of k and a vector $\mathbf{v}$ is $k\mathbf{v} = \left[\begin{array}{cccc} kv_1 & kv_2 & \cdots & kv_n \end{array} \right]^{\mathrm{T}}$.

Theorem B.1. Closure

The set of all vectors in $\mathbb{R}^3$ is closed under vector addition and scalar multiplication.

In three dimensions, the set of **standard basis vectors** is written as

$$\mathbf{i} = \left[\begin{array}{ccc} 1 & 0 & 0 \end{array} \right]^{\mathrm{T}}, \mathbf{j} = \left[\begin{array}{ccc} 0 & 1 & 0 \end{array} \right]^{\mathrm{T}}, \mathbf{k} = \left[\begin{array}{ccc} 0 & 0 & 1 \end{array} \right]^{\mathrm{T}} \tag{B.9}$$

Therefore any vector $\mathbf{v}$ can be written as

$$\mathbf{v} = \begin{bmatrix} v_1 \\ v_2 \\ v_3 \end{bmatrix} = \begin{bmatrix} v_1 \\ 0 \\ 0 \end{bmatrix} + \begin{bmatrix} 0 \\ v_2 \\ 0 \end{bmatrix} + \begin{bmatrix} 0 \\ 0 \\ v_3 \end{bmatrix} = v_1 \mathbf{i} + v_2 \mathbf{j} + v_3 \mathbf{k} \tag{B.10}$$

In higher dimensions we typically use the notation $\mathbf{e}_1$, $\mathbf{e}_2$, ... for the basis vectors, and can break any vector into its components in the same way:

$$\mathbf{v} = v_1 \mathbf{e}_1 + v_2 \mathbf{e}_2 + v_3 \mathbf{e}_3 + \cdots + v_n \mathbf{e}_n \tag{B.11}$$

Definition B.5. Linear Dependence

The vectors $\mathbf{v}_1, \mathbf{v}_2, \ldots, \mathbf{v}_n$ are said to be **linearly dependent** if there exist numbers $a_1, a_2, \ldots, a_n$, not all zero, such that

$$a_1\mathbf{v}_1 + a_2\mathbf{v}_2 + \cdots + a_n\mathbf{v}_n = 0 \tag{B.12}$$

If no such numbers exist the vectors are said to be **linearly independent**.

Matrices

Definition B.6. Matrix

An $m \times n$ (or m by n) **matrix** A is a rectangular array of number with m rows and n columns

---

If we denote the number in the ith row and j^{th} column as a_{ij} then we can write a matrix $\mathbf{A}$ as

$$\mathbf{A} = \begin{bmatrix} a_{11} & a_{12} & \cdots & a_{1n} \\ a_{21} & a_{22} & & a_{2n} \\ \vdots & & & \vdots \\ a_{m1} & a_{m2} & \cdots & a_{mn} \end{bmatrix} \tag{B.13}$$

We will sometimes denote the matrix $\mathbf{A}$ by $[a_{ij}]$.

Definition B.7. Transpose

The **transpose** $\mathbf{A}^{\text{T}}$ of the matrix $\mathbf{A}$ is the matrix obtained by interchanging the row and column indices.

If $\mathbf{A}$ is given by (B.13), then

$$\mathbf{A}^{\text{T}} = \begin{bmatrix} a_{11} & a_{21} & \cdots & a_{m1} \\ a_{12} & a_{22} & & a_{m2} \\ \vdots & & & \vdots \\ a_{1n} & a_{2n} & \cdots & a_{mn} \end{bmatrix} \tag{B.14}$$

The transpose of an $m \times n$ matrix is an $n \times m$ matrix.

Matrix Addition is defined between two matrices of the same size, by adding corresponding elements. Matrices that have different sizes cannot be added.

$$\begin{bmatrix} a_{11} & a_{12} & \cdots \\ a_{21} & a_{22} & \cdots \\ \vdots & & \end{bmatrix} + \begin{bmatrix} b_{11} & b_{12} & \cdots \\ b_{21} & b_{22} & \cdots \\ \vdots & & \end{bmatrix} = \begin{bmatrix} a_{11}+b_{11} & b_{22}+b_{12} & \cdots \\ a_{21}+b_{21} & a_{22}+b_{22} & \cdots \\ \vdots & & \end{bmatrix} \tag{B.15}$$

A **square matrix** is any matrix with the same number of rows as columns. The **order** of the square matrix is the number of rows (or columns).

A **submatrix** of **A** is the matrix **A** with one (or more) rows and/or one (or more) columns deleted.

The **determinant** det **A** of a square $n \times n$ **matrix A** is calculated as follows.

1. If $n = 1$ then $\mathbf{A} = [a]$ and $\det \mathbf{A} = a$.

2. If $n \geq 2$ then

$$\det \mathbf{A} = \sum_{i=1}^{n} a_{ki}(-1)^{i+k} \det(\mathbf{A}'_{ik}) \tag{B.16}$$

where $\mathbf{A}'_{ik}$ is the submatrix of A with the ith row and k^{th} column deleted.

The choice of which k does not matter because the result will be the same.

The determinant is sometimes written as

$$\det \mathbf{A} = \begin{vmatrix} a_{11} & a_{12} & \cdots \\ a_{21} & a_{22} & \cdots \\ \vdots & & \end{vmatrix} \tag{B.17}$$

In particular, for a 2×2 matrix,

$$\begin{vmatrix} a & b \\ c & d \end{vmatrix} = ad - bc \tag{B.18}$$

and for a 3×3 matrix,

$$\begin{vmatrix} A & B & C \\ D & E & F \\ G & H & I \end{vmatrix} = A\begin{vmatrix} E & F \\ H & I \end{vmatrix} - B\begin{vmatrix} D & F \\ G & I \end{vmatrix} + C\begin{vmatrix} D & E \\ G & H \end{vmatrix} \tag{B.19}$$

Definition B.8. Singular Matrix

A square matrix **A** is said to be **singular** if $\det \mathbf{A} = 0$, and **non-singular** if $\det \mathbf{A} \neq 0$.

Theorem B.2.

The n columns (or rows) of an $n \times n$ square matrix A are linearly independent if and only if $\det \mathbf{A} \neq 0$.

Definition B.9. Matrix Multiplication

The product of an $m \times r$ matrix **A** and an $r \times n$ matrix **B** is the $m \times n$ matrix **AB** with elements

$$\mathbf{AB}_{ij} = \sum_{k=1}^{r} a_{ik}b_{kj} = \sum_{k=1}^{r} \mathbf{a}_i \cdot \mathbf{b}_j \tag{B.20}$$

where $\mathbf{a}_i$ is the ith row of **A** and $\mathbf{b}_j$ is the jth column of **B**.

Example B.1.

$$\begin{bmatrix} 1 & 2 & 3 \\ 4 & 5 & 6 \end{bmatrix}\begin{bmatrix} 8 & 9 \\ 10 & 11 \\ 12 & 13 \end{bmatrix} = \begin{bmatrix} (1,2,3) \cdot (8,10,12) & (1,2,3) \cdot (9,11,13) \\ (4,5,6) \cdot (8,10,12) & (4,5,6) \cdot (9,11,13) \end{bmatrix} = \begin{bmatrix} 64 & 70 \\ 156 & 169 \end{bmatrix} \tag{B.21}$$

Theorem B.3. Determinant of Product

If **A** and **B** are square matrices then

$$\det \mathbf{AB} = (\det \mathbf{A})(\det \mathbf{B}) \qquad\qquad (\text{B.22})$$

Definition B.10. Main Diagonal and Diagonal Matrices

The **main diagonal** of a square matrix **A** is the sequence of numbers $a_{11}, a_{22}, \ldots, a_{nn}$. A square matrix is said to be **a diagonal matrix** if its only non-zero elements lie on its main diagonal.

An identity matrix of degree n is a special $n \times n$ diagonal matrix that has 1's on its main diagonal and zeros everywhere else.

Definition B.11. Identity Matrix

The $n \times n$ **identity matrix** is the matrix **I** that satisfies the equation

$$\mathbf{AI} = \mathbf{IA} = \mathbf{A} \qquad\qquad (\text{B.23})$$

for all $n \times n$ matrices**A**

The identity matrix is a diagonal matrix with 1's in the diagonal and zero's everywhere else.

Definition B.12. Matrix Inverse

A square matrix **A** is said to be **invertible** if there exists a matrix $\mathbf{A}^{-1}$, called the **inverse of A**, such that
$$\mathbf{AA}^{-1} = \mathbf{A}^{-1}\mathbf{A} = \mathbf{I} \qquad\qquad (\text{B.24})$$

Theorem B.4. Requirement for Invertibility

A square matrix is invertible if and only if it is nonsingular.

Definition B.13. Matrix Cofactor

Let **A** be a square $n \times n$ matrix. Then the ij **cofactor**, is

$$\operatorname{cof} a_{ij} = (-1)^{i+j} \det \mathbf{M}_{ij} \qquad\qquad (\text{B.25})$$

where $\mathbf{M}_{ij}$ is the submatrix of **A** with row i and column j removed.

Example B.2. Find the cofactor of a_{12} of $A = \begin{bmatrix} 1 & 2 & 3 \\ 4 & 5 & 6 \\ 7 & 8 & 9 \end{bmatrix}$

$$\operatorname{cof} a_{12} = (-1)^{1+2} \begin{vmatrix} 4 & 6 \\ 7 & 9 \end{vmatrix} = (-1)(36 - 42) = 6 \qquad\qquad (\text{B.26})$$

Scientific Computation: Python Hacking for Math Junkies

Definition B.14. Classical Adjoint Matrix

If $\mathbf{A}$ is an $n \times n$ matrix then its **classical adjoint**, denoted by adj $\mathbf{A}$, is the transpose of the matrix that results when every element of $\mathbf{A}$ is replaced by its cofactor.

$$\text{adj } \mathbf{A} = [\text{cof } a_{ij}]^{\text{T}} = (\text{cof } \mathbf{A})^{\text{T}} \tag{B.27}$$

Example B.3. Find the classical adjoint of $\mathbf{A} = \begin{bmatrix} 1 & 0 & 3 \\ 4 & 5 & 0 \\ 0 & 3 & 1 \end{bmatrix}$

$$\text{cof } \mathbf{A} = \begin{bmatrix} (1)\begin{vmatrix} 5 & 0 \\ 3 & 1 \end{vmatrix} & (-1)\begin{vmatrix} 4 & 0 \\ 0 & 1 \end{vmatrix} & (1)\begin{vmatrix} 4 & 5 \\ 0 & 3 \end{vmatrix} \\ (-1)\begin{vmatrix} 0 & 3 \\ 3 & 1 \end{vmatrix} & (1)\begin{vmatrix} 1 & 3 \\ 0 & 1 \end{vmatrix} & (-1)\begin{vmatrix} 1 & 0 \\ 0 & 3 \end{vmatrix} \\ (1)\begin{vmatrix} 0 & 3 \\ 5 & 0 \end{vmatrix} & (-1)\begin{vmatrix} 1 & 3 \\ 4 & 0 \end{vmatrix} & (1)\begin{vmatrix} 1 & 0 \\ 4 & 5 \end{vmatrix} \end{bmatrix} = \begin{bmatrix} 5 & -4 & 12 \\ 9 & 1 & -3 \\ -15 & 12 & 5 \end{bmatrix} \tag{B.28}$$

$$\text{adj } \mathbf{A} = (\text{cof } \mathbf{A})^{\text{T}} = \begin{bmatrix} 5 & -4 & 12 \\ 9 & 1 & -3 \\ -15 & 12 & 5 \end{bmatrix}^{\text{T}} = \begin{bmatrix} 5 & 9 & -15 \\ -4 & 1 & 12 \\ 12 & -3 & 5 \end{bmatrix} \tag{B.29}$$

Theorem B.5. Matrix Inverse

If $\mathbf{A}$ is square and non-singular then $\mathbf{A}^{-1} = \dfrac{1}{\det \mathbf{A}} \text{adj } \mathbf{A}$

Example B.4. Find $\mathbf{A}^{-1}$ where $\mathbf{A}$ is the square matrix defined in example B.3.

$$\det \mathbf{A} = \begin{vmatrix} 1 & 0 & 3 \\ 4 & 5 & 0 \\ 0 & 3 & 1 \end{vmatrix} = (1)\begin{vmatrix} 5 & 0 \\ 3 & 1 \end{vmatrix} - 0\begin{vmatrix} 4 & 0 \\ 0 & 1 \end{vmatrix} + 3\begin{vmatrix} 4 & 5 \\ 0 & 3 \end{vmatrix} = 41 \tag{B.30}$$

$$\mathbf{A}^{-1} = \frac{1}{41}\begin{bmatrix} 5 & 9 & -15 \\ -4 & 1 & 12 \\ 12 & -3 & 5 \end{bmatrix} \tag{B.31}$$

In practical terms, computation of the determinant is computationally inefficient, and there are faster ways to calculate the inverse, such as via Gaussian Elimination. In fact, determinants and matrix inverses are very rarely used computationally because there is almost always a faster method in terms of number of computations required.

Let $\mathbf{A}$ be an $n \times n$ square matrix and $\mathbf{0}$ be an $n \times 1$ vector of zeros, and suppose that

$$\mathbf{Av} = \mathbf{0} \tag{B.32}$$

for some vector $\mathbf{v} \neq \mathbf{0}$. Then it is not possible for $\mathbf{A}$ to have an inverse $\mathbf{A}^{-1}$, because if such an inverse were to exist, we would have

$$\mathbf{0} = \mathbf{A}^{-1}\mathbf{0} = \mathbf{A}^{-1}\mathbf{Av} = \mathbf{Iv} = \mathbf{v} \tag{B.33}$$

The same result follows if we multiply on the right. Together with theorem B.4, this proves the following theorem.

Theorem B.6. Singular Systems

If $\mathbf{v} \neq \mathbf{0}$ then
$$\mathbf{A}\mathbf{v} = \mathbf{0} \iff \det \mathbf{A} = 0 \tag{B.34}$$

Definition B.15. Eigenvalue/Eigenvector

Let $\mathbf{A}$ be a square matrix. Then we say that λ is an **eigenvalue** of $\mathbf{A}$ with corresponding **eigenvector** $\mathbf{v}$ if
$$\mathbf{A}\mathbf{v} = \lambda \mathbf{v} \tag{B.35}$$
The pair $(\lambda, \mathbf{v})$ is called an **eigenvalue-eigenvector pair**.

We can re-write (B.35) by substituting an identity matrix,
$$\mathbf{A}\mathbf{v} = \lambda \mathbf{I}\mathbf{v} \tag{B.36}$$

because $\mathbf{I}\mathbf{v} = \mathbf{v}$. Bringing everything to the left-hand side of the equation and right factoring the $\mathbf{v}$ gives
$$(\mathbf{A} - \lambda \mathbf{I})\mathbf{v} = \mathbf{0} \tag{B.37}$$
where $\mathbf{0}$ is an $n \times 1$ vector of zeros. Thus by theorem B.6, $\det(\mathbf{A} - \lambda \mathbf{I}) = \mathbf{0}$

Theorem B.7. Characteristic Equation

Let $\mathbf{A}$ be a square matrix. Then its eigenvalues are the roots of its **characteristic equation**
$$\det(\mathbf{A} - \lambda \mathbf{I}) = 0 \tag{B.38}$$

Example B.5. Find the eigenvalues of the matrix $\mathbf{A}$ defined in example B.3.
    The characteristic equation is

$$0 = \begin{vmatrix} 1 - \lambda & 0 & 3 \\ 4 & 5 - \lambda & 0 \\ 0 & 3 & 1 - \lambda \end{vmatrix} = 41 - 11\lambda + 7\lambda^2 - \lambda^3 \tag{B.39}$$

The eigenvalues are $\lambda \approx 6.28761$, $\lambda \approx 0.356196 - 2.52861i$ and $\lambda \approx 0.356196 + 2.52861i$.

Theorem B.8. Non-uniqueness of Eigenvectors

If $\mathbf{v}$ is an eigenvector of $\mathbf{A}$ with eigenvalue λ, then so is any multiple of $\mathbf{v}$.

Example B.6. Find the eigenvalues and eigenvectors of $\mathbf{A} = \begin{bmatrix} 2 & -2 & 3 \\ 1 & 1 & 1 \\ 1 & 3 & -1 \end{bmatrix}$ The characteristic equation of $\mathbf{A}$ is

$$0 = \begin{vmatrix} 2 - \lambda & -2 & 3 \\ 1 & 1 - \lambda & 1 \\ 1 & 3 & -1 - \lambda \end{vmatrix} \tag{B.40}$$

$$= \cdots \text{algebra omitted} \cdots \tag{B.41}$$

$$= -(\lambda + 2)(\lambda - 3)(\lambda - 1) \tag{B.42}$$

Therefore the eigenvalues are -2, 3, 1. To find the eigenvector corresponding to -2 we must solve

$$\begin{bmatrix} 2 & -2 & 3 \\ 1 & 1 & 1 \\ 1 & 3 & -1 \end{bmatrix} \begin{bmatrix} x \\ y \\ z \end{bmatrix} = -2 \begin{bmatrix} x \\ y \\ z \end{bmatrix} \tag{B.43}$$

for x, y, and z. This is equivalent to solving the following system of three equations in three unknowns x, y, and z:

$$\left\{ 2x - 2y + 3z = -2x, \; x + y + z = -2y, \; x + 3y - z = -2z \right\} \tag{B.44}$$

Since the eigenvector is only determined up to a direction and not a magnitude (by theorem B.8) we are free to choose any one component of the solution. If we choose a nonzero value for $\mathbf{v}_j$ and it turns out that the remaining system has no solution, that means that $\mathbf{v}$ does not have a projection in the $\mathbf{e}_j$ direction and we should have chosen that component to be zero. Suppose we try $y = 1$. The remaining system becomes

$$\left\{ 2x - 2 + 3z = -2x, \; x + 1 + z = -2, \; x + 3 - z = -2z \right\} \tag{B.45}$$

This simplifies to

$$\left\{ 4x - 2 + 3z = 0, \; x + 3 + z = 0, \; x + 3 + z = 0 \right\} \tag{B.46}$$

The second and third equations are now the same because we have fixed one of the values. The remaining two equations give two equations in two unknowns:

$$\left\{ 4x + 3z = 2, x + z = -3 \right\} \tag{B.47}$$

The solution is $x = 11, z = -14$. Therefore an eigenvalue of A corresponding to $\lambda = -2$ is $\mathbf{v} = [11, 1, -14]^{\mathrm{T}}$, as is any constant multiple of this vector.

A similar procedure can be used to find the two remaining eigenvectors.

Theorem B.9. Eigenvalues of a Diagonal Matrix

The eigenvalues of a diagonal matrix are the elements of the diagonal.

Definition B.16. Triangular Matrices

An **upper (lower) triangular matrix** is a square matrix that only has its only nonzero entries on or above (below) the main diagonal.

Theorem B.10. Eigenvalues of Triangular Matrix

The eigenvalues of an upper (lower) triangular matrix are the numbers on the main diagonal.

Index

slices, 101, 103
slogdet, 246
Sobel filter, 412
sokalmichener, 265
sokalsneath, 265
solve, 245
solve, 246
sort, 107, 141, 142, 155, 163
sort_complex, 142
sorted, 64, 141
sorting, 142
specgram, 172
spigot algorithms, 377
split, 113, 155
spy, 172
sqeuclidean, 265
sqrt, 67
square root algorithm, 17
squeeze, 163
stackplot, 172
standard deviation, 146
starmap, 235
startswith, 113
staticmethod, 64
statsmodels, 309
std, 147, 156, 163
stem, 172
step, 172
str, 64
stream plot, 336
strings, 109
    string conversion, 111
    concatenation, 112
    conversion, 112
    escape sequences, 111
    operations, 113
    prefixes, 110
    string conversion, 110
strip, 113
sub, 73
sum, 64, 103, 163
SVD, 381
svd, 246
swapaxes, 163
swapaxis, 154
swapcase, 113
symmetric_difference, 117
symmetric_difference_update, 117
sys.argv, 209
SystemRandom, 70

tables
    arithmetic operators, 60
    assignment operators, 76
    Basemap keywords, 439
    Basemap map projections, 439, 440, 442
    Basemap methods, 442
    basic colors, 198
    bitwise Boolean operators, 86
    box plots, 187

dictionary operations, 212
Distances in scipy.spatial.distance, 265
fractions library, 69
Image, 404
image attributes, 404
image filtering, 409
image transform, 418
itertools, 235
keywords, 53
legend, 197
list operations, 107
mutable set operations, 117
numpy array manipulation, 154
numpy arrays, boolean operations, 161
numpy arrays, conversion from existing
    data, 152
numpy arrays, ones and zeros, 151
numpy arrays, searching, 156
Numpy arrays, sorting, 155
numpy arrays, statistics, 156
numpy matrices, 162
numpy matrix operations, 163
numpy random sampling, 157
numpy.linalg, 246
ode, 335
odeint, 334
operations on sequential types, 103
operator, 72
operator precedence, 60
pyplot, 170
pyplot axes, 173
pyplot axis scales, 173
pyplot barplots, 184
pyplot eventplot, 193
pyplot line related keywords, 176
pyplot rectangle keywords, 178
pyplot.annotate, 174
pyplot.annotate keywords, 174
pyplot.arrow, 177
pyplot.axhline, 177
pyplot.axvline, 177
Python built in functions, 63–65
Python cmath literary, 67
Python math library, 66, 67
random library, 70
scipy.interpolate.interp1d, 269
searching, numpy, 142
set operations, 117
set_integrator, 336
sorting, numpy, 142
Spatial geometry, 264
string conversion flags, 111
string conversion formats, 112
string escape sequences, 111
string operations, 113
string prefixes, 110
take, 163
takewhile, 235
tan, 67
tanh, 67

Sherwood Forest

The Sherwood Forest imprint evokes the image of Robin Hood, who, in some legends, hid in Sherwood Forest while fighting to help the poor, as they suffered under the oppressive regime of the medieval English aristocracy.

A statue of Robin Hood stands in front of Nottingham Castle, his legendary home. The castle dates to the 17th century; the statue was built in 1952.

Now as we enter the information age, modern university students suffer under the oppression of the expensive traditional publication model. Sherwood Forest Books aims to print low cost, affordable books in hard-copy and DRM-free electronic formats. In the logo, the roots of the tree sink down into the Earth, from which we all arise. The filament on the light bulb is a double helix, representing the DNA that binds all life on Earth and through which we grow, learn, interpret, and communicate our understanding of the world around us. This light of knowledge is spread through the easy and inexpensive dissemination of the printed word, like leaves blowing in the wind. No religious significance should be attributed to any of the symbols in this logo: we like trees, we like castles, we like light bulbs, and most of all, we like DNA. With due deference to William of Ockham and full attribution to Bob Dylan, "the answer, my friend, is blowin' in the wind."

Made in the USA
Lexington, KY
21 January 2016